REMEMBERING BIX

REMEMBERING BIX

A MEMOIR OF THE JAZZ AGE

Ralph Berton

HARPER & ROW, PUBLISHERS

New York, Evanston, San Francisco, London

FIRST EDITION

Designed by Patricia Dunbar

Library of Congress Cataloging in Publication Data

Berton, Ralph.
  Remembering Bix; a memoir of the jazz age.
  Includes bibliographical references.
  1. Beiderbecke, Bix, 1903–1931. 2. Jazz music.
I. Title.
ML419.B25B5   788'.1'0924[B]   72–9107
ISBN 0–06–010304–3

A few passages in this book appeared in somewhat different form in an article "Bix and His Lost Music," *Harper's Magazine,* November, 1968.

Grateful acknowledgment is made to the publishers for permission to reprint excerpts from the following:

The Book Of Jazz by Leonard Feather, Copyright 1947. Published by Horizon Press, New York.

Bugles For Beiderbecke, Copyright 1958 by Charles Wareing & George Garlick. Published by Sidgwick & Jackson Ltd.

Chicago Poems by Carl Sandburg, Copyright 1916 by Holt, Rinehart and Winston, Inc.; renewed, 1944, by Carl Sandburg. Reprinted by permission of Harcourt Brace Jovanovich, Inc.

The Complete Poems Of Emily Dickinson edited by Thomas H. Johnson. Copyright © 1960. Published by Little, Brown and Company.

Early Jazz, Copyright © 1968 by Gunther Schuller. Published by Oxford University Press.

Hear Me Talkin' to Ya edited by Nat Shapiro and Nat Hentoff. Copyright © 1955 by Nat Shapiro and Nat Henoff. Published by Holt, Rinehart and Winston, Inc.

Jazz Masters Of the Twenties, Copyright © 1965 by Richard Hadlock. Published by Macmillan Publishing Company.

My Life in Jazz, Copyright © 1963 by Max Kaminsky and V. E. Hughes. Published by Harper & Row.

"Homage to Sextus Propertius, V. 2" from Ezra Pound, *Personae.* Copyright 1926 by Ezra Pound. Published by New Directions Publishing Corporation.

The Reluctant Art: The Growth of Jazz by Benny Green, Copyright © 1962. Published by Horizon Press, New York.

Sometimes I Wonder, Copyright © 1965 by Hoagy Carmichael and Stephen Longstreet. Published by Farrar, Straus & Giroux, Inc.

"The Road Not Taken" from *The Poetry of Robert Frost* edited by Edward Connery Lathem. Copyright 1916, © 1969 by Holt, Rinehart and Winston, Inc. Copyright 1944 by Robert Frost. Published by Holt, Rinehart and Winston, Inc.

The Story of Jazz, Copyright © 1956 by Marshall W. Stearns. Published by Oxford University Press.

We Called it Music, Copyright 1947 by Eddie Condon and Thomas Sugrue. Published by McIntosh and Otis, Inc.

For Audrey, who wanted a writer
to write . . . within reason

CONTENTS

A section of photographs follows page 144 and 240.

ACKNOWLEDGEMENTS

The word is inadequate; I use it merely out of craven respect for literary tradition.

It would have been impossible for me even to remember, much less mention, all those who in one way or another have helped me get this book done, but I can't refrain from pointing the finger of deep appreciation at a few outstanding examples of helpfulness beyond the ordinary: Charlie Graham, who first insisted I write it; Gene Young, then managing editor of Harper & Row, who gave me the original contract to do so based on nothing but a flattering faith in my prose; to Don O'Dette, guru of the Bix Beiderbecke Memorial Society, Davenport, Iowa, who dug up endless invaluable info & pictures at the eleventh hour; to Evelyn Hayes of the U.S. Passport Office, who most bravely & incredibly cut the Gordian knot of red tape; and to Walter Allen, Bill Challis, Frank Driggs, Reagan Houston, Paul Hutcoe, Bob Mantler, Paul Mertz, Tom Pletcher, Howdy Quicksell, Wayne Rohlf, Frankie Signorelli, Esten Spurrier, and John Steiner, for making available to me pictures I used or didn't as the case might be; finally, to my brother Vic's widow, now Sylvia Kline, for pictures of Vic; to British jazz journalist Jeff Atterton, New York correspondent for the *Melody Maker* and Bix record expert, who patiently gave me needed information, often at 2:00 AM; and to Dan Morgenstern, former editor of *Down Beat,* and very possibly the finest and most knowing jazz critic in the world, a man who always knew where I could reach anyone, provided he was alive.

PREFACE

"... And all of a sudden, Bix stood up and took a solo ... and I'm tellin' you, those pretty notes went all through me. ..."

Louis Armstrong

Bix Beiderbecke, one of the great American jazz musicians, died in 1931, aged twenty-eight.

Like Jesus, Van Gogh, and other gifted outcasts, Bix found the world uninhabitable, and left it, I think, without regrets, dying as he had lived—casually, without ceremony, and of course broke.

Bix's work has influenced, directly or indirectly, two generations of musicians and music-lovers so far, in many countries, and left a permanent imprint on jazz; thirty years before there was a word for it, he was the first "cool" jazzman. How many of his contemporaries came under his spell it is impossible even to guess. One of them said somewhere, in print, that once you heard Bix blow four notes on that horn, your life would never be the same. I know how irritating that sort of rhetoric can be, especially to those who weren't there; but for us who were, it was the simple truth.

It was an irony of ironies that Bix, the least sentimental man I ever met, became known to the general public only via a piece of sentimental popular fiction, *Young Man with a Horn*, by Dorothy Baker, and will most likely go down in history (if at all) with his name forever coupled with that mawkish pseudo-poetic sobriquet.

The novel, with a hero who in no way resembled Bix, was eventually made into a Hollywood movie, with a hero who resembled neither, and a plot and characterization even more absurd, if possible, than the Dorothy Baker original. But the crowning irony is that the real Bix was a far more interesting and dramatic character than either of the invented ones.

In reality these are only seeming paradoxes—actually they embody cultural cause and effect as logically, as inevitably, as any Christian chaplain blessing a shipment of napalm. In an essentially philistine culture, Bix's intelligently conceived art could never hope to attract as much attention from the mob as a drugstore novel that merely used his name as a prop; and that mob (as every self-respecting statesman knows) has always preferred melodrama to drama, fiction to fact.

Another cliché permanently attached to Bix's name is "a legend in his own time," to which one may understandably become allergic. Well, he was; the phrase was never better employed. Anecdote grew upon Bix like ivy on a wall. Everything he did or said, his very silences—and he was mostly silent—were somehow arresting, would be told and retold, by his closest buddies and by people who had never met him. His most ordinary words and acts often took on a fabulous, legendary quality that was very striking, even at second and third hand; like his music, there was something about Bix that was enigmatic, edged, baffling—that made you want to *do something* about him, you couldn't say exactly what. Ask anyone who knew him.

This isn't a "biography" as ordinarily understood, but a personal memoir; for Bix was a boyhood idol of mine, whom I had for one brief spring, summer, and fall the privilege of worshiping at point-blank range (somewhat to his vexation)—a pilgrimage to that boyhood, an age revisited, and what an age! For Bix was notoriously part of the Jazz Age, and it of him; it made him, and it destroyed him.

As the saying goes, *Si jeunesse savait, et vieillesse pouvait!* Would I had known, when I was thirteen and lying under a piano at Bix's feet getting stoned on his music, following him about like a puppy, carrying his horn like the Grail when I could, sometimes sitting in behind him on drums, sharing my bed with him when he had no other, that half a century later I'd be sitting down to write a book about him! (The notes one would have taken!) Today

I'm grateful to the biographers* for many things I never knew, or thought to find out, when Bix was alive and snoring at my side. But the facts qua facts are hardly the point of this book, though I think I have most of them fairly straight; nor the precise order of various events. Avoiding as far as possible that raking of cold ashes called research, I've had to do the best I could with my sometimes slippery memory, and with the maturer judgement supposed to come with age.

My interest was not chronological but psychological. What I cared about was what made this peculiar young man tick, the Strange Case of Bix Beiderbecke, the perennial puzzle of why a human being full of gifts and loaded with admiration by his fellow human beings—the question always raised by the Garlands, Monroes, and Hemingways and their fate—can nevertheless become so alienated that life itself becomes impossible. So, from all I've read and heard about him, but mostly from what I saw myself in that spring, summer, and fall, I've tried to see the reasons, trace the paths by which this lonely knight errant of jazz came to be what he was, to live as he did and die as he did, against the highly colored backdrop of what may well have been the most extraordinary twenty-eight years any land and people ever lived through: America, 1903–1931.

RALPH BERTON

*See Bibliography.

. . . I shall be telling this with a sigh
Somewhere ages and ages hence:
Two roads diverged in a wood, and I—
I took the one less travelled by,
And that has made all the difference.

Robert Frost, *The Road Not Taken*

1
AUGUST 6TH, 1931

Out in L.A., Thursday, August 6th, 1931, was like other Southern California days: at seven in the morning so chilly you needed a sweater to go out in the patio and pick yourself a couple of figs for breakfast, by nine-thirty you were peeling down to your tennis shirt, by eleven o'clock you pretty much stayed out of the sun unless you were up in the hills or down on the beach.

We were living in Hollywood, the three of us and my mother. My brother Vic was I guess thirty-two, playing drums in Victor Young's orchestra at Paramount—the studio house band—and doubling six nights a week at the Coconut Grove with Abe Lyman. Gene, my other brother, twenty-seven, was doing background scores for various studios, free-lance.

At nineteen, I was above all that, the only holdout from what everyone in Hollywood referred to simply as The Industry—what I called the Great All-Night Dream Cafeteria, the Great Second-hand Idea Supermarket, the Great American Mental Whorehouse (&c.)—for I, you see, was a Genius, capital G, in the first throes of what everyone, especially me, assumed would be a brilliant artistic career. Lewis Milestone, Hollywood's new Biggest Director—his *All Quiet on the Western Front* had just been released—had admired a very bad painting of mine at a party at Horace Liveright's house; as a gesture I had given it to him, and it had returned unto me an hundredfold; several of his well-heeled friends came looking for early Bertons; one of the friends was Harry Braxton, owner of the glossy Braxton Gallery, strategically located at the corner of Hollywood and Vine, next door to the Brown Derby—the only avant-garde art gallery west of Chicago in those dark days. Braxton shuffled through my *surréaliste* canvases and malevolent caricatures and offered me, on the spot, a group show with the Blue

Four, no less—Paul Klee, Kandinsky, Feininger, and I forget the fourth. That show was now less than a month away, September first, and I was turning out Dürer still lifes and Chirico nostalgia-scapes (it was my Dürer/Chirico year) at impressive speed, I had a stunning blonde English mistress. . . . In short, life was my oyster.

Mummy had taken a little pink stucco house on a quiet sun-baked dead-end street halfway up the Beechwood Drive hill, as usual taking quietly perfect care of us all, as she had in Milwaukee, Chicago, New York, London, Paris, Woodstock, and on night trains and steamships in between, even though we were now grown up and more or less living with people or bringing them home to live with us. I had pretty much moved across the street into Sybil's place, Vic had his Meeka living with him, and Meeka had recently recruited her somewhat boyish girl friend Frankie to share their bed & board; brother Gene, who generally preferred young men, often brought them home. Mummy set a pretty big table some nights.

For the past two months Vic, caught by the police with a four-ounce can of marijuana in Louis Armstrong's car, had been (with Louis) sleeping downtown in the Los Angeles County Jail five nights a week; it was a story that could only have happened in Hollywood, when Hollywood was really Hollywood, and which I'll tell later. Anyway Vic was home on weekends with his two women, and even managed to run in during the week for a few "matinees," as he called them.

Sybil and I had one of the thousands of brown shingle shacks (in the realtors' jargon, "studio bungalows") that bestrewed the ob-scurer reaches of L.A. and Hollywood, stuck onto the sides of glens and canyons behind the regular houses, every room on a different level, buried in yuccas and banana palms, with bottled-gas tanks out behind the kitchen window. There was one of those shacks anywhere you looked, housing half a dozen striving young actors and actresses sharing the forty-dollar-a-month rent and eating off orange crates, who had come out here dreaming of Beverly Hills castles and swimming pools, and wound up in a shack in the back with bottled-gas tanks. Sybil had arrived four years earlier—twenty, classic British beauty, Miss Pudlington-on-Trent or some-thing, the prize a Hollywood screen test and six-week contract at Metro, with options; but her test was a dud ("That filthy little assistant cameraman deliberately lit me all wrong because I

repulsed his filthy little advahnces") and the studio failed to pick
up her option. Unwilling to go back to England a flop, she had
stuck it out, "making the rounds," her picture composite on file at
Central Casting with the other 8,000 dress extras; getting a day's
shooting at Universal ($65), maybe a month later a day at Co-
lumbia, maybe doing a little hustling on the side—she never admitted it, but a girl must eat—then a couple of weeks as a carhop
out on Ventura Boulevard at night, days sitting by that phone;
unable to hold any square job long because of her lofty British
manner, the other girls calling her Duchess and accidentally spilling sodas on her uniform . . . until she decided to face reality and
do the one thing she could really do well, outside of fucking I
mean: sew.

She really had the touch, running up copies of little $400 origi-
nals for girls just starting to make it in pictures, contract players
and baby starlets who couldn't yet afford the little originals; in six
months she had a solid and growing clientele. It paid the rent on
the shack and the payments on the sewing machine and the dusty
Model A roadster. Empty-headed as a Toby jug, but what a face,
what a body! They were a dime a dozen in Hollywood, looking out
at you from behind every cash register and luncheonette counter,
hoping you might just be a producer or the friend of a friend of
the Third Assistant Casting Director at Pauper Productions, Inc.,
out in the Valley; if you only hinted that you were, you had a date.

All day I would sit painting on my sun porch at the top of the
stairs, naked, sweating under the ragged tarpaulin that was my
awning, with a towel to wipe my chin so I wouldn't drip into my
colors, from "kin see to cain't see," pausing only to eat, make love,
or go to the john; hedged in by our tiny jungle of poinsettia and
bougainvillaea crowding the edges of my porch, a wild profusion
of scarlet and purple, brilliant and blinding where the sun struck;
a print of Dürer's *Hare*, each hair distinct, nailed to the lattice to
keep proper humility before my eyes; Sybil below in her hot little
workroom clattering away on her machine, a week behind on her
orders as usual. Every so often her machine would stop; in the
sudden silence the high-pitched hum of insect life seemed to come
right out of the square patch of hard blue sky I could see through
a torn place in the canvas. Sybil's low cool clear English voice,
from below, *Rafe? I'm randy agayne, are you?* Running lightly up
the rickety brown steps, eyes narrow with lust, tugging me into

the big room, shutting the window on the street side (she was what she called "a noisy one"), Sybil would shuck off her smock and fling herself onto the vast studio bed (never made except for company) for one more "romp." Every hour, on the hour; then a ten-minute cat nap and shower, and so back to work refreshed. Gene said all Sybil and I ever did was fight and fuck, but by God I was turning out an average of two to six paintings a week, none of your post-Pollock dribbles either, but solid representational *pictures*—watercolors, temperas, oils. That sun porch of mine was a factory, all the time Sybil and I were together; broke but happy (when we weren't fighting); who wasn't broke in 1931?

At around six that evening I finished my latest Dürer—*Nature Morte No. 12* (I often titled my works in French, much in the spirit of the American ballerina who changed her name from Winifred Hudnut to "Natacha Rambova")—a big watercolor, 24 × 36, featuring an enormous gladiolus thrusting priapically upward from shards of broken green glass insulators salvaged from the wreckage of a telephone pole. It was one of the few times I ever managed to get down on canvas (or rather illustration board) what I'd visualized in my inward eye; it really was a pip. Even Sybil, whose interest in art was mostly limited to mentioning how many times she'd *bean* to the Tate, was impressed, in her fashion. "Good as a ruddy photo," she pronounced. It took me twenty minutes to mat and frame it; then we went across the street to show it to the family.

Mummy of course loved the flower, and timidly refrained from comment on the rest of the composition. Gene agreed it was my best thing to date, but as usual had to rag me about its derivativeness. "Isn't it about time, darling," he said, "you developed your *own* manner? After *all*, darling, isn't that what Dürer did?" But I was feeling too good to argue tonight, and simply laughed. "Go fuck yourself, brother." Vic arrived from the studio, flanked by his women. Meeka assumed her usual air of mystic wisdom, head well back on her statuesque neck, gazing with halfclosed eyes and Mona Lisa smile. Frankie, cigarette dangling toughly from corner of mouth, winked at me and said nothing.

"What do I know from painting?" said Vic. "I'm just a dumb musician. Flower growing out of broken glass—that's significant, right?"

"It's surrealistic," said my Sybil, serenely proprietary, munching one of Mummy's hors d'oeuvres.

"Guess what," said Vic. "Our sentences were reduced to four months for good behavior."

Mummy laughed. "Good behavior!" she said. "You were never there!"

"Exactly my theory of prison reform," Gene said. "Let the poor buggers out and tell them to behave." He had good news too, but chose to reveal it in his usual dramatic fashion. Producing three cold bottles of Piper Heidsieck *brut,* he announced that Henry King, king of directors at United Artists, had engaged him to do the score and direct the music for his new picture, *Hell Harbor* (starring Lupe Velez, "The Mexican Spitfire"); they'd be leaving next week to start location shooting in the Caribbean; Gene's salary would be $850 a week. It was like him to start spending the money even before the contract was signed.

At quarter to seven we all sat down to one of our jolliest dinners.

Fifteen minutes earlier, 2,455 miles away, in Queens General Hospital, Jamaica, L.I., Bix Beiderbecke had just died, at 9:30 P.M. New York time. The ward nurse on duty rolled a screen around the bed, pulled the sheet up over the pale sweated face and went to notify Dr. Haberski. It was a hot, muggy night; for a week the mercury had been hitting well over ninety. The New York papers had daily stories of deaths from the heat and by drowning.

The death certificate, No. A-25901, Department of Health, City of New York, said his name was Leon Bix Beiderbecke, male, white, 28, musician; last known address 43–30 Forty-sixth Street, Sunnyside, Queens; permanent or usual address, none; cause of death, lobar pneumonia, duration 3 days.

For more than a week Bix had lain alone in the dusty furnished flat like an ownerless dog, his life ebbing away, drinking up what was left in a few bottles of bootleg rum and bathtub gin. It didn't occur to him to let anyone know. Possibly he didn't really know himself; almost certainly he didn't care. Essentially he had been dying for a long time.

Some musician friends across the river in Manhattan had been vaguely aware that he was ill. Hoagy Carmichael was one, but it was a busy time for him; after writing *Stardust, Lazy River, Rockin' Chair,* and several other tunes known mostly to musicians, he had more work than he knew what to do with. He was worried enough, however, to phone a girl he knew saw Bix sometimes, and ask her to go over to Sunnyside and see how he was, but it seems she never got around to it.

At 43–30 Forty-sixth Street, Sunnyside (it's still there, a big, bleak, undistinguished block of elevator apartments), few of Bix's neighbors knew that the quiet young fellow in 2-C had been taken away in a city ambulance and wouldn't be coming back. The old man who lived over him in 3-C had met him sometimes in the elevator, and asked him once if that was him playing on a trumpet all by himself at four o'clock in the morning. Bix was afraid he was disturbing him but the old man begged him not to stop; it was the sweetest sound he'd ever heard.

The landlady thought he must be home because the lights were burning all night, but the old man said he hadn't heard him practicing, which always meant he was away. Still he had several times heard the water running in the bathroom, which was right under his. The landlady decided to knock on Bix's door.

She was shocked at the way he looked and the condition of the flat. Dust everywhere, empty bottles and full ashtrays, in the refrigerator a half bottle of milk blue with mold, half a can of dried-up sardines. Bix lying there in a suit of dirty BVDs, half covered by a dirty sheet, dirty socks under the bed and on the chair, a general look to the place as if no one was living there. The air was hot and close. Bix had fixed up an electric fan on a chair next to the bed to blow directly upon his pillow, which was soaked in sweat; that worried her as much as anything; she said he would "catch his death," but Bix just gazed at her with swollen eyes half glued shut. She asked whether she should call a doctor for him, whether she could get him anything. Bix managed a ghastly grin and mumbled No, he had everything he needed—indicating a half-full bottle of what she took to be gin, and the electric fan going back and forth with a low hum. With some misgivings she left. But on thinking it over she realized she was scared, and decided to call the ambulance.

The death certificate shows he was buried back home in Oakdale Cemetery, Davenport, Iowa. I don't know exactly when his folks broke the news to Paul Whiteman or perhaps Hoagy Carmichael, and the music world.

There was no obituary in *The New York Times*, then or subsequently. In 1931 that respectable organ of information didn't regard a jazz musician's drinking himself obscurely to death as particularly newsworthy. As a fading figure of the already faded Jazz Age, Bix didn't even rate one line of 6-point type.

There was no shortage of news fit to print. At Yankee Stadium, Babe Ruth drove in his 29th homer of the season; Charles Lindbergh and Mrs. Lindbergh took off on a flight to the Pole; Rudy Vallee chalked up a new boxoffice record at the Paramount; Jack Benny and Georgie Jessel headed an all-star vaudeville bill at the Palace. Down the block at Loew's State, the new Joan Crawford film, *Laughing Sinners,* featuring a new male "find," Clark Gable, entered its sixth smash week. In the Bronx, a ten-year-old boy, caught in the crossfire between rival bootlegger mobs, died in the hospital. In Washington, Senator Andrew Volstead called Prohibition "98% effective" and "a blessing of God on our nation."

And yet an imaginative and informed journalist, some contemporary Bret Harte or Ambrose Bierce, had he been there and been hip, might have written one hell of an obituary for Bix Beiderbecke. Even if he had stumbled on the "story" by chance, his writer's hunch might have drawn him on, from clue to clue, headline to subhead.

DIES AT 28

HOSPITAL SAYS ALCOHOL

WAS FACTOR

We can picture him visiting the shabby flat on Forty-sixth Street, gazing with awe and pity on Bix's last "home," asking with mounting curiosity, How? Why?

ADDRESS BOOK YIELDS CELEB NAMES

DECEASED WAS FORMER PROMINENT

MUSICIAN; WHITEMAN, OTHERS

PAY TRIBUTE

Assuming he really went out and got his story, his lead paragraph might have begun:

No jazz was heard last Thursday night at Queens General Hospital as Bix Beiderbecke quietly died. But in a certain sense what was dying, that muggy night, was a significant bit of the Jazz Age itself. . . .

In spite of all the words that have appeared in print about Bix in various parts of the world since his death, somehow, for me, that particular obit never got written. As the reader will doubtless have gathered by this time, what I am trying to do, among other things, is write it now.

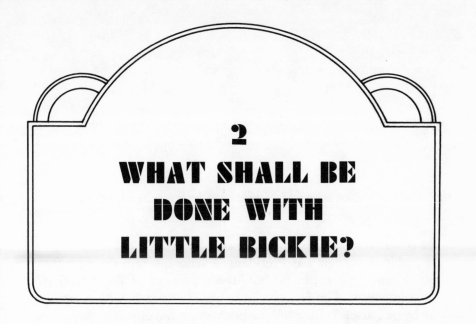

2

WHAT SHALL BE DONE WITH LITTLE BICKIE?

Soap and education are not as sudden as a massacre,
but they are more deadly in the long run.

Mark Twain, *The Facts . . . Concerning The Recent
Resignation*

Bix was born in Davenport, Iowa, March 10, 1903.

Teddy Roosevelt was President. A schooner of beer, with free lunch, cost five cents. Seventy-three percent of the American population lived on farms or in towns of under 50,000, in homes lit by gas or oil lamps; telephones were a novelty. The horseless carriage was still a toy for rich eccentrics. Solid citizens owned horses; young blades rode bicycles, but most people who had to go anywhere nearby, meaning less than five miles, usually walked. In Detroit that year an ex-farmboy with an uncanny feeling for machinery and a total lack of it for people, bought out an old machine shop and started his own factory, the Ford Motor Company. He used the midnight streets near his home to test out the sputtering gas buggies he put together in his backyard tool shed. His neighbors called him, behind his back, Crazy Ford. Later that year at Kitty Hawk, North Carolina, a couple of bicycle mechanics, Wilbur and Orville Wright, flew an airplane for 59 seconds.

A big evening consisted of gathering round the parlor harmonium to sing hymns or, in "peppy" households, ragtime songs. Identities were sharp, distinct clichés: men were brave & strong, girls were weak and fainted, children were seen & not heard or they got a licking when Pa got home; a burglar was a burly fellow in a cap carrying a dark lantern; a tramp had a rum-blossom nose and a four-day beard (the image survives in the circus clown's makeup) and stole Mom's pies off the windowsill, where she put them to cool; a "radical" or "anarchist" (pron. *ar-ny-kist*) was a wild-haired bearded foreigner carrying a lighted, spherical bomb; a Negro (pron. *nigger*) was a happy-go-lucky, childlike chap strumming a banjo, who stole chickens and fainted at the mention of ghosts. A lady's ankle was a daring spectacle, and the word *sophis-*

ticated was no compliment; in 1903 it still meant "tricky," "adulterated." Two big song hits of the day were *Come Josephine (In My Flying Machine)* and *If the Man in the Moon Was a Coon (What Would 'ja Do?)*.

It would have been hard to find a more typical, small, Midwestern American town than Davenport, Iowa, at the turn of the century. Bix's family was solid middle-class German-American, and of course "musical." Great-Grandfather Beiderbecke had been a professional organist in the Old Country; Grandpa, the first Beiderbecke in Davenport, had led the *Deutsche-Amerikanische* choral society there in the 1890s. Bix's mother (*née* Agatha Hilton) won prizes at age ten for playing the piano, and now gave lessons. Uncle Al Petersen, leader of the town band, was a professional cornetist; big sister Alice was a semiprofessional pianist at twelve.

All informants (except Bix himself) seem to agree on Little Bickie's musical precocity. According to his family at least, at two the little toddler, barely able to reach the keyboard on tiptoe, picked out *Yankee Doodle* note-perfect on the family piano; at three, say the same sources, he did the same with the entire theme of Liszt's *Hungarian Rhapsody No. 2* after hearing big sister Alice play it only once. At five he was the "musical pet" of Miss Alice Robinson, his kindergarten teacher at Tyler Elementary School; when the class had sung something, she loved to send "the little boy with the big brown eyes" to the piano, where he would unerringly pick out the whole thing by ear—including the mistakes, if any, to general hilarity and applause. In 1910 the Davenport *Chronicle* carried an item about "little Leon Beiderbecke, this prodigy who at seven can play any selection he hears, on the piano, entirely by ear."

Bix himself always denied any tales of infant prowess as grossly exaggerated—in his own terse prose, "pure family bullshit." It is hard now to decide whom to believe. The family ignored and deplored Bix's musical career when he was alive, but after his death had belatedly apprised them of his fame in the outside world, they all developed a tendency to make a prudent buck out of it by exploiting his memory, shedding crocodile tears over his genius, his sweetness, &c. On the other hand, any sort of praise, including the most temperate and sincere, always made Bix, when I knew him, extremely uncomfortable, and *his* tendency would naturally have been to belittle his own gifts. Both parties are dead now, and we'll never know who was lying. The only solid evidence we have, namely the extraordinary ear and accuracy of musical memory Bix displayed from the time he began to play professionally, suggest that the family might well have been telling the truth about him just this once; let us leave it at that.

As sometimes happens, Bix's phenomenal ear interfered with his learning to read music; easily memorizing the simple-minded tunes on which the ordinary child plods and stumbles, for him the written notes were superfluous baggage which he managed to avoid.

Interviewed twenty-two years after Bix's death, Miss Robinson made a keen observation. "Bix loved to stand by the piano," she recalled, "and play with the class pianist, imitating on the high notes whatever she was playing. He was a dreamy little fellow *and was happy finding his own niche rather than joining the larger group.*"[1]* (My italics.)

Little Bickie was "remembered as a solid and active little boy who enjoyed sports almost as much as music. . . . Bix's older brother, Charles, recalls hearing the piano almost continuously in the years that followed. When the family had all they could stand, Mrs. Beiderbecke . . . would send Bix out to play. He played hard, too, at baseball, ice skating, and especially tennis, but music was always first."[2] The family later claimed they did all an ordinary family could to give their little prodigy a respectable musical education. First Mrs. Beiderbecke herself, then a Miss Holbrook, then a Professor Grade(!), tried their hand at lessons. All eventually gave up. Professor Grade reported tactfully that "his pupil 'responded well for one who played so entirely by ear' "[3]—meaning he couldn't teach him anything. So early in this young genius's career was the pattern being formed whose shape Miss Robinson had already glimpsed; for the rest of his life, such as it was, the dreamy little fellow would be searching for "his own niche," destined never to join "the larger group."

Each moment presents us with a choice, a fork in the road, usually invisible; the story of our life is the story of the choices we made, or that were made for us, each in its matrix of "accident" and "circumstance." In sending Little Bickie to the local yokels for lessons, his well-meaning parents never dreamed they were subtly sealing their boy's fate; but gazing back now on the road he took,

*Source notes are numbered and printed in a separate section, page 403. Fuller details of works briefly cited in notes are in the Bibliography, page 407.

through the mist of years, we cannot help asking ourselves whether this was where the original mischief was done, the tiny but decisive deflection given. Not so much in kindergarten, which appears to have been on the whole rather a happy and productive time, but in that part of his life which, from the day he could toddle to the keyboard, meant most to his dawning consciousness: music. For our Bickie not only got nothing useful from the local yokels; he almost surely got something else—a conviction, unformulated but not the less tenacious, that big people called "teachers" were of no use to him.

It is interesting to speculate—indulging momentarily in the harmless game of hindsight—on what might have happened if, at that moment, Bix had been taken in hand by some creative, imaginative musician, sensitive and responsive to this child's extraordinary gifts. Who can say where the road might have led then? America might even have produced what it never yet has, a major classical composer; and Little Bickie might have still been with us, full of years, to be sure (seventy!), but very much alive and venerated on any number of continents as (why not?) the American Debussy. We know what happened instead: Papa and Mama Beiderbecke, as doggedly as a bee trying to get through a windowpane, continued their foredoomed efforts to give their youngest a "proper" education—musical and otherwise.

(Lest fellow jazz-lovers misunderstand, I hasten to disavow any implication that Bix's becoming a *jazz* musician was ipso facto a lesser destiny, or the world's loss. The greatest classical music is manifestly a "bigger" art than jazz, as a great ancient river is broader and deeper than a mountain freshet; but the fact remains that a jazzman on Bix's level is musically several light-years, in brilliance, inventiveness, and sheer aesthetic horsepower, beyond the Regers and Meyerbeers and other respectable mediocrities for whom the libraries find shelf room. What finished Bix off so young was not jazz per se but what, in his case, went with it; that is, the jazz life with its insecurity and reckless invitation to the alcoholic dance of death, and his own peculiar artistic conflict between the limitations of the fledgeling art he practiced and the splendors of that other, grander idiom which he never ceased to yearn after; and the loss was not the world's so much as Bix's.)

There are few more depressing illustrations of our mass-education machinery's "deadliness," referred to by Mark Twain above, than its well-known paralysis in the face of genius. Like Newton, Shaw, Edison, and Einstein, young Bix was found by his teachers to be unteachable. In school he dreamed away the days, then often squeaked through exams by last-minute cramming. Obviously what was missing wasn't brains. Dick Hadlock[4] thinks Bix was "lazy" and followed "the path of least resistance." But is there really such a thing as a healthy, "solid . . . active little boy" who is also "lazy"? I think not. When a child dreams or looks out the window, he is telling us that what he sees out there or in his head is more interesting than what his teacher is offering. That, as we have got around to recognizing, is the teacher's problem, not the child's. If he happens to be an "unusual" child, he may also be telling us that this time the mold doesn't fit. The routine that suffices to shove the ordinary child along through the system, by a kind of peristalsis, often fails to digest the genius; Bix was a case in point, but a rather special one. My theory about it is intimately related to the very nature of music itself, and to what, for want of a better word, we call its "meaning."

Music is the one art with no direct reference to "reality." Only in the most remote, puzzling way does it even resemble anything we can apprehend of the concrete world. The only truly abstract art, by some deep paradox it is the one that speaks most directly to the darkest, the primordial chambers of the psyche—"this beautiful mute," wrote Gide, "who comes to us, her eyes full of meaning." To try to seize that meaning, and render it *intelligible* (whatever that may mean), is like trying to grasp the terror, the exaltation or hilarity of a dream. That part of us which accepts such experiences lies far beneath the daylight world of the rational, in a place no words can ever penetrate, the submerged seven-eighths of the soul. As Susanne Langer says, in *Philosophy in a New Key:*

The real power of music lies in the fact that it can be "true" to the life of feeling in a way that language cannot; for its significant forms have that *ambivalence* of content which words cannot have. . . . The assignment of meanings is a shifting, kaleidoscopic play, probably below the threshold of consciousness, certainly outside the pale of discursive thinking. The imagination that responds to music is personal and associative and logical, tinged with affect, tinged with bodily rhythm, tinged with dream, but *concerned* with a wealth of formulations for its wealth of wordless knowledge, its whole knowledge of emotional and organic experience, of vital impulse, balance, conflict, the *ways* of living and dying and feeling. Because no assignment of meaning is conventional, none is permanent beyond the sound that passes; yet the brief association was a flash of understanding. . . . Not communication but insight is the gift of music. . . . Music is our myth of the inner life—a young, vital, and meaningful myth. . . .

Now, there are certain temperaments (like Beethoven's, and Bix's) that seem to be at home only in that queer inner world. For them *that* is the real, and what the rest of us call reality is the dreamlike, a glimpsed chaos such as, perhaps, infants perceive, before it has been shaped and formed in the forge of experience. This, it may be, is why so many famous musicians, even more than other artists, have shown themselves so helpless to cope with *our* "reality"; why they sit staring at a schoolbook or a timetable, unable to follow explanations readily grasped by any ordinary ten-year-old—and why we so often find them being looked after all their lives by "practical" women willing to play the role of nurse and baby-sitter.

I feel reasonably sure that Bix was one of these odd souls, and that this, and not a slothful ambling down paths of least resistance, was the true state of affairs, from an age when he was hardly out of diapers. This much, I think, can be said for my theory: it accounts both for Bix's idleness and for his energy, which as we will see in due course was considerable—which Hadlock's "laziness" theory clearly doesn't. In fact, Bix's further history is in itself a sufficient answer to Hadlock's ill-digested notion, but that answer will keep a while.

As Bix grew, he continued healthy, athletic, good-looking, and well liked, though rather quiet and seemingly shy. He continued also to "fool around" at the piano, but without making anything his folks could consider progress. His schoolwork was alarming, and grew worse as he got older. The more he tried, the less able he was to put his mind to it. In June, 1914, he failed for the first time to pass at all, and was left back. He was eleven years old.

A little more than one month afterward, on the night of August 4th, World War I began. In New York City that year, a fifteen-year-old Neapolitan immigrant was booked on charges of malicious mischief; the magistrate suspended sentence, hoping "this would be the first and last time his name would appear on a police blotter." The youngster's name was Alfonso Capone.

On July 4th, 1914, in faraway New Orleans, a chubby black
half-orphan named Daniel Louis Armstrong was arrested for firing
a pistol belonging to his mama, a part-time domestic and two-
dollar prostitute in the cribhouses of Storyville; mostly for his own
good, the judge "sentenced" him to the Colored Waifs' Home. The
couple who ran the Home were musical; Little Louis with his nice
manners and sunny smile was an immediate favorite. He was
given a trumpet to play in the Home's band. That would prove a
memorable day—for America, for musical history, and for Bix.

Nineteen fourteen was also the year the word "Victrola" entered the language; Tom Edison's remarkable toy had suddenly
become big business, like those other toys of his, the electric light
and the movies.

For young Bix the three years from 1914 to 1917 went by like
a dream—for the thirty hours of school every week, a bad dream.
He was now fourteen, and only in the fifth grade.

There was nothing wrong with his reading ability; he enjoyed
reading. But arithmetic was a nightmare; answering questions,
any questions, a nightmare; at the sound of the teacher's voice,
breaking into his reverie, his "mind would go blank," his spine
limp. Music ran in his head much of the time, unorganized, vague,
troublous. In 1917 he again failed to pass. Desperate, his parents
sent him to summer school to try to make up his grade; he went
dutifully enough, but the short "cram" course only made things
worse; he failed again. It began to look as though he would never
get out of grammar school.

Grownups who never went through it can scarcely conceive the
misery of an adolescent boy in such a predicament. Added to the
usual problems of just being fourteen (and let us not underestimate them) was the special, crushing problem of being, in everyone's eyes including his own, good for nothing, not even for the
one thing he loved best; for by all conventional standards (and at
fourteen you have no others) he had strikingly failed to prove
himself worthy to become a musician. He could only draw still
further into his shell of shyness and silence. Even his "fooling" at
the piano, once so admired, had become an aimless, guilty thing:
now no longer the fussed-over *Wunderkind*, he was that most
inglorious of objects, the prodigy *manqué*.

Looking back from the perspective of half a century, we can see
that Bix at fourteen was like some storybook Frog Prince or Beast

under an enchantment, waiting for an as yet unknown Beauty to break the spell that bound him, and set free the bright spirit imprisoned in the dull shell of his adolescence in Smalltown, U.S.A.

His deliverance was even then on the way, following its own curious path of choice and accident. Unknown to Bix, it had already, more than once, brushed him with its wing, but he had failed to recognize it the first time around.

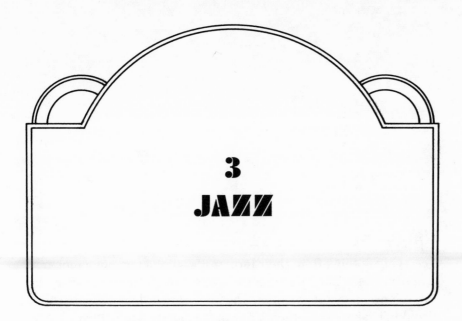

3
JAZZ

Without the American Negro there would be no jazz, and without the white man there would be no jazz. Jazz has never existed in Africa, and it doesn't exist there today. It was formed from the two musical cultures: from the African, which has the highest development of rhythm in the world, and from the European, which has the greatest development of harmony in the world; and it happened in America.

Max Kaminsky, *My Life in Jazz*

The first slaves came to America in 1619, naked and in chains, carrying nothing from their former life—not a rag, not a tool, not an ornament. They were, however, carrying something after all, it seems: a secret weapon, the one thing their new masters couldn't take away—their African memories, embedded in attitudes, reflexes, in speech, motor, and musical habits that were part of the very fiber of their society. Not much, but, as it turned out, enough. Enough to place an indelible stamp on the society of their captors and give birth to a new musical idiom destined to conquer the world, the only indigenous American art worth a damn, mankind's first global art form.

Along the way it would be called many names, most of them defamatory—slave songs, nigger music, minstrel, cakewalk, ragtime, coonsong, lowdown music, sportin'-house music, barrelhouse, honky-tonk, gutbucket, hot—before it got the name that would stick, and would eventually supply the name for an entire epoch of American history: jazz. Ironically, that word too was originally an insult—a low slang synonym for "fuck" (what could be worse?); around Chicago where I grew up, as late as 1922 a *jazz baby* was an accessible girl, a loose woman; a *jazz hound* meant a craver of loose women. But in 1915 a vaudeville hoofer-&-comic named Joe Frisco, playing a date in New Orleans, heard a white *spasm band*, as it was called locally (homemade instruments & komic kapers), playing a kind of cheerful burlesque of the music they'd learned in black red-light districts, *et cetera*. Frisco got them a gig at Lamb's Café, in Chicago, billed as "Tom Brown's Band From Dixieland." Business was good; they were held over.

Respectable union musicians resented the invaders, and placed an ad denouncing them as players of "nothing but cheap, shame-

22

less JASS music." The shocking four-letter word had a predictable effect. The next week Lamb had to put in forty extra tables, and thoughtfully changed their billing to "Brown's JASS BAND From Dixieland." It was the first known public use of the phrase.

Nobody saw any connection between that obscure event and certain far-reaching changes taking place in the national life, which had begun to dig the grave of the horse-&-buggy, *Sweet Adeline* America that would soon exist only in Norman Rockwell's *Saturday Evening Post* covers. The tidal wave of the new society had already swept away the foundations of the world Bix had been born into; soon it would level the enchanted tower in which he still remained stuck like a fly in amber, becalmed in the void of his middle-class mudflat; Bix himself would become one more bit of flotsam in the resulting wreckage. But the hectic New Order would demand a new music, and that music would be called jazz.

A hip historian might well ask at this point, Why jazz? Was there anything inherently hectic, or rebellious, or "immoral," about the jazz *idiom?*

Not for the black Americans who had spawned it. For them its associations were just as much with Sunday mornings in church, funerals, and quiet evenings on the front porch, as with tonks and whorehouses. But for most whites it was inextricably interwoven with alcohol, loose ladies, pelvic dance, and the sinful mixing of races after dark. (For the square white world that association has proved permanent; to this day, any child watching a film or TV drama can usually tell by ear alone when the plot is about to take a sinister, dark-alley turn, because the music track will segue to jazz.)

When and where did Bix first hear jazz?

Davenport, Iowa, really is a port, on the Mississippi, upriver from Mark Twain's Hannibal, Missouri, and from Saint Louis, Vicksburg, Natchez, and New Orleans. In Bix's boyhood the river was a major artery of commerce; up from the South came the riverboats tooting and churning, with cotton, tobacco, turpentine, lumber, and, since minstrel days, musicians, many of them black. The celebrated Streckfus Line, which had its home office for the entire upper Mississippi right in Davenport, exulted in the services of Fate Marable, pianist and leader, holding his orchestras together with an iron hand.

The musicians had to play music strictly for dancing (Marable actually set the tempos *with a stopwatch*), and that music included popular waltzes and other styles not dear to the hearts of jazzmen —but they always managed, of course, to get their jazz licks in whenever, so to speak, the boss wasn't looking. Louis Armstrong's first job away from home was in Fate's band on the packet *Dixie Belle*, getting as far north as Saint Paul, and making Davenport on the way. Bix said he used to play hooky on warm afternoons, a favorite haunt the narrow streets of the old Lower Town along the waterfront. Legendmongers notwithstanding, there is no evidence that he ever happened to hear young Louis—not that he could recall—but he must have heard plenty of jazz, the real thing, played by "those colored guys on the riverboats," a weird, exciting sound, compelling and unforgettable. But it remained, for the time being, an alien phenomenon, "it had nothing to do with my life." For this scion of a respectable white family in that day and age, it would have been no more conceivable to get personally involved with it than if they had been a touring Chinese opera company. Still it stayed somewhere in his mind, latent, germinal.

In 1917 Bix reached the decisive crossroads in his life—an event which had had its origins twenty-eight years earlier and a thousand miles away.

In 1889, in New Orleans, had been born one Dominick LaRocca, destined by name and nationality to grow up on the wrong side of the tracks, as we used to say. Like a lot of other poor kids in his neighborhood, little Nick used to follow the street bands around, both black and white, at funerals and other social occasions, hung around the tailgate wagons filled with musicians advertising the next Saturday night's attractions. Soon he started playing trumpet himself. By the time he was in his teens he was in one of the most famous early marching bands, Papa Jack Laine's Reliance Brass Band. In 1915 some of Laine's boys broke away to form the aforementioned Tom Brown's Band From Dixieland that played at Lamb's Café. Nick LaRocca wasn't one of them, but some who had had a taste of "up North" came back and talked about the amazing money to be made there. By 1916 Nick LaRocca, twenty-seven years old and a seasoned Dixielander, had put together a quintet of kindred spirits—Larry Shields (clarinet), Daddy Edwards (trombone), Andy Ragas (piano), and Tony Sbarbaro (drums). Their style was formed on the street and tailgate bands and on the rowdy spasm bands of the black urchins who followed them around, the so-called Second Liners, and on the raggy piano "professors" of the sporting houses and honky-tonks, all adding up to their own raucous, jaunty, go-to-hell-in-a-barrel brand of "jass" or "jazz," as the musicians themselves had now started to call it. They named themselves, not quite accurately, the Original Dixieland Jass Band. Right after New Year's Eve, 1916, they landed a booking at Reisenweber's Café in New York, just off Columbus Circle. It happened to be exactly the place, and the time, for what was about to happen.

They opened the night of January 26th, 1917. Interviewed forty years later by Marshall Stearns, Tony Sbarbaro told him:

> "We had a good press agent—he squeezed us in on the 2nd floor—Gus Edwards and a big revue on the 1st and Emil Coleman and high society on the 3rd."[5]

In 1917 those were big names in entertainment. Edwards had a kid revue that played every first-class vaudeville theater in America; Emil Coleman's was the number one "society" orchestra, which dowagers automatically engaged for the annual Junior League Ball; our five roughnecks found themselves in high-toned company, and the combination was magic. The Social Register crowd that came to dance to the subdued strains of Emil Coleman had never been exposed to such extraordinary noises; they were bewildered, but the electrifying pulse of jazz was irresistible. The oldest and most efficient type of advertising, i.e., word of mouth, did the rest:

> "We sweated it out for two weeks and then we hit solid, the place was jammed."[6]

Stearns continues:

> Reporting the big news with such haste that a clarinet was referred to as a piccolo, *Variety* commented:
>
> > "There is one thing that is certain, and that is that the melodies as played by the Jazz organization at Reisenweber's are quite conducive to making the dancers on the floor loosen up and go quite the limit in their stepping."

And Jimmy Durante . . . just beginning his career as a ragtime-playing entertainer, added: "It wasn't only an innovation; it was a revolution!" . . . Still other bands . . . white and Negro, had preceded the Original Dixieland . . . but this band played the right spot at the right time and hit the headlines from coast to coast. More important, the band made the first out-and-out jazz recordings, which were issued on Victor's popular lists and sold in the millions. . . . Almost overnight, the word "jazz" entered the American vocabulary . . . a rackety musical novelty with barnyard—or worse—antecedents.[7]

A few weeks after their first record was released by the Victor Talking Machine Company *(Livery Stable Blues | Dixie Jass Band One-Step)** it became next to impossible to walk into any American home able to afford a "Victrola" and not find a copy of it in the parlor. That smash hit was quickly followed by others, by the ODJB, by imitators, by worse bands (white) and better (black). Jazz was in, ragtime was dead.

For years afterward jazz, as played by whites for whites in any commercial situation, would remain essentially a music of burlesque, of caricature, zany humor, rough and violent. Whereas a black musician might be any kind of man including a respectable sober family man, white jazz musicians tended to be more like social outcasts, tough nomads living a hand-to-mouth, job-to-job existence bare of such ornaments as family and future, in cheap hotels or furnished rooms, borrowing money and clothes from each other like kids in frat houses, part Bohemian, part bum, knowing little in the world but their music and caring less, with a general level of culture resembling a fight gymnasium, except that there were always girls around—not, of course, the kind of girls who cared about families and futures, but all the others— dancers, singers, waitresses, checkroom cuties, and the usual crop of juvenile strays from the faraway world of respectability, the Jazz Age forerunners of our contemporary East Village runaways.

So for the general (i.e., white) public, the swinging beat of jazz, its raucous, uninhibited, free-wheeling atmosphere *as it appeared to whites,* were made to order as expressions of the New Era of rapid change, the shattering of old moral and social shackles. The older generation, still stuck in the Gay Nineties-ragtime-barber-shop-quartet era, shrank from the new sound, just as parents of our 1960s and '70s shrink from the rock holocaust. So much the worse for the older generation: their rejection only reinforced the young's identification of it with everything they wanted in life.

In at least two homes, the week *Livery Stable Blues* was

*Victor 18255; reissued on LPV–547, January, 1968.

released, the effect on the boy of the house was considerably more than his elders who had brought the record home had bargained for.

I was six, living in Milwaukee, Wisconsin, and I can still recall my sensations as I heard for the first time the sardonic, driving horn of Nick LaRocca, the impudent smears and growls of Daddy Edwards, the barnyard crowings and whinnyings of Larry Shields, the slaphappy poundings of Ragas and Sbarbaro. I must have played it a hundred times before I remembered to breathe. It was the first thing I did in the morning when I ran downstairs in my nightie, the last thing at night before being dragged pleading off to bed. I quickly wore out two copies, not a hard thing to do in that day when the "tone arm" weighed half a pound and carried a steel needle which, after half a minute's wear, developed a knife edge that chewed up the gritty black grooves (at 78 rpm) in short order. I learned every note by heart, picked it out on the piano, sang it at the top of my lungs, whistled it at the top of my embouchure, and acquired other jazz records as fast as they appeared. For better or worse, jazz had entered my life.

A hundred and fifty miles away in Davenport, Iowa, much the same thing was going on in the Beiderbecke household, with certain important differences. We were a show-biz family; my older brother Vic was already a well-known jazz drummer (among other things); they found my enthusiasm entirely natural, and even (moderately) shared it. Vickie had already begun my instruction in the art of the drums, should I care to pursue it. But at the Beiderbeckes' of Davenport, there was dawning consternation as Papa and Mama realized that their youngest (Bix was just turning fourteen) had been injected with a dangerous virus. For, within the space of a few days, Bix's life had acquired, for the first time, a purpose; he knew now, simply and with certitude, that what he wanted to do was play the cornet like Nick LaRocca. He immediately asked his papa to buy him one. His family's response was something like panic.

Like millions of other papas from Maine to California, Mr. Beiderbecke had brought the record home as a joke, never dreaming what a stick of dynamite he was carrying. When he and Mama Beiderbecke realized that their unfortunate backward boy was taking it not only seriously but as a beacon for his future, they tried at first to dismiss the whole thing as a childish whim. They soon

saw that it wasn't to be dismissed that easily—and now they had
something new to worry about: their son *a jazz musician!* They
could scarcely have been more alarmed if Bix had announced his
intention to become a pickpocket.

For the moment then Bix appeared to desist; as always, he tried
to live by his family's lights. But now—so say the legends, and it
may be so—he found himself spending every hour he could steal
hanging around the waterfront, making sure to meet the incoming
riverboats, whose sounds he drank in with awakened senses, and
to listen at the doors of the riverside saloons, which had already
begun to employ "professors" who could imitate the new "jass,"
a sound no longer remote or alien to him, but the pulse of his
future lifework.

Next he tried Uncle Al, who after all was a cornetist himself, but
Uncle Al too ridiculed the idea, and Bix's idol, LaRocca, as a mere
caricature of a musician, assuring little Leon that the whole jazz
fad would be forgotten as soon as people tired of the novelty. He
advised his young nephew to forget these fly-by-night bums and
Buckle Down and Make Something of Himself. Music was at best
a doubtful trade for a sensible man—a hobby or avocation, why
not? but a profession? And as for this noise called (ugh!) *jazz*—why,
the very word should warn any self-respecting person to shun it.
Clearly, little Leon saw, there would be no help from that quarter,
or indeed any quarter; so far as his family were concerned, the
matter was closed.

They were very much aware of *this* fork in the road, nor did
they underestimate its critical importance; indeed, they thought
they were doing everything possible to push him the "right way"
—completely misjudging the inevitable effect of their efforts,
which was only to reinforce what Bix already knew, that he could
get no help from them at the only point where it really mattered,
the point at which his soul met music—and thus to push him one
more crucial step along "his own" path. What none of them apparently realized was that, unnoticed by anyone, their dreamy little
boy's character had acquired a certain underlying hardness. Un-
deterred by their Dutch-uncle lectures and attempts to discour-
age his ambitions, Bix figuratively set his jaw and quietly went
about solving the problem all by himself.

Ironically, one consequence of this silent decision was a noticeable improvement in his "marks." There's nothing like having a

purpose in life. Young Leon visibly Buckled Down, and apparently stopped "dreaming." To his folks it looked as if their exhortations had actually hit home; their boy had never acted this "sensible" before. Papa even permitted himself once again to dream that some day Leon might take his rightful place beside him in the Davenport Fuel & Lumber Co., mentally adding "& Son" to the black-and-gold sign over the office door.

Nothing of course could have been further from Bix's mind. He had simply realized that what he needed most now was freedom —especially freedom from hourly surveillance by parents and teachers—and everyone knew that in high school a boy had that sort of freedom to a degree undreamed of in grammar school. Bix's newfound purpose required two things: a horn, and getting into high school, the sooner the better. His mind was full of visions, not of lumber, but of big cities (he'd never seen one), pulsing with bright, soaring jazz and people as crazy for it as he was. Of course, Bix being Bix, few of these projections ever attained the level of conscious planning; they were just "there."

By one of history's most lavish ironies, Bix's visions were about to prove only too timely.

In faroff Washington, D.C., a momentous event was preparing that would precipitate a total revolution in American morals and manners; a new law of the land that would overnight make law itself a joke, and the land an international laughingstock; would profoundly affect American lifestyles in general, and Bix's in particular. On December 18th, 1917, Congressman Andrew Volstead submitted to the Congress a measure that would enforce the Eighteenth Amendment prohibiting the making, selling, or swallowing of any alcoholic beverage. Praying for its passage were two oddly assorted groups of Americans: on the one hand the righteous cretins comprising the WCTU (Women's Christian Temperance Union) and the Anti-Saloon League—on the other, the organized mobs. With a clarity the WCTU hadn't the brains to envy, the mobs foresaw that if this insanity ever became law, the take from gambling, prostitution, and the hard rackets would look like peanuts alongside the revenue from booze and beer. To render "illegal" something nine out of ten citizens did every day was to hand the mobs a taxfree income of a hundred million a month, and they knew it if the WCTU ladies didn't. In New York, Johnny Torrio and friends licked their lips impatiently, and provided copious quiet funding to the Prohibition fanatics; in Brooklyn, Al Capone, who at eighteen had risen, by his handy fists and reliable marksmanship, to second in command, prayed daily and, it is reported, lit a thousand candles at a local church as celestial insurance; he'd been promised the Chicago territory if the Eighteenth Amendment became law. Some older, more conservative hoods refused to chip in, but only because it seemed too good to be true; even American lawmakers, they argued, couldn't be that stupid. As we know, they were mistaken.

One man who knew the younger mobsters were right was President Wilson. He fought the Eighteenth Amendment as both wrong in principle and unenforceable, an outrage against personal liberty, sure to achieve an effect opposite to its proponents' intentions. But in 1917 and '18 Mr. Wilson had other matters to occupy him, including a world war he completely failed to understand and a "peace" that aggravated the problems that had caused the war in the first place. Wilson, who was responsible for the slogan "Make the World Safe for Democracy"—a fantasy that killed more people than the Black Plague—saw too late that he had only helped make the world safe for the winning side's millionaires and political wolves, and that he had been a credulous fool to imagine anything else. The truth of what he had done crushed him, and his efforts to salvage something from the peace finished him off. In vain he fought for "a just peace" against the wise old European wolf pack; he couldn't even get his own Congress's support. He took his case directly to the people, touring the country like a candidate; the people's answer was to return a Republican majority to Congress, dooming Wilson's efforts. On September 25th, 1919, following an impassioned speech to an impassive audience, he suffered a stroke. On January 16th, 1920, Prohibition became law, at least on paper.

Bix was just going on seventeen. He had at long last escaped from Tyler Elementary and entered Davenport High.

A boy in high school is already half a man. With new decision in his manner, Bix again asked his folks to get him a horn, again asked Uncle Al to give him lessons, and indicated that jazz was—as he would have said fifty years later—his bag. Again they rebuffed him, whereupon Bix took $8 of his own allowance money he had carefully saved up for just this occasion, went down to a hockshop "downtown" and bought himself an aging, beat-up cornet he'd been looking at in the window. He brought it home in a paper bag, saying nothing to anyone.

When next Uncle Al visited, Bix had a little surprise for him. Without a word Bix took the battered horn out, put it to his lips, and blew, without a mistake, the verse and refrain of the current hit *Margie.*

Uncle Al was floored. Rather grudgingly he congratulated his nephew, then volunteered to show him an easier fingering than the one Bix had taught himself out in the woodshed. Characteristically, Bix preferred his own; he never did learn conventional fingering.

What his family expressed on that occasion he never could recall, but it wasn't enthusiasm. Clearly if young Leon was ever to get anywhere, in the only calling to which he had ever felt called, it would have to be on his own nerve and muscle.

But—the thing had happened. The enchantment was broken; he was no longer the mute prisoner, mewed up in a wall of isolation, confused, procrastinating. Mute, to a degree, he would always be; verbal communication would never be his medium, though his words could be clear, sharp, and caustic when he chose. But he now had his aim in life. Not with clarity—that would never be—but with sufficient force to burst open the Iron Maiden his world had (always with the best intentions) forged around him, compacted of all the square small-town conventions and expectations automatically accepted by the "normal" child—in fact, its *norms.*

Like an eaglet pecking through its shell, he had broken out into the open air, peered for the first time into a new sky, trying to make out his future in its blue depths. But there was a considerable strengthening of his wings still to come before he could venture out upon them.

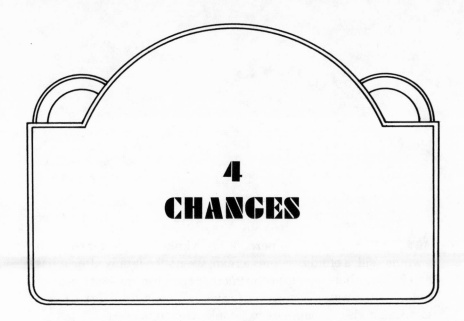

4
CHANGES

How this miracle of fire and ice was to be created, and to sustain itself in a harsh world, he had never taken the time to think out.

Edith Wharton, *The Age of Innocence*

Many things change imperceptibly: a knife rusts, water cools on a windowsill, a child becomes a man; we notice it only after it has happened. There are also the moments of the qualitative leap; suddenly the water is ice; it has, as we say, been *transformed* into something else. It happens to people, and to nations.

Between the years 1919 and 1920 two things happened—in America's life and in Bix's—that were closely connected. America was forbidden to drink, and Bix learned to drink.

Of course that was only one conspicuous bubble on a very deep-flowing current. Change, profound change, was everywhere; everywhere, for those who could read them, were signs of the times—a kind of hardening, a disappearance of innocence, a rise in speed and pressure. A way of life was dying, perhaps already dead; on its corpse a new way was triumphantly rearing itself—a shiny, garishly colored, massproduced gadget culture that would swiftly remake in its own image first the country, then the whole world.

Many and complex were the signs, and of some it would be hard to say what was cause and what was effect. Four million "dough-boys" (as the World War I GIs were called) were coming home, having been irrevocably exposed to the European experience—a sort of massproduction musical comedy version of Henry James's favorite theme—and they too would never be the same. A song hit of the day was *How Ya Gonna Keep 'Em Down on the Farm (After They've Seen Par-ee)?* It posed rather a deeper question than the writers had intended. The reasons were more basic, more cogent, than even the seductions of Par-ee. They were economic, very American, and irreversible.

Quite simply, the City had begun to devour the rest of America.

34

The old family farm and small town, with their quasi-bucolic, leisurely, artisan-based life and outlook, were being swallowed piecemeal by the big town and the factory; the countryside was vanishing under an advancing tide of technological obsolescence. To survive at all, the farm would itself become in effect a giant outdoor factory, producing cash crops with more and more machines and fewer and fewer people. For most farm and small-town boys, whether or not they had seen Par-ee, there would soon be no place on the land or in the old small-town businesses and gently decaying "mills" along the riversides. A mass exodus to the City was under way, by the millions. Young Bix, though driven, to be sure, by a passion quite different from that of most of the herd, would nevertheless become one of those millions.

The principal architects of change were the inventors, the busy mechanics and technicians, the Edisons and Fords. Over the years Mr. Ford, the Great Cheapener, had perfected his masterpiece, the assembly line, to force the price of his ugly, indestructible Model T down, down, down, to a precedent-shattering, incredible $300, an event that probably had a greater impact on American life than anything since the Confederates fired on Fort Sumter. As Mr.Ford had accurately foreseen, the "auto," from a costly toy, became overnight a family necessity. Anyone with a job could afford one, and the assembly lines ground them out like frankfurters. ("Any color you want," quipped the ads, "as long as it's black.") Ten million flivvers needed paved roads to run on, and lo! they appeared, 21,000 miles in some eighteen months, an irresistible flow of asphalt and concrete crisscrossing the country like a network of varicosities. They were known as *arteries,* and strange and new was the ichor they pumped to the remotest extremities of the nation. The horse and his faithful valet-diaperer, the "White Wing," the street cleaner, vanished from the earth; likewise the village smithy, his spreading chestnut tree cut down to make room for a parking lot. They weren't calling Mr. Ford "Crazy" Ford any more.

For the young, what those arteries pumped was freedom, mostly freedom from the surveillance of parents and neighbors, which meant among other things that the long dreaded Sexual Revolution was suddenly a fact of life. After 2,000 years of Judaeo-Christian moral imprisonment, the young of Western Man were triumphantly sprung, not by the Romantic poets' lofty sentiments

or the ringing words of the anarchists and freethinking philosophers, but by Tin Lizzie's dependable 4-cylinder power plant—as
the leering cartoons and thundering pulpits of the day convincingly attest. They thundered in vain. A young couple sitting
primly behind the rear end of a horse going clip-clop at 5 miles
per hour is nothing at all like the same couple joyously fleeing the
vicinity at 50 miles per hour; two hours and they are beyond the
reach of thunderbolts and nosy neighbors. Sex was here to stay,
and short skirts, bobbed hair, rolled stockings, loose panties, and
a ripening acquaintance with birth control were at no great distance. In this as in other ways, America on wheels was a new
America. The doughboys who had left eighteen months before to
Make the World Safe, &c., came back to a land they scarcely
recognized.

Bix too had won his war; he had his horn, his objective, and his
eye on the ball.

Bix's freshman year at Davenport High was a refreshing change
from the misery of his previous school experience, and, apparently, a triumphant one in at least two areas, music and sports. His
interest in his horn and the newly popular Dixieland idiom was
shared by a growing segment of his fellow students; in baseball he
was a sought-after teammate. He was universally liked—it was, I
should imagine, as impossible then as later for anyone to *dis*like
him.

He also took up tennis in a more serious way, aided by the fact
that about this time the Beiderbecke family joined an exclusive
club out in the suburbs, which not many other families could
afford. This club had a tennis court, and Bix must have spent some
fruitful hours on it, developing a "modern" style.

The game had undergone a remarkable metamorphosis precisely during the years when Bix was growing up, had come in fact
to resemble other aspects of the age. Gone was the pattycake,
fun-on-the-lawn *divertissement* (imported from Bermuda, *c.* 1874,
by a Miss Outerbridge), a ladylike affair played in long skirts and
blazers; like the new vehicles, it now went faster. The serve, formerly a polite way of putting the ball in play, had evolved into a
weapon, frankly intended to put the receiver instantly on the
defensive, or if possible win the point outright with an "ace." It
had a logical sequel—rushing the net, another idea unthought of
in a gentler age—and another equally logical follow-up, the over-

head smash: a more lethal version of the serve, executed ideally from the net or at least midcourt, and virtually unreturnable. The effect was to curtail or put an end to the long polite rallies from the baseline; the deadly serve, rush, and volley were meant to force an immediate error or kill the ball altogether. By about 1913, when Bix was ten, Big Bill Tilden & friends had made of tennis what it has remained ever since, a combat sport featuring speed, muscle, and premeditated aggression.

Surprisingly, young Bix, so seemingly shy and unaggressive, took to the new tennis as he had to sandlot baseball. He was, I think, still a freshman when he was picked to represent the school in a Tri-Cities match and walked off with the cup.

Remembering the little that Bix himself said—he wasn't prone to reminisce about his childhood with me—and browsing now through the biographies, I've been able to piece together in my own mind a picture of Bix in his teens that I think rings true, is in fact immediately recognizable to anyone who knew him a few years later on.

His popularity at Davenport High, with both boys and girls, would also appear a bit surprising in a way, in view of two aspects in particular of his personality: his "shyness" (if any), and the fact that he was largely devoid of that wellnigh universal anxiety to be one of the gang, to conform, to be approved of by one's peers, for which the young are especially conspicuous. In fact Bix may well have been, even at that early age, already something of an eccentric, but if so his eccentricities probably added to his charm. Wareing and Garlick[8] even go so far as to tell how Bix was always forgetting his horn outside Maher's ice cream parlor, whereupon somebody would take it inside for safekeeping, to be handed to Bix the next morning on his way to school by kindly old Mr. Maher; but I have recently been informed by one of Bix's old schoolmates, Esten Spurrier, that this is just some more bullshit, concocted to make the Bix legend more interesting; he says Bix would as soon have forgotten his left arm. Again, you pays your money and takes your choice. As will be seen, the Bix I knew a few years later was absentminded enough to have forgotten the arm as well, had it been unattached.

As to Bix's frequently alleged "shyness," I think it has been somewhat misunderstood. He certainly had a lifelong tendency to speak only when spoken to, and absolutely no smalltalk; my impression was that he just didn't think a lot of things were worth talking about. I also reject the notion that he was "afraid of girls." Then as afterward, girls played a minor role in Bix's life; he himself said more than once that in his school days he went in very little for what he called "the boy-and-girl stuff," as he brushed off my curious questions on that subject. The amateur psychological sleuths have diagnosed this "deficiency" as everything from acute terror to latent homosexuality, but my guess is simpler: I think Bix, generally speaking, was just too busy to bother much with girls. He didn't exactly avoid them, and he also never pursued them to my knowledge. Girls liked him, but everybody liked Bix; later on, more than one must have loved him, and I'm sure Bix, in his quiet way, loved some of them back. I think he accepted girls as he did other nice things in the world—sunlight and shade, food and drink and friends—without anxiety or overwhelming need; but as a boy he had more urgent matters on his mind. On that point at least the authors of those turn-of-the-century texts on Clean Living and Sex Hygiene would have loved Bix. They would have been less happy about the hours he'd begun to keep, of which more in a moment.

Not long after he entered Davenport High, he and some other students put on a vaudeville show, which may have been the very first time Bix Beiderbecke performed in public. Bix first sang as part of a vocal quartet (who wouldn't give half his kingdom for a recording of *that?*),

. . . then, to round off the entertainment, while the remaining members . . . kept time by clapping their hands, the colored boy broke into a tap dance, accompanied by Bix's immature cornet improvisations.[9]

His schoolwork wasn't brilliant, but he was doing his best to keep it at least adequate; the surge of energy that had got him out of Tyler Elementary still sustained him. There was perhaps another element, a kind of mute act of thanksgiving for this new freedom to work at his future career. The fact is that "lazy" Bix was now, in effect, going to school by night too, and with a zeal not even a Victorian schoolmaster (or Dick Hadlock) could find fault with.

It was after school, and often far into the night, that his real life went on: sitting at the piano working out a thought that had been running in his head all day; alone in his room with his horn and a beat-up phonograph purchased from the same pawnshop, end-lessly and laboriously shaping the figures and arpeggios* that are the matériel of the jazzman's counterpoint; having to be called half a dozen times for dinner (I seem to see the sad, resigned expressions of the normally cheerful Beiderbecke family as they peer covertly at their lost sheep for signs of weariness or weaken-ing), getting his food down as fast as good manners allowed (they were always a well-behaved family), and disappearing as soon afterward as decency dictated—destination Jazz.

For young Leon Beiderbecke as for the rest of young America, Mr. Ford's faithful Model T meant liberty—for them sexual, for him musical. Four or five nights a week he would go rattling around the countryside in a borrowed flivver, to any roadhouse or cabaret within 200 miles that had a band, to listen and sit in; for lovers of place names and local color, I offer the Terrace Gardens in Davenport, the Poppy Gardens near Geneseo, Illinois (not "Genesco," as one biographer spells it), and, somewhat later, the Tokyo Gardens in South Bend, Indiana. That was how you learned the art of jazz then (things haven't changed much in the interven-ing years): by screwing up your nerve to get on the bandstand alongside the pros, ready to do or die, and no matter how badly you loused it up or how many times your skill or inspiration failed you and made you want the earth to open and swallow you, going right back the next night and trying again—and in every available hour in between those ordeals continue your wood-shedding, day by day increasing your command of the instrument, going back over last night's tunes, sharpening your wit and invention—in short the hard way, the only way there was.

According to the aforementioned Esten Spurrier, whom I have no reason to disbelieve, Bix's cornet improvisations at that time *were* "immature" (we have no recordings to prove it one way or the other). Esten, Bix's closest friend and fellow musician at Davenport High, loved and palled around with Bix as few others were privileged to do; he was a few years ahead of Bix as a trum-petplayer, but says Bix soon left him far behind in musical accom-plishment. Even then, before Bix had any real command of his horn, his tireless dedication and enthusiasm made him the out-standing musician of his peer group—it was obvious to the rest of

*The notes of a chord played in succession instead of simultaneously (Ital., "harp-ing").

them that they were seeing genius at work, albeit still unripe and at the awkward age. So persuasive was Bix's influence on those around him, even as a teen-ager, that not only Esten but quite a few other budding trumpetplayers in the Davenport area grew up sounding a lot like him—we might almost call it "Davenport style" horn. Esten himself told me he "owed his whole musical career" to the fact of his long association with Bix, then and at intervals throughout the later years. Describing himself as "the best cheap imitation that was available" of his famous buddy, whom he still idolizes as the greatest human being he ever knew, Esten was always the first trumpetplayer sought after "when they couldn't get Bix," at least in the Tri-Cities area and around Chicago. Doubtless Esten Spurrier would have become far better known, on the strength of that reflected glory, but for the fact that he acquired, early in life, a family and the responsibilities that went with it, refused to travel, refused to drink or smoke tea or lead the jazz-man's nomad existence; but Bix soon became his god, and has remained so (he is now sixty-nine, but he still becomes moist-eyed at the sound of Bix's horn).

Another story related by Wareing and Garlick,[10] if true, offers a crucial insight into Bix's musical mind and what became his musical problems:

Wilbur Hatch, a student at the University of Chicago, engaged him . . . to play . . . weekends in a four-piece band at Delavan Lake, Wisconsin. . . . During the intermission Bix would move over to the piano; but his harmonies . . . sixth, ninth, and thirteenth chords . . . common in modern dance orchestrations, were then so revolutionary as to prove a source of much irritation to his companions . . . his efforts were condemned as mere progressions of discords.

These remarks, in conjunction with a map and our later knowledge of Bix's *modus operandi*, tell us a great deal. Spurrier, to whom I repeated the story, doubts it strongly. For one thing, he thinks he'd have known about it if Bix ever went that far away on a gig at sixteen—they traveled around together on jobs or just sitting in, almost every night of their lives during that couple of years; for another, he doesn't think Bix was as yet good enough to inspire Mr. Hatch to go a couple of hundred miles out of his way every weekend all summer just for a trumpet player to play his dances.

But the business of Bix and the piano has an authentic ring to it nonetheless. Something like it must have been happening somewhere; and if that is so, we have already a clear glimpse of an inner conflict, then still germinal, that was to play a crucial role in his subsequent lifelong dissatisfaction with his own creative work. It is a safe bet that there weren't many jazz musicians, circa 1919–1923, annoying their companions with harmonies that even in contemporary classical music were regarded as bold and experimental. We are reminded again of Miss Robinson's curiously prophetic insight into the mind of her dreamy little kindergartner—but when did genius ever take the traveled road? For Bix there was never, it seems, even such a possibility. Offered the conventional musical education, he had chosen instead the renegade path of jazz; now, having scarcely set foot in it, he was already finding that even that rough wild way had its clichés and commonplaces, perfectly acceptable to his "companions"—but not to Bix. Here too, while yet a raw apprentice, he felt the compulsion to create something fresh, to seek challenges to his musical imagination that were incomprehensible to the more ordinary minds around him, perfectly content to go from C to G and (by way of a G seventh) back to C again, ad infinitum; he was like the spirited boy who cannot walk down the stairs like any sensible person, but must slide down the banister or climb down the side, and generally risk his neck. And, ironically, the "foreign element" he strove to inject into jazz as he found it, in its then comparatively rudimentary state, was derived precisely from that classical background he had supposedly forsaken but would, as we will see, never forget. Eventually the whole world of jazz would take that path, the effort to combine in various ways the virtues of jazz and "classical"; in 1919 no one imagined such a direction—except sixteen-year-old Bix.

Life, Marx said, is struggle; but some lives are more so than others. The conflicts that beset Bix's soul, from early childhood on, were unusual in both quantity and quality; between force-fed education and his peculiar private needs, between conventional music education and his peculiar private ear, between a decent bourgeois vocation and jazz, with all the inevitable accompanying contradictions which in the end came down to day life versus night life—not to mention the more subtle but nonetheless harrowing struggle within his own musical psyche. For Bix now there was no turning back; for the first time since kindergarten days he had found, as it were, an atmosphere that would support life, an air he could breathe, and it was the smoky jazz-filled air of cabarets and nightclubs; he could no more have decided now to live as his parents thought fit than a bird could decide to live under water. Not surprisingly, it was during this time, according to Bix himself, that he first began to drink—not very much at first. It would have been strange if he hadn't.

On January 16, 1920, the Volstead Act became law; America was now officially dry, which meant it had become a point of honor with most Americans to serve and consume alcohol at roughly twenty times the rate they had ever done before. People who had never touched it before now drank openly, at home and abroad; those who had always drunk drank more. Even the frank alcoholic was no longer so much pitied as wryly admired—"Too bad he doesn't know when to stop" became "Boy! he can sure put it away!" To refuse a drink became square; not to offer one, rude. For the first time in the history of modern man it became chic to carry liquor in one's pocket; the *hip flask* became a routine item of commerce. Except in what H. L. Mencken used to call the Bible Belt, it became unusual to spend an evening out without being offered a drink—or a lot of drinks.

Naturally this was particularly true in the jazz world. The cabaret was traditionally on the margin of the law, even before Prohibition; now its links with the underworld, the only source of its main commodity, hardened into a permanent structure; as for jazz, the white man's version of it, it had been born in the cabaret, and for another half century would have no other home. Alcohol was as much part of the nightclub's atmosphere as stale smoke and velour drapes.

Bix, as the youngest in any crowd, would at first have done, in simple sociability, what everyone else did; but, as the reader will have gathered, Bix at seventeen already had better reasons to drink than most. We will come in due course to his relationship to alcohol, which was as special as everything else about his personality; here we may just note that night, freedom, the glow of alcohol, and the throb of jazz wove themselves into an indispensable psychic fabric, his nightly magic carpet.

Exactly when he started drinking "too much" I don't know. How much is too much? Everyone has a different answer to that question, generally based on how much he drinks himself (or thinks he should). Abraham Lincoln was prepared to grant Grant personal discretion; in reply to a complaint that the general drank two quarts of whiskey a day, Lincoln telegraphed, "Find out his brand—I would like to send some to my other generals," or words to that effect. For adolescent Bix, who had begun his noctambulations on Friday and Saturday nights and soon progressed to other nights as well, the appetite for the whole mélange was one which, as the French say, grows with the eating—with predictable effects on his daytime life. All things considered, it is astonishing how long he managed to burn that candle at both ends—nearly two and a half years—before something had to give. The something, of course, was his schoolwork.

Bix himself was always hazy as to the precise date of the disaster —a sort of gradual crisis. It is a depressing picture: the progressive decay of attention and understanding, the gradual engulfment by torpor and blank stupidity, the sporadic attempts to catch up, and —on this point alone Bix betrayed a rare ruefulness—the strenuous efforts, foredoomed, of some teachers to cover for him, overlook, ignore, stretch a grade. In vain. By the end of the 1921 spring term, as near as I can judge, it was clear that he wasn't going to make it at Davenport High. He was just past his eighteenth birthday.

It didn't exactly come as a surprise to his family. For quite a while now they had watched, with sorrow and helpless anxiety, their boy going wrong. Their saddest forebodings were indeed come true: sweet, quiet, well-behaved Leon had before their eyes turned into an alcoholic loafer, a jazz-crazy bum. Clearly something had to be done—but what?

5
LAKE FOREST

So he had passed beyond the challenge of the sentries who had stood as guardians of his boyhood . . . to escape by an unseen path: a new adventure was about to be opened to him. It seemed to him that he heard notes of a fitful music leaping upwards a tone and downwards a diminished fourth, upwards a tone and downwards a major third, like triple-branching flames leaping fitfully, flame after flame, out of a midnight wood. . . . This was the call of life to his soul and not the dull gross voice of duties and despair. . . . His soul had arisen from the grave of boyhood, spurning her graveclothes. Yes! Yes! Yes! He would create proudly out of the freedom and power of his soul . . . a living thing, new and soaring and beautiful, impalpable, imperishable.

James Joyce, *A Portrait of the Artist as a Young Man*

Military school has always appealed to certain parents as the way to "straighten out," as they say, a more than usually unrectilinear boy; a sort of dilute reform school. How well these institutions do the job has been much debated; today they are a dying industry, an idea whose time has come—and gone; but fifty years ago, to a conservative German-American family like the Beiderbeckes of Davenport, Iowa, that idea must have seemed eminently reasonable.

Having been during my own childhood the occasional object of similar parental anxieties, of sporadic (and vain) attempts to turn an eccentric *Wunderkind* into a Regular Boy, and later on a parent myself, I can sympathize with both parties to these tragicomedies—with the drive of parents to tow their rudderless offspring into some safe harbor, and the equally urgent need of the young to cut the rope and head for open water.

It is no trick for us now, at this distance, to see that Papa and Mama Beiderbecke's calculations were exactly 180 degrees out of phase with psychological reality, that the results must be the opposite of their intentions. The trick would have been to see it then, to descry the future through the turbulence of immediate problems. In defense of their fumbling, let us note that no one else ever did much better, including his best friends and loudest admirers. Not once in Bix's lifetime would any of us offer any clear, coherent view of what our confused hero was all about, or how he was to steer a rational course toward a rational goal. As one of them sadly remarked long afterward, none of us ever really knew who Bix was —least of all, of course, himself.

So for the last time Mr. and Mrs. Beiderbecke made that desperate effort to set their son's feet back on the road to respectability:

they decided to send him to a military academy.

They might have chosen any of a score of reputable schools scattered around the Midwest. The one they did choose was as good as any, a sedate establishment that flourishes to this day— Lake Forest Academy. That choice, however, strikes us today as a final ironic joke of the gods, the prank of a perverse fate, a plot device too pat for any selfrespecting novelist. For, as you may verify by glancing at a map, Lake Forest, Illinois, is less than forty miles away—about an hour's ride on the North Shore Electric— from what was then the jazz capital of the world: Chicago, Illinois.

Possibly Bix's fate was already sealed, his peculiar personality too well crystallized to be pressed into any very different shape; but it is tempting to speculate, for example, on how things might have turned out if the nearest center of attraction had been not Chicago, but some quiet little college town—preferably of a progressive, liberal-arts hue—with a good Music Department and some pretty music majors. One bright sensitive girl, one perceptive young instructor with a point of view, can change a boy's life. Nothing like that ever happened. Bix was destined to go on as he had begun, groping toward obscure goals, with only the haziest picture of what they ought to be.

Bix Beiderbecke at military school sounds to us today like a surrealist joke—Oscar Wilde as Tarzan, Woody Allen playing half-back with the Pittsburgh Steelers—but it is a fact that Bix himself saw nothing absurd in the suggestion at the time. From the little he ever said, I'm sure he went along with the idea, hoping, like his parents, that good would somehow come of it. Unlike young Dedalus, so stirringly depicted in the epigraph to this chapter, young Leon was no proud renegade, consciously challenging the shibboleths of the respectable world (writers as a rule know what they're up to, musicians as a rule don't); nor on the other hand was he the defiant truant, the tough little runaway telling the old man to go to hell. On the contrary, he was what in essence he would always be, the good boy, glad to please his loving papa and mama if he could, silently disgraced when he couldn't—which he felt was practically all the time. He probably felt in his heart that Mama and Papa and Professor Grade were right, that it was likely he'd never amount to anything, and must try harder. Also, the latest fiasco couldn't have been too pleasant; in his vague way Bix might well have felt any change was welcome—whatever Lake Forest

Academy might have in store, it could hardly be worse than the daily doze at Davenport; the catalogue had shown some fine pictures of cadets playing tennis and playing instruments.

I suspect there was something else too, a thought perhaps only half formed, lurking somewhere at the back of Bix's foggy unconscious. In his wanderings around the local jazz circuit, he could scarcely have failed to hear repeated tales of that fabulous Windy City, so near and yet (to a teen-age boy still under the parental roof) so far. Chi, as we called it (pron. *shy*), was "the place" so far as jazz musicians were concerned. The magic names were all there—King Oliver, Kid Ory, Johnny Dodds, Jimmy Blythe, Freddie Keppard, the New Orleans Rhythm Kings (a white band that *played just like niggers, man!*). In Chi, out on the South Side, blacks and whites mingled boldly in the "black & tan joints"; nobody cared; jazz was king. Nor could Bix fail to realize that a boy away at school is far more on his own than he would be living at home—and that Lake Forest, Illinois, was a lot nearer Chi than Davenport, Iowa. . . . Be that as it may, and however mortifying to idolaters of the Bix Beiderbecke legend, the lonely Free Soul imprisoned by heartless parental decree, the reality is that their hero saw nothing very dreadful about it, and duly arrived on campus, rather cheerful at the thought of being away from home for the first time, and also rather eager to unpack his horn and his rackets in fresh territory.

His induction at Lake Forest was quite auspicious. As I have already indicated, I never heard of anyone who didn't like him, and the people at Lake Forest, both students and faculty, were no exception. He was immediately popular even with *seniors*. Only readers who have attended a boarding school themselves, particularly a military school, can fully appreciate what that means, or understand how fiercely the upperclassmen guard their priceless protocol. Even for them to notice the very existence of an underclassman—let alone a new boy, a rookie, a fish—is almost unheard of; judge, then, the social revolution implied when not one but *two* of those exalted beings, Cadets Welge and Stewart, "took him up" the very first week, and overnight became his best friends on campus. There could be no accolade more absolute. It happened that Cy Welge and Sam Stewart had both been bitten hard, the previous year, by the jazz microbe—Cy played drums, Sam saxophone—and like every other musician or would-be musician that

been a glutton for punishment, or possibly determined to vindi-
cate his honor, but he never had a chance; I think Bix made a few
errors in the first few games, but after that Rodney was lucky to
get one or two points in a game—the score was something like 6–1,
6–0. Toward the end, Rodney blew up completely, which is understandable, and threw away his service in double faults, Bix repeatedly acing him and running him ragged with placements and drop
shots—in short, a slaughter of classic dimensions: "and Bix wasn't
even sweating" (it was a beautiful fall morning, and Bix's style
wasn't laborious), whereas Rodney . . . But over Rodney's condition and behavior—apparently he wasn't a graceful loser—and the
exultation of the gallery at his long overdue comeuppance, let us
(to swipe another line from Mark Twain) "draw the veil of Char-
ity."

I loved the story when I heard it (I was thirteen), for obvious
reasons, but in retelling it now I am struck by a small but mysterious circumstance that came out later, in a conversation with Bix.
I'm quite sure Bix said on that occasion that he and "the only other
good tennis player at Lake Forest" were amiable rivals during
Bix's whole time at the Academy. He even, I'm equally sure, told
me of a harmless practical joke they collaborated on, to put the
athletic director on—something to do with substituting dead balls
for fresh ones during a match. I think Bix said too that this rival
invited him to his home for a weekend; it had a private tennis
court and was otherwise "pretty swell," the swellest Bix had seen,
which suggests it must have been Rodney's, all right—everything
fits. What is a bit puzzling now is the idea that, with such a beginning, the classic case of making a lifelong enemy, Rodney could
ever have been turned into a friend. I don't suppose this trivial
mystery will ever be solved, since I don't even know who Rodney
was, nor whether "Bill" was perhaps exaggerating the temperature of the confrontation (or even the glee of the gallery); my own
opinion on the whole affair is that Bix's offhand modesty and total
lack of self-importance could charm away the churlishness of an
overdriven traffic court magistrate, and I find it hard to picture
even a "Rodney" (as described by "Bill") staying mad at him for
very long, especially as they had after all a common passion.

Cadet Beiderbecke didn't need tennis victories to clinch his
popularity. Jazz, as already remarked, was the universal rage
among the young in 1921 (though not much of it would perhaps

ever came in contact with Bix, they only had to hear h
time to be transfixed as by Cupid's arrow.

Another incident that occurred during Bix's second
did nothing to diminish his general popularity. One
seniors, who was rather generally disliked, *(a)* becaus
richest family, and *(b)* because he never let any of his f
forget it, was also Lake Forest's tennis champ, anothe
which he could be equally obnoxious.

As I heard the story several years later, not from F
but from another ex-Lake Forester, who came out
Municipal Pavilion one night, Bix had arrived on c
Wednesday or Thursday, and on Saturday morning
the first time to put on his tennis shoes and wande
courts in quest of a game. My informant—let's call hi
little more than a novice at tennis, and was lounging o
when Bix came up, watching the school champ—le
Rodney—practicing his serve. Bix asked Bill if he wai
but Bill begged off. Rodney then came over, ostensi
his sweater, more likely to look the new boy over; he
and decided to ignore him. He could hardly be blai
snap judgement. In contrast to Rodney's ultra-correc
whites, Bix must have looked like a farmboy who hap
wearing sneakers—old greasy pants, a moth-eaten swe
sizes too small, and tennis shoes that looked as if the
worn while lying under an automobile, which indee
have been. Bix, who probably never noticed he was bei
asked Rodney if he'd care to hit a few. Rodney in retu
how long Bix had been playing; Bix said a couple of ye
point a couple of Saturday girl visitors appeared—F
added, was also a formidable ladykiller. Rodney chang
and told Bix O.K., he'd play him a set.

While they were warming up, the news that Rodne
had deigned to take on the New Boy must have spr
crowd of spectators began to appear, which soon grew
gallery. The contrast between the two gladiators must
hilarious. Bill said he felt sorry for the new boy, everyoi
ing about his old pants and the girls tittering at the s

I no longer recall the details of this match, whic
counted to me with relish—only that the New Boy poli
champ in straight sets, two or perhaps three. Rodney

be classed by today's connoisseurs as *jazz*), and Bix blew just about the most exciting jazz most of these students had ever heard.

The musical director was a Professor Koepke (Bix, believe it or not, didn't even remember his name three years later), who was ever on the watch for recruits to the school orchestra—forty pieces, give or take a few trombones. Finding that Cadet Beiderbecke came of a family both German and musical, and played the cornet, he lost no time; all in his first week, Bix was signed up for tennis, baseball, football, and as Professor Koepke's forty-first piece.

Had Dr. Koepke known what brand of music Cadet Beiderbecke was really into, he might have been less eager to invite this hawk into his dovecote. It never occurred to Bix to conceal his lowbrow leanings, and we can imagine the good Strasbourger musician's dismay as he listened for the first time to his new find rip into the audition repertory of Waldteufel waltzes, Napoleonic marches, and other light standards, as they are known in the trade —all with an unmistakable jazz beat. He was also appalled to observe that this youth with the faultless ear was faking everything, and couldn't read a note. Bix's own role couldn't have been any more rewarding; the professor's menu of musical *Kartoffel-küchen* was not exactly refreshing to his palate: Professor Grade all over again.

Professor Koepke, an ex-officer in the German army as well as a conductor, was not accustomed to having to speak twice. He let young Cadet Beiderbecke know in unambiguous terms that there would be no Dixielanding under his baton. Bix did his best to (literally) play it straight for a few days, but in the end the good Herr Doktor's solemnity, plus the persistent egging-on of his fellow players, proved too much for his wry sense of humor; the temptation was more than flesh could resist. The debacle came at a particularly outrageous moment, when the professor was showing off his orchestra to some musical visitors. To the opening measures of Elgar's familiar "Pomp and Circumstance" March no. 1 Bix saw fit to add, as counterpoint, with a hot-jazz beat, the refrain of *How Ya Gonna Keep 'Em Down on the Farm*. Professor Koepke must have narrowly missed having a stroke. Cadet Beiderbecke was soundly chewed out in front of his giggling comrades, excused from practice for ten days, and permanently excused from taking any more solos. But Bix said he behaved himself after that one prank, more a reflex of musical nerves than a case of malicious mischief. Bix after all enjoyed any musical activity, at this point, better than none at all; and the frequent practice was excellent for his lip, though his highly personal fingering may have caused the professor a few added gray hairs.

Like many "quiet" people, Bix had plenty of his own sort of energy and persistence of purpose; he was also, in his quiet way, a capable and methodical organizing force. He quickly got up some musical activities that more than made up for Professor Koepke's menu. Within a fortnight of his coming to Lake Forest he had put together a nine-piece dance band (the contemporary euphemism for a jazz combo), with Cy Welge, Sam Stewart, and himself as nucleus, and their own book* and rehearsal schedule. Since the term *dance* could mean anything from the hottest Dixie-land to the pallidest ricky-ticky hotel-tea-hop music, the faculty were caught napping, and at first made no objection to this Fifth Column forming under their very noses, using, moreover, the school's own instruments and facilities. Knowing that the least taint of jazz was *streng verboten,* Bix made a manful effort to repress the irrepressible, but—even at that early age, evidently— he could hardly put horn to lip without "cooking," as can be inferred from an explicit paragraph that appeared in *Caxy,* the Lake Forest student magazine, issue of October 29, 1921, less than two months after Bix's matriculation:

Bix Beiderbecke, one of our "home talents," furnished the music, which was declared to be unexcelled by his fellow students;

and from a subsequent revelation by one of those fellow students, as quoted in Wareing and Garlick:

"Bix succeeded in obtaining official approval for his band and trotting it out [for them]. . . . The result was pandemonium, as Bix and his gang really shelled out. . . . The staid old building rocked like Lunceford night at the Savoy.†

It all culminated in the Principal climbing the ladder to the balcony,

*The current repertory of a dance or jazz band, comprising either printed stock arrangements or "originals," put together by the band—and not necessarily all on paper.
†The Savoy opened sometime in 1926, and quickly became Harlem's leading ballroom ("The Home of Happy Feet"), the mecca for every first-class black band and dancer in the country. Playing "the Track" was being on the jazz Big Time. The reference in the text is evidently to what used to happen there when the dancers got swinging and jumping at a certain tempo, which happened to corre-

from which the blast was blowing, and clamping an official . . . soft pedal on the proceedings."[11]

Presumably the instructors at Lake Forest Academy were no worse than any other conventional pedagogues of the time and place. The principal, Mr. Richards, and Professor Koepke, like most men in their position, had probably come to regard, from long habit, any vessel they couldn't steer as unsafe; but they couldn't steer Bix Beiderbecke's. Who could have? The hour was already very late. Considering the age they lived in, they all tried pretty hard. It was an age when most schools were frankly custodial institutions—by no accident, they looked a lot like prisons and asylums. Students were expected to speak only when spoken to, and many were unaware that teachers had first names. Any sympathizing with a child's difficulties was frowned on as "coddling"; the tool most employed for driving facts into his head was the drill. Bix must have got very special handling, for he recalled, with a guilty shake of the head, that some of his officer-instructors went far out of their way to try to crank that reluctant engine. But right from the first they had severe competition for their attention.

By 1921 jazz had entirely displaced ragtime as the popular music of America. Much of what the white public listened to would hardly measure up to the standards of today, including those of the most rabid collectors of early jazz, but what it lacked in quality it more than made up in quantity. Every café, roadhouse, upstairs restaurant, and chop suey joint, in town and out in the country, felt compelled to provide its patrons with some variety of jazz band —hot or "sweet," rough or smooth, pure or diluted. And, predictably, the nearer to Chi, the thicker and hotter were the jazz bands.

No sooner had Bix settled into the Academy's routine than he embarked on his previously established practice of night roving, in quest of places to listen and sit in. If by day he showed only mediocre application in math, history, &c, by night he once more found energy and diligence enough for ten—in the only kind of school that ever made any sense to him. Violating a military school's strictest rule, Bix would sneak out after taps two or three

---

spond to the natural (resonance) period of the dance floor: the entire floor could be seen vibrating up and down like a guitar string. Jimmy Lunceford's big band was a hardy perennial at the Track, and the above-described phenomenon often occurred while they were playing.

nights a week, alone or with some vassal he had corrupted, carrying his horn in a paper bag, and head for one of the neighboring
Nachtlokale, in all of which he soon became a familiar face.

Once there, we can be sure, he had no trouble getting himself
invited onto the bandstand. Even then, every musician with an
ear for jazz must have sensed instantly that it was this youngster's
natural element. As with great chess players, so with great musicians; most of them give early glimpses of what is to come. As
Bobby Fischer's and Paul Morphy's first recorded games already
exhibit the stigmata of genius, as Stravinsky's First Symphony,
openly a student imitation of Tchaikovsky, is nevertheless recognizably Stravinsky, so Bix, earwitnesses say, was already Bix in
1921. What we all heard pouring out of his horn only a couple of
years later, the sharply etched style and astonishing conception
that so stunned the jazz world, must all have been there, in essence, when he was an eighteen-year-old cadet skulking out of
grounds at night to dumfound the natives.

I would guess too that this must have been the time of Bix's most
rapid growth as a musician. Everyone around him could feel the
heat from that inner fire. His room in East House quickly became
hangout and headquarters for every cadet with a musical ear, as
well as quite a few professional jazzmen working in the vicinity.
Hours of every day of Bix's life were spent practicing, listening to
records the boys pooled their allowances to buy, or running
through the Dixieland and popular repertory with anyone who
cared to join in. It was characteristic of Bix that he would, as often
as not, go on practicing right through mess call and the dinner
hour, or after taps, frequently carrying several admiring companions along on the tide of shattered regulations. They reaped a
harvest of warnings, demerits, and penalties; they muffled the
music but wouldn't stop it. "Cy Welge would tap out his rhythms
on the study table, and Bix would continue playing with a handkerchief or towel stuffed down the bell of his cornet. . . ."[12]

As had happened before in Bix's life, his new surge of energy,
spreading outward from its musical center, sent forth ripples that
were reflected in other areas, mainly tennis, football, and baseball.
On the courts he was considered "a terror"; on the football field,
though only a sophomore and weighing less than 140 pounds, he
was such a tiger that other players complained to the coach that
he and Sam Stewart, a senior, ought not to be playing on the same

squad; Bix was duly transferred from the Orange Team to the Black. In the classroom he again made a determined effort to tackle his studies; the results were, to quote one teacher, "erratic"; he seldom did well on exams, achieving a passing grade only by the skin of his teeth, and possibly a bit of illicit help from devoted friends. Even so, his efforts were appreciated by his teachers, who had not failed to detect, from the very first week, which way the wind blew in this strange boy's head.

On his Christmas visit home, Bix managed to give his folks the impression that all was well at Lake Forest, and no doubt he thought so himself. But on returning there in January, 1922, he, Cy, and fellow conspirators sharply expanded their jazz activities. Bix was rapidly attaining professional status on cornet, and also playing a good deal of piano. He and his henchmen now formed the Cy-Bix Orchestra, which included several ringers from Chicago, and began to advertise their services in the local newspapers; they soon had paid engagements, on and off campus, and became known up and down the North Shore (as for some reason unknown the eastern shore of Illinois and Wisconsin on Lake Michigan is called), as far away as Milwaukee. Not only did fellow students playing alongside Bix look up to him as their musical god, but professional musicians made no secret of the fact that they felt honored to sit on the same stand with him. Those who were around to hear him then agree that there was no longer any question of equality or rivalry. Bix was the unchallenged star; they were happy to shine as satellites in his reflected radiance. About that time too, Professor Koepke regretfully gave up his attempts to interest or guide this young genius, for whom he had cherished such high hope, in his own kind of music; he abandoned the renegade to his fate.

However, Bix's other teachers, during this brief false dawn, were optimistic enough about his progress to give Papa Beiderbecke, who paid the Academy a surprise visit early in the 1922 spring semester, an encouraging report. But at that same time Bix was so naïve as to brag to his father, with a pride he obviously expected him to share, that he, Bix, was a welcome guest in every nightspot in the vicinity that featured jazz! Both father and son must have played their roles in this little scene perfectly, a mutually tacit game of voluntary self-deception, or nonperception: either father managed not to hear this good news or not to draw

the obvious inferences from it, or son managed not to observe
father's reaction—or perhaps a little of each; for Bix said he
remembered Dad leaving for Davenport well satisfied that the
military school magic was working, his youngest's dangerous "idleness" had been exorcised—a major miracle! By the way, Bix seems
to have thought all this too—one more instance of that essential
trait that, along with the power to symbolize, sets the human
animal apart from all others: the ability (and need) to *rationalize*
—to believe that if we want something to happen, it will, or that
if we want to do something, it must be right to do it.

Needless to say, the miracle was a mirage. (Bix himself never
saw through his own little game until I inadvertently pointed it out
to him a few years later—something I had been uniquely
equipped to do by both nature and nurture, as we will see. As a
boy I regarded teachers as an unnecessary evil, something to be
avoided, like tsetse flies, and couldn't understand why any decent
chap like Bix would ever have wanted to *please* one.) The truth
was simple enough. Just as Bix had needed to get out of Tyler
Elementary into the comparative freedom of high school, so he
now needed, with ever intensified urgency and passion, to go on
living away from home, to continue his nightly apprenticeship to
the one thing in life that mattered; in both instances the path to
that freedom, so far as Bix could make it out, lay through a kind
of bramble thicket of books and "subjects" in which he could take
neither pleasure nor interest, and of well-meaning "teachers" who
couldn't teach him anything but who must somehow be cajoled
into scribbling "C" for "correct" at the top edges of a certain
indispensable number of test papers; and he would have to—or
still believed he would have to—somehow crawl and scramble his
way through that thicket . . . if only he could stay awake.

In short, whatever effort Bix was presently making in school was
almost wholly motivated by his underlying resolve to make the
grade as a jazz musician (which doesn't mean he was necessarily
conscious of his reasons); and by what must by now have become
a really desperate (if not conscious) realization that he could never
go home again, never again make even a pretense of leading the
square, futureless life that would be his lot if he ever did go back,
a failure, to the parental roof. He had indeed reached a point of
no return; there was only one way he could go now.

The next step in our hero's odyssey was not far—only thirty-five miles due south, to be exact—and now about to happen any moment. Only a mind like Bix's, with its curious assortment of drives and defenses, aspirations, evasions, and preoccupations, could have managed so long to remain unaware of where it must take him: to that unique and rather intimidating city of the plains, an hour's ride on the North Shore Electric—Chicago, Illinois, *c.* 1922.

6
THE WINDY CITY

Hog Butcher for the World,
Tool Maker, Stacker of Wheat,
Player with Railroads and the Nation's Freight Handler;
Stormy, husky, brawling,
City of the Big Shoulders:
They tell me you are wicked, and I believe them . . .
And they tell me you are crooked, and I answer: Yes, it is true I have
    seen the gunman kill and go free to kill again.
And they tell me you are brutal, and my reply is: On the faces of
    women and children I have seen the marks of wanton hunger.
And having answered so I turn once more to those who sneer at this
    my city, and I give them back the sneer and say to them:
Come and show me another city with lifted head singing so proud
    to be alive and coarse and strong and cunning.
Flinging magnetic curses amid the toil of piling job on job, here is
    a tall bold slugger set vivid against the soft little cities . . .
Bareheaded,
Shoveling,
Wrecking,
Planning,
Building, breaking, rebuilding,
Under the smoke, dust all over his mouth, laughing with white
    teeth,

Under the terrible burden of destiny laughing as a young man
laughs,
Laughing even as an ignorant fighter laughs who has never lost a
battle,
Bragging and laughing that under his wrist is the pulse, and under
his ribs the heart of the people,
Laughing!
Laughing the stormy, husky, brawling laughter of Youth, half-
naked, sweating, proud to be Hog Butcher, Tool Maker, Stacker
of Wheat, Player with Railroads and Freight Handler to the Nation.

Carl Sandburg, *Chicago* (1916)

Chicago, Chicago,
That toddlin' town! . . .

Fred Fisher, *Chicago**

The Union Stock Yards stretched from Thirty-sixth Street south to Fifty-first, and from State Street all the way to Kedzie, nineteen square miles of bleating, groaning animals, pens and stockades funneling them into the houses of death, giant killing wheels that caught them by a foot and hoisted them, shrieking and bellowing, to confront the hulking Swedes and Polacks and Hunkies with their long bright knives, their high boots crimsoned and slippery, splashed from head to foot with blood and guts and shit, straddling the steaming gutters bubbling with fresh hot red blood. Nights when the wind was from the south the heavy stink of guts and glue and hides would drift over the city like a memo, over the miles of back-porch slums along the South Side L tracks, all the way to the shining palaces of the North Shore millionaires and lakefront luxury hotels, to remind all Chicago how much of its wealth depended on blood, guts, shit, and death. Upton Sinclair's greatest book took its title from what the men who worked in the stockyards in 1906 called it, The Jungle; it told how men fell into the vats and got boiled up into soap, one of the more kindly things that happened to workers there. International scandal, indignant congressmen, investigations, new laws (among others the Pure Food & Drug Act, 1906—look it up). The millionaire butchers shrugged and passed the word: no more people in the soap. No one really gave a damn one way or the other, and Chicago went right on making its principal product, money.

Anywhere in Chicago, you were never far from the sound, sight, and smell of a railroad. Chicago was the biggest rail center in the world, with I forget how many lines coming in from every corner of the North American continent—the figure 72 sticks in my mind; is that possible? anyhow a lot. You came smoothly rushing and swaying toward the big ugly town across miles of prairie, then suddenly you were passing a few smoking factories, then more farm and prairie, the telegraph wires outside the Pullman window smoothly rising and abruptly dropping like miles of music paper, birds dotting them like black sixteenth notes racing by in a swift silent melody over the never-ending rhythm of the wheels, then without any warning you were right in it, still going fast and smooth, past long stretches of grimy warehouses and blackened steel mills, the roadway at your side suddenly sinking down between gloomy streets and clattering across black iron bridges, getting more and more entangled in the wilderness of steel ribbons crisscrossing like giant tick-tack-toe boards; now gradually drifting to lesser speeds, rumbling over more miles of switches and curving track, everything around you getting blacker and smokier every minute, the long powerful train running at half speed now through the yards, passing with a sudden rush of sound another train, another train overtaking you and swaying alongside for a moment and then curving widely away on its own track, and another and another, converging, diverging, vanishing. "Chicago! . . . Chicago!" . . . The conductor's drone as he strode calm through the swaying cars, their overhead lamps swinging in perspective down the long aisle. "Chicago! . . . *Chicago!*" . . . It had a quickening, almost ominous note. *"Chicago! . . . LaSalle Street Station!"*. . .

That was the first thing you saw in Chicago—hugeness, smoke, noise, the caverned darkness of the enormous station dim with smoke above you; smoke, noise, casual indifference, a veiled ferocity and hard glare, extremes of shabbiness and luxury, a vast sprawl of steel, stone, concrete, glass; glittering, grimy, rich, poor, neither knowing nor caring how anybody had got rich or stayed poor; that and the hard seamed faces of the taxi drivers, faces that had seen everything and would see it again.

Big Bill Thompson, William Hale Thompson, was our mayor. If there had been no such man as Big Bill Thompson, Chicago would have had to invent him. From 1902 on he had been a power in Cook County politics, riding a rising tide of easy graft and cheerful corruption that finally put him right where he'd always belonged, in City Hall, three terms including the time of World War I, when he campaigned, if I remember right, on the urgent issue of keeping America pure and safe from the dastardly designs of (no kidding) England. Why England is a bit more than I can recall, but I have a vivid picture of Mayor Thompson, looking exactly like a Mississippi redneck sheriff at a lynching, standing on an open platform with American flags draped all over everything, shooting off firecrackers (I suppose it was the Fourth of July) and displaying a picket sign that read something like WE KICKED THEM OUT IN 1776/DON'T LET THEM BACK IN NOW. William Hale Thompson, Big Bill to his friends, and who wasn't his friend? Every pimp, racketeer, blue-sky stock swindler, and grafting truckman on the Cook County secret payroll could swear they never had a better friend in this world, especially of course the Irish; the Sicilian gorillas and beer runners and the Jewish gamblers he learned to love later, and none of them ever forgot to reciprocate, making sure every ballot box on the North Side knew which way to lean, come the first Tuesday in November. Yes, as long as Big Bill was in office, Carl Sandburg might well strum his guitar and rhapsodize on the gunman going free to kill again (probably knocking off one of Big Bill's do-gooder critics; Chi wasn't a healthy place for reformers to get too uppity in). That long happy reign was no accident; in a way you'd have to have lived there to understand, Big Bill Thompson *was* Chicago.

Another unique feature, when I lived there—and it is little changed today—was the Lake.

Unlike many American cities, Chicago never murdered its waterfront, neither burying it behind a wilderness of wharf and warehouse nor selling its soul to the garish electric whorehouse of the Coney Island boardwalk culture. When I lived there, Lake Michigan in its majesty was simply and majestically *there*, running the length of the city north and south, and northward for another hundred miles of mysteriously unspoiled shoreline. From a considerable area of the huge city, you could walk down any cross street and sit at the water's edge, put your feet on sand and pebbles or grassy bank, look at lapping waves and listen to the ancient cry of shore birds. Beaches were everywhere, and they were free. Anywhere within a mile or so of the Lake, all summer long, you could see people in bathing suits—grownups might add a robe—heading for it, many of them barefoot.

There is a special ambience about a city from which you can see blue water and distant steamers. The sheer noble presence of the great lake—actually a sizable inland sea, 307 miles long and 118 miles wide, a thousand feet deep—was a pervasive influence, an enlargement of the soul. Sparkling blue in the summer sunlight, gray and threatening under the sullen storm scud, laced with wild fierce whitecaps in the winter gales, the Lake too was always there, was Chicago. To the deadening pressures of big-city life it opposed the casual freedom of beach towns, in the long hot Chicago summer; in the terrible Chicago winter it turned on the city with impartial savagery, pounding the miles of creaking breakwaters with mountainous seas and eighty-mile winds, bringing to our lives a note of wild challenge as if we all inhabited some lone lighthouse on a rock.

A few blocks west of the Lake ran the L—Chicago Elevated Rapid Transit Railroad—roaring and rumbling over the streets it had darkened, stretching its black iron trestles for miles north, south, and west from the Loop—so named because all lines met there, circled, and diverged again to the far corners of the city— north to Evanston and Winnetka, west to Oak Park, Ravenswood, and Cicero, south to Calumet and the Indiana border. Twice a day five days a week, a million Chicagoans packed themselves into its crude wooden cars like sardines, bulging from the open platforms in all weathers, hanging perilously over the hand-operated iron gates, rocking and rumbling to the factories and blast furnaces and slaughterhouses and offices, the biggest, noisiest industrial machine in history, and back again at night over the dark streets. Every city with an L knows the dreary right-of-way it darkens, the grim resignation of those poor enough to live under it, its uneasy shadows by night, its grimy wooden stations, soot-blackened and weathered until they melt into the squalid cityscape. In its L as in many big-city features, Chicago was much like New York; but the differences were even more striking.

It is often said that New York isn't America. But what is? which is to say, what big, complex city is?

Memphis, Tennessee, and Bend, Oregon, are unquestionably America, but could a transvestite photographer, a Neapolitan gunman, a Hindu poet, America's best symphony orchestra, most exciting opera company, best classical composer, greatest con man, toughest jazz bands, and farthest-out "little" magazines—plus the IWW, Eugene V. Debs, and the inventors of the skyscraper and Pullman car—find happiness there? In Chicago they could, and I never heard anyone say Chicago wasn't America; on the contrary.

Sandburg, with his ungovernable Whitmanesque raptures over everything and anything "American," was far from being Chicago's only literary celebrant. Before and after World War I, the town was crawling with avant-garde poets, revolutionary writers, artists, critics, and assorted free-form intelligentsia. Most famous were the "Chicago group"—Theodore Dreiser, Sherwood Anderson, Ben Hecht, Floyd Dell, et al.—but there were many, many others.

Harriet Monroe's pioneering magazine, *Poetry* (b. Chicago, 1912; d. New York City, 1924), was first published there; so was the *Little Review* (b. Chicago, 1914; d. Paris, 1929), of which more in a moment. On North Clark Street, not far from the garage where seven gang chiefs died in that many seconds in the Saint Valentine's Day massacre ordered by Al Capone, was a saloon called the Dill Pickle Club, which spawned more musical, art, and literary projects than the slopes of Parnassus. After 1920 it became a speakeasy. Ben Hecht's celebrated *Daily News* column, "1001 Afternoons in Chicago," was often written there at a table behind the bar. Arthur Weil, the notorious Yellow Kid, hatched his most elaborate con games there, and, when he had made a big score, was its grandest spender.

It was in the Dill Pickle that John Alden Carpenter, one of the few American classical composers worth remembering, first met Rabindranath Tagore (or so my brother told me), whose beautiful *Children's Songs* he set beautifully to music; at a corner table, I was told, he sketched out the themes for the three most interesting and original ballet scores ever created in this country: *Skyscrapers, Krazy Kat,* and *The Birthday of the Infanta*.

It was also the place where Jane Heap and Margaret Anderson, openly and militantly living as husband & wife, mostly edited the aforementioned *Little Review,* the most vigorously avant-garde magazine ever seen on this continent; its cover, printed on a different-color art paper each month, bore the belligerent subtitle, in 36-point type: A MAGAZINE OF THE ARTS/MAKING NO COMPROMISE WITH THE PUBLIC TASTE. Reader, guess where James Joyce's *Ulysses* first saw print. Dublin? London? Paris? New York? Not at all. *Chicago.* Yes; our two dauntless dykes, Anderson & Heap, were absolutely the first people in the syphilized world (to swipe a joke from Mr. Joyce) with the courage to publish that rather important work—the first eleven "episodes" as Joyce called them, one a month—probably the first appearance in public of such good old English words as "fuck" and "cunt." Eleven history-making episodes, before the cops awoke to the nation's peril and shut down the magazine—but that was in New York, whither it had rashly migrated. The *Little Review*'s contributors included Picasso, Marcel Duchamp, T. S. Eliot, Djuna Barnes, Sean O'Casey, André Gide, Jean Cocteau, Amy Lowell, Vachel Lindsay, and of course its London editor, Ezra Pound, along with the entire gang of Left Bank expatriates around Gertrude Stein. It was also the first to publish the poems and Dada collages of the Mad Baroness, Else von Freytag, who anticipated the *surréalistes* by some years—she who announced to the Berlin police (I think in 1921) that on her birthday she would shave and shellac her head and walk naked down the Kurfürstendamm (she did); but it was Chicago, not Berlin, that gave her an audience.

It was no accident that Mary Garden, the tiny but puissant redhead who stormed the Opéra Comique at twenty-five, became Debussy's first and favorite Mélisande, and then made a similar conquest of the Met, found only in Chicago the definitive setting for her natural gifts—and so did "Scarface" Al Capone. Capone did it with a hail of bullets and pineapple bombs that made him the undisputed crime king of Prohibition America, his thoughtful blend of murder and merger netting him for more than a decade a $100,000,000-a-year income from booze and broads alone. Garden made her killing just as effectively, by "joining" (i.e., capturing) the Chicago Civic Opera and remodeling it to her taste, replacing what she rudely called "wopera" with modern French and Russian repertory; in 1921, cowed, they made her general director; she promptly produced *Louise, Pelléas et Mélisande,* the world premiere of Prokofiev's *Love for Three Oranges,* and a $3,000,000 deficit for the year—a world record at the time—then swiftly got it all back by extorting it, with a mixture of charm, insults, and threats from the meat packers' wives who had originally nurtured this viper by paying for her education and sending her to Paris.

At home & abroad, the standard-bearers of the Chicago Culture behaved in a certain way, the Dill Pickle Club & *Little Review* way—a Chicago way. A few further anecdotes from the annals of the irrepressible Miss Garden, and others, will suggest the flavor better than any mere adjective. Garden was a crushing ad-libber, whose *lustige Streiche* and fearsome squelches were legendary; I reluctantly limit myself to three. (1) Producing Strauss's *Salome* in Boston(!) with herself in the title role, she let it be known in a newspaper interview that in the famous Dance of the Seven Veils there would be nothing under the seventh but Miss Garden, who by the way was extremely good-looking and stacked like a *Playboy* centerfold (I attended a lecture she gave at sixty, and can testify that those astonishing convexities were still defying gravity). Naturally the city fathers were in shock. On the morning of the fatal day the mayor and a deputation of councilmen personally visited the diva to beg her not to. Miss G. welcomed them at the door of her hotel suite nude; they fled; that night she did her dance as scheduled. (2) Invited as co-guest of honor with Chauncey M. Depew to a Washington banquet celebrating his ninety-second birthday, Garden arrived in a gown so ruthlessly *décolleté* that even hardened newsmen were shaken. Depew, himself no mean wit, stood it as long as he could, then at last, with a courtly twinkle, quavered, "Forgive me, Miss Garden, if I have seemed to stare; but I have been wondering all evening just what it is that is keeping that gown of yours *up!*" and, as reported by the journalists, received the now legendary reply (with a demure tap of her fan upon his arm): "Only your extreme old age, Mr. Depew!" (3) One of the Chicago meat-packer queens, I think Mrs. Potter Palmer, asked Miss Garden—to whom, over the years, she'd probably given cash donations totaling $100,000—to an afternoon musicale at her palatial Lake Shore Drive home, an affair glittering with international musical celebrities. At what she judged to be a right moment, and with someone of the order of Paderewski or Rachmaninoff seated at the piano, Mrs. Potter Palmer cooed, "Dearest Mary, won't you sing something for us?" Miss Garden rose graciously and obliged with *Depuis le Jour* and a couple of little songs by Fauré (as always in her faultless Scottish accent); then, in the hush that followed the applause, turned to her hostess and remarked amiably, "That will be five thousand dollars." Mrs. Potter Palmer paled, but managed to say, "Certainly. My secretary will send you a check," but then unwisely added, "Naturally I shall *not* expect you to mingle with my guests," to which Garden unhesitantly replied, in those silver tones that carried to the farthest potted palm, "Oh! In that case the fee will be only four thousand dollars!"

That was pure Chicago style, which can be sensed also in Al Capone's response to a summons from the Cook County DA: arriving at the head of a cavalcade of a dozen brand-new black armored Cadillacs filled with his bodyguards, all wearing expensive new suits, Scarface walked into the DA's office flanked by four stone-faced companions—and emerged an hour later to boast, at an impromptu press conference, "Dey got nuttin on Capone. Capone is clean. Capone is strickly legit. Dis ain't prosecution, it's poisecution." This was about one month after he was reliably reported to have personally beaten an associate to death with a baseball bat.

It was equally visible in the behavior of Ben Hecht in Hollywood, where he and Charlie MacArthur were doing the screenplay of their Broadway hit *The Front Page;* they not only wrote into their contract with MGM that the studio must decorate their office as an authentic French whorehouse, complete with red flowered wallpaper, brass bed, & crucifix, but imported a real-life French whore to play the piano while they worked and accommodate them both in the intermissions. When Irving Thalberg, head of the studio, sent them a reprimand, they returned it with a marginal comment: "Not strong enough."

There was a definite Chicago flavor, also, in the way Ralph Shackley, famous fashion photographer and drag queen (and a close friend of my brother Gene's), chose to execute Helena Rubinstein's commission to create the Ideal Eternal Feminine as her product symbol: Ralph took a shot of his own gorgeous face, suitably creamed and swathed in gauze from brow to chin, which looked out enigmatically at all of us for the next forty years in ten thousand Helena Rubinstein ads, possibly the most publicly displayed hoax of all time.

There was more than a touch of it in the way the Yellow Kid (a good friend of my mother's), awaiting trial in Cook County Jail on one of his celebrated million-dollar swindles, whiled away the time by selling one of the jailers a money machine. (Incidentally, he beat that rap—as he usually did—and saved himself a tidy sum by acting as his own attorney. "The mere thought," he subsequently boasted in the Dill Pickle Club, to my mother and a circle of other admirers, "that any man should be *paid* to hypnotize a judge and jury *with words,* in the presence of the *Yellow Kid,* was mortifying.")

The Chicago jazz scene was likewise unique. To understand it, it is necessary to know something about the "state of the art" as a whole at that period.

Beginning about 1915, jazz had been undergoing a remarkable transformation, from an essentially regional and racial folk music —southern U.S., black—into a major national art, our first and only, destined soon to cross the remotest frontiers of the globe. A variety of factors combined to make Chicago, after 1917, its most active hotbed. In the previous thirty years, that singular metropolis on the Delta, New Orleans, one of the most sophisticated cities of the Western world—multilingual, polyglot, permissive, cynical, urbane—had become a paradise for jazzmen; its celebrated red-light district, Storyville, offered them more gainful employment per square foot than any other area in the country. Nor was the nexus between music and milieu accidental, nor the fact that when puritan America, Land of the Pilgrims' Pride, finally found a name for that music, it was the obscene epithet *jazz*. To the folks of Storyville, whores and johns alike, the name can hardly have come as a shock: had they not been looked down upon for decades as jazz babies and jazz hounds? To anyone given to reflection on such matters—"soc." majors and visiting anthropologists please note—this name borne by our national music is profoundly instructive: in effect, "music to copulate by," with permanent, built-in overtones of scorn & defiance, the hypocritical scorn of the respectable who so named it, the sardonic defiance of those who picked up the dirty name and would wear it ever after as a badge of (to borrow a Marxist locution) class-conscious honor.

It is important to see places like Storyville in proper perspective, for their contribution to "jazz history." It is by no means my intention to add fuel to the fable that jazz was "born" in New Orleans (which is like saying the English language was born in London), "came up the river to Chicago," *etcetera, etcetera.* The truth of course is that the gestation process was going on simultaneously, if unevenly, all over America, especially in sizable black communities. (Ma Rainey, b. 1886, was from Columbus, Ga.; Eubie Blake, b. 1883, Baltimore, Md.; James P. Johnson, b. 1891, New Brunswick, N.J.; Mamie Smith— the first recorded blues singer— b. 1890, Cincinnati, O.; Bessie Smith, "Empress of the Blues," b. 1894, from Chattanooga, Tenn.; Willie "The Lion" Smith, b. 1897, from Goshen, N.Y. and the Haverstraw, N.Y., brickyards, where, Willie said, "those colored people . . . sang blues all day. Men older than I will tell you that."[13]) But it is no fable that where you found blacks & whites united in celebration of those two essential seque-lae of the Christian morality, whores and night life, you were pretty sure to find jazz; and Storyville was for three decades a fine example. Then, in 1917, Storyville was suddenly shut down; hun-dreds of jazz musicians migrated northward to Chicago, though not "up the river" (the Mississippi is over 100 miles from Chicago at Lincolnville, Illinois, the nearest point); like Louis Armstrong, they took the Illinois Central; so much for popular fables.

They had lost their jobs largely because of another popular fable, the notion that licensed prostitution promotes venereal dis-ease (the opposite is true), but also because three years before, on June 28, 1914, an eighteen-year-old Serbian high school student named Gavrilo Princip shot and killed the Archduke Francis Fer-dinand of Austria, and his wife, at Sarajevo, Bosnia. One thing led to another, as the saying goes, and thirty-six days later, a million and a half German troops were marching through Belgium on their way to conquer France; World War I had begun.

On April 6, 1917, the United States declared war on Germany and, a few weeks later, on the wicked women of Storyville. Secre-tary of the Navy Josephus Daniels, as upright a blockhead as ever drew a bureaucratic breath, ever zealous to protect the health and morals of Our Boys in Blue, and horrified by the existence of such facilities so near an important naval base, primly decreed that the girls must go. In vain the mayor of New Orleans protested that the "cure" was an illusion:

. . . [recognizing] prostitution as a necessary evil in a seaport the size of New Orleans, our city . . . has believed that the situation could be adminis-tered more easily . . . by confining it within a prescribed area. Our experi-ence has taught us that the reasons . . . are unanswerable, but the Navy Department . . . has decided otherwise.[14]

As regularly happens, mere experience made no impression on the Official Mind, and on November 12, 1917, Storyville, weeping, expired; an eyewitness described the last day:

The scene was pitiful. Basin Street, Franklin, Iberville . . . became a veritable shambles of Negro and white prostitutes moving out. With all they had in the world . . . in two-wheel carts or wheelbarrows . . . the once proud Red Light Queens were making their way out of Storyville to the strains of *Nearer My God To Thee,* played by a massed combination of all the Negro jazzmen of the Red Light dance halls. By nightfall, the once notorious District was only a ghost—mere rows of empty cribs.[15]

Louis Armstrong, then a boy of seventeen, later said of that day:

The people of that section spreaded out all over the city . . . nice and reformed . . . bootlegging the same thing . . . savvy? . . . In the Third Ward . . . there were always a lot of honky-tonks. . . . Where it would cost you from three to five dollars to see a woman in Storyville—it didn't cost but fifty to seventy-five cents . . . in the Third Ward.[16]

The reader can judge for himself whether the public hygiene and safety were better served by seventy-five-cent streetwalkers sneaking up an alley to support desperate and hungry pimps, than by the proud and glittering *maisons de joie* of Storyville run by haughty madams jealous of their reputations. The destruction was permanent—and Storyville's loss was Chicago's gain.

But again, why Chicago?

When the celebrated bank robber Willie Sutton was asked by a reporter why a clever and amiable little fellow like himself had chosen to rob banks, he replied with classic simplicity, "Because that's where the money was." The jazz musicians of 1917 might have said the same of Chicago. In 1914, when American industry went on three shifts to supply the Allies with war matériel, there was such a labor shortage that even women and Negroes were welcomed. Thousands of black sharecropper families from the Southern farmlands, who had never known what it felt like to have a full stomach, suddenly found themselves earning union wages. Chicago got the biggest influx; its South Side became the largest black city in America (813,000 population) and, relatively speaking, probably the most cheerful. Up here, a black man could earn himself $5 a day in a war plant, or $500 a day as a pimp if he knew how, and nobody would begrudge it to him; he could ride around in a solid gold Cadillac if he could pay for it, and nobody would call him "uppity" or a "dress-up nigger" or expect him to call anyone Sir; nobody would call him Uncle or Boy; he could vote, shop where he chose, sit beside white folks in any streetcar or theater, send his kids to the neighborhood school—and the same Irish or Italian bigot who called him nigger behind his back would never dream of refusing him service in a restaurant (though he would draw the line at renting him an apartment or selling him a house next door); he could even marry a white woman, if he could stand the strain; he might get stared at, but he wouldn't get lynched. It wasn't heaven by a long shot, but it certainly beat life in Mississippi. Each month the South Side grew more flourishing as friends and relatives arrived from the South; every month it had more money to spend on necessities like music.

The new black affluence wasn't the only factor aiding jazz growth in Chicago. Like New Orleans, Chicago had the right sort of mayor; however solemnly he might moralize in public, Big Bill was hardly the man to give whores and their hangouts a hard time —which meant more work for musicians.

In Chi, the two races were free to mix without harassment, to the advantage of all concerned, as they never had been able to in the South. Black and white musicians still belonged to different union locals, and there were no mixed bands; but after hours, which has always been the time of greatest enjoyment for many jazz artists, white musicians came in swarms to visit and sit in with the black bands, though their hospitality could hardly be recip-rocated; the manager of a lily-white hotel lounge or nightclub would have had a heart attack if he ever saw a black sitting in. After about 1918 it became less necessary to import white jazz musicians from the South, the native Northern crop had grown so well. Then came a new and powerful booster shot: Prohibition. Crime and "vice" flourished as never before; Chicago, which had a head start, became after 1920 the gangland capital of the world, and even friendlier to jazz and the shady ladies.

Even a few of Chicago's avant-garde intellectuals were begin-ning to sense that jazz was a new art form, and incorporated jazz themes, or what they thought were jazz themes, into classical pieces, paintings, or writings, attempted "jazz ballets," etc.

In sum, it was there that jazz acquired not only its name but much of its permanent shape and flavor; Chicago became within a ten-year period, 1917–1927, the mecca for various types of jazz-men, black and white, the crucible in which jazz was annealed into the form of things to come.

7
THE REAL
THING

A healthy eighteen-year-old body can take a lot of punishment. If Bix had continued to confine his noctambulations to the neighborhood *boîtes,* there is no telling how much longer he might have stuck out the double life he was leading. But a boy like Bix and a city like Chicago couldn't be kept apart very long; indeed one might wonder that he hadn't got there sooner. Bix once explained it to me in his oblique way: up to that point he had preferred to "stay out of *that* argument." Even so, there were times when he'd found himself in pretty fast company; the suburbs and nearby towns were crawling with good musicians. In itself that wouldn't have bothered Bix, I'm sure; he had absolutely no ego in the usual sense of the word; he wasn't out to "cut" (outshine) anybody, nor was he miffed when they cut him—rather, he was admiring and *instructed.* He was there to learn, and in turn try to "say something." Dixieland is basically an ensemble style of improvisation, demanding close teamwork; and anyone who ever played alongside Bix remembered it with exhilaration—"Man, he *made* you swing!" It was an exacting school, the jazz world's College of Hard Knocks, full of stimulation and frustration; only those who have, as musicians say, "paid their dues" can know its rewards and rebuffs, challenges and fiascos, and the insidious elixir it distills, which has saturated the souls of uncounted millions all over the world, often to the exclusion of all else. Bix had been paying dues, all right, but Chi was something special. You just didn't go into the sacred grove until you felt spiritually prepared.

One night when the Cy-Bix Orchestra was playing a dance in Evanston, a suburb just north of the city, one of the "alligators," as we called the aficionados around the bandstand, heard Bix bite into his first ensemble lead—he'd never heard Bix before—and, as so many did, "went out of his mind." Between sets he raved to Bix and the others about a band they just had to hear, who had just started at the Friars' Inn, a flashy clip joint down on Wabash Street and Jackson Boulevard, in the heart of the Loop (the Chicago equivalent of the Times Square area). Bix had heard about that band, the New Orleans Rhythm Kings; musicians had taken to calling them "the Friars' Inn gang"; on some of their later recordings they were "The Friars Society Orchestra." Bix's informant said they played the dirtiest jazz ever heard from white guys, and insisted particularly on the virtues of their trumpet man, whose low-down growl style "sounded just like King Oliver, man." He couldn't understand why Bix hadn't already caught him.

Bix couldn't talk Cy or Sam Stewart into going down into Chi that night after their own gig ended, and wasn't quite willing to make the journey alone. But next evening all three were at the Friars' Inn when the New Orleans Rhythm Kings hit for their first set: Leon Rappolo, clarinet; George Brunies, trombone; Jack Pettis, tenor & C-melody sax; Elmer Schoebel, pianist and leader; Lew Black, banjo; Arnie Loyocano, string bass; Frankie Snyder, drums; and the man Bix had *really* come to hear, Paul Mares, trumpet—all of them *from* New Orleans except Pettis, who came from my home town, Danville, Illinois, and Schoebel, who hailed from East Saint Louis, Illinois, and had been playing theater and vaude gigs since he was fourteen—at twenty-six he was an all-round veteran musician, who had authored a sizable hunk of the jazz "standards" repertory of his day, including *Nobody's Sweetheart, Bugle Call Rag, Farewell Blues, Prince of Wails,* and I don't know how many others. All in all, quite a crew.

Bix had heard a lot of jazz, but nothing like this. The guy at the Evanston dance hadn't exaggerated. It wasn't only that they had a little more of this or that—it was their *attitude.* Among themselves they went in for the same deadpan kidding and horseplay you saw everywhere in the jazz world in those days; but when they sat down to play, the kidding stopped. They played not in the zany, tongue-in-cheek spirit of the white bands Bix had come in contact with until now, but *seriously*—mean and low-down, pretty or funky, driving or lyrical, but always *for real.* As we said in those days—and there was no higher praise—*they played like niggers.*

Without being consciously aware of it, Bix had always felt that

way about jazz; it had been one of the things that had obscurely
separated him from all others he had sat down and played alongside. Now he knew; he had for the first time, in a new sense, come
home. The process that had begun so long ago for him, as a little
toddler in a dress, picking out tunes on tiptoe at the family piano,
then stumbling upon jazz, then feeling his way through his early
experience—the long process of trial & error and selection, feeling
himself somehow "different," often finding his own conceptions
somehow too personal, too thoughtful, too something-or-other to
fit easily into the carefree pattern of the customary jocular white
Dixieland mood, yet so compelling that other musicians found
themselves caught up by them; while, all the time, Bix had gone
on polishing his technique, striving to command those strange
notions of his, seeking "his own niche"—now, all at once, that
journey had come to a landing stage. Before him were six or seven
other musicians, white like himself, but speaking a musical language straight from the heart just like his own, every note *meant,*
and no joking. Not that their *sound,* particularly the sound of their
trumpet man, Paul Mares, was anything like his; but that wasn't
the point. The *feeling* was there, true, hard, and hot, as never
before in his listening; and the feeling was everything.

Was Bix—vague, fuzzy, absentminded, dreamy Bix, the silent
one, all music and little talk—really conscious of all this? I'd say
yes. Not in logical sentences, I'm sure; but he knew, as only an
artist could, what the Rhythm Kings had that no other band he'd
heard had. In after years, when we spoke of them, he managed,
in his own laconic, dry, Bixian prose, to convey his impression:
"They didn't give a shit, they just swung . . . every guy up there
was a real tough viper* . . . they weren't there for laughs . . . every
note, they were saying something." And the most penetrating
observation of all: "They weren't kidding someone else's idea—
they were too busy laying down their own." To express it another
way, it was no burlesque, but an original creation, expressed in its
own language—the jazz language.

The Original Dixieland Jass Band had swept us all off our feet
on first hearing, because we'd never heard *any* jazz before. But
hard, no-nonsense swinging wasn't the essence of their message;
that message was "Let's all get loaded and see how nutty we can

*1920s musicians' argot for "pot-smoker"; by extension, "hard-core jazzman."
Much used then.

act"; the swinging was incidental, a kind of musical nose-thumbing at the authority of nonswinging respectability.

The Friars' Inn gang swung fifty times as much as the ODJB, and, as might be expected, earned one-fiftieth as much money. All of them had done, from childhood, what Bix was doing now: dedicated themselves to jazz as a way of life, forsaking all others. I would imagine they all came from families that didn't worry too much about the loss of social status incurred by being jazz musicians, not having that much of it to lose in the first place. Perhaps that was one reason why there was nothing of the facetious in their brand of jazz; facetiousness is often a mask for self-disparagement, and these men saw nothing in jazz to disparage. The face their jazz wore was no mask: it was the real thing, and Bix knew it, right down to the bones of his heels, the instant they started to play.

Bix and his friends stayed until closing; the next night they were back for more, and the next. After that Bix was there whenever he was physically able to get there, with or without Cy or Sam.

The difference between their response and Bix's to the Rhythm Kings aptly illuminates the difference between amateur and professional, or, even better, between the genius, meaning fanatic, and the "reasonable man." As upperclassmen and honor students, Cy Welge and Sam Stewart had many more privileges than that very marginal sophomore Cadet Beiderbecke, and could far more easily afford a few demerits—but Cy and Sam weren't about to do anything that might seriously compromise them with the school authorities, or jeopardize their fundamental respectability—which is what their kind of life is, after all, really about. The brilliance of Bix's personal bonfire had momentarily dazzled them, the glamour of his music charmed them, into stepping just a little distance off the cowpath of conformity; but when the chips were down (they always are, eventually), for boys like Cy and Sam there could be only one choice—the safe road. For Bix too, of course, there could be only one—the other, "the one less travelled by"; and this time, at this rather final fork in the road, that choice would indeed make all the difference. There have been innumerable attempts to say what peculiar set or combination of traits goes to make up what we call the genius; I like Marianne Moore's terse line: he is the man for whom *"nothing is too much trouble."* That, in five words, was Bix; when it came to music, nothing was too much trouble; and no lack of trouble was just around the corner

now. Bix's point of view was presently undergoing such retemper-
ing, in the heat of his new passion and revelation at the shrine at
the corner of Jackson and Wabash, that, for the first time, trouble
—of the conventional sort—was beginning to lose definition, was
becoming blurred and meaningless.

Putting it as simply as possible, I think the advent in Bix's life
of the Friars' Inn gang, the combination of his new sense of dedication and the endless late-night hours it demanded, were what
finally pushed him over the line into full-time professionalism. For
after the first night or so, he became a fixture of the joint.

To most jazz musicians, nothing—not even money or security—
is more precious than good listeners, as a close look at their personal lives and behavior will abundantly confirm (if money and
security were what they were really after, they wouldn't be jazz
musicians in the first place, but would have all gone "commercial"
long ago). They will not degrade their music for the sake of pleas-
ing square listeners; when all else fails, they just play for each other
—watch them some time.

There are no better listeners, generally speaking, than other
jazz musicians; but Bix was the best I ever saw. I can picture the
Friars' Inn gang, within a night or two, getting so accustomed to
playing to and for that popeyed, openmouthed face continuously
registering every nuance of delight and astonishment, reacting
with micrometer precision to the varying intensity of every note
—that ear on which nothing was ever lost—that, on nights when
he failed to show up, they must have experienced withdrawal
symptoms.

According to Bix, he made no attempt at first to sit in. Not, I
believe, out of shyness—Bix was never shy that way. His own
explanation was characteristic. "Your first time in church, you
don't get up there with the minister and say, 'Hey, Dad, can I give
you a hand?' " Like any pilgrim, Bix knelt and worshiped with the
rest, and the band had of course no way of knowing what manner
of musical mind lay behind that boyish moon face. Bix had been
for several evenings on a first-name (or nickname) footing with the
whole band before anyone thought to ask what was in that paper
bag.

Even in our own calculating age, the jazz fraternity remains a
relatively free-and-easy tribe, notably lacking in formality and
ceremony. In 1921 it was a sect like the Christians in the cata-

combs. There were no jealous cliques, no selfconscious schisms in style or period to divide jazzmen, no union delegates to harry and fine them for playing for free. Even more essential was their *attitude*, which was elitist and absolute. There were two kinds of people—those who dug jazz and those who didn't, or what today we would call the hip and the square (whom we called *tin-eared*, or *cornfed*). If you dug, or, especially, played, jazz, it was instant brotherhood; you were welcome to share whatever another brother had at the moment: his last five bucks, a sandwich, a jug, a bed, maybe even a girl. There was little or no exclusionist snobbism; if you could play an instrument even passably, you were welcome to get up on the stand and do your best; if you loused it up it wasn't the end of the world; the worst you might get was some deadpan kidding or goodnatured groans from the pros. Even hardened veterans like the Rhythm Kings would cheerfully make room for an unknown, ready to take the intention for the deed. The moment came when Bix was invited to get out his $8 horn and sit in.

It was a memorable night in the annals of jazz when Bix Beiderbecke sat down and played for the first time with his equals. Nobody was expecting anything out of the ordinary from the dreamy youngster with the baby complexion and clothes that looked as if they'd been slept in (they probably had). They were in for a surprise.

It is one of the sorrows of my life that I wasn't present that night; I might so easily have been—my big brother Vic used to take me often.

Bix himself brushed off that first session, saying, *Christ, I only knew one tune of theirs*, and adding (as usual) that he never did get his lip together and had probably loused it up—but then Bix never would concede that anything he did was "that great." I never knew whether to believe that "only knew one tune" story (later spread also by Paul Mares), since Bix always had peculiar definitions of "knowing" a tune; and Mares, a good roughneck trumpet player but a man totally without subtlety, wasn't the one best fitted to take the musical measure of one of the subtlest musical minds ever to appear on the jazz scene. Certainly Bix's technical polish must have been crude compared with what I heard a couple of years later, but the consensus of those present, including the other musicians, was that they were stunned by what they heard from this "farmboy"; there was no mistaking the power and freshness of his ideas, the arresting individuality of his whole style; above all, it was his *tone* that got them "whacked out of their mind," a tone nobody had heard before from any horn—of which more in due course. How long it took Bix to "learn the rest" of the NORK's book I don't know; but after that Bix was no longer just another customer; he soon became more like an unpaid member of the band—and his days as a schoolboy were numbered.

Among the regulars at the Friars' was a group of five or six kids from—I think—Northwestern (in Evanston) and the University of Michigan, who had already formed a jazz band they called, in honor of that state, the Wolverines, playing dances all around the Lake region—probably a good deal above the level, musically, of the Cy-Bix bunch. Knocked out by Bix's playing, they became his inseparable companions and, not many months later, gave him his first fulltime professional job—a debt Bix repaid with compound interest: because of their association with him, their names are blazoned permanently in the annals of jazz history. As I remember they were all older than Bix; more important, they'd been out of school and working together long enough to accumulate a sizable book, more than 100 numbers. Bix, though incomparably the superior musician, was still green enough to feel more comfortable with them than with hardened pros like the Rhythm Kings; I imagine they were also more "his kind," coming as they did from middleclass homes, in contrast to the rougher origins of the guys from New Orleans. In fact while Bix was still (nominally) a student at Lake Forest, he and four of the Wolverines—Jimmy Hartwell (clarinet, alto sax), George Johnson (tenor sax), Min Leibrook (tuba), and Vic Moore (drums)—formed a new group they named, in the jocund style of the time, the Ten Foot Band (5 people = 10 feet—get it?). So besides the "legitimate" 40-piece orchestra of Professor Koepke, Bix was now distributing his energies among three different bands, when he wasn't sitting in with the Rhythm Kings or some local combo around Lake Forest. What did he do in his spare time? I suppose he practiced. Meanwhile, his relationship with the Academy had become increasingly dreamlike.

For some weeks after Papa's last visit, Bix had again tried hard to be a student, with diminishing results. Out nearly every night till early morning, his mind full of music, he began dozing through the days; his marks slipped sharply downward, and this time there would be no recovery. By April, 1922—just after his nineteenth birthday—Bix was finding it impossible to keep up any pretense of schoolwork. More than half the time now he was late for class, or had the wrong books; most of the time he hadn't done the preparatory work. It was all he could do to stay awake, let alone follow what the rest of the class were doing. He began to fail to show up at all; he was in his room sleeping off the night before. The authorities must have liked him a lot to put up with him as long as they did—eight months in all—for his presence didn't encourage discipline; Bix at this point in his life had as much business in a classroom as a mermaid. There came a limit to what they could tolerate. News of his nightly doings had reached Mr. Richards, and early in May Bix was called into the office for a little talk.

I would guess that few older men could look upon that round, vague, innocent face, those clear, brown eyes, without experiencing fatherly feelings; Mr. Richards seems to have succumbed to the fatal charm. With all the evidence clear before him of the most outrageous rules-flouting in Lake Forest history, Mr. Richards temporized. Instead of canning Bix then and there, as he had intended, he found himself treating him like a stray lamb—letting him off, in fact, with a mild lecture and warning. The nighttime doings must cease, for the remainder of the semester—Bix could of course do as he liked with his summer vacation. From now on, his attendance at every class would be strictly enforced, every assignment reviewed to make sure it was done, every test carefully monitored. In short, there in Mr. Richards's office that bright May morning in 1922, young Leon Beiderbecke was being offered what would prove to have been his very last chance in this life to go straight. Mr. Richards might just as well have offered to rescue a fish from drowning.

He could hardly have been expected to foresee that within a few years the contrite youth in the unpressed uniform would become the icon of an international cult, the creator of a totally new musical concept, about whom books, plays, and movies would be made, every scrap of information sifted like goldbearing sand, legends told and retold from his native Davenport to Tokyo, Paris, Bombay, and Belgrade—and incidentally would render the name of Lake Forest Academy immortal. In fairness to Mr. Richards, neither did the contrite young cadet; *his* sole concern at the moment was to atone for his sins—which (also for the moment) he saw through the righteous eyes of Mr. Richards—and to go and sin no more.

Mr. Richards was completely taken in by Bix's sincere remorse and fervent determination to mend his ways. So was Bix. As we know, he had had years of practice at this game; his performance, which had the conviction and authority of a Moscow Art Theater actor's, would have gulled a shrewder man than Mr. Richards. There was no faking—Bix meant every word; Stanislavsky could have demanded no more. Sitting in the principal's office, Bix wanted only to become a good boy, and was perfectly sure he could. He had managed to forget all about that thing in the paper bag at the foot of his bed. The reality of course was that Bix could no more have stopped his nightly musicmaking than he could have stopped breathing; but, as always, he managed not to let his left hand know what the right was up to. Thus he could with a clear conscience agree readily to Mr. Richards's edict—no more off-campus playing, for fee or for free, until June, on pain of immediate expulsion—and then, without missing a beat of the metronome, turn around and violate the whole spirit of the agreement before, so to speak, the ink had dried on it—all with the same innocent sincerity.

This was the situation: According to the historians, the Cy-Bix Orchestra was invited to play Lake Forest Academy's junior prom that year, but turned it down because Bix had already accepted a paid gig for the same night, May 6, all the way out in Gary, Indiana. The implications are crystal clear. The music for a formal school affair like a junior prom is arranged for, as a rule, far in advance of the big night, which means Bix must have been offered this one no later than March; his refusing it could only mean he had already booked the Gary engagement long before the moving atonement scene in Mr. Richards's office, and—this is the point—he never made the slightest move to cancel the Gary job! In fact, on the night of May 6, right after he had promised to love, honor, and obey the rules, he was in Gary, playing that job, quite as if the scene had never occurred; and according to report, he was similarly engaged on a number of other May nights. As further proof of Bix's double dealing, back in April Bix had placed an ad in *Caxy* offering the Cy-Bix band's services and giving Cy's and Bix's dormitory phone numbers—and that ad was never withdrawn. It must be obvious that Bix in his heart had no intention of giving up his night journeys—not from deliberate duplicity; rather a kind of inexorable blind tropism, like a vine seeking water. Sam Stewart and Cy Welge, by the way, received the same ultimatum Bix did. Sam forsook his evil ways at once; Cy, apparently torn between two gravitational forces, followed Bix's erratic orbit a while longer —a short while; then he too was back where he belonged.

Wareing & Garlick[17] tell what happened next:

On the 17th May the Principal issued instructions for Bix to attend upon him in his office—but Bix was away from school that afternoon. That night . . . about midnight, Mr. Richards decided to call upon Bix in his room— but the room was empty. On the 19th May Bix failed again to answer a summons, and on the 20th he slept all day, not appearing at a single class. . . . On the following day . . . with his eyes still half closed, Bix was marched before the Principal and told in no uncertain terms that he need no longer consider himself a member of the Academy.

His family weren't surprised:

. . . to the contrary, his mother confessed surprise that he had stayed there so long. Yet . . . his amiable nature, his unselfishness and his popularity among the students were long remembered; and, as a memento . . . he did bring away with him a lyre-engraved locket . . . presented to him . . . in recognition of his outstanding musical ability.

So ended Bix Beiderbecke's academic career, not with a bang but a yawn. His parents and teachers had, at long last, given up trying to saddle this zebra. It must have been quite a relief for all concerned. For Bix, it was like waking from a bad dream; but it is revealing of his character, once again, that the square world, in evicting him, had finally done for him what he had been too ambivalent to do for himself—release him from his cell.

No doubt if there had been some way of going on trying to live up to his father's and mother's idea of what a boy should be, without giving up the other half of his double life, he would have remained at Lake Forest another two years; his anxiety not to let them down was too deep to allow him any forthright action.

For Bix's real career the expulsion from Paradise could scarcely have come at a more opportune moment. Had it come earlier he would have had to take shelter again in the family bosom—exchanging one cell for another—with perhaps unfortunate consequences. As it was, besides being nearly out of his teens, he also had just enough professional experience under his belt to set out on his own in comparative emotional—and financial—security. And he would be far too busy with that career, during the next couple of years, to waste any regrets on a way of life he never could have followed in any case.

I'm sorry to say I don't know exactly what Bix did on the last day of his sentence, his first day of real freedom. Probably he just packed up his few belongings—if I know Bix, forgetting half of them in various drawers, closets, and friends' rooms—and headed for Chi, where his new friends were waiting for him. Or maybe he put in a call to his folks, who might have asked him to come home for a while and regroup before taking any definite step toward permanent independence; there is some evidence that he did go back to Davenport sometime that spring. The precise order of his movements isn't important; Bix's first experience as a full-time professional is.

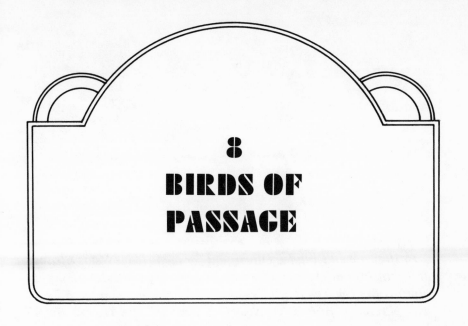

8
BIRDS OF
PASSAGE

Louis Armstrong:

In 1922, when King Joe Oliver sent for me to leave New Orleans and join him at the Lincoln Gardens to play second trumpet, I jumped for joy. The day I received the telegram from Papa Joe I was playing a funeral in New Orleans with the Tuxedo Brass Band. . . .

I arrived in Chicago about eleven o'clock the night of July 8th, 1922, I'll never forget it, at the Illinois Central Station at 12th and Michigan; I had no one to meet me. I took a cab right to the Gardens. When I was getting out of the cab, I could hear the King's band jumpin'. I said to myself "My Gawd, I wonder if I'm good enough to play in that band." I hesitated about going inside, but finally I did. Chicago was really jumping around that time. The Dreamland was in full bloom. . . . The Plantation was another hot spot . . . the Sunset. . . . A lot of after-hours spots was real groovy too. There was the Apex, where Jimmy Noone and that great piano man, Earl Hines, started all this fine stuff. . . . The tune Sweet Lorraine *used to gas everybody. They had a place on State Street called the Fiume where they had a small ofay band, right in the heart of the South Side. They were really fine. All the musicians, nightlifers, and everybody plunged in there in the wee hours. . . . I used to meet a lot of the boys there after we would finish at the Lincoln Gardens.*[18]

Joe Glaser:

All the young musicians in town would come to hear Louis—Benny Goodman, Muggsy Spanier . . . I used to let them in free. Hell, they were kids and never had any money.[19]

Paul Mares:

Abbie Brunies got a telegram to come to Chi to work in a new
*Dixieland band. Abbie figured the cab business was a better deal,
so I packed my horn and suitcase and came up to take the job. I
played around here at Camel Gardens with Tom Brown and a lot
of other places. Then came the Friars' Inn job. I sent for George
Brunies to take the trombone chair. George had to have train fare
and a new overcoat.... Something happened every night at Friars'. There was always lots of clowning ... we used to put oil of
mustard on each other's chairs. The boss could never figure out
what all the confusion was about at the beginning of a set. Jack
Pettis would always go to sleep on the stand during the floor show,
and we'd wake him up by holding the oil of mustard under his
nose.... Friars' was a hangout of the big money guys. Al Capone
and Dion O'Bannion used to come in.... The band had lots of
offers for better money, but no one would leave. We used to try to
hold rehearsals, but no one would show up. So we did our rehearsing on the job. The crowd never knew the difference. Elmer Schoebel was the only one who could read, and he made arrangements
for us. We'd kid Elmer and play it all wrong, with lots of bad
notes, the first time, just to make him sore. Elmer wrote and arranged* Nobody's Sweetheart, *which we introduced.... We used
to play* Farewell Blues *a lot;* Rappolo *wrote that one—and* Bugle
Call Rag *and* Tin Roof. *Bix—he was in school at Lake Forest
Academy then—used to sneak down and pester us to play* Angry
*so he could sit in. At the time, it was the only tune of ours he knew.
... We did our best to copy the colored music we'd heard at home.
We did the best we could, but naturally we couldn't play real
colored style.* [20]

Mezz Mezzrow:

Burnham was a small town on the Illinois boundary line, not
*far from Hammond, Indiana, a hop and a skip from Chicago, with
more whores per square foot than any town in the U.S.A.... about
two hundred girls who worked 8-hour shifts on weekdays and 12
hours straight on Saturdays and legal holidays. Pimps and simps
would fall in from here and there and everywhere, grabbing
$1000 advances from the madams and leaving their lady friends
in pawn until they ground out the thousand or got a slap from Mr.
Clap. This was one place where business and pleasure were bud-*

dies—and it was a block from the Arrowhead Inn, where we played. Business jumped all the time . . . you could always dig whether a cat was on his way to or from one of the houses when he dropped in at the Arrowhead for a bracer. . . . The girls leaving the 8 PM and 4 AM shifts would stop off at the cabaret . . . they were good-natured and sociable even after eight hours of grinding at the mill. . . . Al Capone's syndicate owned a piece of the Arrowhead, as well as the whole town, including the suburbs. . . . There never was a town sewed up as tight as Burnham . . . the chief of police was our bartender, and all the waiters were aldermen, so we never had any trouble with the law. The only time the board of aldermen ever had a meeting was when the waiters ganged up around the bar to talk about the laines* they clipped. . . .[21]

Eddie Condon:

One day Pee Wee Rank, a drummer, called me from Chicago. "How would you like to play in Syracuse?" He was on his way to the Tri-Cities—Rock Island, Moline, and Davenport—to round up talent. . . . "Meet me at the LaSalle Street Station at eight o'clock tomorrow night." At eight o'clock the next night I stood in the station and watched Pee Wee come at me with three other guys. One of them was a kid in a cap with the peak broken. He had on a green overcoat from the walk-up-and-save-ten district; the collar was off his neck. He had a round face and eyes that had no desire to focus on what was in front of him. Pee Wee introduced us.

"This is Bix Beiderbecke."

I've made a mistake, I thought. I'm stuck with this clamdigger for two months.

"Hello," Beiderbecke said. Great talker, I thought.

"We have a couple of hours before the train leaves for Syracuse," Pee Wee said. "Bix wants to go to the College Inn and see Louis Panico. . . ."

The College Inn was in the Sherman House, a Loop hotel. Louis Panico was playing trumpet in Isham Jones's band. He . . . had written Wabash Blues, and was getting $350 a week. They'll never let us in, I thought. This corncobber probably has heard Louis on a record and hasn't any better sense than to think he can march

*Suckers.

in wearing that cap and hear him play. I fell back and walked with Hostetter.

"Is Beiderbecke our cornet player?" I asked.

"By way of understatement, yes," Hostetter said. "Wait until you hear him play. You'll go nuts."

I can believe it, I thought. What kind of music have these guys heard? . . . How can a guy in a cap and a green overcoat play anything civilized?*

We walked right into the College Inn without being stopped. . . . I spotted Panico about the time he saw Beiderbecke. His face lighted up like a drunk on Christmas Eve.

"Bix!" he yelled. . . . The boys in the band looked around as if free drinks had been announced. Beiderbecke must be something, I thought, but what? . . . My eyes were just getting used to the glare when Pee Wee said, "Bix wants to go to the Friars' Inn."

Well, I thought, they let us in here, why not the Friars' Inn? The Friars' Inn was a flashy cabaret for big spenders. For music it had the New Orleans Rhythm Kings, the famous white jazz band. I had heard their records on Gennett. . . . They had Leon Rappolo on clarinet; he was already a legend. Jack Pettis on C-melody saxophone, Elmer Schoebel on piano, Frank Snyder on drums, George Brunies trombone, banjo Lew Black. On string bass was Arnold Loyocano; Don Murray on tenor sax. Hostetter repeated their names as if he were nominating an all-American football team. "There's nothing better," he said. Then he added, as if it was something I ought to know and keep quiet about, "Schoebel reads music."

. . . The players fell over themselves greeting Beiderbecke. . . . "How about sitting in, Bix?" one of them said. Beiderbecke smiled like an embarrassed kid and muttered something. . . . He sat down —at the piano. Clarinet Marmalade, *someone said. Bix nodded and hit the keys.*

Then it happened. All my life I had been listening to music. . . . But I had never heard anything remotely like what Beiderbecke played. For the first time I realized music isn't all the same, it had become an entirely new set of sounds. . . .

The next day we got up as the train came into Cleveland. With

*In 1922 only children, proles, and peasants wore caps. Eddie Condon was always a "sharp," if somewhat boyish, dresser.

nothing to do but stare at the scenery from there to Buffalo, I began to wonder again about the cornet. I got out my banjo. Eberhardt dug up his saxophone and doodled along with me. Finally Beiderbecke took out a silver cornet. He put it to his lips and blew a phrase. The sound came out like a girl saying yes. [22]

Hoagy Carmichael:

The Wolverines were organized in the spring of 1923 . . . Dick Voynow, piano; Bobby Gillette, banjo; Vic Moore, drums; Min Leibrook, bass; George Johnson, tenor sax; Jimmy Hartwell, clarinet; Bix Beiderbecke, cornet; Al Gandee, trombone, who joined the band in Cincinnati. Ole Vangness was the original drummer when they played the Stockton Club in Hamilton, Ohio. . . . The Stockton job blew up in a wild melee on New Year's Eve, 1923. . . .

In Chicago we found George Johnson, Bix, and Vic Moore in a hotel room, all primed for a big night. Bix, sleepy-eyed, said, "We got the mixings." "A couple of quarts of gin and a package of muggles.* It's enough to start," said Gene Fosdick.

We went to the Lincoln Gardens, a southside black-&-tan place. King Oliver's Band was there . . . the real solid jazz. Louis Armstrong played second trumpet. . . . His white teeth showed when Bix gave him the high-sign.

. . . The joint stank of body musk, bootleg booze, excited people, platform sweat. . . . The muggles took effect, making my body feel as light as my Ma's biscuits. I ran to the piano and played Royal Garden Blues *with the band. . . . The rest of the night I have no memory of.*

. . . In the spring of 1923 I booked the Wolverines at Indiana University for several dance dates. They didn't bother with waltzes or sweet arrangements. Other bands were playing stock orchestrations. . . . Contrary to the general impression, the Wolverines were not strictly a jam band. They had arrangements, even though the actual parts weren't written out. Bix and Voynow worked out the arrangements at the piano and the boys learned their parts by ear. . . .

Bix and I were becoming friendly and I could see the tragic note deep in him. He had a kind of despair about him, even then.

*Marijuana cigarettes.

*. . . I tried to explain Bix to the gang. . . . It was no good, like
the telling of a vivid, personal dream . . . the emotion couldn't be
transmitted. . . . It was best just to hear Bix, sloppy, souped up; he'd
look around him, always the enigma.*[23]

James Joyce, a man who knew the right word when he saw it,
named his only play—its two protagonists were writers—*Exiles;*
indeed the increasing alienation of the artist is one of the most
striking symptoms of contemporary society's (and the artist's)
progressive decay. The exile may be "only" spiritual, like
Baudelaire's, or literal, as with the Left Bank expatriates (anywhere was better than home) or with Joyce himself, who never set
foot in his native Ireland after 1912. Society may actively perse-
cute the honest artist, who is, as a matter of course, at odds with
it (the "socialist" society often seems to favor this approach), or just
let him starve, go mad, or—more prudently—go commercial, unless he happens to be one of the lucky few "names" for whom we
always have room in our star system, and whose very doodles, once
he reaches a certain plane of notoriety, are worth as much as a
painting or concerto by "lesser" lights.

Since the end of the eighteenth century, when the artist ceased
to have any essential function in our society, he has lived not so
much in it as in spite of it—in its interstices, as it were, "free" to
scratch out a living any way he can, free as an alley cat (I can
remember some of the good old days in Greenwich Village when
more than one artist was literally eating out of garbage cans, giving the alley cats some competition). Lest we forget, Joyce dryly
titled one collection *Pomes Penyeach;* Vachel Lindsay had one
called *Rhymes to Be Traded for Bread,* and he wasn't kidding; I
often saw my old friend Max Bodenheim (this was *after* he'd published *Replenishing Jessica*) peddling verses in the streets and
coffeehouses for whatever the tourists would give him, and
damned glad to get it.

Still it is one of the standing paradoxes of our status culture that
art gets a certain grudging respect even when it doesn't command
much cash. The threadbare painter or composer can at least walk
in hollow dignity, "consoled" by the probability that the dealers
or publishers will be clawing each other over his works, once he
is safely dead; in life, the title "artist" is no mean compensation for
the dirty looks we get from our unpaid landlady and tradesmen;

for—let us be candid about it—in a snob society we are, as Shaw observed, all snobs one way or another. We who have chosen to get our bread on the rocky road of the creative arts may begin innocently enough, in "artless" youth, but by the time we're old enough to don beards and corduroy jackets (in the 1830s it was the tam-o'-shanter and Windsor tie),* we know quite well we are not made of the same clay as the clods around us; what is even more gratifying is that the clods—tacitly, to be sure—agree. The Man in the Street looks with a certain grudging awe upon the man who can write or paint, and will hush his voice in the concert hall just as he does in church, indicating that the grave chap about to assault the Steinway grand is in some way a sacred being too.

No such redeeming status and respect were bestowed on the jazz musician during the first forty years of this century. He was a mere Entertainer, was so regarded by all sensible people and so regarded himself; he would have laughed in your face, adding "unprintable" comments (the adjective itself dates the period like an atom of carbon 14), had you ventured to call him Artist. Certainly back in the twenties only some discerning Europeans, a few bold freethinking Stravinskys, Ansermets, and Milhauds, plus a rare native kook or two (I was one) dared be so bizarre in their thinking as to see in jazz an art form; and as I say, the "artists" themselves were only made derisive or uneasy by such extravagances. So the jazzman led a twice-strange life, simultaneously over- and underground, and to some extent getting the worst of both worlds. On the one hand, since he was lumped, and lumped himself, with vaudeville hoofers and dog acts, he got none of the artist's kudos; on the other, since he really *was* an artist, "Making No Compromise with the Public Taste," he seldom got much of the true entertainer's cash reward; few jazz musicians, then or now, have risen far, or for long, above a precarious, hand-to-mouth, job-to-job existence.

But—"Are we downhearted?" Their ego defense to this uncomfortable fate was exactly like that of Aesop's well-known fox (by the

*The whole beatnik-hippie revolution in dress and hair styles was precisely a demand by "ordinary" youth for the rebel, "unconventional" status proudly sported by the Bohemian intellectual since the Romantic uprising. As a result, you can no longer tell just by looking who's an intellectual and who isn't: Dumb Dick and Dumb Dora, IQ 68, now parade the same unshaven and unshorn look formerly reserved for "creative" types—and don't think the creative ones don't resent the upstarts!

way, what was a *fox* doing trying to eat *grapes?*—but let that go): they positively celebrated their nomad life; doubly exiled, they were doubly defiant—of both square society as a whole and the classical music world, whose scorn they returned with interest. The square public were beneath notice, and any non-jazz-playing musician was "nowhere," the "long-underwear gang." Aggressively vagabond, proudly and sardonically broke, the typical white jazz musician boozed all night and slept all day, and drank his breakfast (at 4 P.M.) from a bottle of bathtub gin. Beneath the bravado was a legitimate point: their rags—to use a figure of speech—their mean, hobo life in trains and shabby furnished rooms, were medals of valor, battle ribbons, won by their steadfast refusal to make any music but the kind they felt in their souls.

They were, in those early days, an amazingly insular clan. Few knew anything about anything but jazz; a jazz musician who had read a book, or could play chess or tennis or develop photographs, was a freak, an object of wonder and admiration. Jazz musicians had no interests, no hobbies, no politics, no families; if the world exiled them, they exiled it right back, with a vengeance. For any man outside their own tight world, be he poet, peasant, or President, they had always up their sleeves the ultimate put-down: *"I'll bet he can't swing!"* Of course there were some notable exceptions, jazzmen who were literate, men of parts, just as there are two-headed calves, but they were almost as rare.

Into this very odd lot, this embattled brotherhood of birds of passage, where exactly did our fledgling exile Bix Beiderbecke fit? As we know, they accepted him at once, and with enthusiasm, as one of themselves, to the manner born—there was no doubt that *he* could swing!—but how deeply *he* accepted *them*, and the art of jazz "as was," even in this first flight among them, is debatable. No doubt Bix thought he did. He must have assumed—as he assumed so many things, without reflection or conscious critical thought—that Dixieland jazz and the life that went with it were just what he'd always wanted, precisely that freedom toward which he'd been tunneling ever since he got that $8 horn.

To the naked eye, it is true, there couldn't have been a marriage more plainly made in heaven than this one. The casual, upside-down hours, the unprobing, undemanding, do-your-own-thing camaraderie, suited Bix down to the ground. In this world of fierce nonconformists, his eccentricities bothered no one, his vagueness about times and places was noticed, if at all, only with an indulgent grin, his indifference to clothes was . . . just Bix. Above all, to his comrades as to himself, all that really mattered in the world was the thing to which Bix had already irrevocably committed his life. In short, paradise.

Or was it?

As anyone who was born poor and got rich can tell you, once you solve one set of problems others generally arise—such is life. Bix had been freed of his first great problem, the irksome dominion of well-meaning adults trying to form him into a conventional citizen; freed at last *to be himself*—which raised a new and totally unanticipated question: Who was that?—a question no one was then equipped to recognize or deal with.

What I believe is that, once more, Bix and everyone around him were—pardonably—deceived. Because Bix was so obviously a jazzman and swinger, it was taken for granted that he belonged; but it was an illusion—let us call it an oversimplification. I believe that though Bix himself was scarcely aware of it, he was already searching for something else, some species of musical synthesis as yet undreamed of, far removed from jazz as he found it. Many people sensed this, in one way or another—even Dorothy Baker in her own muddled fashion, in that masterpiece of point-missing *Young Man with a Horn*. ("Everyone is right *some way,*" Wilhelm Reich once told me.) It emerged there in ludicrous caricature: her hero, "Rick Martin," who as she informs us in the front matter was "inspired by the music, but not the life, of the late Bix Beiderbecke," is searching too; in fact he burns himself out at an early age, physically and emotionally, reaching for—guess what?—*high notes*(!); eventually, Mrs. Baker tells us solemnly, notes so high they didn't exist, "at least, not on a trumpet." (Presumably if "Rick" had only known enough to choose a dog whistle as his instrument, everything would have turned out O.K.) Perhaps some new Dorothy Baker will one day favor us with another corner drugstore thriller "inspired by the music of " Ludwig van Beethoven, in which the composer destroys himself seeking the ultimate in selfexpression—an orchestra that plays louder than any other orchestra in the world. Since the real-life Bix, almost alone among jazz trumpeters, was conspicuous precisely for seldom playing above the middle register of the instrument, one wonders just which music of "the late Bix Beiderbecke" Mrs.

Baker was inspired by; maybe she had Bix confused with some-body else (Bobby Starks?*).

To return from the world of fantasy to the world of fact, even a superficial scrutiny of Bix's musical tendencies, beginning with his earliest doings in jazz, throws a clear light on Bix's "different-ness." There was the matter of harmonies, already cited† in the recollections of Wilbur Hatch, wherein the chords teen-age Bix heard so plainly in his head and searched out on the piano were "condemned as mere progressions of discords"; intervals that, we may be certain, must have appeared almost at once in the ar-peggio figures he was blowing on cornet. Another obvious clue is the whole-tone scale he introduced into jazz; another—it is a ques-tion which of these items is more obvious than others—is his rejec-tion of nearly all the mute and "vocal" effects so much used by his contemporaries and even his idols, in favor of a quite rigorous open, natural, *classical* approach to tone production.

In short, Bix's musical apartheid was no late-blooming flower, but must have been perceptible, in its essentials, long before he even became a professional musician.

But there is one great fundamental trait that underlies all these others, that unifies and explains them—a trait of *character* that set him apart from all predecessors: I mean his introversion.

The musical waters into which Bix had plunged in becoming a jazz musician, and in which he was forced to swim, were at that epoch a sea of purest extroversion. In 1920, '21, '22, there were no doubt just as many introverts around as there are today, *but they didn't become jazz musicians.* Except for Bix, there were no introverts in jazz, just as there were virtually no homosexuals—I don't really know why.

To illuminate that contrast, we need think only of the greatest and most typical jazzman of all time, the young man who was just about to teach the whole world to swing—*his way*—young Louis Armstrong, the living archetype and apotheosis of fiery im-petuosity and joyous, soaring exuberance. Bix was, as far as we know, the first man, ever, to show that jazz could go another way; and though the sheer beauty of what he personally discovered *his way* soon begat imitators and disciples by the dozen—including

*An all but unsung hero of Fletcher Henderson's band, who can be heard, e.g., and very excitingly, on *Yeah Man* (Columbia C4L-19).
†See p. 40.

some of genuine distinction like Jimmy McPartland, Bobby Hackett, Max Kaminsky, Rex Stewart—it would be many years, and Bix would be long in his grave, before a *school of jazz* could come into being, peopled by, and attracting into jazz, fellow quietists and introverts. It would come about through the mediation of such a genius as Lester Young, who was able, a few years later, in the mid-twenties, to hear what Bix and his loyal "adopted father," Frankie Trumbauer, were "saying," and said to himself in effect, *Yeah—right—that's it.* Many events, musical and otherwise, would have to occur before Bix's way could become *the* way, before groups could exist with whom Bix could have sat down and played as an equal and compatible fellow temperament.

Bix in the twenties was so far ahead of his time musically that he had literally nowhere to put his marvelous inventions to work. He played with Dixieland musicians, because they were the only kind around then. He was, if you like, very much in the same predicament as Leonardo da Vinci with his model airplanes and his correct intuition that man could fly; as in A.D. 1500 there was no internal combustion engine to make his idea work, in 1922 there was no rhythm section, no group support, to make Bix's musical airplane fly. And like Leonardo, he didn't even have a clear idea of what was missing.

In sum, what we have in Bix Beiderbecke, dimly visible even before he had fairly reached his majority, is *exile*, raised, as it were, to the third power. For if art was an exile from society, and jazz an exile from the accredited arts, Bix was truly an exile from all three. And as jazz was the only world in which he even *thought* he belonged, where then was this solitary spirit to find a home?

The answer, all too obvious today, also answers a number of other questions about Bix: Nowhere.

But no one, during Bix's lifetime, was able even to formulate the question properly, let alone discover the answer.

9
FAMILY PORTRAIT

... my boy, Vic Berton, whom I still think is the greatest drummer of all times.

Max Jones and John Chilton, *Louis: The Louis Armstrong Story*.

By 1924, the Berton family had been living in Chicago—except for six months in London and Paris and about a year in New York —for nearly seven years; the longest, I think, that we'd ever lived in one place; but what could you expect from people who worked in vaudeville? Our rich relations called us "the gypsies."

Vic was as usual playing a "society" job—I think this one was at the swanky Edgewater Beach Hotel on Sheridan Road, 5700 North, not far from our home at 945 Argyle. It was one of the bitterest ironies of his life that he could never really afford to work at the two kinds of music he loved, symphony music and jazz; then as now, the steady jobs and good money were only in commercial dance music, which no doubt is why it's called commercial; and Vic always had a family to support, namely us.

Vic had been the family breadwinner since age seven, when he won a statewide contest for the vacant chair of first percussionist at Milwaukee's Alhambra Theater, the fanciest new movie palace in the Middle West. It was Vic's dependable weekly check that supported Gene's career (a word heard often in our house) and brilliant caprices and sent him to study with the best singing teachers in Europe. For Vic, by the time he reached his teens, was widely acknowledged as the best drummer in America, with his pick of jobs, the only rub being that he was always compelled to pick the most lucrative, not the ones he liked.

With his phenomenal energy, he managed to squeeze in an occasional afternoon as extra man with the Chicago Symphony, on cymbals, snare drum, etc.; and a couple of nights a week, after the hotel job, he would drive out to the South Side to sit in with the great black jazz bands, often taking me along. Though I was twelve years his junior, where Vic went I went, and had since I was seven, and just starting on drums myself. All three of us boys, you see, were Talented.

That was our only household god: Talent.

Talent was the fairy godmother's wand that would turn rags to riches, pumpkins to limousines; Talent justified every whim and eccentricity. A Talented child need not be bothered with such humdrum burdens as going to school or to bed. Talent was the magic river in which Thetis dipped the infant Achilles, making us immune to the rules of life governing "ordinary" people. As the devout grow up believing the Lord will provide, we believed Talent would provide—provide everything including its own soil, sun, and gardeners—and, in the fullness of time, its own inevitable, dazzling public triumph. My family would never have profaned such a sacred gift by finding out, for example, how to market it. All one need do was feed it, fan it, and admire it; events would do the rest.

So deeply was this faith ingrained in the family character—one might say it *was* the family character—that it was in effect experience-proof. Even when more prudent voices spoke a warning, when reality inflicted its hard lessons, we managed not to understand. *Our* talent was different. Like a mighty river it would make its own channel, carving out the resplendent future, overturning all petty obstacles. And the worst of it was that our early exploits only seemed to confirm these fatuous convictions, which thereafter clung to our careers like a witch's curse, to a large extent dissipating the effects of the talent itself.

Vic's career as an inventor is an apt illustration. Fortunately his unquestioned supremacy as a musician guaranteed him a living anyway, for he never made a nickel out of his remarkable ideas, which went a good way toward ushering in the modern age in jazz and dance drumming, a fact known only to a limited circle of his friends and admirers.

His first major idea wasn't even patentable.

If you look at old pictures of dance orchestras, say before about 1920, you will see that the drummer has only two cymbals. One hangs from a contraption atop the bass drum; the other, smaller one is screwed to the rim of the bass drum, a relic of the old marching band, going *zing-zing-oompah-oompah.* So far as I know, my brother Vic was the first man in the world to realize there was no place in the modern dance sound for that square tinkle, and that the little zinger must go. He removed it from its old spot and put it on top of the bass drum alongside the big crash cymbal, where it could be played as an independent instrument. The little striker on the bass-drum pedal was at first simply folded back out of the way; then, as Vic's idea swiftly spread through the drummers' world, it disappeared altogether. (Look at any later photographs; the zinger is gone.)

Next Vic became dissatisfied with the way the cymbals were suspended—by a rawhide thong hanging from a hook atop the bass drum. That was good enough for the old crash cymbal *(Drum roll . . . Crash! . . . "Ladeeeze and gennlemen, may I have your attention?");* but the emerging jazz style demanded better control; clean fast licks couldn't be played on a cymbal bouncing wildly around at the end of a thong. Vic made a rude sketch of an improvement: a vertical *rod* on which the cymbal would fit, snug enough for control yet loose enough to ring freely. He showed it to his favorite manufacturer of drums and "traps," as the drummer's accessories are called. That manufacturer must have thought Vic had a pretty good idea, because soon every drummer in the world had cymbals sitting up on those vertical rods, Vic Berton style—and still has, as you may verify by looking at the next orchestra you see. I assume somebody somewhere took out a patent, and made a bundle, but it wasn't Vickie. I'm not sure it even occurred to Vic that the world owed him anything for that idea.

His next business triumph occurred around 1921, when I was ten.

At informal jazz sessions in musicians' homes, which often take place "after hours"—i.e., between 2 A.M. and 6 A.M.—the drummer would use, instead of snare drum and drumsticks, which would have awakened the neighborhood, an upended suitcase and a pair of whisk brooms, probably an idea borrowed from the old spasm bands. Vic dug the sound, and again devised a professional improvement: in our garage he hammered together, onto a pair of flat wooden sticks, two fan-shaped bundles of short thin steel wires, clamped together at their vertexes. He had just invented wire brushes.

These too quickly became obligatory equipment for the jazz drummer, spreading like a prairie fire through the music business. For the unvarying hollow thud of the conventional drumstick—another heritage from the brass band—they substituted a crisp, agreeable swish that struck exactly the right note in the new, swinging, increasingly subtle jazz beat. For Vic had once more taken his little idea to his manufacturer friend, who again thought it was just dandy; in fact he took care to improve on Vic's crude design by attaching the sheaf of wires to a metal tube, before taking out a patent and going into production. Today, fifty years later, wire brushes are taken for granted as an indispensable ingredient of the sound of jazz drums—many drummers use them exclusively—and again Vic Berton never made a nickel out of it, nor, so far as I know, even got official credit.

A year later came Vic's crowning invention, which I helped him put together in that same garage one summer evening, by the light of the headlamps in our brand-new Model T Ford coupe.

He took a matched pair of medium-small "zinger" cymbals and mounted them on a couple of two-by-fours, hinged at one end, with a spring from an old couch between them. It was the first backbeat foot cymbal, now known as a *sock cymbal.*

This device, in the most precise sense, completed the constellation of sounds demanded of the rhythm section by the modern jazz combo, and in dilute versions by all commercial, theater, and society bands. Played with the left foot, on the *afterbeat*, it "answered" the downbeat of the bass drum with a crisp, authoritative *sock;* a sound every rhythm section in the world, from Troy to Tokyo, has taken for granted now for half a century.

Vic was working one of his rare jazz gigs that year (circa 1922), with Arnold Johnson at the Green Mill, a gangster hangout on the Near North Side. We could hardly wait to try out the new gadget.

The band hit at nine o'clock at the Green Mill. At a quarter of, Vic started setting up; I took up my usual position next to the bandstand. Johnson, a tough, swinging piano player from the St. Louis cathouse district, with tow-color hair and the face of a race track tout, stared at the foot cymbal; the others surrounded Vic.

"What for Christsake is that thing?" Johnson asked.

"Little idea of mine," said Vic lightly, seating himself on his stool. "Come on, Arnie, stomp off, let's go."

Arnie stomped off, in an easy walking tempo, played the intro to *Ballin' the Jack*, Vic cut in behind him with a flashy press roll, and then, for the first time on any stage, came the Modern Sound of Jazz Rhythm: mmm-*sock,* mmm-*sock,* mmm-*sock.* . . . Oh boy. The rest of the band fell in—everyone got the message. First the musicians, then the alligators, crowding round the stand open-mouthed. Johnson turned his pale blue eyes to wink down upon me, jigging ecstatically in my corner, and said out of the corner of deadpan lips, prison-yard style, *jesus that fucken brotherayours*. He was one of the few musicians in our set who'd talk that way to an eleven-year-old kid. A great cat.

The whole set went like that, each number more swinging than the last; the new sock beat was murder. All the musicians were in there, riding that beat, inspired, the dancers hollering encouragement: *Oh yes . . . Hit it, baby . . .* mmm-*sock*, mmm-*sock*, mmm-*sock*. . . . All agreed. Vic's foot cymbal was "the berries."

The second set, Arnie let me sit in, with the usual deadpan kidding. "Come on, Vic, get your ass out of there and let a real drummer sit down. . . . Fuck off, man. I thought you retired last year." (Vic was all of twenty-three.) "You all set, Frenchy?" (My nickname.)

"All set." I was ready, all right, my foot snugly strapped into the foot cymbal, touching the drumhead lightly with my brushes.

"Call it, kid," said Arnie. It was the ultimate courtesy.

"*Tiger Rag*," I said, the sweetish taste of excitement in my mouth.

Arnie stomped it off, I shut my eyes and laid down that sock beat under the swish of the brushes, the whole ensemble blasted into the first strain; my heart jumped like a live rabbit, I added a steady lick, a grace note just ahead of the downbeat, *cha-faaa, cha-faaa*. . . . I opened my eyes as I felt the trumpet lead take hold of my insistent accent. Arnie winked out of that dead mask. Vic was grinning up at me from the musicians' table in the corner; he winked too. Heaven. Whew. That foot cymbal was murder.

The next night the Green Mill was crawling with drummers. Everyone wanted to sit in, try out the new gadget. "Shit, man, somebody should've done this years ago." "Man. What a beat." "C'mon, Arnie, just one more number." It was a parade, one drummer following another onto the stand. And all everyone wanted to know was where they could get one of those God damn things, and how soon.

This time even Vic Berton realized he had something. This time he did a most un-Bertonlike thing: he actually got himself a lawyer.

But the family curse still clung, though in subtler form. In his ignorance, Vic handed over his precious brainchild to the first young schmuck fresh out of law school that he met at a party, some friend of a friend; the fact that he was young and needed the work was doubtless a point in his favor in goodhearted Vickie's eyes.

The outcome was one more example of what we came to call "the Berton luck," meaning monumental bad judgement + naïve trustfulness + rash premature action, with their predictable consequences. Someone who had the brains to hire a real patent lawyer instantly got round Vickie's pathetic two-bit patent by "inventing" a patentable improvement; it's known as the hi-hat cymbal. That of course was the one that got manufactured and marketed, the one you see every drummer in the world using today, from Troy to Tokyo, and on every bandstand in between. Once again (need I add?), the only money Vic ever made out of it was the wages he earned while using it. It's been fifty years, but I still get a metaphorical ulcer every time I see one on a stand or in a music store.

Vickie's management of World War I was equally impressive.

On April 6, 1917, the United States of America declared war on Germany, and so did my brother Vic. We were still living in Chicago. Gullible as a child at a carnival booth, eighteen-year-old Vickie swallowed the War Office's propaganda whole, atrocities and all. Bursting into the house (at 1122 Sunnyside Avenue) one afternoon after listening to some Liberty Bond Drive spellbinder, he startled timid Mama by announcing his resolution to enlist forthwith. Not one more Belgian child should have her hands cut off by a grinning Hun soldier if he, Vic Berton, could prevent it. He burned to go Over There and personally shoot Kaiser Wilhelm II—a popular ambition among young Americans in those dreamy days. He also made it clear to brother Gene, busy at the piano as usual, that henceforth Schumann lieder and other enemy art would no longer be tolerated in our 100 percent American home.

Thirteen-year-old Gene, already firmly apolitical, and incurably skeptical toward "official" pronouncements regardless of source or subject matter, laughed at Vic's dramatics, and reminded him that it wasn't Schumann who had invaded Belgium; he also doubted whether Beethoven would have wanted to cut off anybody's hands, except possibly certain pianists'. Vic, about to give his life

for democracy, was not amused, and Gene might have become an
early war casualty, but Mummy winked at him to put away the
lieder, &c., until the air cooled.

Lest young readers suspect that I exaggerate, or that Vic's imbe-
cile behavior was anything unusual, I suggest they glance at any
1917 American daily journal, where they may read of fights and
arrests because somebody said *Gesundheit* to a sneeze. Families
with names like Schultz and Schmidt prudently changed them to
Shaw and Smith, frankfurters became "Texas hots," hamburger
became "Salisbury steak," sauerkraut became—no kidding—"liberty cabbage." Vickie was right in style.

The Army, and a rifle company, obviously offered the best
chance for a shot at Kaiser Bill, but the Army turned Vic down on
discovering a double hernia he'd had for years. (Wags alleged Vic
had acquired his hernia by fucking the entire line of showgirls at
the Green Mill in a single night. I don't put the feat past him, but
I happen to know he got the injury less romantically—by slipping
on an icy step while carrying his heavy trapcase and bass drum
home early one wintry morn.)

He next tried the Marines, but they didn't want a warrior with
a truss either. As a last resort he tried the Navy, willing to settle
for a shot at Admiral von Tirpitz; they were reputed to be taking
anyone who could walk into the recruiting station unaided. The
Navy accepted him, and clapped him instantly into surgery.

The posters said JOIN THE NAVY AND SEE THE WORLD ("through
a porthole," ran the popular postscript), but all Vic ever saw was
the training station at Great Lakes, a suburb of Chicago; and the
only shots he ever fired were rimshots* under the baton of Commander John Philip Sousa, leader of the USN band and celebrated
composer of *Stars and Stripes Forever, The Washington Post,* and
some ninety-five other march evergreens. For while Vic was con-
valescing from his hernia operation—his first vacation in eleven
years—Commander Sousa chanced to walk through the ward, and
could hardly believe his luck when he spotted the number one
percussionist of America lying there within his grasp. In less time
than it took to type this sentence, Vic was assigned to band duty
"for the duration"; doubtless a break for both Vic and the Kaiser,

*Loud strokes, used to simulate pistol shots, made by holding one drumstick firmly
against the rim and head of the snare drum and hitting it sharply with the other
stick.

who were thereby spared to die in their beds.

Vic took out his frustration on the world by becoming one of the Navy's better lightweight boxers, until Sousa had him barred from that form of combat too; he didn't want him risking his priceless hands.

Playing under Sousa meant playing a lot of tympani, and though Sousa was satisfied with Vic's playing, Vic wasn't. He was, like Arnold Bennett, "a simple man, perfectly satisfied with the best of everything." Right after his discharge, Vic went to the greatest tympanist in America, Josef Zettelmann, first percussionist with the Chicago Symphony. After three or four lessons, Dr. Zettelmann refused further payment, declaring it an honor to instruct the most brilliant drummer he had ever known. He also told Dr. Frederick Stock, the Chicago's famed director, that when the time arrived for him, Zettelmann, to retire, there would be only one man worthy to succeed him in the chair—Vic Berton.

In reality, of course, nothing of the kind could happen; Vic could never have gone on supporting his family—a responsibility he never questioned—on a symphony sideman's* salary; I think union scale at the time was around seventy-eight dollars a week. By the time Zettelmann did retire, in the late twenties, Vic would be in New York, playing for Paul Whiteman and making four or five times that much.

Studying with Zettelmann meant three lessons a week and at least six hours' daily practicing. Vic was then working at the Winter Garden, a Loop cabaret, 7 P.M. to 2 A.M. every night, three floor shows with dancing in between; plus a lunchtime jazz gig at the roof cafeteria of The Boston Store. (That was a weird gig: a tough group sharked up from two of the hottest jazz spots in Chicago—the Friars' Inn and the Midway Gardens—Elmer Schoebel on piano, Steve "Red" Brown on bass, Frankie Quartell on trumpet, Vic on drums. The way they swung was scary. In reality it amounted to a daily command performance for the store manager, an ex-jazz musician who dug having jazz free every day with his lunch, but the setting was bizarre: four hundred ladies wolfing a fattening snack, too busy screaming at each other about bargains to even notice the musicians, let alone pester them with requests for the Missouri Waltz—almost the ideal audience, but if

*Any musician in an orchestra except the leader.

they had ever actually stopped to listen to what Frankie Quartell was putting down on that trumpet and bathroom plunger, they would have phoned for the vice squad.) By the time Vic got home, showered, and caught a couple of hours' sleep, it was time to get into his tux and rush back downtown to the Winter Garden; he ate his dinner with the waiters after the first floor show. Even those few hours of afternoon sleep would be sacrificed if Vic brought home a "thrill" (girl), usually a dancer or waitress from wherever he was working, but she might as easily be a music student, a rescued call girl, an heiress slumming, a black chambermaid, a pair of Chinese twins from a balancing act, or the little widow next door; rich and varied was the pussy parade through Vic's busy boudoir, even when he had a "steady" already living there. I recall one period of some months when there were *two* steadies, who not only tolerated guests but, I am convinced, sometimes recruited them.

But when did Vic find time to practice tympani six hours a day?

Simple: he practiced all night. A pair of brand-new machine kettledrums, provided gratis by Ludwig & Ludwig in return for his endorsement, were installed in the Winter Garden basement. At 2 A.M., when the last customer had departed and the waiters were totting up the night's larceny, Vic would go downstairs, strip to his BVDs, and practice on his tympani till 8:30 A.M., only pausing at six to have coffee with the watchman. Then he would drive home, catch an hour in the sack, shower, and go to his Boston Store gig; *und so weiter.* . . .

Two years of that regime, and he had made himself master of the tympani "as no man ever before, or ever again," so said Dr. Zettelmann. That was no empty rhetoric. Besides acquiring the conventional tympani technique—which might have been thought an arduous enough task for any normal man—Vic had, as usual, got another "little idea of his own," which he called "hot tympani." What he had done was teach himself to play bass parts on the pair of drums.

When Vic's first tympani recordings appeared, about 1926, drummers and jazz listeners in every part of the globe were roweling their brains trying to figure out what was going on. Many wrote puzzled letters to music magazines, to the Pathé Record Company, and to Vic himself. Magazines interviewed him; the

London *Melody Maker* sent a special correspondent and a photographer. Despite much earnest effort, no other drummer, as far as I know, ever managed to attain the required skill; hot tympani was a one-man art, and died with Vic Berton.

To understand what a very singular fellow brother Vic was in the music world, it is necessary to recall that in that era there was virtually no communication of any kind between the thoroughly disreputable jazz milieu and the world of concert music. In the 1920s a classical musician of any reputation would no more have dreamed of consorting with jazz musicians than he would have brought a hooker home to dine with his family. I believe my eccentric brother was the first "bilingual" musician, of any stature, at home in both languages, and moreover supreme in both. To jazz he brought an authority and technical polish never before heard outside the concert hall or opera house ("Them hands—them *hands!*" was all one great black drummer could repeat, shaking his head in awe, as he watched Vic play), as well as a driving beat, an unpredictable musical imagination, an effervescent wit and irresistible *joie de vivre*. I saw another famous drummer get down on his knees, one night at the Savoy Ballroom, and, in front of the whole crowd, raise his hands in prayer and bleat, "Have mercy, Vic! No *more!*" And conceivably the very fact of his jazz feeling, his ability to do what no other symphony man could do—swing—added some indefinable spark of brilliance to his concert work.

But by 1924 Vic Berton was a restless man. At twenty-five he had run out of worlds to conquer. He was getting fed up with being a mere drummer, even the best. For eighteen years there had been no letup, even in the Navy. He was so good at the job that no one would let him do anything else—and as the family breadwinner he couldn't even pause to try—in the hope of one day "getting off the God damned drums." As the child of two socialists, Vic knew free enterprise doesn't smile on the employee, and like any child who could add two and two, he knew you don't get rich working for someone else. His dream was to become independent by becoming a leader, like Paul Whiteman and George Olsen; better yet, like Husk O'Hare or Joe Glaser, put bands together, manage them, book them. Had he been anyone but a Berton, one might have suspected him of being about to do something businesslike.

One day in March, Vic came bounding up the stairs of 945 Argyle, clutching a new 10-inch test pressing.* I recognized the Gennett colophon.

"Come here, guy," he said, trying, unsuccessfully, to repress the excitement in his voice (Vic never could dissemble worth a damn). He put the disc on the Victrola turntable and wound the machine vigorously. "I want you to hear a cornet player."

While Vic put in a fresh needle I scrutinized the label, blank except for a penciled scrawl: *Wolverines. Matrix #11751, Fidgety Feet.*

"New band, Vickie?"

Vic grinned slyly, not looking at me directly, as he started the turntable going. "Yeah . . . never mind the band," he said. "Just siddown, guy, and listen to this boy play cornet."

He carefully lowered the tone arm onto the spinning record.

*Preliminary copy of a new recording, usually with the label blank except for handwritten indispensable information—artist, date, matrix number—in advance of a general pressing and release of multiple copies.

10
LISTENING

What any music *I* like expresses for me is not *thoughts too indefinite* to clothe in words, but *too definite*. If you ask me what I thought on the occasion in question, I say, the song itself precisely as it stands. . . . Because words do not mean for one person what they mean for another . . . the song alone can say to one, can awake in him, the same feelings it can in another—feelings, however, not to be expressed by the same words.

Felix Mendelssohn, quoted in Edward Gurney,
The Power of Sound

There is a kind of anguish in listening to certain pieces of music, which is unlike any other sensation. It acts upon some inner sense, with a force intangible and penetrating as an unknown perfume, arresting as the distant whistle of a train in the night (the haunting triad of the old steam locomotive, not the brazen honk of the diesel). Even the note of an unseen bird in the green depths of a forest, some tentative broken phrase of two or three warbling tones, querying the silence like the faraway yellowed glimmer of a ship's riding light in the darkness, can awaken in us a yearning, profound, inexpressible, for we know not what: it is a question without an answer, leaving us with a subtle sense of mystery and loss. Ravel's *Ondine* has this quality, the E minor fugue in the first book of *The Well-Tempered Clavier,* almost any passage at random of Stravinsky's *Oedipus Rex* or *Les Noces.*

I felt that anguish as I listened to the unknown test pressing, hearing for the first time that astonishing sound*—clear, precise, round and full like ripe golden fruit, emerging like a string of matched pearls, and with such an effortless swinging beat that I literally leaped from my chair in startled laughter, while Vic sat smirking complacently.† My God! Who was that? What was he? Where had he been hiding?

His name, Vic told me, was Bix Beiderbecke, and he was a young kid—from Iowa, he thought.

Bix Beiderbecke. What kind of name was that? I put the needle

*"Bix's tone was so pure, so devoid of any tinge of sentimentality or personal ego, that it was the nearest thing to perfect beauty I have ever heard." —Max Kaminsky, with Virginia Hughes, *My Life in Jazz.*
†Readers who would like to know what I'm talking about should at this point drop everything and listen (if they can) to tracks 1 and 2, side 1, of *Bix Beiderbecke with the Wolverines,* available on Jazz Treasury S–1003.

back to the beginning. I did that a few times.

"You haven't heard the other side," Vic said.

Matrix #11754, Jazz Me Blues (an X-rated title). I wound the Victrola again and put it on.

An easy tempo, walkin' and swingin'. The whole band sounded pretty good, but I was listening for that cornet, impatient of the mortals surrounding it. It came again, that tone, a thing of beauty and power in itself, quite apart from its nominal function as a vehicle of melody. It was tantalizing: somehow simultaneously excitingly hot and quietly cool and detached; a controlled ardor, a passion veiled in reticence. It had a chaste *understatement* never heard before in jazz, flowing yet so naturally from an open horn, staying modestly and casually within the middle register. The *attack* was like nothing I'd ever heard on any brass instrument, in classical music or jazz—each note not as though blown, but *struck:* "as a mallet hits a chime" (Carmichael); "like shooting bullets at a bell" (Berton). For once I found myself speechless, baffled.

Vic just laughed, and said, "Wait till you hear him in person."

"Where did *you* hear him in person?" I asked, wounded.

He must have answered me, but I was so upset I hardly heard. "Don't worry, guy," he was saying. "You'll be hearing him, plenty. Didn't I tell you? I'm going to manage this band." I blinked; my soul revived. "Yeah. They're going places, this band. I've already got a couple of jobs lined up for them. And some more record dates for Gennett."

And there was nobody to say to my poor eager brother, *You're kidding.* For years this would-be entrepreneur had been gazing with envy on the leaders and bookers of the commercial dance bands; characteristically, it seems not to have occurred to him to notice *what type of music* Paul Biese, Husk O'Hare, and Paul Whiteman were selling so successfully, or to ask himself why those men (whose music he detested) could afford to hire him, Vic, at top wages, while the bands playing real jazz were lucky to be working at all; now, on deciding at last to venture into business himself, what would he pick but a young, unknown *jazz* band?—an investment risk, in the hierarchy of risks, somewhat on a par with a child's sidewalk lemonade stand.

The reason for Vic's enthusiasm was obvious; the reason was Bix. Like other men of taste with no gift for business, Vic was confusing merit with salability; any millionaire executive, any pushcart peddler could have told him that any connection between the two is purely coincidental—but Vic didn't ask. Once again, like a true Berton, he was making the unconscious assumption that Talent, like murder, will out.

Meanwhile—business didn't interest me either—there was only one thing I wanted to know: When would I . . . ?

"Tomorrow!" Vic cut in jubilantly. "I called the first rehearsal for tomorrow afternoon, two o'clock," he added importantly, now the big businessman.

I said tonelessly, "Good."

The problem now was to live until two o'clock tomorrow afternoon.

Children, a poet friend once pointed out to me, live in a continuous present. Yesterday is a dream, tomorrow never comes. I resolved to seek oblivion in my favorite narcotic, chess, and went across the street to the Somerset Arms, at the corner of Sheridan Road and Argyle, then a swanky Jewish apartment hotel. I had an older friend there, Artie Klein, a brainy senior at Senn High, the only nonadult I knew that I could talk to about books and music; also the strongest chess player—he always beat me. He must be home from school by now.

I made him play with me the rest of the day, but at dinnertime Artie's mother put her foot down. "Frenchy, go home," she said. "Artie has to do his homework—and," she added pointedly, "*he* has *school* tomorrow." It was well known that I was the most outrageous hooky player on the North Side, and, scandalously, with my family's open connivance.

Six-thirty. Nineteen and a half hours to go.

Fortunately it was one of my nights to go out working with Jack Goss. Jack was a boy about my own age from Paducah, Kentucky, whose folks, like mine, had been in vaudeville, and who was, like me, a precocious performer; he and I had got up an embryo nightclub act in imitation of Gallagher & Shean; we played ukeleles, sang, in harmony, the song hits of the day, and told "crossfire" jokes swiped from popular comics; for a big finish Jack would tap-dance while providing his own stop-time chords on the uke, while I sat down at the drums and echoed his tap effects with my sticks. We billed ourselves as The Jazz Juniors, going around to whichever North Side clubs and speakeasies would let us in, adding our act to the regular floor show; the patrons would throw money on the dance floor—usually our sole pay, though some managers would add a buck or two on their own if we had made an obvious hit. We were both thirteen, but looked younger, and were considered "cute."

In preparation for that night's work, I did something unusual for me—went down into the basement, where my drum set was, and spent a good hour practicing. Unlike my famous brother, I hated to practice (one important reason why I never got very far as a drummer, or on any other instrument), but tonight I was cramming as if for a crucial exam. In fact the whole time from hearing that record to the promised meeting with my new hero was for me, in retrospect, much like the vigil of the last night undergone by the medieval squire, his final shriving and spiritual preparation before being knighted. What if during tomorrow's rehearsal I should be invited to sit in? All my ineptitudes loomed in my mind, like chickens come home to roost. How was I to face my hero? At any rate I was determined to outdo myself tonight in our round of the clubs, so much so that I hurried into my "working clothes" (the only time I ever "dressed up," as ordinary kids did, say, for church or going visiting, was for such performances), took especial trouble with my impossible hair, vaselining it till it shone like a lacquered floor mop, donned a new bow tie I'd been "saving," &c.

"What's gotten into you, sonny?" my mother wanted to know.

"Nothing," I said, annoyed. "Can't I comb my hair back for once?"

"He must have met a new girl," Mummy said. "He's been acting funny all day."

Gene scrutinized me keenly. "Or a new hero," he said. My succession of heroes had long provided subject matter for amused comment at home, and had included, so far, a retired amateur astronomer, a female chemistry professor at Lewis Institute, a demobilized U.S. Navy radio operator, the world's lightweight boxing champion, and assorted musicians, jazz and classical. "Who is it this time?"

"N-nobody. Leave me alone," I said, blushing—for two reasons. In our home, nobody ever lied; I was furious with Gene, and with myself in my new role as fibber. I avoided their eyes.

Jack and I outdid ourselves, and each other, that night. At one garish dump on Wilson Avenue, known as Bimini Bay and featuring supposedly Caribbean décor and a chorus line in grass skirts, we actually stopped the show with our rendition of *Lovin' Sam (He's Just a Two-Time Man)*, followed by my "impression" of Bessie Smith in *You Gotta See Mama Every Night (Or You Won't See Mama at All)*, with harmonica obbligato by Jack. The pickings from the floor alone added up to nearly twenty dollars, and the management, a three-hundred-pound Sicilian hood from Cicero named Boom Boom, added another ten dollars. It was the most we'd ever earned in one joint, and we were properly overwhelmed.

But when we got out onto the sidewalk Jack looked unhappy, and turning on me, said, "Hey, Frenchy, what you trying to do, cut me?"

I was astounded. "Cut you? Me?"

Jack shrugged, and walked on. "Ah don't git it," he muttered. "Ah ain't never seen you so steamed up and razzmatazz. . . . What's got into you anyhow?" he added, echoing my mother.

I was tongue-tied on that subject; I couldn't share such a sacred feeling with anyone, not even Jack, my best friend. I said lamely, "Jeez, you were great too; you killed 'em."

The rest of the night, in the interest of dissimulating my passion, I was more moderate. But when I finally got home, along toward two in the morning, I felt drained. I got into bed by 2:30 A.M. Eleven and a half hours to go. Mummy was asleep, Gene was asleep, keeping voice student's hours (roughly equivalent to a fighter's in training), Vickie wasn't home yet.

I couldn't fall asleep. That was nothing new; it was well known I was "high-strung," also excitable, and stubborn as a yak. Until I was nine I had been really skinny and sickly, became nauseous in the face of the most trivial emotional problem, feverish on slight provocation—too much agitation over a new piece of music, for instance (*Le Sacre du Printemps* put me out of commission for several days, first time around)—and with a degree or two elevation of body temperature I invariably became delirious as well, with terrifying hallucinations. Thank God that was all over now. I'd left the skinny-sickly phase behind at age ten and was strong as a cat, but still extremely nervous and an erratic sleeper. My poor mother often had to settle for my "resting," meaning staying up reading till I dropped from sheer exhaustion. This looked like that kind of night. I turned on the light and got out my well-thumbed McPherson & Henderson (*A First Course in Chemistry*).

As a child I could never understand the popular phrase "read yourself to sleep." It was above all "illogical" (my favorite word). A book was either exciting or dull. If exciting it would keep me awake, if dull I wouldn't read it at all. Brother Gene had taught me to read at three, and it soon became a health menace. By the time I was five, the bookish habit had undermined any normal juvenile social life or perspective I might have developed, erecting an almost palpable barrier between other children and me; what my head was filled with, they knew nothing about; and vice versa. There were days when I seldom had a book out of my hand. I read while dressing, I read brushing my teeth with one hand, I read on the john and in the tub and walking along the street—a real nut. My reading was unhampered, unguided, omnivorous. Where I was, books accumulated like dead leaves; I could never bear to throw one away (I still can't). Reference works were my especial passion, particularly rival dictionaries, in which I would compare definitions. I think in my whole life, from infancy onward, I never skipped over a new word without bothering to look it up (in at least one dictionary). When, later in life, I met a fellow writer (Gersh Legman) who told me that as a child he had set out to read the *Encyclopaedia Britannica* from AARDVARK to ZYRIAN (see KOMI), I recognized a soul brother. I went on binges—all kinds: I once devoured all 108 Horatio Alger, Jr., novels *(Ragged Dick, Sink or Swim, Luck & Pluck*, &c., &c.) in something like a week, a curious exploit for a lad who had begun reading Joyce at nine. At times, fearful for my sallow cheeks and fevered look, my mother would literally chase me out the door—"Go and play, for God's sake!"—little suspecting that under my coat was a copy of *Principles Underlying Radio Communication* (or *Riders of the Purple Sage*, or *Murders in the Rue Morgue & Other Tales*), and that I never got nearer the playground than the second-floor landing. As music was Bix's reality, so for me was the stuff I read in my books; my fictional heroes were as real to me as any others. (The previous year I had gone through a Hopalong Cassidy period— *Danger at Bar-20 Ranch, Bar-20 Days, Bar-20 Curse, Hopalong at Rustler's Canyon*, &c.—wearing two life-size six-shooters and walking with a limp . . . and woe to the stranger who called Hopalong Cassidy "Gimpy"!)

This night I tried quite a few of my ancient favorites, from *Introduction to Astronomy* to *Black Beauty*, but nothing helped.

At 4:30 AM. I was out in the kitchen making myself a hard salami sandwich—I grew up on a diet of equal parts Jewish cold cuts and health food—when Vic came home from his job and caught me *in flagrante delicatesso.* Luckily for me he was (literally) in high spirits, i.e., full of booze, and with a new girl—so he didn't yell the way he often did when he found me "up late," meaning I hadn't been out with *him.* This time all he said was "Guy! are you still up?" and gave me a hug. "Honey, this is my crazy kid brother. . . . Hey, guy, I've got a new lick to show you." I got my practice pad and sticks and put them on the kitchen table. While the girl sat yawning and gazing with unbelief on the scene before her, Vic showed me the new lick: *You keep the eighth notes going in the left hand, see. . . .*

Vic eventually chased me off to bed; I fell asleep watching the first pinkish-gray streaks in the sky over the Lake. Maybe I'd just been waiting for him to come home.

I awoke from heavy dreamless sleep. It was raining pitchforks outside, the sky was lead gray. I leaped up in panic: morning or evening? I could easily picture my mother telling Vic, "Sonny, his sleep is more important, he's so high-strung anyway," and my missing the rehearsal. But the clock said quarter to eleven; it was only the rain clouds making it so dark out. I was so thankful tears came to my eyes. Three hours and a quarter to go.

I could hear Mummy's voice from the kitchen: "Birdie? Are you up?" and delicious breakfast smells. I ran in on wingèd feet.

Mummy was at the stove grilling sausages and mixing a vast bowl of buckwheat batter, one of her rainy-March-day specials. A pot of oatmeal simmered on a back burner, bubbling slowly like a miniature crater of lava; I loved to put butter, banana slices, and raisins in my bowl first, then pour the hot oatmeal slowly on one side and watch the lava engulf them one by one, a toy Pompeii.

I asked whether Vic was up yet.

"Er . . . just getting up, I think." Mummy hesitated, then said delicately, "I think he has someone."

This tactfulness of hers always irked me. "I know," I said impatiently. "I met her when they came home last night; I think her name's Judy."

Mom sighed. "Again a new one. Is she pretty?"

"Not as pretty as Ada."

Mummy didn't answer. Ada—my favorite, so far, of all Vic's

sweeties—had been a bit *too* "free" even for my liberal mama—
drinking, coming out of the bathroom without a stitch with the
iceman right there, and in front of me. . . . Then on Christmas Eve
morning last year, my thirteenth birthday, waking up hung over
& horny, finding me all alone in the house, Mummy out last minute Christmas shopping, Vic at an early rehearsal, Ada had decided to give me "the nicest birthday gift a boy ever got," un-
quote. . . . After that I was madly in love with her, she was the most
beautiful girl in the world (and I'd seen the best, growing up
backstage). I thought it was our beautiful secret, but leave it to
cheerful, innocent Ada to brag about it that same afternoon to my
mama right in front of me, how "cute" I was, "the little devil!" Not
many inhibitions, my nineteen-year-old Ada. Even Mummy, who
theoretically approved of complete freedom, was a bit taken
aback.

"Don't you think Birdie is a little . . . young yet?"

Ada laughed her silvery laugh and said, *Ask him,* and kissed me
right on the mouth.

"I hope you didn't give him any kind of a disease," Mummy
brought out. I could have killed her.

"Mummy! Really!"

But Ada shrieked with laughter and hugged Mummy and said,
"Oh, Flo, you're the limit!" and sauntered in to take a shower, robe
floating open behind her as usual, trilling like a mockingbird—
impossible girl! She'd been on the road with the show now for four
months, but Vickie still teased me about her, showing me a letter
from Detroit or Cincinnati, all big loops and *i*'s dotted with big
circles . . . watching me flush at the mention of her name. Hopeless
love!

"Vickie, breakfast!" Mummy called as she ladled the speckled
liquid slabs onto the griddle. I could hear Vic coaxing and reassur-
ing Judy, about the shower and so on; finally they came out, Vic
of course in a robe, the girl all dressed and proper; Mummy said
good morning and hoped she was hungry, but the girl was so
formal and ladylike it put a damper on everything. She hardly
would eat anything, and kept saying, "I beg pardon?" Even Vic
finally shut up. Mummy said to him afterward, "I felt like saying
to her, 'Oh for God's sake, you'd think it was the first time two
people ever slept together.'" A real Dumb Dora.

Still two hours to go, nearly. Then an hour and a half. When I

realized Vic was taking that Judy to the rehearsal too, I was unhappy. If ever I wanted Vic all to myself it was today. First that
weary night, then the rain and my scare, and now this damn girl.
To me it meant everything would go wrong today. Bix might not
even show. . . . That's how I was sometimes, a real pain in the ass.

Driving over there was more of the same. Because it was raining
Vic wouldn't let me drive; and because of her sitting between us
I couldn't say anything I was feeling about the approaching meet-
ing with my hero. One look at that genteel puss and you knew she
couldn't possibly dig jazz. We didn't have the word *square* then.
This was one time we sure could have used it.

Damned if I know now, or for that matter knew then, whose pad
the rehearsal session was at. It could have been Paul Mares's—he
was there, getting drinks and standing around as he always did,
but was he host or guest?—not that it matters. It was like all the
musicians' places—nondescript furnished-flat furniture, dusty
daybed with a torn cushion, telephone on the floor next to a big
sagging bed that hadn't been changed for a month; icebox full of
homebrew beer, half a blue-moldy bottle of what had been milk,
the drip pan under the icebox brim full and starting to spill over
onto the frayed linoleum floor. The two things that counted were
in the living room: the piano, a battle-fatigued upright with no
front board, ivories off some of the white keys like missing front
teeth, its dusty top strewn with empty bottles and full ashtrays;
and the Victrola, equally beat up and dusty, with a stack of jacketless records standing on the floor against it, a leaning tower of jazz.
I knelt at once to shuffle through them; most of these piles were
about the same, in our house or any house of jazz: King Oliver, the
Original Dixieland, Jelly Roll Morton, Fats Waller, James P. Johnson, Fletcher Henderson's Hot Six, Clarence Williams's Blue Five,
Mamie Smith's Jazz Hounds, and the other blues women—Bessie
Smith ("Empress of the Blues"), Ivy Smith, Trixie Smith, Ma
Rainey, Monette Moore, Ida Cox, Sara Martin, Aunt Jemima,
Amanda Brown, Katie Crippen, Birleanna Blanks, and a hundred
groups now forgotten—Benny Peyton's Jazz Kings, Jazzbo's Cali-
fornia Serenaders, the Scrap Iron Jazz Band, the Jazz Wizards, the
Jazzola Boys. . . .

Paul Mares, a chubby, indolent man who looked vaguely Creole,
grinned at me. "You heard this Bix fella blow yet?"

I nodded. "Just that record on Gennett, *Fidgety Feet* and *Jazz Me Blues.*"

Paul shook his head. "That record ain't nothin'," he drawled. "He can blow better'n *that*. Lots of folks *fussin'* 'bout this boy, but Ah don' know—he kina *peculiar*. But he can blow all right. Ah don' always know what he's *sayin'*, but he sure is sayin' *somethin'*."

"You gonna play some today too, Paul?" I asked cautiously.

"Oh, sure, Ah guess so," Paul said genially. "Cain' let these Yankees hawg it all." He drifted away to refill his glass.

Did I detect a note of subtle disparagement, the possibility of a cutting session* between two of my heroes (Paul Mares had been one, ever since the Rhythm Kings' record *Milenburg Joys* was released)? My spirits wavered upward a bit. This could turn out to be a memorable session after all.

Several members of the Wolverines were there already. Victor Moore was setting up his drums, a cheerful, energetic youth with a mop of curly black hair and—a rarity in those days except on slick salesmen types and he-done-her-wrong movie "villians"—a mustache; Min (actually Wilfred) Leibrook (tuba), a tall, quiet, dreamy, peach-complexioned chap, his mouth always slightly crinkled as if at some private joke, who managed to make his elephantine instrument into a thing almost graceful. Others were arriving: Jimmy Hartwell (clarinet), Bobby Gillette (banjo), Dick Voynow (piano, arranger, and den mother). But—my forebodings returned —no Bix. "Where the hell is he?" they were asking each other, and replying, "I thought he was with *you.*"

"Don't worry, guy, Bix'll be here," Vic said. I blushed and turned away, gazing out at the rain, coming down in buckets.

The others laughed. "Catch Bix missing a session!"

While they were tuning up, Vic brought out a publisher's printed arrangement of a song he'd written with Art Kassell, *Sobbin' Blues*, and gave it to Dick Voynow, a black-browed fellow built like a Greek weightlifter. Dick, who could read, sat down at the piano—obviously pleasantly surprised to find it in perfect tune and all keys working, despite appearances—and played the

*"Cutting"=outdoing, outplaying, outmusicking. Also "carving." These contests among jazzmen are generally quite amiable, but they can get as viciously competitive as any other ego or skill displays.

melody over for the others, who immediately picked it up by ear and fell in behind Dick as fast as each got his instrument out and fitted together. They ran it down a couple of times like that— George Johnson had come in meanwhile and joined in on tenor sax —nodding approval, ironing out the clinkers, including the printed ones (I never saw one of those publisher's copies without wrong notes), then, once they had it under their belts, began swinging it. As I'd anticipated, they sounded much better in person than on the record. For half an hour or more they continued warming up their chops. Muggles were rolled, lighted, and passed around (skipping me); some of the guys were drinking *and* blowing gage,* and were soon feeling no pain.

At the moment they weren't really rehearsing, just jamming†— mostly Dixieland standards like *Panama, Copenhagen, Eccentric, Tiger Rag, Tin Roof,* and pop tunes—*Margie, All by Myself, Who?, Alabamy Bound, Oh Sister Ain't That Hot?, Linger Awhile, The Sheik of Araby.* They stuck to the easier, "natural" keys, C, B♭, E♭, F natural, G natural. Mares got out his horn, Vic sat in, and the musical temperature rose perceptibly. Vic's Judy dozed in a corner. Mares was blowing so great I forgot about Bix for a while.

Paul Mares was famous in those days as one of the *dirtiest* trumpets of any white man around, the nearest thing to his model, King Oliver. The words we used are revelatory of how we all thought of the jazz essence: dirty, mean, lowdown, funky, nasty, gutbucket, barrelhouse, tough, bad, terrible, scary. And apt. Jazz had begun on the bottom rung of the social ladder—nigger music, lower, as they say down South, than a rattlesnake's ass in a wagon rut. No white family would countenance a son's choosing a jazz career unless they were so poor and *déclassées* that they were glad of any occupation that would get one of their kids off the street or out of the pool hall. A boy became a jazz musician not by formal study, but as he would get to be a pickpocket or a package thief —by showing an aptitude and keeping bad company. That's the way it was, all the time I was growing up, and generally speaking it hasn't changed too much today.

Paul Mares, like most of the other cats in the New Orleans Rhythm Kings band, was a perfect representative of the breed: tough, cheerfully uncultured, unencumbered by any interests out-

*Marijuana cigarettes.
†Improvising freely on agreed-upon songs.

side jazz. His rough, hoarse growl style was a projection of his personality.

He was in great form today; even without Bix, it was already a fine session. But underneath it all, I think all of us were—waiting. We all sensed it. Even Mares. You felt it in the lulls between numbers, the frequent glances at the door. Where was he?

I knew it, I said to myself finally. I knew it was too good to be true. Like many high-strung people I was often intuitive to the point of being considered "psychic"; my hunches were often right. Bix wasn't coming. But just as I was settling for that glum satisfaction the doorbell rang, someone hollered down through the speaking tube (then a feature of most Chicago multiple dwellings), and a minute later my hero entered, looking like a five-foot-ten-inch drowned chicken.

I don't know how I'd expected Bix to look. Something ethereal, I suppose, otherworldly, soulful, darkly romantic—one-third Lord Byron, two-thirds Hamlet (as played by John Barrymore). I saw instead a husky young fellow of above-average height, with light brown hair and brown eyes, a round, wellfed, open, nicelooking face, the classic Clean Cut American Boy, the kind you'd see hanging around a rural gas station or delivering the *Sioux City Evening Register* on a bike. Was this the face that had launched that mysterious tone—this rather blanklooking choirboy?

I must say he *looked* somewhat like a boy delivering newspapers; he was wearing that cap (or perhaps another) and carrying a brown paper bag, wet and coming apart. Who wore a cap in those days except a kid or a yokel? His first words weren't very romantic either. Delivered in a flat Iowa twang, what he said was, "Shit, I got lost again."

There was a chorus of *Oh, nos* from his fellow workers.

"For some God damn reason I always wind up on Cottage Grove Avenue," Bix said sourly.

"You *walked* here from Cottage Grove Avenue?"

Bix shrugged. "There weren't any cabs," he said.

"No, but they's a trolley car runs raht paste this cohnuh," said Mares.

"Yeah," Jimmy Hartwell chipped in. "We rode on it together just two days ago—remember? We got off at the corner where you stopped to talk to that dog?"

Bix said vacantly, "Oh, yeah. We did, didn't we?"

Dick meanwhile was getting the wet things off him. Bix was certainly a sight. No rubbers, no raincoat, no umbrella, soaked to the skin; his shoes leaked little puddles at every step, his cheap green suit had shrunk in the rain, and his wrists, raw with cold, stuck out of his sleeves four inches—the country bumpkin in a vaudeville skit. Somebody took the paper bag from him, and it did fall apart; it contained his horn.

"Bix, for God's sake get out of those wet rags before you catch your death of pneumonia!" Dick scolded him, in words he had frequent occasion to use, and pushed him into the bedroom. Judy had awakened and was looking on with interest. The others just grinned and shook their heads. *Wouldn't you know. Well, that's Bix for you. Remember the time he . . .* And everyone did remember the time he . . .

A few minutes later Bix emerged from the bedroom wearing dry faded pants and a shirt that had been made for a shorter, fatter man; they fitted Bix like a chair cover. His damp dirty feet were stained blueblack from the socks he had just peeled off. His hair, plastered wet to his head, stuck up in some places like broom-straws, a trivial point that caused me private distress. Having only recently emerged from the chrysalis of childhood into Girls & Grooming, I'd just won a two-year war to train my own stubborn fright wig to lie down in a pompadour, and was the neighborhood authority on such burning questions as pomades versus vaseline, belts versus suspenders, bow tie versus four-in-hand, and so on. Vic was an invaluable big brother, having long been a "sharp" dresser. The fact that my hero seemed utterly unconscious of such vital concerns *with a pretty girl in the room* was appalling. My mind was full of confusion; could this yokel be the author of the aesthetic delights I was painfully anticipating? Had my first impressions of the record been an illusion?

Our first exchange of words wasn't momentous. Something like, "Hey, Bix, this is my kid brother, Ralph. He's a musician too."

"Oh, yeah? Hi, kid."

"Hi, Bix."

I shrank into a corner next to Vic, watching Bix with burning gaze, looking for signs of greatness. Someone handed him a full water glass of alcohol and orange juice. Bix drank it like orange juice, making the obligatory grimace followed by the obligatory jest "Gosh, that was good!" and sat down to put his horn together.

He took a tarnished silver cornet out of the shredded wet bag and wiped it on his sleeve; Dick handed him his mouthpiece, which he had rescued from Bix's coat pocket.

Bix blew a couple of vulgar noises through the mouthpiece, then fitted it to the horn and examined it, twiddling the keys. He turned and asked Paul Mares something. Paul produced a little vial of yellow oil from his trumpet case and handed it to Bix. I smelled its lemony bouquet as Bix oiled up the valves and ran his fingers over them again, corked up the oil and gave it back to Paul. It was a hard two minutes for me to sit through. Vickie's eye met mine; he winked and punched me playfully on the chin.

I was suddenly aware of the silence in the room. I wasn't the only one, brother. Dick had been doodling quietly at the keyboard, but now paused also and like everyone else looked at Bix. I found myself holding my breath; I could hear the rain rustling against the windows.

Bix thought a second and said quietly, *"Royal Garden,"* stomped off, put the horn to his lips and blew the intro; the rest of the band fell in.

Jesus.

With his very first notes I felt the hairs rising along the back of my neck, the gooseflesh along my arms. And all he was doing was playing the melody lead, straight, according to the usual custom —but every note went through you like a shaft of light, making you feel all clear and clean and open. Vic's eyes shone, we exchanged a swift glance, he gave my arm a squeeze. They were playing now with new zip; Moore hunched over his drums, hammering out a steady pulse, Hartwell bouncing a light obbligato around Bix's forceful lead. This was what we'd all been waiting for. Even Dick, so serious and unsmiling under his black brow, had a half smile on his swarthy countenance.

After the opening ensemble chorus came the customary two-bar break;* and then Bix, crossing one leg over the other knee, halfclosed one eye, his gaze focused somewhere outside the solar system, and sliced into his first solo.

Tears started to my eyes, a lump into my throat as big as a pear. It wasn't one more white facsimile of King Oliver or Freddie Keppard or any other superb New Orleans trumpet player; it

*Suspension of the pulse by the "rhythm section" (drums, piano, bass, banjo).

certainly wasn't remotely like young Louis Armstrong's exultant fireworks—it was, if anything, the exact opposite. In fact, it was unlike anything I'd heard in jazz. It was itself: *sui generis*.

Superimposed on its hot, swinging beat was a coolly logical structure coherent in form as a Mozart sonata, a crystal lattice seen under an electron microscope. The melodic line had a beginning, a middle, and an end; the beginning moved, like Act One of a well-made play, straight toward its logical climax in Act Three; the beginning implied the end, the end was an inevitable comment on the beginning. Within that structure each part implied the whole, each individual phrase partook of the same cool, consistent style, each partial episode had its own little surprise denouement—and all of it fitted together like—I was about to say like a fine Swiss watch, except that in its inspired blending of the ingeniously intricate and beautifully simple there was nothing of the mechanical; its symmetry was functional, organic, the symmetry of a seashell, an opened leaf—and it had that kind of freshness too, the freshness of something just born and never to be duplicated, like a new daybreak, each idea flowing as inexorably out of the previous one as the sequent rills in a running brook, effortless and graceful as the motion of a waterfall, a field of grain ruffled by a breeze.

It was too much, too new; I couldn't take it all in, my mind was on fire. Even the record had been nothing compared to this.

They played on, tune after tune; in between they drank alcohol-&-orange juice, or homebrew, or passed a joint* around. Bix drank more than anyone, but never showed it; two hours later he was blowing with the same relaxed precision. Bix had missed the rundown on Vic's *Sobbin' Blues;* Dick got it out again and played it. Halfway through it, Bix picked up his cornet and began blowing a soft background accompaniment of broken chords, making Vic's banal melody (which by the way wasn't a blues at all) sound suddenly pretty and lyrical; it was as if Vic hadn't really known what his own tune "meant," and Bix was, ever so gracefully and gently, explaining it to him. Vic looked at me with bright eyes, grinned, and whispered, "Gee, I write pretty melodies!"

Then Bix said, "Wait a second. Let's do something with that middle strain." He sat down at the piano next to Dick, and fished around on the keys until he found a weird, haunting sequence of

*Marijuana cigarette.

chords to go with Vic's tune—odd off-harmonies, but growing out
of each other like artichoke leaves. He gave the individual notes
of the chords to everybody—"Jimmy, you take this—what is it?—
F; George, you got the D below it . . ."—working patiently, finding
each change note by note, all strictly by ear (he couldn't read well
enough at sight, but Dick helped him out), the others dutifully
working it all out till they had it nice and smooth, Bix getting in
at last on cornet. They ran it over then, three or four times, in
tempo. I had a glow of fraternal pride. I'd been at a recording
session the previous year when King Oliver had made *Sobbin'
Blues*—on the Okeh label, I think—not, I regret to add, one of the
King's better efforts; Louis Armstrong, unfathomably, chose to
take a solo on, of all things, a *song whistle*(!). I couldn't help comparing that rendition of *Sobbin' Blues* with Bix's beautiful idea.
. . . The same year, in August, Paul Mares and the Friars' Inn gang
had also made Vic's tune, on Gennett, not a bad record either, but
to my ear the way the Wolverines did it, under Bix's and Dick's
guidance, was incomparably better—I don't know why they never
recorded it.

They played *Tiger Rag*. I'd heard it played by the greatest, but
Bix gave it a whole new slant, moving the others around like so
many chessmen. Then *Muskrat Ramble;* Bix took hold of that
well-worn Dixie standard, and it became something rich and
strange. *Jesus Christ, what's happening?* Vic was sitting in now,
Vic Moore was in the bedroom phoning some girl, the Wolverines
were blowing joyously. I'd lost track of time, I felt as stoned as they
were (you could get high just breathing that air, to say nothing of
listening to Bix). I was undergoing one of my frequent crises of
compulsion to *understand,* to analyze (meaning verbalize) my
sensations—God knows why—sensations more sensible people
took for granted. In what maddening ways was this music of Bix's
so different, what was he doing to turn my head inside out?

After that Bix looked around, swallowing a new drink, and asked
Paul, "Hey, man, why don't you get your horn out?" I had been
wondering the same thing myself; but this is always a moment of
a certain delicacy; I've seen the giants of jazz become coy and
hesitant, reluctant to upset the fine adjustment of a group. Perhaps
Bix had had something to get out of his system first, or perhaps
Paul had thought so; anyway he nodded amiably, polished off his
own drink, and got his horn out.

Cutting sessions, whether lovingly cooperative or viciously competitive, traditionally produce some of the great moments in jazz, and this one rather more than lived up to my expectations. They started off at an easy clip, with a blues in B flat and a couple of modest pop standards. They played *Tin Roof* and *Milenburg Joys,* on which Paul was of course supreme; Bix confined himself to supporting him with a background riff. Bix was fine on some unpretentious songs of the day, *Blues My Naughty Sweetie Gave to Me, Hard-Hearted Hannah (That Gal from Savannah),* and some of the Dixieland flag wavers* like *Shimmeshewabble* and *At the Jazz Band Ball,* and was particularly good on *Eccentric,* a tune the Friars' Inn gang had made themselves on Gennett a year and a half before, one of my favorites.

Then Bix called *Bugle Call Rag,* which features a series of 8-bar stanzas punctuated by 4-bar breaks, offering unlimited scope for self-expression to each soloist. Each took his turn on the breaks, including Bobby on banjo (groans, as he hit a clinker) and Min on tuba (laughter), but then, all at once, it settled down for the first time to a true cutting session between Paul Mares and Bix, the others just accompanying as the two stars warmed to their work. It did not begin in any spirit of hard competition, rather it was as if the fundamental differences between their temperaments began to show themselves, with dramatic clarity. The two protagonists themselves seemed aware of them, seemed even to be deliberately stressing them, not invidiously but with a mixture of pride and humor that was very attractive.

Paul was no *flat tire,* as we used to say. He blew as great that day as I ever heard him, at times hilariously rough, always highly colored. He used, as mutes, first a regular Harmon mute, then, in succession, a brass buzz mute, a water glass, and the rubber cup of a bathroom plunger, getting a dirtier tone with each one. Some of his effects broke us all up in uncontrollable laughter, including Bix; his breaks became successively wilder, zanier, deeper "into the barrel," "in the gutter." Bix laughed with us but made no attempt to follow Paul in that vein. He used no mute at all (I'm not sure he owned one then); once or twice he cupped one hand over the bell to make a certain quick crescendo effect, once he picked

*Up-tempo jazz songs.

up somebody's hat to get a wah-wah; otherwise, it was all straight open horn as usual.

What he did do was something extremely subtle, cryptic, and unexpected. His "answers" to Paul's earthy roughhouse began with some offhand, hardboiled kidding of the whole concept of *Bugle Call Rag,* a sort of surrealist tabulation of bugle phraseology, alternating between the absurdly complex and mockingly simple. It was like certain dreams, wherein ordinary things are hilarious, though we cannot explain why on waking. His use of *swing* was odd too, in fact unique: he would deliberately play one or two bars very straight, no swinging, fragile as the notes of a music box— then without pause switch to the dirtiest, swingingest beat, some- how integrating the contrasting idioms into one unified statement. It was delicious; there was no other word for it. The *Bugle Call* form, with its built-in inanities of interval and rhythm, was made to order for this kind of joke, which came out both profoundly funny and satisfyingly hot, like certain sexy surrealist montages. The cumulative effect was weird, and made you aware of an aspect of jazz and its possibilities that was entirely new; Bix had just done with its musical clichés what Buster Keaton was doing, around the same time, on film, with certain familiar objects—a balloon, a cookstove, a diver's suit, an ancient locomotive—demonstrating unexpected potentials for humor and surprise in apparently trite material, the usual way of genius with the commonplace.

Having thoroughly explored that vein, Bix with unerring taste shifted abruptly to another, even drier one: he started to com- ment, musically, on Paul's alternating breaks—without malice, but in adroit caricature, elaborately understated. The more extrava- gant Paul's became, the more economical were Bix's "footnotes." Everyone realized instantly what Bix was up to: once more, but in a different direction, witty contrast. If Paul's gutty horn snarled of gin & sin, Bix's caroled a sly reference to some maudlin ballad; if Paul's growled a rude oath, Bix's cracked out a jazzy distortion of some nursery jingle, clear and bare—but never forgot to swing just as hard. Paul got tougher and rougher, Bix got wittier and prettier, finding small delicate figures like snowflakes . . . then suddenly, uncrossing his legs and opening his eyes, stood up. Eyes popping, not missing a beat, he turned to face Paul with his horn pointed straight at him like an artillery piece, and blasted out a searing gut-tearing lead into an eight-bar finale that caught every-body including Paul completely off guard, a wrap-up phrase no one could top; so ended the session.

Laughter and wild enthusiasm filled the room like a flight of birds. Paul shook with laughter, wiping tears from his chubby face. Voynow smiled morosely at Vic and shook his head, muttering, *Some rehearsal;* Vic Moore and Bobby Gillette clasped each other in an impromptu tango routine, shrieking the tune of *La Paloma* at the top of their lungs. Paul punched Bix in the ribs and then salaamed in mock humility, saying, *Hey man, where was you?* Bix conceded, "Hey, Paul, I liked that. We really got off there." I was to discover how rare were such admissions from Bix.

I took a breath; it felt like my first in half an hour. I felt dazed; my mouth was so dry I could hardly swallow. I ran to the kitchen and put my mouth under the cold tap (I didn't see a glass clean enough for the way my mother had raised me), and drank and drank. I couldn't face anyone or speak to anyone just yet. I was sure I must be feverish.

When at last I went back into the living room, Vic collared me and yanked me with him into the group surrounding Bix, who was leaning against the piano swallowing a drink. I could have killed Vic when he said to Bix, "You should have seen Ralphie when he heard that test of *Jazz Me Blues* yesterday. He almost had a fit." I flushed and bit my lip, but Bix made a face and replied, "Yeh, I had one too."

"Y-you didn't like it?" I ventured, shocked.

"Like it?" Bix said wryly. "We sounded like we were playing under a rug."

I felt myself grinning inanely and saying something equally inane; I was experiencing a rare emotion: shyness. For a wonder, I had for once no desire to shine, to be shown off; all I wanted was to become invisible. As for parading my slender accomplishments at the drums or singing, I would rather have been quartered. I sat as near Bix as I could do unobtrusively, but avoided meeting his eyes. (Jehovah knew what He was about when He veiled His face in a cloud, or was it a pillar of fire?) With downcast eyes I sat and listened, but there wasn't much to listen to; seemingly, everyone had something to say but Bix, who opened his mouth only to swallow another drink, or make some rare practical remark *(Hey, we oughta put that second chorus in a lower key, then come back to the original on the out chorus).*

Voynow, looking after them all like a brood hen, had phoned out
for sandwiches, pickles, and potato salad; soon everyone was going
back and forth to the dining table munching and opening bottles
of home-brew. I trembled as I found myself next to Bix, and
flushed when he offered me half his sandwich. Back in the living
room, I chose a corner next to Judy, where I could look my fill at
my hero unobserved.

His features had undergone, for me, a miraculous metamorphosis. Externally he was still the All American Boy, but that somehow
was no longer incongruous. On the contrary, that now seemed the
only way to look and dress. His small, sensitive mouth, like a
child's, already showed the permanent lacerations of the self-
taught brass player. His gaze rested on some object lost in space
—perhaps inner space. Whatever he did have to say was prosaic
enough, though I also caught the notes of irony and sardonic nega-
tion. Unlike so many of the jazz tribe, Bix had an outdoor look, an
agreeable tan. As for his "style" of dress, hadn't I read only the
other week that Beethoven had been "extremely slovenly, often
to the mortification of his friends"? And ditto Schubert? Here he
was, barefoot, carelessly clad in cast-off rags, only because—wasn't
it obvious?—his mind was on higher things. Therefore had he
wandered in the rain, lost, a stranger among men (my internal
monologue's prose style often owed a good deal to Joyce). (I
couldn't know, that first evening, how intuitively my boyish fantasy had hit the mark.) Now his very name had a glamorous, inci-
sive ring to it: *Bix Beiderbecke.* I longed to know how it was
spelled, but thumbscrews wouldn't have made me ask anyone,
even Vic.

Vic had in fact already made a casual attempt to bring us together, to instigate the kind of dialogue I would ordinarily have
with an admired musician, thinking to force me out of my shyness.
In vain. I stayed tongue-tied, and Bix was no help. Like a cornered
animal, my mind found a way out of its predicament. I got suddenly very sleepy, nearly fell asleep with my eyes wide open like
a tired motorist. Doubtless the fact that I'd been up almost all
night, and a glass or two of home-brew, plus the emotional drain
of that session, all contributed—in any event, escape I did; seeing
my glazed eyes, Vic at once sent me to the bedroom, where I fell

down and slept like a corpse for four hours. I vaguely recall waking once, with a raging thirst and a full bladder, and staggering to the living room. Paul was snoring on the sofa; Vic's Judy was curled up in a big chair asleep; Vic and the boys sat around the dining room table, littered with overflowed ashtrays and the remains of the food. Vic had a stack of union contracts in front of him and was explaining something to them all—except Bix, who was off in a corner by himself, sitting with his horn pointed straight down between his knees, blowing a triplet figure over and over, so softly he could hardly be heard over the buzz of conversation.

I stumbled through to the kitchen, amid some ribald comments, and drank until I was waterlogged, then into the bathroom, where I stood urinating, in a stupor, for what seemed like a quarter of an hour; then back to the bed again and fell down to sleep. That home-brew was powerful. Once I woke with heaven music in my ears. I got heavily to my feet and peered into the living room. Vic, Voynow, and some others were on the sofa, in earnest conference; Judy sat next to Vic, her arm around him, looking a little drunk herself; some new piano player whom I recognized (Mel Stitzel?) was at the piano, chording softly some tune like *Ja Da* or *Squeeze Me;* Bix squatted on a cushion next to him, blowing soft but intense, his eyes bulging, staring at nothing. They were trying some idea of Bix's; every few bars Bix would break off to murmur something—*O.K. now . . . this note . . . what is that, F sharp?*—then a few more notes—*All right, now into that other key. . . .* I fell back and slept some more.

I was awakened gently by Vic. "Wake up, guy, we're going home. . . . You awake, guy?"

It was midnight. They were packing up their instruments. Dick Voynow was emptying plates and ashtrays and cleaning up. I helped Vic Moore strip his bass drum and stow everything in his trapcase. Everyone was bleary-eyed and looked pretty smashed, except Vic Moore and the irrepressible Bobby Gillette. Out of a clear sky, as I stood up to catch my breath after helping Moore, genteel Judy, now really squiffy, staggering on her high heels, came up and grabbed me around the waist and gave me a big deep amorous kiss on the mouth, muttering, *Jesus you're beautiful, Ralphie, didn't anybody ever tell you?* in front of everyone; I could smell pot on her breath; she got me excited as hell in those ten seconds. Vic just laughed and said to her, *Take it easy, baby, the night is young.*

Bix was again wearing his own clothes, such as they were: deplorably shrunk, probably still damp, the comedy cap stuck on the back of his poll like a yarmulke, the coat so tight he could hardly move his arms. We all laughed. So did Bix, and said with that twist of his little red mouth, *Look at the dough I'm saving on a strait jacket.* Somebody, probably Dick, had dug up a piece of cloth and tied his horn into it like a bandanna. We all trooped downstairs and out into the night.

The stars were out in a dark clear sky, the breeze smelled of wet fresh earth. The streets glistened in the bluish light of an arc lamp high up over the street corner; little gusts of wind shook sprinkles onto us from the rain-heavy trees. The musicians were all piling into a couple of decrepit-looking open touring cars. One of them was an old Franklin Six, aircooled, with the sloping hood.

Vic and Dick Voynow and Bix were standing a little away from the others talking; I could hear Bix's flat accent. Bix suddenly laughed loudly at something Vic said, clapped him on the arm, and turned to get into the Franklin beside Min Leibrook; he saw me looking at him and waved, with his small twisted grin just discernible in the ghostly half-light from the street lamp. This time I didn't blush or shrink. I grinned and waved back, and a warm glow of quiet elation suffused my soul (somewhere in the thoracic region). Now I could have found my tongue, could actually have talked; there was so much I had to say! Possibly this was what the ironic French would call *le courage des adieux;* but no, there was infinitely more to it. All at once I could look at my hero without tremors, *rationally* (another favorite word).

For something momentous had happened to me during that long sleep, something marvelous. It wasn't only that I felt rested now, calm, alert, fresh, quiet, elated. All those things, and something more: a qualitative change had taken place in my relationship to the music. It was as if all the music I'd heard before, all my life, had taken on some new and deeper meaning—had "sunk in." It was no longer something outside myself, that shook me or left me indifferent; now I had somehow digested it, assimilated it into my psychic fiber, like some magic elixir that changes us into gods. I had indeed heard Bix blow, not four notes, but many hundreds, on that horn of his, and assuredly my life would never be the same again. I had in some subtle way *grown up*. (Had Judy's kiss been an intuitive seal and symbol?)

I looked on the world and seemed to see it all for the first time. I saw the rainwashed city, the cobbled street (how many iron hooves and leathern heels had they outlived?), the touching variety of man's makeshifts, the walls of brick and clapboard for his shelter, the patiently fashioned vehicles for his movement, the ingenious arc light sputtering high above for his seeing, fed by the silent miles of wire strung overhead, bringing us their freight of power from the far-off dynamos and humming substations. I noted the cement poured in shapes of steps, measured to man's stride, the crude initials lettered into them by some childish hand (back door to immortality). I smelled Judy's ineffable girlsmell as she stood near me, alcohol and perfume and something indefinable, female; I breathed in life, and life throbbed quietly in my veins, powerful and precious, overwhelming me with new meaning and perspective. It stretched before me, infinite in length and promise, mine to do with as I would! O power! O youth! O illusion!

. . . The cars chugged away, coughing and missing and backfiring, passengers and watchers laughing in unison at the noise, the musicians shouting goodbye and waving, loud and receding down the quiet midnight street. Vickie came back toward us, twirling the car keys. I saw him, too, as if for the first time; his impetuous stride vibrant with life and hope, his small square strong hands, infinitely skilled, his fingers forever curled around a pair of invisible drumsticks, his goodnatured face and eager dark eyes, head always a little forward like a pointer straining at a leash—O how I loved him at that moment!

Our eyes met, and for no reason I started to laugh; he stood an instant nonplused, then he too started laughing; as Judy watched, astonished, we laughed and laughed, hugging like performing bears, dancing around, laughing until tears came. A lone passer-by on the other side of the street stopped to stare—resentfully, I think —and went on; we released each other at last, breathless, leaning helplessly against our little black Model T.

"Well, guy? How about Bix Beiderbecke?" Vic said.

I sighed. "Yeah, how *about* Bix Beiderbecke?" We started laughing again; even ladylike tipsy Judy tittered; we were a pair!

Wiping my eyes, I echoed again in my head *How about Bix*

Beiderbecke? while Vic opened the car door and Judy got in. On an impulse Vic turned to me and said, "Like to drive this heap home tonight, guy?" and handed me the keys.

It was the first time he'd ever let me drive at night.

11
SURPRISES

Some weeks went by before I could maneuver Bix over to our house, or rather maneuver Vic into having him over. Not that either would have had any objections, but both were pretty busy. When wasn't Vic busy?—but now his new role as the Wolverines' manager kept him busier than ever, up all afternoon on the phone with agents and bookers, dashing out between sets to see club owners, &c. Naturally there could be no thought for the present of giving up his regular work; he kept the Edgewater Beach job going, and continued to take the "extra" engagements as they came. As for the Wolverines, the release of their first record was causing a minor sensation among musicians, and some of the excitement was spilling over to the job market; Vic's "contacts" were promising more work.

Vic had no real occasion to have Bix or any of them over to the house. For the little rehearsing they ever did or were willing to do—Bix and Dick Voynow were the only ones who cared about that anyway—they would feel far more at ease in some musician's carefree pad than in my mama's well-ordered home, having to worry about dropping ashes or leaving a butt burning on the piano or rings from wet glasses on the furniture. There was also the fact that Bix, according to Vickie, was "sort of a funny guy," seemingly shy and uncommunicative, not easy to get close to—so opposite to Vic's ready ebullience. "To tell you the truth," Vic said, "I don't really know him that well. . . . Keep your shirt on, guy. He'll be around plenty this summer." I said O.K., O.K., I just thought it would be fun to . . .

The way, and the reason, Bix first came over—incidentally, I have no idea where or how he was living then, or whether he even had a place of his own—were somewhat accidental. Some patroness of Gene's—I really don't remember which one, but I have a feeling it was Mrs. Samuel Insull, wife of the Midwest's biggest utilities magnate (the same one who was indicted in the thirties in a three-billion-dollar stock swindle and fled to Greece)—had heard Gene remark that his piano at home was "a horrible old upright, a menace to music." Mrs. I. (or whoever it was) had a reputation for rather flamboyant generosity, and she more than lived up to it on this occasion. The next morning our telephone rang; it was the Mason & Hamlin warehouse, wanting to know if we were at home for a delivery. An hour later three piano movers arrived. They made the switch (I rescued the old piano stool, which I still liked to spin up and down on), and twenty minutes later were taking the quilts off a brand-new Mason & Hamlin baby grand. Vic tried it—Gene wasn't home—and joked, "We'll have to send it back; this is too good to *play* on!"

Shortly after the movers had left, the phone rang; it was Gene's benefactress, eager to let him know who had done this deed.

When Gene opened the front door, a little while later, we all hid to watch. He did a double take, dashed to the piano, read the *HAPPY BIRTHDAY!* card, saw us standing there beaming, and burst into tears; we all hugged each other; then he sat down and struck a chord, exclaimed, "My God, my *God!*" and burst into fresh tears. . . .

The same patroness sent him back to Paris a couple of days later, to spend a final month with his voice teacher, Lilli Lehmann. Mummy cried as usual when he left—as much, I think, because he was now "big enough" to travel around Europe by himself (he was twenty) as for anything else—but I had mixed feelings, which I probably wasn't even aware of then. Gene, as it happened, had absolutely no feeling for jazz; he regarded Vic's and my involvement with it as some species of low taste, "incomprehensible," like a duchess's taste for stableboys; he had long given up commenting on it, seeing we were hopeless. Vic and I had similarly given up on Gene and jazz; *he* was hopeless; we simply accepted it as "one of those things."

What would happen when *Bix* discovered this shocking insensitivity, this tin ear, in the bosom of an otherwise swinging family? I knew too well how jazz musicians made fun of other musicians; and Bix Beiderbecke was certainly a jazz musician. I also (I blush to write it) had my eye on Gene's empty room. I knew the way these musicians lived; it wasn't inconceivable that Bix could wind up as our house guest. Oh, I was deep! But children's crushes are no halfway affair.

I kept these fantasies to myself—not, I must add, without remorse; but I had emotions now I simply could not share with anyone, not even Vickie. (Which didn't, however, prevent me from bragging to Jack Goss, and others, somewhat prematurely, about "this famous cornet player who'll probably be staying with us—my brother's his manager now.")

That evening the famous cornetist's manager happened to mention Gene's extraordinary "birthday" present, adding, "March tenth wasn't Gene's birthday, but he decided to be nice and accept it anyway!" At which Bix—Vic said—made a wry face and replied, "I wish he'd introduce *me* to that lady—March tenth *is* *my* birthday!" whereupon, on an impulse, and doubtless influenced by my constant nagging to "get Bix over here," Vic piped up and said, "Hey, why don't you come over and try it out this afternoon?"

I could have killed Vickie for not calling to let me know; as it was, I wasted part of the afternoon playing baseball. When I finally walked in, the first thing I heard was the piano—Bix had been there for nearly an hour.

To my astonishment, what he was playing on our beautiful Mason & Hamlin wasn't jazz at all. It was some piece of "semiclassical" piano music I vaguely recognized—some American composer, I thought disparagingly (it turned out to be Eastwood Lane's *Adirondack Sketches*). "Astonishment" is putting it mildly. Except for Vic—and of course myself—I'd literally never met a jazz musician who even dug classical music, let alone could play it. Bix of all people! Once again my appraisal of him had to undergo radical emergency surgery.

Bix gave me only the barest nod of recognition and went on playing. It was an hour I would never forget: Bix at the piano, oblivious of everything including the bottle of my mama's homebrew standing near him on the floor and going flat while, eyes closed, he groped for the remembered notes; myself listening and gazing from the sofa, clutching a bottle of my own in grown-up propinquity, two silent kindred spirits. Bix played on, while the light outside slowly failed. . . .

I wish I could say he played exquisitely; on the contrary, he stumbled often, swearing at himself, *shit, I don't know why I can never . . .* and would go back over it again and again until he got it right, at least until the next clinker. . . . There is a special magic in twilight—*l'heure exquise,* some French poet called it. I became aware that the street lights had gone on. Bix stopped to take a long swig of his beer. I was loath to break the spell.

How could Bix ever know what that hour meant to me? My immediate anxiety was that it not end, ever—though I knew of course it must, but *Oh, please, not yet, not yet!* And in that tremulous yearning not to disturb it, not to be noticed, like a still hunter unseen by some wild creature, the words of a little song of Ravel that Gene had taught me rose into my mind, an unpretentious and profound moment of insight by some rather obscure French poet:

Ça n'a pas mordu ce soir,
Mais je rapporte une rare émotion.
Comme je tenais ma perche de ligne tendue,
Un martin-pêcheur est venu s'y poser.
Nous n'avons pas d'oiseau plus éclatant!
Il semblait une grosse fleur bleue au bout d'une longue tige.
La perche pliait sous le poids.
Je ne respirais plus,
Tout fier d'être pris pour un arbre par un martin-pêcheur.

Et je suis sûr qu'il ne s'est pas envolé de peur,
Mais qu'il a cru qu'il ne faisait que passer d'une branche à une autre.*

Roughly (which is as well as French poetry can be approximated in English):

They weren't biting this evening,
But I came away with a rare emotion.
As I sat holding my fishing rod,
A kingfisher came to alight on it.
Most dazzling of our birds!
He looked like a great blue flower at the end of a long stem.
The rod bent beneath his weight.
I didn't dare breathe,
So proud to be mistaken for a tree by a kingfisher.
And when he flew away, I'm sure it wasn't from fear,

*Le Martin-Pêcheur, poem by Jules Renard, music by Maurice Ravel (Paris: Durand et Fils, 1906).

But he thought all he was doing was passing from one branch to another.

Purely in the interest of preserving this delicate status quo, and knowing my kingfisher to be so enamored of minor American composers, I ventured to say to him, "We've got quite a lot of John Alden Carpenter, if you'd like to look through it," opened the chest Gene kept his music in and took out several volumes of songs and piano pieces.

"Uh huh," Bix said, shifting uncomfortably, and barely glancing at them. "You play piano?"

"No," I said, "not piano, just drums and xylophone," and put them on the piano.

Bix shook his head. "I can't read," he said casually, lighting a cigarette.

"No kidding."

He nodded.

"You mean you just picked that all up *by ear?*"

Bix nodded again. "I mean, I guess I could dope it out if I tried; take me quite a while, though . . . it's easier to pick it up. Usually I just have to hear it one time—you know." He turned a page. "Hey, I know this one." He laid the music down and began to play, from memory. He knew it, all right. As before, he hit a few clinkers, went back, swearing, ironed them out, finished the piece in style.

He went back to Gene's music chest and started pulling out scores: operas; the Stravinsky ballets in reductions for piano, four hands; ballets by de Falla and Ravel; and hundreds of songs, from the classical Italians and German lieder to modern French, Russian, and English. One by one, Bix took them out, piling them up, muttering "Hah!" and "Huh!" to himself, leafing through them hungrily, reading the titles and composers half aloud to himself.

He helped me put them all back neatly, and looked at me searchingly with his bright, slightly protruding eyes. "All this stuff belong to your brother Gene?" he said.

"Yep."

He took another long swig from the bottle. "He play all that on the piano and sing all those songs?"

"He sure does. He's considered," I enlarged, seeing he was in this vein, "one of the best singers of modern French and Russian songs in the world. He's only twenty years old, but they consider him one of the best there is."

"How about that," Bix said. "What do you mean by 'they'?"

"Lots of people. *Les Six*, for instance."

"Lay *who?*"

"*Les Six*. That's what they call themselves. They're the most famous young composers in modern French music right now. It means 'The Six.' There's six of them."

"I never heard of them," Bix said, looking at me oddly.

I was in my element now, i.e., showing off. And to my hero! "Maybe you've heard of some of them," I said, enumerating on my fingers, in alphabetic order, and in my best French, inflections and all: "Georges Auric, Louis Durey—but I think he's out of the group now—Arthur Honegger, Darius Milhaud, Francis Poulenc, Germaine Tailleferre—she's the only girl. They're all about twenty-six or twenty-eight years old, I guess."

"I never heard of any of them," Bix said. "You know all this stuff too?"

"Sure," I said, riding the crest of the wave now. "I know lots of it by heart. I met some of them too."

"These composers?"

"Gene introduced me to them when we were all in Paris a few years ago," I added casually.

"You were in Paris?"

"For six or seven months." I wouldn't have traded places at that moment with the Prince of Wales or Charlie Chaplin, the two most popular men in the world. "Mummy had to go there to look after Gene because he was only sixteen, so I had to go along too. And I had to be my mother's interpreter whenever she went shopping or we had to go anywhere because she couldn't speak French."

"How about that," Bix said. "When was all this?"

"We sailed from Portland, Maine, January 22, 1920," I said promptly, rattling it off like a quiz kid, "on the S.S. *Canada*—ten thousand tons. We stayed in London a couple of months, and it rained every day. Gene didn't like his teacher there, so we went to Paris, and Lilli Lehmann auditioned him and accepted him right away. She's the most famous voice teacher in the world."

"No shit," Bix said, fascinated. "Keep going, kid."

"That's where he got in with *les Six*," I said. "He sang for Nadia

Boulanger and she told them about Gene. He was only sixteen, but he sang their music better than anybody they knew, so they chose him to be the vocalist at the first concert of their music they ever gave."

"For Christ sake."

"That's right—at the Salle Pleyel, the most famous concert hall in Paris." I didn't know whether it was or not, but I was in no mood to split hairs. (Was this the brother Gene I'd been ashamed to introduce Bix to?)

"Want to hear some of their music? We've got some records."

"Sure," Bix said with alacrity. While I got out the records Bix squatted down to inspect our record cabinet. He pulled out *The Firebird, Petrouchka, Le Sacre du Printemps, Images pour Orchestre.* . . .

We put on Stravinsky. I started singing along with the record, and Bix stared and said, "You know all this stuff by heart? You got a pretty good ear, kid."

"I've been listening to it since I was about nine," I said. "I met Stravinsky in Paris too. I'll tell you afterward. Listen to what he does here!" I broke in, pointing out favorite highlights. Bix was amazed. I was in seventh heaven. *I was his guide! Bix's guide!* Delight upon delight, unexpected and unalloyed . . .

My mother came home from marketing; I suddenly realized how hungry I was. Bix made a move to leave, but Mummy of course made him stay to dinner. "You boys go ahead and listen to your music," she said cheerfully. "I'll call you when it's ready."

We got through *Petrouchka, Le Sacre, The Firebird,* Debussy's *Ibéria* and *Fêtes* and *Nuages,* before Mummy called us. Everybody used to say it was a riot listening to music with me. I responded to every "significant" passage with exclamations and physical gesture. Now I had a listening companion who was the same way. "Hah!" . . . "Wow!" . . . "Hello!" were some of Bix's greetings to the composer's message. Many passages had to be replayed, with my exegeses: "Hey, get this now—listen to the figure he starts going in the basses" and "Watch this trumpet section entrance now, taking off over the whole orchestra."

Mummy had made one of her great, simple dinners—broiled sirloin steak, creamy mashed potatoes with a big lump of fresh sweet butter melting in the center, fresh green beans steamed just soft, a big romaine salad with tomatoes and cucumbers tossed in oil, garlic, and wine vinegar; for dessert a homemade green-apple pie sweetened with honey and brown sugar, under a whole-wheat crust shortened with pure butter, topped with homemade ice cream—I'd turned the freezer myself for an hour that morning. It was Mummy's boast that we didn't use a can opener in our home half a dozen times a year.

There was nothing wrong with Bix's appetite. He ate slowly, quietly, eyes down; nothing to say. Mummy, who wasn't used to silent mealtimes, put the conversational ball into play.

"Did you know Eugene made his debut at the age of twelve?"

"No kidding," said Bix.

"At Aeolian Hall, in New York," Mummy said. "You should hear what the critics said about him."

"Yeah?" Bix said, and stopped to look at her. He was genuinely interested.

Mummy said, "Oh, if you'd really like to hear," a little surprised, and Bix nodded vigorously. Mummy excused herself and came back with a big black scrapbook.

Bix stared at it. "Is that all about Gene's . . . what'd you call it?"

"Debut," I said quickly. "That's what they call your first public concert."

"Oh. Yeah, I get it," Bix said.

Mummy began telling Bix about Gene being in vaudeville with Gus Edwards, and then getting so big in the act he went out on his own on the Orpheum circuit, the "Big Time," as a single, and killed everybody. I think she had every review from every newspaper in the Midwest from every town Gene ever played.

Bix is so bugeyed and openmouthed over it all he forgets to chew.

"Bix," Mummy stops to remind him, suddenly the Jewish mama, "you're not eating."

Then she gets to the part she really digs, Gene's concert career. By this time she has her glasses on and is reading aloud what Leonard Liebling said about Gene's debut in the *Musical Courier* —"a tasteful and demanding program of songs in five languages, sensitively accompanying himself at the piano. . . . We predict that this amazing young man from Chicago, whose age we are not at liberty to reveal, will take New York by storm."

"Wow," Bix said.

"Bix, you're not eating."

Bix had indeed stopped to listen, staring at Mummy with his brown eyes wide and popping, and not in silence, but rather like the congregation of a black shoutin' church, punctuating Mummy's reading with responsive cries and ejaculations—"Hey!" . . . "Wow!" . . . "How about that!" . . . "Hah!"—a most satisfactory audience. Mummy remarked that it was a pleasure to see him eat. He also put away a remarkable quantity of Mummy's home-brew, which she'd been manufacturing in our various basements since Prohibition began.

"Where's Gene now?" Bix asked, after polishing off a third helping of Mom's Apple Pie. (I experienced a twinge of jealousy at this question.)

"Right now?" Mummy smiled. "Let's see. Tonight he's still in New York. But ten o'clock tomorrow morning—"

"New York time," I put in.

"Yes, ten o'clock tomorrow morning he'll be on a boat sailing for Paris."

"S.S. *Dauphine*," I supplied promptly. "Twenty-seven thousand tons."

"Oh, yeah? He's going back to Paris?"

We explained that Gene wanted a last polishing up of his fall recital program with Madame Lehmann, while Bix's face, transparent as a mountain lake, lighted with comprehension of each point as the water ruffles under every breeze. "Hah!" . . . "How about that!"

"When does Gene get back to Chi?" Bix asked, giving me another small twinge. Mummy said it wasn't definite, maybe three weeks to a month.

"Hey, that was some dinner," Bix said, leaning back at last with a sigh. "I haven't ate like that since I left home."

"I'll bet you haven't!" Mummy laughed, and asked him where was home.

"Davenport? I know Davenport," she said. "Vickie and Eugene played Davenport. What's the name of that theater?"

Bix told her some name, the Columbia or something. Mummy nodded.

"That's the one. Tiny dark little dressing rooms smelling of pee. Isn't there a bank across the street?"

Bix nodded seriously.

"Are your people in show business?" Mummy asked.

Middle America respectability epitomized: Bix's birthplace, 1934, Grand Avenue, Davenport, Iowa.

"The little boy with the big brown eyes." Leon Bismarck Beiderbecke, three years old.

A symbolic tableau: Little Bickie ("...this prodigy, who at seven can play any selection he hears, on the piano, entirely by ear") with the one really important woman in his life, the beautiful Agatha Beiderbecke, c. 1909.

First official recognition of Bix's growing star status. On January 26, 1925, Bix returned to the Gennett Studio as "leader" with this pickup group, casually labeled "Bix & His Rhythm Jugglers." Among other titles they cut that day was Bix's first composition, *Davenport Blues*. Left to right: Howdy Quicksell, banjo; Tommy Gargano, drums; Paul Mertz, piano; Don Murray, clarinet; Bix, in sweater and pants in their usual just-crawled-out-from-under-a-car state; Tommy Dorsey, trombone. (Thomas S. Pletcher)

Bix with the Frankie Trumbauer Band in St. Louis, probably early in 1926. (Thomas S. Pletcher)

The good old days, when railroads were supreme and the Golden State
Limited was famous. Seated left to right: Pee Wee Russell, Mezz Mezzrow,
Bix, Eddie Condon. (I don't know the two standees.) 1926 or '27.

Bix, and his adopted "foster
father," "Tram," somewhere on
a railroad station platform—
possibly catching a train Bix
might have missed if Tram
hadn't brought him there
personally. c. 1926–27.
(Paul Hutcoe)

The Goldkette Band on its New England tour, c. 1927. Bix, looking unusually clean and well groomed, is seen high up, fourth from the right. "Red" Brown, everybody's favorite bass player of the period, is second from right.

Bix and Red Ingle, a fellow member of the Goldkette Band, relaxing during a tour.

Bix in Atlantic City, probably early in 1927. (Thomas S. Pletcher)

Bix at an amusement park, clowning with Howdy Quicksell (on horse) and Don Murray.

Me and my brother Gene, probably in Milwaukee, c. 1914. Gene, about ten, was already a vaudeville star.

The donkey shot again—Milwaukee, c. 1916. The expressions are representative: Gene, chubby and cheerful, Ralph, at right, already somewhat apprehensive about having been born into the wrong world.

Vic Berton at the hot tympani: the Five Pennies Band, about 1926. Left to right: Red Nichols ("the poor man's Beiderbecke"), Jimmy Dorsey, Bill Haid, brother Vic, Miff Mole, Eddie Lang.

In my teens, taken in the studio I shared for a season in Woodstock, New York, with Billy de Kooning, Anton Refregier, and a couple of other struggling painters.

Gene Berton. A passport photo taken in 1920.

Bix made a face. "I'll tell the world they ain't. Just the opposite." After a moment he added, "Dad's in the lumber business." Another pause. "They think I'm a nut."

"Oh, dear," Mummy said quickly, "that's too bad. Aren't they musical?"

"Sure, I'll say they are. Mom is a piano teacher. Everybody in my house plays or sings. My big sister plays in the church, and all that stuff."

"Then why . . ."

"They just don't understand hot music," Bix said. (Musicians avoided the term *jazz* in those days, as insufficiently selective.)

"Well, maybe they'll change one of these days," said Mummy sympathetically. Bix didn't respond to this optimism. "People have to do what they're cut out for in life. Especially when they have talent. And Vickie and Birdie are so crazy about your playing."

Bix looked uncomfortable and muttered, "Huh, I'm not that great."

"Well, I don't know much about it. But with all that talent, you can't just go and give it all up. That would be a crime!" Mummy finished solemnly.

Bix looked up eagerly. "You think so?"

Mummy nodded energetically. "A crime. How can they expect you to just throw away . . . No, that would be crazy!"

Bix shrugged gloomily. "Huh. I wish . . ." But he never said what he wished.

"You miss your papa and mama?" Bix nodded soberly. "You write to them?"

Bix looked abashed. "I'm not so good on writing, and that stuff. Guess I'll get around to it one of these days."

"Oh, don't say that," Mummy said with emphasis, and repeated one of her "sayings": " 'One of these days' never comes. You have to give yourself a time—make a date with yourself. 'Tuesday I'll write to them.' You don't know how much a little letter means. Wait till you have children of your own." I tried to picture Bix with children of his own. "Promise you'll write to them soon." Bix looked away and squirmed a little, but finally said, "Sure, I'm gonna write to 'em. It's just, I've been pretty busy, we're getting quite a few jobs now." He broke off, with a startled look. "Hey! Jeez, what time is it?" I ran into the dining room to look.

"A quarter to nine."

Bix jumped up out of his chair. "Jesus Christ!" he cried. "I mean —excuse me, Mrs. Berton—holy cow, I'm supposed to be somewhere in fifteen minutes. . . ." He was fishing in his coat pocket. "Where the hell did I put that piece of paper now? . . . Excuse me."

Mummy laughed. "You're excused. Where is it you have to be?"

"Jeez, I don't know, somewhere down in the Loop. . . . No, wait a minute, that was yesterday. Some place on the North Side. . . ."

"This is the North Side," Mummy said. "Where on the North Side? The North Side is a pretty big place."

Bix finally found the piece of paper in his overcoat pocket. "Lawrence Avenue—where's Lawrence Avenue?"

"Oh, that's not far," Mummy said. "How should he get there, Birdie?"

"What number on Lawrence Avenue? Lawrence is seven miles long."

"Lemme see. Looks like . . . yeah, 2620 Lawrence Avenue."

"Well," I began expertly, "Kedzie is 3200 west, Western Avenue is 2400 west, so 2620 would be between Kedzie and Western, nearer to Kedzie, on the right-hand side of the street—the north side of Lawrence Avenue, in other words."

"How far is that from here?" Bix asked anxiously.

I made a mental calculation. "Just a little under five miles, I'd guess. You could take the L right here at Argyle, get off at Lawrence—that's the next stop—then take the Lawrence Avenue streetcar—"

"Holy cow, I haven't got time for all that. I'll have to get a taxi."

"Do you have money for a taxi?" asked practical Mummy.

"That's a good question," Bix said, pulling out an assortment of crumpled greenbacks and silver from various pockets. He counted it up, with Mummy's help—about twelve dollars. "Where do you get a taxi out here? Can I phone for one?"

"You don't have to, this time of night," I said. "You can always find one right out here on Sheridan Road—in front of the Somerset Hotel. There's a taxi stand there."

"O.K., I guess I'll make it all right. Hey, thanks for dinner!" Bix paused in the doorway, wrestling into his overcoat. "It was the nuts!" He turned to me. "Mind if I come back and hear some more of those records, kid?"

"No. No, I don't mind. Tomorrow?"

"Oh? Yeah! Ha ha! No, wait a minute . . . I'll call you, O.K.? Frenchy? Ralph? Birdie? Ha ha!"

"Bix, go, go, you'll be late!" Mummy said, pushing him.

"It's O.K., they can play without me for a couple of numbers. Hey, I'll see you!" He ran down the stairs.

On general principles and out of long habit, my mother walked into the living room and looked around. "Hmm, look at the mess they left me." She spotted a paper bag on the couch. "What's that? Did Bix forget something?"

"Oh, Jesus, his horn!" I ran to the window and yelled down at Bix's figure receding down the street. "Bix! Bix!" He looked up, turned back. "Your horn!"

He dashed back. I leaned on the buzzer to let him in, grabbed the bag and ran down to meet him halfway. His eyes shone in the dim light of the landing.

"Hey, Jesus, thanks, kid. You're O.K." He vanished down the steps, two at a time.

I reentered, glowing.

"Sit down, sonny, you're all out of breath," Mummy said, busy straightening up the living room, collecting ashtrays and bottles. I hurried to help, still dazed. I had a lot to think about.

"A nice boy," said my mama. "A little *meshugana*."

"What do you mean? He's a musician."

"That's right," Mummy said gently, and sighed. "A musician. Oh, well, we're all a little meshugana, or we wouldn't be in this business."

"He was just in a hurry, that's all," I said defensively.

Mummy smiled. "What's the matter, sonny, I can't say anything, nobody should criticize your new hero?" I blushed and made an impatient gesture. She ruffled my hair playfully; I ducked, irritated, but Mummy put down her dustcloth and drew me to her, kissing my sacred head.

"Akh, sonny, sonny, I know. He's . . . different, hm?"

This time I didn't pull away; I put my arms around her. I realized I hadn't done that for quite a while, weeks maybe. Was I *growing up?* For no reason at all tears sprang to my eyes; I hugged her tighter. Why did people have to grow up? Life was so sad somehow. I remembered how Mummy had cried a couple of years ago, the day she took me to buy my first long pants. So sad, so sad! I could find no words for my profound, confused feelings.

"Gee . . . Ma . . ." was all I could find to say.

She went on stroking my hair.

12
A RELUCTANT
HERO

Every human relationship is a kind of barter agreement, a sort of exchange of gifts. In this one between Bix and me, Bix and my family, there were some absurd conflicts, cross-purposes, "contradictions" as the Marxists would say.

What, specifically, at thirteen, did I want from Bix? What could I hope for? What could he give? What did he want?

I had fallen in love with a sound—so it had all begun—a kind of jazz never heard before, enigmatic, haunting. . . . Like a traveler following some unseen shepherd's pipe, I needed desperately to trace it to its source, to understand its creator. The tracing took twenty-four hours; the understanding would take fifty years.

Hearing Bix play in the flesh that day, so incomparably more intensely and poignantly than on the recording, had only made matters worse, sharpened the anguish, the need to unriddle the riddle. It helped not at all to rub one's eyes and stare again at the reality in which this fragile art had its origin—this "husky farmer boy," as someone (Mezz Mezzrow?) once described him, with his simple, open face, uncalculating as a two-year-old's, who mostly uttered only banalities when he bothered to talk at all—to find *this* at the center of my anguish was only to deepen it, make the mystery more so. How was I to get at the core of what Bix was? Had I been of opposite sex, I might have simplified the problem in a familiar way, or at least deluded myself that I had, as so many women do. As it was, I could only blunder on, in the classic tradition of hero worship, knowing only that I must get close to my idol, touch him spiritually at least, somehow satisfy my confused and indefinable yearnings.

The triumph of luring Bix to my lair had only turned to further confusion, when I got from him, in that first visit, not the gift of more jazz, but instead some semiclassical *patisserie*, mediocre music badly played (I could put on a record of Alfred Cortot playing Ravel—I didn't need Bix Beiderbecke trying to play Eastwood Lane). Now I was thrown off the scent completely, our roles suddenly reversed: it was Bix who hungered after something, something *I* (or we) could give *him*—great modern classical music (excuse the paradox), informed guidance. I was proud to play my new role to the hilt—while it lasted. Again I had mixed feelings about my brother Gene's imminent return from Europe. My involvement with modern French and Russian music had been mainly a reflection of his. I hadn't exaggerated; Gene Berton was indeed considered one of the very finest interpreters of such music; when the master appeared, what role would be left for the apprentice? Well in advance of the event, I tasted the bitter bread of hopeless rivalry, all the more galling in that Gene would be totally unaware that any "rivalry" existed; in fact Bix would probably be of little interest to him musically; just one more admirer, and a passably ignorant one. Jazz, as I've said, didn't exist for Gene.

Meanwhile I made the most of having Bix to myself.

About eleven one morning, a few days after that first visit, our bell rang; up came Bix, wearing exactly the same clothes he'd had on before—I'm not sure he'd had them off. The only change I noted was a new paper bag for his horn, with the name of some bakery on it.

I never would have asked, but Mummy did at once. "Bix, were you up all night?" Bix thought a moment, blinked, and said, "Oh . . . yeah. There was this rich jane in the joint. . . ." He yawned, and didn't elaborate. Mummy told him to go in and take a shower if he wanted to (I must say he looked as though he could use one), and lie down. Bix didn't seem too eager, but yielded to an offer of some breakfast. He smelled of fresh alcohol. (There are two kinds of people—those whose breath, after one drink, smells like vomit, and those who, no matter how much they've had, just smell like an alcohol lamp—doubtless something to do with bile production. Fortunately Bix was the second kind.) He put away a couple of eggs with ham; asked where Vic was (asleep); then asked if he could hear Debussy's *Ibéria*.

I went to dig out the record while he dropped onto the couch. By the time I had found it and put it on the turntable, he was fast asleep. Mummy took off his shoes, pursed her lips at the state of his socks, put a clean pillow under his head (he opened his eyes for a moment, but immediately shut them again), looked at me expressively and shrugged, and went back to the kitchen shaking her head and sighing.

I put on *Ibéria* anyhow, but using a soft fiber needle and with the little doors of the "horn" (as we still called the soundbox) shut. I played the whole thing through, also *Fêtes* and *Rondes de printemps*. Bix never stirred for four hours. I discovered that my hero snored a little. Mummy had at some point put a blanket over him.

When Bix woke, Vic had already left for work—I think he was doubling then at the Senate Theater, out on Kedzie Avenue, in Art Kahn's orchestra; Mummy was taking a nap, as she often did in the afternoon; I was in my room busy with my ham radio, trying to raise an operator in Fond du Lac, Wisconsin, with whom I was in the middle of a radio chess game. At that epoch my room looked like the radio room of a naval vessel (easily the most glamorous interior décor in the world to me then): my transmitter had the maximum power allowed by the Department of Commerce, one kilowatt, embodied in a sure-enough U.S. Navy government-issue rotary spark gap set with all the accessories, also USN—doubtless one of the very last of the type in the civilized world; terribly exciting-looking and -sounding, with highly satisfactory blue sparks crackling through the room, and huge high-voltage bus bars and two-foot insulators running up the wall and out to the outdoor antenna, a thirty-foot tower affair—but then rapidly becoming obsolete in the face of the irresistible onward march of the power vacuum tube.

I looked up, to see Bix staring popeyed at the scene. I didn't know how long he'd been standing there. I waved, but couldn't talk to him just then—the ham in Fond du Lac had just answered me. I was busy writing his message (regular paper wasn't good enough for me; I had to write away for the special Radio Message Pads supplied by *QST* magazine, official organ of the American Radio Relay Association, to which all hams belonged). I made his move on my chessboard, then switched my selector from RECV to XMIT and closed the power switch, causing a gratifying blue flash and *click-click-clack* of the remote relays, followed by the rising hum of the rotary as it got up to speed. Oh, the sound effects were really the cat's pajamas, as we used to say in those days; you couldn't beat a rotary gap for either visual or auditory glamour.

The best was yet to come: I now had to reply to my æther pal in Fond du Lac. Let me explain that each time I depressed my sending key to make a dot or (especially) dash, not only would the resulting high-voltage spark crackle visibly across the three-inch gap, but the accompanying sound was good enough for a Frankenstein movie. *Dit-dit-dah, dit-dit-dah, dit-dit-dah,* I greeted him, then went on to explain that I had company and would call him later, and signed off, *dah-dah-dit-dit-dit, dit-dit-dit-dah-dah* ("73," the official signoff signal among amateur radio operators). I removed the earphones, switched everything off, and stood up, looking as casual as I could under Bix's fascinated stare.

As the reader will have gathered, I was not exactly displeased to have my hero catch my act, so to speak. He proved to be an appreciative audience, gazing at my exotic equipment with literally openmouthed awe. It was apparent that he'd never seen a transmitter before.

"What's all this?" he asked, blinking and still bleary-eyed. "You a wireless operator?"

"Ham radio—amateur," I said carelessly. "You know anything about it?"

"Shit, no," said Bix. "Where'd you get all this stuff?" He was staring at the seven-foot-tall louvered steel cabinet, battleship gray like all the other equipment in the room, with USS SHARKFIN stenciled large across every unit.

"Guess!" I laughed and eagerly explained. "When we lived over on Sunnyside Avenue a couple of years ago, this guy moved in across the hall, Tom Seese—he was a radio operator on board a destroyer" (actually a supply ship, but I liked "destroyer" better) "and when he got his discharge he practically dismantled the radio room. The quartermaster let him get it all out; he said it only cost him a case of whiskey." I went on to tell Bix how I'd practically moved across the hall into Tom's apartment, helped him put his station together while he taught me all about radio and gave me all his old Navy tech books and manuals (*The Principles Underlying Radio Communication,* a dark-red limp-leather volume, was my bible and bedmate for a year—I still remember it as one of the best I've ever read)—then went back to his old quartermaster in my behalf, taking me along as added persuasion, and succeeded in liberating another thousand dollars' worth of equipment; helped me build a station of my own; drilled me in the Interna-

tional Morse Code till I was ready to pass my government test—
and (I left out this part) became, naturally, my hero. My family
used to rib me, all that year, about my newly acquired traits—the
rolling, sauntering gait, the generalized Southern drawl that
marks all true members of our Armed Forces, a trick of scratching
my left cheek when puzzled. . . . Gene wondered aloud when I
would also manage to become five foot nine, slightly chubby and
dirty-blond, get stewed every night on home-brew, &c. I even
began to chew gum, surreptitiously, when Gene wasn't around.
. . . That was a lengthy romance. Even when Tom Seese got
married and moved out to Ravenswood, it lived on, if only in my
doodles, which still ran heavily to electronic symbols and circuit
diagrams, and TOM SEESE (a terrific name—I envied it) in elaborately shaded lettering. . . .

La giovanezza è mobile. I will not say I'd forgotten Tom Seese;
was I not living among his souvenirs? Each dot and dash I sent
radiating out into space were symbols of my debt to him, reminders of his patient instruction and lazy good humor. Forget Tom
Seese! But I had a new hero now, and this one . . . I had said it each
time, but this one was *really* different. This one touched something in me so deep—something I had not known was even there
—that I couldn't understand, but only had this feeling about: about
music, and life, and the life in music; if this seems incoherent, well,
it *was*— I could see no further into it. . . .

"Hey, could I listen in?" Bix asked.

"Sure." I handed him the earphones. Bix listened intently.

"There's some guy sending something," he said. "Where's that
coming from? Is he far away?"

I plugged in a spare earphone set and listened.

"That's a guy named Crawley right out here in Oak Park. His
transmitter's only got maybe fifteen watts—his range is about
eighteen miles at night, right now maybe ten or twelve."

"How could you tell who it was so quick?" Bix asked.

"I know what his signal sounds like," I said. "I hear it all the time.
Anyhow I recognized his 'fist'—you know, the way he pounds his
key. Every operator does it a little different."

"Huh," Bix said. "That's a darb!"*

"He didn't spend that much on his station," I said, sort of su-

*From *darby* (adj.), 1920s slang for "terrific"; i.e., "a beaut."

perior. "Sounds like a little power buzzer. The whole thing probably didn't cost him fifty dollars."

Bix looked at me. "Yours didn't cost you much either," he said dryly. He could be sharp, I was finding.

"Yeah," I said, a little sheepish. "You want to send?"

I switched over to BROAD BAND. We could hear a couple of guys talking—not code, ordinary speech. "Phone radio" was just starting to come in among hams; some ships already had it; but code died hard. For years after everything was phone, every licensed station had to maintain a standby key (code) transmitter, and you still had to know code to get an operator's license.

"Couple of johnny-come-latelies with microphones," I said scornfully, echoing Tom Seese. Needless to say, for me the whole romance was in *the sound of code.* I regarded phone transmission as a North Woods Indian guide might have regarded a party of drunken playboys roaring about in a snowmobile. "Phone is only good for short ranges," I added, which was true at the time. "I can get Mexico City on this set at night."

We fooled around with the radio for nearly an hour. I was glad to show off my accomplishments, but now I wanted some *Bix.*

"Hey, Bix, how about some hot piano? Come on," I said, dragging him into the living room.

"Shit, I can't really play piano," said Bix, but sat down anyway; for a moment after I opened up the keyboard, all the life he'd been displaying seemed to go out of him. "My mind's a blank," he muttered.

"How about *Aunt Hagar?*"

He thought a moment, then began to chord softly. It was a full minute before I recognized *Aunt Hagar's Children Blues* (which by the way is not a blues), as Bix warmed up and began to put original melodies over the chords. I listened in growing amazement to Bix's conception of this curious little tune, which combines a down-homey, bluesy introductory strain with a strange modulation into minor. I'd never heard it treated any other way but in a rough, earthy one. Bix brought out a lyrical, melancholy character I'd never thought of in connection with it—nor had anyone else—mostly by means of a subtle progression of chords that dug deep into the minor strain and came up with unexpectedly rich harmonic inferences. He had forgotten I was there, concentrating his gaze on the keyboard, wincing when his fingers failed to find what his mind was seeking, but I noticed that—unlike his "classical" efforts—when playing jazz on the piano he almost always would go right on, errors and all, not breaking the beat, getting farther and farther into the variations, until a particular number was, as it were, played out. He must have played *Aunt Hagar* a good quarter of an hour.

I suggested *Eccentric*, which I knew was a favorite of his, and went to fetch some beer from the icebox. Once he got warmed up he would keep on playing. He started playing other songs, from the Wolverines' book, Dixieland standards, blues, pop tunes— magically transmuting the crass Tin Pan Alley ditties into fresh, surprising musical gems. Alas, he was *not* a good pianist, frequently blurring and hitting outright clinkers, but what he lacked in facility he more than made up for in imagination and sheer musical power. On slow, pretty-type numbers he explored the harmonic depths, then would often invent a fresh, lilting new "second subject" in lightly stepping double time that would blow through the original theme like a cool breeze; on "up" or walkin' tempos, he swung with a beat that hit you in the guts, right down the centerline of *jazz*, its swinging essence. Where did all that come from? Nothing is more mysterious than the gift of music, nothing. . . .

All at once he stood up, stretched, blinked, shook his head, finished his beer, and said, "How about that *Ibéria* thing?"

I put the Debussy on. Bix squatted down next to the Victrola, his head right in the "horn" almost like the little black-&-white terrier in the "His Master's Voice" trademark picture, and listened, frozen, every few moments erupting with a "Hah!" or a "Jesus!" When the first side ended he said, "Wait a second," went directly to the piano and began fishing for the themes and chords he had just heard. To my astonishment, he had practically the whole thing by heart—stumbling often, to be sure, but invariably going back and finding the right notes. *I* knew it by heart too, but I'd heard it a hundred times. I began to understand why Bix had never learned to read.

Mummy was up by that time, and gone shopping; she had stolen out almost unobserved. ("Talent" was never to be disturbed.) We played the rest of *Ibéria;* Bix could now stumble through the whole thing. It was getting dark. Bix had again, to all appearances, forgotten my presence. After getting all the way to the end of his ear rendition, Bix began to improvise on one of the sequences ("In the Streets and Byways"). It wasn't exactly jazz, and it wasn't exactly Debussy; it was—Bix. Jazz was suggested rather than given overt expression. Again I was having a wholly new experience, hearing a new kind of sound. Where did the two musical languages fit together?

Then, and often thereafter, I observed that this delving into new musical depths brought Bix no visible satisfaction. On the contrary, he seemed to experience mostly a deep sense of frustration. He scowled, winced, exclaimed in muttered bursts of self-disgust and exasperation. It did not matter that what he was finding struck the listener—me, for example—as charming, arresting, beautiful. Listeners not only didn't count; they simply weren't there—I often had that sense. I didn't know the word "introvert" then, but one of my frequently used dictionaries today defines it as though trying to describe Bix Beiderbecke: "*n.* a person concerned primarily with things or feelings within the self, as opposed to things in the external world." Indeed one got the sense of a person whose inner life was in such turmoil that real or lasting resolutions of it could not readily be found; a turmoil that really expressed itself only in music, compared with which all the rest of his life seemed little more than a shadowy dream.

Bix came often that spring. Sometimes Vic was home, sometimes not. He came at odd hours, usually without phoning; for all I know, he may have come sometimes when no one was home, and simply went away again. Once he didn't show up for several weeks; then I learned that Vic had got the Wolverines a gig out of town; another time, that he had been staying at some girl's apartment, a girl none of the other musicians seemed to know. I've forgotten her name if I ever knew it, but it doesn't matter—he never seemed to get very friendly with the type of girl who hangs around jazz musicians; I have no idea how "serious" any of those relationships were, but I imagine if they had been "serious" we would at some point have seen the girls.

Occasionally, during a visit to our house, Bix would get out his cornet and play along behind a jazz record; I don't recall his ever doing it with a classical record.

Sometimes he would sit at the piano toying with chords for a few minutes, and then, as though unconsciously, drift into some part of a record I'd played for him a week before, Ravel or Milhaud or

Fauré, but oftenest Debussy. He was crazy about *L'Après-midi d'un faune* and couldn't get enough of it; he seemed to discover something new every time we listened to it. A succession of far-out harmonies, seemingly unrelated, and suddenly I'd become aware that they had led subtly but inevitably into, say, *L'Après-midi*— not necessarily the opening measures of it.

Those improvisations of his, straying over the keyboard apparently at random, then carried along on one of the currents of his interior musical monologue, were the strangest of all, unlike anything previously heard on land or sea. They'd start invariably in the most hesitant, reticent, coolest, most classic style—often ad lib tempo—Bix looking vacantly out into space; were marred by frequent errors, which he'd usually go back over and correct, ten times if need be (swearing softly at himself); not what you could call brilliantly played, but in the less demanding passages a rather surprisingly delicate touch could emerge . . . then you would realize you were hearing the first theme being repeated, but it was now putting forth modest buds, natural and consistent as a green leaf opening; often, at that point, something else happened: a pulse developed in the left hand, perhaps "walking" upward from the low bass, that soon hardened into an insistent swinging beat, and now the language had become jazz; the original theme would start to lose itself in little whorls and eddies of melody, cast in the slurred intervals of the blues scale, though deformed echoes of the original still clung to the new sound, more like reminders than literal references. That first eruption into jazz always made my skin tingle; it was a birth, an ever new something flashing up into the sun. . . . Not long ago I'd seen a "nature film," shot in stop-motion, of metamorphosis: caterpillar into butterfly, all the days of slow change magically condensed into a few hundred feet of film —suddenly the humble creeping creature was a winged dancer, floating upward, freed from the earth. That was the image that leaped to my mind the first time I heard Bix do *his* unique musical metamorphosis—the sudden, jarring, swinging stride of jazz was like a pair of wings, which literally lifted me up off my chair and made me laugh aloud, as I had the first time I heard Bix's horn on the record (was it possible that was only a few weeks ago?). *What was he "saying"? What did it all "mean"?*

But just as we were properly launched and flying, just as that line of thought seemed about to achieve some sort of climax, the jazz muse would be abruptly abandoned, and the voice of Debussy, or of Debussy-cum-Beiderbecke, would once more be heard in the land. So it would go, classical/jazz/classical, with passages in between that were neither or both; and all—jazz, classical, and what-is-it—were cut from the same fabric, and the fabric was Bix. Another image that comes to mind now, as I remember Bix's oddly alternating modes, is of some curiously wrought column, carved on opposite sides, Janus-like, with twin masks—à la Tragedy & Comedy—both carved recognizably by the same hand, the column turning and turning, lit by some ambiguous and changing light that now sharpened, now blurred their features to an ambiguous resemblance, as first one face, then the other, stared out at one. . . .

In truth it was less simple—I say this *now*. For the "two faces of Bix" were no simple opposites; in certain ways yes—but just what ways? To this day I know of no really good qualitative analysis of the jazz aesthetic—of wherein precisely it differs from that of classical music, if indeed anything so elusive and manysided would be found to lend itself to dissection and formulation. It is one of that vast category of experiences, easy to feel and identify, hard to describe.

In any event, there soon emerged a discernible pattern in these visits, a tacit *quid pro quo*. Bix would arrive—it might be any time of day, rarely in the morning; nights he was generally working. If I was doing something at the moment that he found intriguing—playing with my radio set or chemicals, or stargazing—he might or might not watch or join me or ask questions. In due course either he would ask to hear some record or I would want him to hear one he hadn't heard—classical, jazz, ethnic (I had not long before gone through a Chinese period, which had duly left its jetsam on the shores of my life—several dozen records, fascinatingly labeled in Chinese characters, of Cantonese orchestras and popular singers); after an hour or so at the Victrola he would drift, or I would nudge him, over to the piano—less often, induce him to get out his horn, if we ran across a particularly enticing jazz record. If I was less fortunate, Bix might wander off into some of his musical memoirs with Eastwood Lane et al. Coward that I was, I could never let my hero see how little I liked these efforts, but waited tactfully (and hopefully) for him to doodle his fill of these mediocrities and get onto some "real" music.

Often, especially if Mummy was at home or came home, we fed
him; on one occasion he slept nine hours straight, in Gene's room;
always he drank, whatever alcoholic was offered; I never knew
him to *ask* for anything, not so much as a glass of water—indeed
he was no friend to water. I don't know that it was shyness that
explained this notable lack of initiative, if that's the word. Rather
I would say it was a kind of chronic unawareness of need, arising
from a chronic mental preoccupation—as busy children must be
reminded to eat, rest, or urinate. Except, of course, where music
was concerned. He would ask to hear records, any time, day or
night; he would, if so inclined, go very directly indeed to the piano;
once immersed in listening or playing, he would forget everything
and everyone. He never thought to ask if his playing bothered
anyone (but I must suppose my immediate and continual urging
precluded any such thought), just as it never occurred to him that
anyone was enchanted by it; I doubt that he even thought about
it; it was simply part of his metabolism, like breathing.

Several other Wolverines records were released, also on the
Gennett label. Those recording sessions were held at the Starr
Piano Company's studios in Richmond, Indiana, a two-hundred-
mile drive from Chi. I recall *Oh Baby* and *Copenhagen* was one
coupling; another—the best, my favorite—*Riverboat Shuffle,* with
a terrible pop tune on the other side they never should have cut
at all, *Susie.* That was even a bad take—it had a real clinker on it
by George Johnson toward the end of his tenor solo. At the time
we all laughed about it, no one gave a damn how good or bad it
was (Bix thought they were all pretty bad, judging by his sour
expression); but now that these sides have become history, and any
record with even an apocryphal two bars of Bix on it is a collector's
item, bid for at auctions, &c., it really hurts to listen to some of the
things they dashed off, obviously with little concern for posterity.
There was another date later on that had *Tiger Rag,* which I don't
think ever came out for some reason; I only heard the test pressing
but thought it was "the berries," though again Bix just shook his
head and said, *Shit, what's good about it?* Several times I tried to
draw him out about the record dates, but he so evidently disliked
talking about it that I desisted.

The only time I'd heard Bix and the band live was at that first
"rehearsal." I was dying to go along on the jobs they were starting
to get with increasing frequency in and around Chi.

I could see no logical reason why I shouldn't. I was no stranger to the club circuit; had been doing the best & worst from age seven, when I first started playing drums, with Vic as my sponsor and guardian; had regularly sat in, and played and sung, with some of the best jazz bands, black & white—including King Oliver's (with Louis playing second cornet) and the Friars' Inn gang—and been hailed as a sensational kid performer (almost anything is forgiven a ten-year-old child who looks eight). As we also know, I had more recently, dizzy with these triumphs, been doing the North Side spots with Jack Goss, and no big brother Vic around. But in those situations I had a real excuse for being in such an unlikely place as a Prohibition-era Chicago nightclub. As the Jazz Juniors, we sat around in the dressing rooms, or the Green Room, if there was one, until it was time to do our number, collected our winnings, and scrammed, not waiting around to get the management in trouble in the event of a raid or gunplay.

But what excuse did I have to tag along on a Wolverines date? It's times like those you feel your age. I couldn't bring myself to ask Bix; I didn't enjoy bringing up anything that emphasized our age difference. I sang with other bands; why not the Wolverines? one might ask; but nothing would have induced me at that stage of our acquaintance to open my mouth in front of Bix; brash everywhere else, I just felt unworthy with him.

But one night the problem unexpectedly solved itself. Vic had got them a gig and, this time, had to go along to talk business with the club owners. I'd been pestering him to death, despite my reticence with Bix. He was hesitant at first, but seeing my agony relented and took me along.

The joint was out in the toughest part of Cicero; most of the customers looked like gorillas and hookers. It was a real speak; you had to give your name through a hole in the steel door to get in. Well, at least nobody was going to request a waltz; the band could play as rough as they liked.

That kind of atmosphere usually turned jazz musicians on. This certainly did; the boys outdid themselves, and the customers loved it. Bix was a gas, ripping out chorus after chorus, eyes shut, or staring madly at the ceiling, which had one of those revolving things with a couple of hundred mirrors on it reflecting the blue & red spotlights hitting it from the walls. The waiters, who all looked like bodyguards, served the drinks in coffee cups; root beer bottles full of whiskey and gin stood around on the tables. The management must have taken it for granted that all jazz musicians were lushes; between all the chairs on the bandstand stood more bottles of gin or some other white dynamite, courtesy of the club.

They danced pretty rough there. The harder the band swung, the better they liked it; quite a few of them must have dug jazz, by the way they stood around in front of the stand listening and clapping after every number. Bix had that crowd in the hollow of his hand after the first number. To me Bix's playing was a very subtle and inside thing, but it's a fact that wherever he played, in those days, the most unsubtle-looking people seemed to fall all over him. I have no idea what it was they heard (do we ever know that about other people?), but whatever it was they went crazy about it that night. I saw more than one of those blue-chinned gorillas frowning at his rather unsteady steady, growling at her not to get so goddamn friendly with the musicians. Even Vic Moore, who found all girls irresistible (they often reciprocated), was on his good behavior tonight; I suppose my brother Vic had warned him off.

We sat with the bosses at a table near the stand. I was in seventh heaven. The bosses' girlfriends thought I was "cute" (how I hated that word), asked how old I was, was I a musician too, tried to get me to sit in, and sing (Vic as usual had bragged about my gifts), and so forth, until their chatter got on their gentlemen friends' nerves and they were unceremoniously told to "git lost." They pouted but obeyed. Vic and the bosses were discussing some future engagements, but I wasn't hearing anything but the band, which meant mostly Bix.

It didn't occur to me then, but it should have: no wonder Bix didn't like record dates. The difference between the way he sounded on records and live was like night and day. For one thing, a 10-inch 78-speed record had a maximum of three and one-quarter minutes playing time on it; for a musician with a lot to say it was like telling Dostoevsky to do *The Brothers Karamazov* as a short story. Bix on a bandstand, if he was going good, would really stretch out—ten choruses were nothing, everybody including his fellow musicians egging him on: *Yeah, Bix! Go on, man, don't quit now!*

Between sets the band sat at the next table. The waiter brought them homemade wine in coffee cups, a subtle class distinction: Vic and the bosses were drinking Scotch, which they boasted was "right off the boat from Canada." I was dying to go and sit with Bix, but felt I needed an excuse. I leaned over to say, "Hey, Bix, how come you guys haven't played any blues yet?"

Bix looked at me vaguely and replied, "We didn't? Oh, yeah. Well, I guess Dick's been trying out these new things for the book —you know."

That was sufficient pretext for me to come over and squeeze into a chair between him and Voynow. "Yes, Dick, how come?" I persisted. "How come you guys don't play those blues?"

Voynow fended me off, deadpan: "I don't know, how come we don't?" But I wasn't to be put off with banter.

"You guys are always hollering about how great King Oliver is, and all those nigger musicians," I said. "In case you haven't noticed, about half the tunes all those bands play are blues—right?" I had begun all this as a ploy, but now the subject had come up, I realized I'd long nursed this gripe, sort of in the back of my mind.

They looked at each other. Voynow shrugged it off, but Jimmy Hartwell said seriously, "I guess we just don't know that many. Let's face it, we're not going to catch those niggers." That was most white jazzmen's attitude. I looked at Bix, who was drinking his wine and saying nothing. Finally he looked up at me.

"Niggers play different," he said. "They're . . . the real thing. I mean the *real* thing." Then to my astonishment he looked around at the others and said, "Frenchy's right. We ought to be playing the blues more."

"I don't know," said Vic Moore, his eye on a pair of cute gams at the next table. "We play blues. We play *Tin Roof* and *Farewell Blues.*"

"*Farewell!* That's not a real blues," I said, getting excited. "I'm talking about *blues*—like Bessie sings, and Mamie Smith—you know what I mean. Like when a nigger band just says, 'Let's play a blues,' and somebody says, 'What key?' and somebody else says, 'B flat,' and that's it. I don't mean just these name blues like *Saint Louis Blues* and *Memphis Blues* and *Tin Roof.* I mean just *blues,*" I finished, still glowing from what Bix had said, trying not to show it.

"I know what Frenchy means, all right," he said again. "We ought to get into that more. The nigger bands've got that thing down."

My heart pounding with pride and love, I hardly heard the rest of the discussion, which led to a kind of general vague decision to "really get into those nigger things more."

Voynow said to me, "How'd you get that nickname 'Frenchy'?"

Bobby Gillette said, "Because he can talk French, dopey."

They all looked at me with interest. "I could," I said, "when we first came back from France—that's three years ago. I've forgotten a lot of it now, I guess."

"How do you say 'Which way to the men's room?' " asked Dick, deadpan.

I translated, but added, "They don't usually have men's rooms and ladies' rooms. They just have a little old woman who sits outside; you pay her a tip when you come out." Astonishing!

The talk became general. Somebody gave me a cup of wine (after annoyingly checking with my brother Vic that it was all right). I was still floating on air, not daring to look at Bix.

When they went back on the stand and started playing again, I became aware of a more critical attitude toward the rest of the band. None of them were really anywhere near being on Bix's level. Moore and Bobby Gillette (banjo) had a habit of rushing the beat, especially on their breaks, thereby effectively destroying any jazz feeling. How about a *rhythm section* that doesn't *swing?* I asked myself dispiritedly as I listened to their ministrations. Bobby, one of the most charming and enthusiastic fellows I ever met, was a pure unadulterated *ragtime* musician; the incongruity of his sound, behind or before and after the indescribable subtlety and swing of Bix, was grotesque. Voynow wasn't that bad, but had absolutely nothing to contribute except a discreet background of chords; I don't think I ever heard him take a solo, which was probably just as well. Min Leibrook happened to be a fine musician too—but how much can you swing on a *tuba?* It was no accident that by 1924 the better jazzmen were already dropping it in favor of the (plucked) string bass; in a few more years it would be a museum piece. Min was so far ahead of his time he actually could, and did, play little solo breaks on it, which reminded one of an elephant doing an entrechat—fun's fun, but that too was just one more failure to swing. So much for the (alleged) rhythm section. As for the other horns, I don't remember ever hearing or meeting Al Gandee in person, but he sounded, on the couple of records where he played trombone, just adequate, in a—let's face it—

archaic, Kid-Ory*-ish vein. George Johnson played fair tenor sax, but his technique was uncertain, and he often lacked the sure-footed authority over his instrument that is the improvising jazz-man's most indispensable tool. The best of the lot, after Bix, was Jimmy Hartwell on clarinet; not a hard swinger, but fluent and graceful in a New Orleans street band way. All of it added up to not much support for a musician like Bix; but I can't remember ever hearing Bix say a word against anyone except himself. All, Bix included, accepted their fellow bandsmen just as they were; they were buddies, and chuckled over each other's frailties and limitations like the members of a goodhumored family. Voynow was nominally the "leader," but I'm sure he too would no more have thought of replacing one of them to improve the band than you would think of replacing your little boy to improve the family. Such as they were, they were stuck with each other—and having a high old time of it; their stumbling onto a musician of the caliber of Bix had been the merest accident, and did nothing to change their cheerfully uncritical attitude. Even Bix, I believe, thought of himself as one of them, and as having the time of his life—and it was true that he'd never had it so good. If I, or Vic, or others who were inclined to carp, felt otherwise, we either did so half-unconsciously or kept our carping to ourselves; for the moment, the Wolverines were the Wolverines, and doing very well for themselves.

They certainly were doing all right on this club date. Those Chicago racketeers and bootleggers weren't noted for their generosity to each other, but many of them were very good to jazz musicians. The ones in this club must have laid something like $500 in tips on the band before the night was over, probably more than the pay for the whole gig. One of them, a short, chunky Sicilian with a mashed nose—the one who had told the "broads" to "git lost"—fed the kitty† every time he got up to dance with *his* broad later on, and the more he drank, the bigger the tips he dropped in the kitty. He seemed especially fond of Bix, and during one set stuffed a fifty-dollar bill in the bell of Bix's cornet, which Bix unobtrusively dropped into the kitty's common fund the moment the man's back was turned.

*Kid Ory (1886–1970), pioneer jazz trombonist who played with Buddy Bolden, Oliver, Armstrong, et al.
†A box for tips, usually cut out in the shape of a cat's head.

One of the bosses must have said something to my brother about sitting in; at the start of the third or fourth set Vic signaled to Vic Moore, who gladly relinquished the stool and was soon deep in "conference" with an unattached girl.

What a difference when Vic Berton took over at the drums! The casual power with which he kicked it off, the brilliance of his playing, breathtaking licks coming one on top of the other like storm waves rolling in, lifted everyone right out of his chair, guys and dolls as well as musicians; the reaction was something you could feel run through the place like an electric current; even Bobby's banjo seemed almost to swing with Vic driving him, Dick Voynow laid down a decent stride; Bix was . . . indescribable.

After the set, Vic Moore grinned his most sheepish grin, shaking his head ruefully, and said, "You mean now *I* gotta get up there?"

Fortunately for him, then came the floor show, a mini-floor show, with a "line" of only four buxom cuties in costumes best described as the bare minimum, and a "singer" who must have been somebody's sister-in-law—and, for the big finale, the inevitable shake dancer, who emerged onto the floor clad only in a few feathers, to "Oriental" accompaniment on Vic Moore's tom-toms. One of the waiters, doubling as light man, killed all the lights except for half a dozen baby spots mounted on the side walls of the establishment and equipped with deep blue and red gels* that rotated in alternation, casting a dim, weirdly changing illumination on her performance—a combined "tribal rite" and striptease that ended with her on the floor, entirely naked and apparently having sex with an imaginary partner who must have been, judging by the tempo of her movements, part vibrator. At the conclusion of this one-girl orgy, she was borne offstage, supposedly swooning, by the other four "dancers," who dashed in on cue, with all the grace of a squad of medics under fire; so ended the floor show. (Toward the end of this performance, Bix, having apparently had all he could take, picked up his cornet and contributed some satirical "growl" effects, using a derby hat as a mute, which I'm sure the customers in the joint took seriously as an auxiliary aphrodisiac.)

That was the first time I'd watched Bix in a commercial setting. It was also the first time I'd watched him drink—I guess I just

*Transparent colored sheets (formerly made of gelatin) in square or circular metal frames, for stage lighting.

wasn't really looking at that first "rehearsal" (or whatever it was). The whole band drank plenty, all except Dick Voynow, who neither drank nor smoked (he carried barbells as part of his luggage), but Bix seemed to put away twice as much as anyone else. The remarkable thing was that, while the others soon began to show the effects of alcohol, Bix remained as he always was, drunk or sober—quiet, polite, preoccupied, contributing little to the conversation and much to the music.

Subsequently I was able to get taken along on other Wolverines jobs. One of them was really hilarious, a Jewish wedding, a catered affair at some fancy North Side establishment that Vic had got wind of through our rich relatives. The caterer must have thought he was hiring a regular society orchestra. Dick Voynow gave them all a serious lecture while they were setting up, which gave Vic Moore and Bobby Gillette a fit of uncontrollable giggles, so that for the first couple of numbers they didn't dare look at each other. As the sole Jewish member of the band, Dick (an atheist, by the way) felt it was up to him to impress a certain minimum decorum on their behavior; he also pointed out to them that these gigs paid well, for a relatively brief span of hours, and didn't even interfere with regular club jobs since many of them were held in the afternoon. It was no use. Moore and Gillette continued to sputter with ill-suppressed laughter, and ended by making even Dick break up, as they received the various "requests" from the floor, and "suggestions" from the boss of the catering place, for waltzes, polkas, &c., which they actually tried to play; luckily Dick knew them all, and would play them through once on the piano, whereupon the others would quickly pick up the tune (approximately) and start to harmonize in the corniest possible barbershop quartet style, doing their best to keep a straight face (try giggling while playing a wind instrument sometime). The guests ate it up. The cornier the boys played, the more syrupy the clichés, the more pleased were the wedding guests.

There was a tense moment when, after the very first number, the bride's father came over, introduced himself with a self-important air, and then asked in some bewilderment, glancing about, "Where is the music?" Dick explained it had been lost in a fire two weeks ago, and they were accumulating a new book as fast as funds would permit. The man clucked sympathetically over their plight, remarking, "You're a nice bunch of boys. You Jewish?"

"Oh, of course," Dick said.

"That's nice, that's nice," the man said, and added in a whisper, "They fix you up yet with a little schnapps?"

"Not yet," Dick said.

The man went to the bar and came back with a couple of bottles. "Right off the boat!" he whispered. "Put it away, put it away!" and strolled off. Bix said out of the side of his mouth, "We'll put it away, all right."

They exercised remarkable self-control until the very end, when Bix, who had "put away" one of the bottles virtually single-handed, said to Dick, "How about waking these people up a lit-tle?"

Seeing they'd already been paid, with a handsome tip besides, Dick shrugged and said, "Call it!"

"Eccentric," Bix said, and stomped off, tearing into the first lead, eyes popping out, louder and harder than I'd ever heard him blow. The manager was staring at us from the other side of the room; the guests stopped dancing one by one, or couple by couple, blinking in bewilderment, except some of the young people, who started dancing "real crazy," their yarmulkes sliding off their heads, while their elders glared at them in stern admonition. When it was over and we were packing up, one bearded patriarch approached with great dignity.

"From where you learn such music?" he inquired severely. "From a saloon?" and strode away again without waiting for an answer. I felt we'd got off lightly. But that was the first and last Jewish wedding engagement the Wolverines got, as far as I know, and I heard later that the rich relative called Vic up and gave him hell for engaging "a bunch of bums, jazz musicians, what are you, crazy?" and so on. Vic regarded the whole affair as a good joke, which may help to explain why he was never going to get rich in the orchestra business. (My mother could see both sides of the question; she really didn't approve of offending anyone, but her sense of humor always got the best of her when such scenes were described to her.) Naturally these doings only confirmed the pre-vailing view of our respectable relations that "those gypsies" were incurable lost souls who would come to no good end—and proba-bly have no very pleasant journey getting to it.

On Bix's next visit to our house, I tried lightly to broach the subject of how differently he played in person, with the band, and how great he sounded. To my surprise Bix refused to discuss it at all, and got really sarcastic, almost nasty for him.

In reply to my encomiums, he cracked, "I must be the Paderewski of hot music," using a name that was on every tongue at the time, the most celebrated pianist since Liszt. "Shit, I don't even know what the hell I'm doing half the time."

I must have said something like, "Well, *I* know what you're doing, and it's not like any other musician," to which Bix said sardonically, "I guess one's enough, huh?"

My feelings were hurt; he had managed in effect to imply there was something wrong with my ear or my musical judgement. Well, I wasn't the only one in the world who thought he was "something." How come so many bands liked to have him sit in? How come so many other musicians . . . ? Bix only withdrew further behind his defensive armor of sarcasm and then changed the subject, obviously irritated; and I had to face for the first time, without equivocation, the bleak truth that my hero simply didn't share, and was never going to, the attitude that for me formed the principal basis of our whole relationship—my good opinion of his musical gifts.

Consciously or not, I came to realize that whether on piano or cornet, alone or with the band, live or on record, Bix Beiderbecke got little satisfaction or pleasure out of his own playing. The only expressions of real delight I had ever seen drawn from him were about *other people's* work, *other people's* interests—Paul Mares's or Louis Armstrong's playing, Debussy's writings, my radio shack, Gene's scrapbook. For others, Bix was the world's greatest audience, with a sensitive appreciation not often found in our fellow man; it was as if he possessed special antennae whose function it was to find the good in things. But when it came to his own work, this marvelous sensibility of Bix's, to talent, to achievement, failed utterly—was as if turned upside down. Nothing was good enough, nothing—to his ear—came right.

I see him now, at the piano, exploring the keyboard, eyes closed, like a blind man in a familiar room, his small mouth pursed in a peculiar twisted way he had; finding strange harmonies, fragments of a melodic idea that would start and stop, start and peter out, like the frayed end of a rope in the wind, ending nowhere— but often along the way it had *said something*, something poignant or, at times, wayward and enigmatic, something perhaps whimsical and puzzling. . . . Now he would open his eyes, suddenly, his gaze wandering over the keys just ahead of his fingers, his bulging eyes vacant, his mouth falling a little open like a child's (sometimes just the tip of his tongue visible at the corner), the gaze unfocused, just skimming the keys; then all at once he would get hold of something, an elusive idea would suddenly get pinned down under his fingers like a butterfly. Usually at that point, or as soon as he *had it safe* in his hands, he would shift gears, into the jazz mode; his jaw would set (as if to say *I've got you this time*) and —this I think was the nearest I saw him come to anything that could be called satisfaction (but not really), these moments when his searching mind *found it,* the blind man's groping hand suddenly closed around something solid—and now he would take his "find" along with him like a retriever clutching a bird in its jaws, back into the world of jazz (was *that* "his" world after all?).

Now would come at last that burst of rhythmic power I too had been waiting for, an extended passage of purest jazz, budding and branching out of the previous classical gropings like fireworks, like the sudden clusters of stars exploding from the rocket against a dark sky. And I noticed again, without knowing I noticed, that once he had set his feet on the track of jazz, there was to be no halting until that passage was *complete;* now there was no pausing over mistakes or blurred figures, to hell with them, to hell with everything, his onward drive careened straight ahead, drove headlong over skipped notes and clinkers like a runaway truck pounding over potholes.

Those jazz solos of his did not go on, develop "naturally," chorus on chorus, variation following variation, in the familiar vein of the normal jazzman. It was not as though inspiration flagged—rather that *he withdrew it,* to point it once again in that other direction, in among the stranger trees and flowers of the garden of the classical, once more tentative and groping its way, seeking, searching—but for what?—until, frustrated and recoiling upon itself, once more it swung about, "hard about," into the rough swinging waves of jazz, like a savage answer to a tender question. . . .

If what I was witnessing was indeed a search, I never had the sense of his having found whatever it was he was seeking. But I had learned better than to try to share with Bix my pleasure in and admiration of the bright moments, great and small, the often gorgeous flowers he plucked and threw away so impatiently along the way. I learned to accept his eternal vexation with himself, though it made me unhappy to see it, as I would learn to accept his drinking, his self-neglect, and a hundred other things about which I, like many others, eventually decided there was nothing to be done. They were just—Bix; and they were, like Bix, my despair and my anxiety.

And in learning that uncomfortable lesson, though I couldn't know it then, I was only joining that considerable legion of well-wishers—family, teachers, friends, admirers, fellow musicians, lovers—who, from Bix's infancy onward, had felt those same emotions toward him: admiration, love, anxiety, hope, and at last despair (*What shall be done with Little Bickie?* they had cried once upon a time, and come to no useful answer).

But I wasn't one to give up easily, not at thirteen.

13
SOME CHICAGO
AFTERNOONS

April. The warmest day yet.

I was a big baseball fan and the second-best hitter on our block. Chi was a red-hot town for baseball, with two of the best clubs in the country, the Cubs and the White Sox. The 1919 Black Sox scandal had put an almost fatal crimp in the White Sox. I was at Comiskey Park for those infamous games, every day they played (I'd have gone to Cincinnati for the rest if I could have), and cried the first day the Reds won on the White Sox "errors"—but we still had the Cubs (remember "Tinker to Evers to Chance"?). April; another season about to begin.

As I came out wearing my "Jr. Cubs" uniform (I loved those spiked shoes) and carrying my bat, &c., Bix was climbing out of a taxi. He paid the hackie (from the usual assortment of pockets), blinked at me out of small, reddened eyes (smoking weed all night, my mind registered automatically), and greeted me in his usual offhand way. "I was just on my way to play some ball," I said.

"No shit," said Bix with mild irony. "I thought sure you were heading for a violin lesson."

I grinned and asked if he wanted to go back upstairs; he yawned and said, "Where do you play ball around here?" I pointed down the block and said without thinking, "Want to come along and watch?" Bix nodded, tucking the inevitable paper bag under his arm, and started walking with me toward the lot. Only then did I realize the way he looked—but it was too late. What should I do?

Bix was wearing a wrinkled tux that looked slept in, cigarette ashes all over one sleeve, and patent leather pumps; his boiled shirtfront was coffee-stained, his snap-on bow tie askew. I was ashamed to have my friends see him, and ashamed of being ashamed. I went through a scarlet, scalding moment when I almost made up some excuse to abandon the ballgame and go back to the house; then I stiffened mentally. *This was my hero—a musician, a genius, for Christ's sake. What the hell did I care what Arnie and those other snot-nosed kids thought? To hell with what they thought!*

We had the lot to ourselves. The rest of the kids must have been just getting out of school. Bix stowed his horn in the crotch of a tree. "Want me to toss you a few?" he asked unexpectedly. It hadn't occurred to me to connect this alcoholic, night-owl musician, in tux and patent leather pumps, with outdoor life, but I said sure, I'd like to hit a few fungoes. I threw him the ball and a fielder's mitt; he stuck it on and walked out to the pitcher's mound. On top of everything else, he needed a shave—his neatly parted hair only emphasized his stubbly chin. He was a sight, all right. Could he really throw a ball sixty feet, and put it somewhere within reach?

He tossed me a nice easy one, which I popped up for a high fly. Bix went back just enough, shading his eyes like a real ballplayer; the ball dropped into his glove like a nickel into a slot. The next one I caught on the end of my bat for a line drive that flew straight for his face like a bullet. He caught that one too, just right, casually lifting his hand exactly in time, like a cat putting its paw on a moving string. "Gee," I said, "you're O.K." I wasn't feeling so bad any more.

Some of the others were arriving, from all directions—Arnie Auerbach, Jack Roesch, Phil Sharpe, Limpy Scholtz. Phil and I were the best hitters and base runners on the block, unless Artie Klein showed up. He was nearly seventeen, and completely out of our class, but sometimes he came around on Saturdays and played with us for an hour or so. He was getting ready to graduate, go to Northwestern, and law school, and didn't allow himself much time for things like baseball. I was hoping he might come around today, to balance off Bix so we could have a fairly even division of forces. Meanwhile Phil—my best friend on the block—was whispering to me.

"Who's that funnylooking gink?"

"That's the cornet player I told you about," I whispered back, blushing. "You know, Bix."

"Boy! he's a darb,"* said Phil, unable to restrain giggles. "How come he's dressed so funny?" Others too, I saw miserably, were staring and tittering.

"He . . . he's a musician," I said lamely. "He just came from playing at some big theater," I added, hoping to impress them.

"A the-ayter? Dressed like *that?*" said Arnie scornfully. His father, as it happened, was the manager of a local *the-ayter*, a fact I'd forgotten.

"Hey, Frenchy, is he gonna *play* in them shoes?" asked Limpy loudly. Bix meanwhile, ignoring everyone, was still out on the pitcher's mound, tossing the ball idly in the air and catching it. I had to admit he certainly did look strange in that bow tie and those shoes, which by now were covered with dust.

"I don't know," I said, annoyed. "Sure, I guess so. He catches pretty good," I added.

"Yeh, he looks it!" Limpy said, good and loud again. Bix paid no attention.

By now there were ten or twelve, enough to start a game. Just as we were starting to choose up, Artie Klein came around the corner. He was wearing his Senn High uniform and looked like a real big-leaguer. He must have come from after-school batting practice.

"Hey, Artie!"

"Hey, Frenchy!"

"We got Artie!" cried Arnie Auerbach. "*We* got Artie!" hollered the others he'd already picked.

"O.K., we got Bix," I hollered right back, wondering whether that was good or bad.

"Can you pitch?" I whispered to Bix when he came in at my signal.

"I guess so," said Bix. "I ain't done it since school, but I guess I'll make out. You want me to play?"

"Sure, sure I do!" I said, hoping for the best. How was he going to run in those shoes? I had a vague idea of running back up to the house and seeing if I couldn't fix him up with a pair of Vic's or Gene's sneakers, or maybe Vic's old ring shoes.

"Yeah, I guess I'd better take 'em off," Bix said, yawning, and, in front of the assembled, goggle-eyed kids, proceeded to sit down

*From "*darby*" (*adj.*), 1920s slang for "terrific"; i.e., "a beaut."

on the ground and remove his shoes and socks and roll up his pants legs, as calmly as if he were alone in his bedroom.

At this spectacle, and it was a spectacle, the boys' mirth became uncontrollable. I thought Phil would have to be carried home on a stretcher. I set my teeth and tried not to hear the gibes.

"Holy jeez! Looka that!"

"What're you gonna do, go swimmin'?"

"He's gonna do a toe dance!"

Bix grinned mildly and stowed his shoes and socks back where he had already put his jacket; as an afterthought he removed his bow tie and stuffed it in his jacket, opened his detachable collar and took it off, and rolled up his shirt sleeves. The boys exhausted themselves laughing at last, and chose up for first-at-bat. We won the toss. Determined to show my confidence, I put Bix fourth in the lineup. If he could hit at all, with any luck we ought to have at least one man on then. After all, he *was* a grownup. I put myself third, just ahead of him. I usually got a base hit every time at bat. I prayed for full bases.

Phil was first up for our side. "Take it easy, Artie!" he yelled, as Artie wound up for the first pitch.

Artie just smiled sourly and put one right across the plate, a sizzler. "Strike!" yelled Jack, umpiring until his turn at bat.

But having put a second one past him, Artie, showing off as usual, refused to strike Phil out, and contemptuously walked him. One on! Jack was up next; Artie allowed him a pop fly, which Limpy miraculously dropped. Two on!

I got up to the plate, swinging my bat and praying for a nice low one. I never could predict what Artie Klein would do; he was a queer duck. If he happened to be sharp and right on his game, he might fan me six times running; but if he was even the slightest bit off or overconfident, I might knock one into the next block, and he knew it. Bix was watching me curiously, a little smile on his face. I felt flushed and determined. *I couldn't fan out in front of Bix. Please, please!*

Artie, incomprehensibly—maybe he thought to catch me napping, since his first pitch was usually a fast ball—threw me a nice slow floater. I couldn't believe my eyes—but there was nothing wrong with my reflexes. I hit right from my toes, putting everything I had into the swing. My bat caught the apple square, just a little low, and lifted it straight over Artie's head, high over center field and, unbelievably, still rising, but I was already nearing first base, running like a deer. If nobody caught it, it was a sure homer. The *crackkkk!* of my bat meeting that ball was still ringing in my ears, everybody on my team yelling advice, Phil and Jack practically on top of each other racing for home, Phil had already scored, then Jack, I was almost at third, when I heard a concerted groan go up, and an answering yell from Arnie's team. "Frenchy! Frenchy! No homer! No homer!"

My fly had landed on the roof of the apartment house back of center field. Since it was so close to the lot, we had made a rule —no home run if you hit it on the roof; it was only a three-bagger. I pulled up at third, disappointed. Well, anyway, I'd certainly shown Bix the power of my bat. I was happy now, and looked across at Bix, already up at bat and measuring the field with his eye. Despite his dirty bare feet and rolled-up pants and shirt with no collar, all at once I had faith. Bix grinned back at me and winked. Somebody had gone up to get the ball off the roof; Arnie tossed Artie another ball.

Arnie's whole team was yelling advice at Artie. "Fan him," hollered Arnie. "He can't hit! Give him your fast one, Art!"

Artie smiled his provoking smile, nodded, and steamed one in, hard as he could throw it. He was on his mettle to show up this barefoot clown.

There was a crack like a rifle shot as Bix swung—a line drive going straight for DoDo Pollack at first base. DoDo made no attempt to catch it, but dived for the deck for dear life. It whizzed over him and slammed into the fence, just outside the foul line.

"Foul—strike one!" called Whitey Van, who was umping, in an awed voice. "Jeez, take it easy, fella! You'll kill somebody!" Bix's swing hadn't looked that hard, but there was a splintered spot where his ball had struck the green fence.

Bix nodded. "I'm a little rusty," he replied. "I ain't had a bat in my hand for two years."

Arnie had walked out to Artie for a little conference. I didn't need to hear what they were whispering about; it was obvious. We had two runs in already, I was on third. If Bix hit safely, that could easily wrap up the ballgame; and judging by that first whistling foul, which was only inches away from turning into at least a two-bagger, he might knock the next one into the lake. Obviously Arnie was telling Artie to walk him, but he didn't know Artie

Klein. If Arnie had said nothing, which was what he should have done, and let Artie pitch his own game, Artie, who had fifty times the brains Arnie had, would probably have decided to walk Bix on general principles, and also just to be provoking. But who was Arnie, a fourteen-year-old snotnose, to tell Artie how to handle a batter? If I knew Artie, he would surely pitch to Bix now, hoping to strike him out.

Sure enough, he steamed one right across the plate. I don't know where Bix's head was; he just looked at it and blinked. "Strike!" yelled Whitey. "Strrrrike *two!*"

"Nice pitch," Bix said approvingly, as though it were his own team he was praising. I groaned.

He can't do this to me! I moaned inwardly. *Not with those bare feet!* I had a sudden brainstorm. "Hold everything!" I hollered to Artie Klein. "Time out! Time out!"

"What?" everybody yelled at once.

"Time out!" I yelled back, running toward Bix.

"Hey, c'mon!" Arnie said. "What is this? Your guy has two strikes on him; you can't stop the game!"

"Oh, yeah?" I cried angrily. "What did you just do with Artie after strike one?"

I took Bix aside. "What happened to that second pitch?"

"I don't know," Bix said, grinning. "I guess I wasn't thinking. Don't worry, I'll hit the next one. This guy's got nothing, believe me. I'll take him for a home run this time."

"He throws that apple pretty fast," I said doubtfully. "Shouldn't you bunt, maybe? Two and nothing! And I can score on a bunt; I'm very fast on my feet."

"I saw that," Bix said. "No, we'll both come in. What's that about the roof?"

"Oh, God, yes," I said rapidly. "Whatever you do, try not to hit it on that roof back of center. Three-base limit. And this is our only other ball."

Bix looked around. "Right between those buildings, O.K.?" he asked, as though we were discussing where to pitch a tent.

"You think you can hit it that far?" I asked, dumfounded.

"Sure, why not?" Bix said, blinking. "This boy's got nothing on it. Anybody could hit him."

I shook my head, stumped. "All right," I said. "Go ahead. Good luck. Watch out for his floater, though. He's tricky."

Arnie and Limpy were yelling their heads off by this time. "For cryin' out loud!" "Why don't you marry 'm?" "What're you doin', sayin' the Lord's Prayer backwards?" "Hey, Shoeless? How about playin' ball before it gets dark?" The whole team was yelling.

I walked back to third. Two and nothing. Now or never. I knew now that Artie would never in the world walk Bix. He'd put everything he had on this next pitch, and in my opinion, with all due respect to Bix's easy answers, Artie had plenty. Artie just smiled.

"Is it all right to play ball, your lordship?" hollered Arnie in a falsetto voice. How I hated him! How could I ever have been friends with that moron?

"Play ball!" I called back, putting my foot on third and then taking a big lead-off.

Artie took a deep breath. Bix stood at the plate, watching him now, his bare feet squared for the swing. He looked so relaxed I wouldn't have been surprised to see him yawn.

He held his bat a funny way too, resting back on his shoulder, not tense and ready like everybody else, but loose, as if he could just as easily drop it out of his hands, and his feet pretty close together, not tense either, just—standing there. I couldn't say the same for myself. I was ten feet off third, poised like a runner for the 50-yard dash, on my toes, determined to score on this pitch.

Artie wound up and threw right from his socks, and simultaneously I leaped and took off for home. I heard a crack like a whip, but didn't stop to look up. If that ball was fair, it was *gone.* The air was filled with shrieks in all shades and tones of adolescent timbres. I crossed the plate, slamming into Whitey and almost knocking him down, and then looked back. The ball was nowhere in sight, and Bix was trotting negligently around the bases, just rounding toward second in his bare feet. Phil was hugging me and laughing insanely, Charlie Bormann was punching Phil in the back and jumping up and down.

Bix had hit that ball exactly where he had said he would—right between those two buildings. It must have flown all the way into Margate Terrace. I couldn't contain myself. "How about those bare feet now?" I was yelling at Arnie. "How about the shoeless wonder?"

Artie smiled urbanely, and called to Bix, who had just crossed over the plate, "Nice homer, mister." Bix grinned and nodded. He was puffing like a hippopotamus. "Boy, am I out of condition," he panted. "It's a good thing they don't have five bases."

Arnie was almost crying. "Wise guy!" he was shrieking at Artie, who looked at the sky, bored. "Wise guy! Looka this! Four to nothing, no outs! Wise guy!"

Our team had surrounded Bix. "Wow!" "Boy oh boy, some sockaroo!" "You're the bee's knees!" "You're the cat's whiskers!" "Boy! was that the berries?" "Hey, Frenchy, where'd you find this gink?"

I wouldn't have traded places with Benny Leonard.* "C'mon, let's play ball," I said importantly. "Four to nothing, let's go."

Artie Klein took it out on the next three batters; nobody got near the ball except Sonny Farkas, who hit a pop fly right into Arnie's glove, and now it was our turn in the field.

We were all talking at once. "Hey, Shoeless, can you pitch too?" "Yeah, Bix, what about it?" I asked him. As far as I was concerned, his word was law from now on. Some shoeless wonder! I thought of Shoeless Joe Jackson, every Chicago kid's idol before the horrible Black Sox disaster ("Say it ain't so, Joe!" one ten-year-old kid had cried out to him, after the first bribery charges had been published, and all Chicago had echoed the cry). Some shoeless wonder!

"I guess I could pitch," Bix said, flexing his fingers. "Might take me a couple innings to get the kinks out—I don't know."

"I vote for Shoeless," Freddie Aiello said. "If he thinks he can, that's good enough for me."

"Me too," I said. That was putting it mildly. I would have entrusted a World Series to him unhesitatingly. My ears burned and sang with pride, but I would have thought it in poor taste to gloat about my find.

Bix warmed up with a few indifferent pitches to Freddie, tried a fast ball which was very wide, and another that almost struck the plate. He shook his head and stretched his arms. "O.K., I guess," he called to us, "I'll just have to pitch a few. Let's play." And to me he said, "Don't let it bother you if they hit me a few times; I'm just rusty."

"O.K., Bix," I said, and from first base I signaled everyone to be on the alert for flies.

That first inning turned into a nightmare for me. Bix walked the

*World lightweight champion (1917–1925), retired undefeated; unexcelled in technique and ring strategy; famous for K.O.'ing one top contender after another without mussing his elegant pompadour.

first two batters, not intentionally, just throwing wild fast balls. I kept telling myself he had to throw those to warm up his arm. Limpy was up next and hit a long one that could have been a two-bagger but Sonny just managed to get under it. Arnie came up and hit safely, a fast grounder that got past me; the bases were loaded, one out, and naturally Artie Klein is up. *Walk him, walk him,* I prayed, but nothing would have induced me to presume to give Bix advice on the mound, or anywhere else. Bix did walk him, forcing in a run. . . . *One's better than four,* I consoled myself. He pulled himself together then and struck out the next batter, but the next—Beany, a tough little Polish kid—bunted to force in another run, all the men on base ran, and Bix's throw to first was wild, and before the confusion ended the score was 5–4.

"Don't let it bother you," Bix said as we came in to take our next turn at bat. "My arm's O.K. now. I'm going to try to hold 'em down to these five runs, or maybe another one or two at the most. And this guy—what's his name, Artie? He isn't hard to hit. . . . "

"For you, maybe," I said, "but he just about strikes everybody here out every time when he's sharp, and I think he's sharp today."

Bix shook his head. "There's nothing on that fast one of his," he insisted. "You gotta wait for it, don't swing too quick. Take your time and get your bat right under it, you'll knock it right out of the park. Do that a few times, he's bound to get rattled, and what else has he got? A floater? Once he starts that we'll murder him. And these kids aren't going to hit me any more; my arm's feeling O.K. This game'll be over in an hour. . . . It better be," he added, shaking his head. He did look pale and winded.

The others were all gathered around listening to these pearls of wisdom. I could see they were doubtful. Freddie and Phil and I had faith. Bix gave them some more advice on how to hit Artie Klein's supposed killer ball, and then we went to work on him. Neither Bix nor I got up to the plate this trip, but Phil hit a two-bagger and Freddie a home run right behind him, and both of them were glowing when they trotted back in, slapping Bix on the shoulder and exulting. "He's right! Shoeless got Artie's number, all right. Boy! Didja see me connect with that fast ball?"

Bix turned out to be right all around. He walked one more in the fifth, and Artie hit a three-bagger, scoring him, and then scored himself on an error. The score was 8–7, our favor, and that was the last run they got. Bix's pitching improved as he went along. Nobody got anything better than a single off him, and when anyone was on, Bix bore down and invariably struck out the following batters. Artie managed to get only a couple of pop flies, and a beautiful liner which Bix speared without moving more than a step or two off the mound. That one seemed to get Artie so rattled that he lost all his savvy and started swinging furiously at anything he could reach; Bix struck him out three times, and Artie was fit to be tied.

His pitching went to hell too, just as Bix had said it would. He must have thrown his arm out trying to get one past Bix, who homered twice, once with the bases loaded and two out. It was a slaughter. The final score was 17–7. It was the first time I'd ever seen Artie lose that snotty superior smile, like nothing could bother him. This bothered him, all right, but after the game he pulled himself together and came over and congratulated Bix.

"You're quite a fella, Shoeless," he said, shaking hands. "Where'd you learn to play like that?"

"Oh . . . you know, school . . ." Bix said vaguely. Any kind of praise seemed to embarrass him; he always managed a quick exit. Even Arnie came up, chanting, "Shoeless Joe from Kokomo," or something asinine like that. Our team was doing an Indian war dance around Arnie, trying to get his goat, but Arnie tripped a couple of them and they gave up.

I helped Bix collect his discarded bits of clothing and waved everyone off as we started back to the house, I with a superior expression on my face, securely possessive of my champ. *They ought to hear him play cornet,* I said to myself.

Bix Beiderbecke was the greatest living American. What couldn't he do when he chose? I carried his shoes myself. I didn't care now who saw him walking barefoot in his dusty tux with the pants rolled up like a kid going wading and the shirt collar off. The nuttier he looked, the more defiant I felt. *Take a good look,* was my attitude as homeward-bound housewives and respectable Jewish CPAs stared through their glasses from across the street. *You just wish you could do what he can do, you untalented bastards.* I wasn't my papa's and mama's son for nothing. *Gather round, morons, step right up, folks, ten cents a peek, one dime, the tenth part of a dollar. First time you ever saw a man's bare feet? Come on down to the beach and I'll show you ten thousand of 'em.* How

I hated them, the booboisie, as H. L. Mencken, my latest literary god, had christened them. (In January I had proudly become a charter subscriber to his new magazine, *The American Mercury*.) Bix, suddenly very fagged out, just plodded along at my side, the famous bare feet all but invisible for the gray dust that covered them and half his once-black pants legs.

"Jesus, am I out of shape," he said. "I don't know how the hell I finished that game. I couldn't've gone one more inning."

"You were the absolute berries," I said sincerely. Suddenly I looked down at everything we were carrying. "Where's your horn?"

"Oh, shit. I left it on the lot."

It was still up there in the crotch of the tree. Some of the kids were still there, horsing around. They greeted Bix with a mixture of hilarity and respect. "Hey, Shoeless! You comin' out tomorrow?"

"Hey, you live around here? How about givin' us some pointers?"

"If I'm around," Bix said vaguely.

I waved them away. "See you after school tomorrow."

"So long, Frenchy. . . . So long, Shoeless."

Walking back this time, a thought struck Bix. It was bound to come up sooner or later; it always did. "Say, Frenchy, don't you go to school?"

"Huh uh," I said, shaking my head.

He blinked. "How come?"

Where shall I begin, a grownup might have begun. I gave the simplest answer. "The truant officers don't know about me," I said, which was true, but raised more questions than it answered.

For the first time I saw Bix pursue a topic (other than a musical one) with aroused interest. I had evidently touched a nerve.

It was a topic I myself had never really analyzed, though the bare facts were, I knew, sufficiently bizarre. Then and in subsequent conversations, Bix succeeded in eliciting most of them. I think the very first one floored him as much as any: that, in all my thirteen years, perhaps two—scattered among various schools here and in Milwaukee—had been spent in schoolrooms; despite which, I had nevertheless graduated at the age of eleven (W. G. Goudy Elementary, Winthrop Avenue at Foster, Chicago, June, 1922). My diploma was not earned by any burst of academic brilliance. "They were happy to see me go," I said, smirking.

Unlike poor Bix, I had never considered it my place to placate the authorities; I was determined to make them pay dearly for the crime of having imprisoned me, and my teachers bore the brunt of my vengeance. I don't know what they'd done to deserve me, those poor hardworking maiden ladies. I regaled Bix with tales of my exploits, now appalling in retrospect: correcting their English in front of the class *(All right, children—everyone take their seat. Uh, Miss Hattrem, shouldn't it be 'Everyone take* his *seat'?);* asking trick questions on subjects I knew they knew less about than I did *(Miss Pierce, is air a compound or a mixture?),* "innocent" questions on embarrassing subjects—remember this was 1920 *(Miss Clark, what's the difference between an ox and a bull?) (Miss Deely, what's a strumpet?)* ... for good old Shakespeare was a gold mine of painful passages, though I never quite had the nerve to tackle my harried instructresses on *Merry Wives of Windsor,* Act V, Scene 5: *"Send me a cool rut-time, Jove,"* cries Falstaff, *"or who can blame me to piss my tallow?"* Needless to say, I was a hero to my fellow captives, but it may be imagined how glad the authorities were to hand me that precious bit of ribboned paper and say, with Groucho Marx, "Go, and never darken my towels again."

During my growth from five to ten, I had managed to play hooky most of the time, with my family's connivance—notes from my mother, notes from the doctor—until they got more used to my absence than my presence. To my mother, who had only made it to the third grade herself (all she could stand), a hike in the woods outside Cicero was a far more important use of a lovely spring day than "sitting inside" (always spoken with a shudder); as for my papa, who was around until I was seven, Nature was his god, any interference with it the cardinal sin.

How well I succeeded in conveying all this to Bix is questionable. That there could be any way around the long torment of going to school, never in a thousand years could such a thought even arise. What wouldn't Bix have given, as a boy, for such a deliverance?

All of us, in fact, Vic and Gene too, had grown up outside the walls of school and church, had got whatever education we got at home or at work, and by hanging around with complaisant grownups. We were also spared other sacred institutions we saw imposed on all other kids, such as "dressing up" and taking medicine. Even vaccination had been inflicted on us over my parents' strenuous protests, at gunpoint, as it were; for Pa and Ma had a rooted mistrust of that other priesthood too, the one in white, with its pills and its needles. ("Did you ever see a deer take a pill?" Mummy would ask triumphantly, adding the crushing sequel, "Or use a can opener?") "Nature" was *their* religion, meaning lots of raw foods, fresh air, &c. (Papa died at eighty-six of a pneumonia he got swimming through the Lake Michigan ice in January—a good fourteen years short of his expectations; the week before, he'd swum his usual nine miles.)

My nonschooling explained both the woeful holes in my education (if that's the word) and my precocious "vocabulary" (my admirers' favorite word), as well as my remarkable repertory of remembered music, my familiarity with college-level astronomy, chemistry, &c., and my surefooted ability to get around any city by myself after a few days' investigation. No doubt my eidetic memory helped, but it was afforded unusual opportunities for use: the time other kids had to waste in school, learning Palmer Method Penmanship and catalogues of dates & battles that would be gratefully forgotten two days after the "tests" for which they had been memorized, I could spend learning, or doing, exactly what I wanted. If I wanted to read the entire collected *Works of Thomas Hardy* (I did, during one of my childhood illnesses), that was O.K., and if a month later I felt like rereading the whole set (which I also did), I could do that too. I could spend all day and evening listening to *Le Sacre* if I chose, or the latest New Orleans Rhythm Kings record (I did, for three days, when Leon Rappolo, their clarinetist, became my Hero of the Month). Was it surprising that I soon knew them by heart? So would you, if you weren't packed off to school for 30 hours a week. I said as much to Bix, who asked, "What about your pa?"

I was also blessed with a delightful schlemiel of a papa who would rather go exploring with his little boy any day than bother about such trivia as making a living. He took me for star walks until all hours, igniting my infant interest in astronomy (of which, however, he could tell me little); days we often spent poring over maps of whatever town we were in, marking promising-sounding places and then, by God, *going* there (usually on foot), a practice that equipped me with a lifelong love of walking and of finding my way about—all this before I was six. At five I was allowed to travel alone from Milwaukee to Chicago—90 miles—on the North Shore Electric, to visit Cousin Elwood—and no nonsense about pinning notes on my coat—which also involved my taking the then unfamiliar Chicago L out to my aunt's house, and finally walking six blocks there. ("That crazy meshuganah family!" my aunt Annie shrieked when she opened the front door to my ring. "Sends a five-year-old snotnose a hundred miles on a train alone? To get lost? Crazy gypsies! My crazy sister!" All I could think of in reply was "Well, I didn't get lost, did I?" which only threw gasoline on the blaze of her hysterics.) But I had already fallen in love with the L.

When a year later we moved to Chicago, I spent the first few weeks riding around (alone, of course) on the L until I knew it like our kitchen, every station, switch, and curve. (At home, I played "L train" as other kids play cowboy.) And walking strange neighborhoods, black, Italian, Irish, Polish, the Jewish pushcart ghetto of Halstead Street, the neat German neighborhood out west.

All this gave me an unequaled opportunity to show off yet again for Bix. He was the ideal audience for this particular skill of mine; Bix could live in a place ten years and manage to get lost three blocks from home. The area I chose for this display of virtuosity was the South Side.

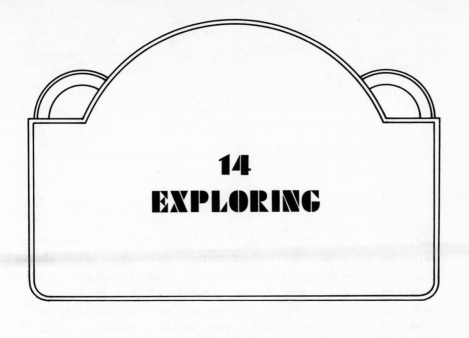

14
EXPLORING

By an inexorable inverse-ratio law of motion of our fucked-up, upsidedown, anticultural culture, in those dawn years of jazz the "worst" places always had the best music. That is to say, you could hear jazz at its feeblest, its most diluted and bleached, at some white middleclass high school prom, aflutter with organdied virgins and summer formals—and at its gutbucket best in some nigger dice joint, tonk, or whorehouse deep in the heart of the black ghetto. "The devil has all the best tunes," as Shaw reminds us somewhere.* In 1924, the very best jazz tunes were to be heard on Chicago's South Side, a community unlike any other in the world.

It was the biggest black city in America—813,000—bigger than the black populations of all the leading Southern U.S. cities put together; nearly a third bigger than Harlem, its nearest rival. But there was much more to it than mere size.

In contrast to the extremely urbanized, hardboiled, sophisticated atmosphere of Harlem, the community that invented the word "hip" (and needed to), Chicago's South Side was more like a giant-size projection of some Southern darktown. Most Harlemites gave one the feeling of being city folks; even if they weren't they soon learned to act like it. But a large fraction of the South Side residents, probably a majority, were openly (and recently) country folks, and had made themselves thoroughly at home, country-style, in Chicago.

There was also the fact that the South Side wasn't entirely a ghetto, if by ghetto we mean a depressed area. There was total

*The Oxford Dictionary of Quotations, 2d ed. (London: Oxford University Press, 1966), p. 248, has "He did not see any reason why the devil should have all the good tunes." —E. W. Broome, Rev. Rowland Hill, vii (1744–1833).

segregation of course—the Black Belt proper was, to the best of my recollection, 100 percent black—but not much of the terrible vertical overcrowding that distinguished the slums of Harlem; there was visible prosperity at the top end of the financial scale, and a considerable middle segment in between, working families who were neither very well nor very badly off, most of them much better than they'd been down South. A principal factor was the relatively large availability of *space* in Chi, a factor that affected every social class; it took me a long time, after we moved to New York, to get used to the cramped quarters of Manhattan.

These black Southern ex-peasants had naturally brought their music north with them, along with their cuisine and their iron wash kettles, making the South Side, for me, easily the most inter-esting part of the world, to which I now became Bix's guide. I was telling him one day about the varieties of native music to be heard there, and he looked so interested that I said on an impulse, "Hey, Bix, how about going out there right now? A day like this, the kids'll be out on the sidewalk jazzin' it up!" He hesitated just a beat —he looked half asleep, as he so often did—but then said, "O.K., kid, lead the way."

I was gratified to discover that Bix, though he'd been living in and around Chicago for several years, knew very little about it except for the Loop cabarets he'd frequented, and a few blocks around the places where he'd hung his hat along with other musicians. When we walked up Argyle Street to catch an L train bound for the South Side, it turned out that he'd been on the L only a few times and knew nothing about getting from one part of town to another on it.

It was the same with the streetcars. The way Bix went somewhere was to give the address to a cab driver. For all he could tell you afterward about how he got there, he might as well have been taken there blindfolded, like the children in certain fairy tales. It was all he could do to remember the address. He was stunned when two different motormen (they were more accessible in those days, a fact of which I'd been taking full advantage for nearly six years) greeted me by name. Showing off as usual, I made a point of telling Bix the name of every stop, in advance, and before the conductor called it out, information Bix must have found less than invaluable. . . . For me, though, once we had got fairly away from my own neighborhood, every name had a mysterious romance:

*Belmont, Wellington, Diversey, Wrightwood, Fullerton, Webster,
Armitage* ... But it was only when we had gone right through and
around the Loop, only when we passed Congress Street and actually set our wheels into the *south* numbers, that my soul expanded:
we gazed out at that wholly different world as our train roared and
clacketed between the rows and rows of backyards with black
children playing among clotheslines and rusting skeletons of
ruined automobiles. . . . Now the L stops were all numbers. Four-
teenth Street—that was the real beginning of the Black Belt—
Eighteenth Street . . . Twenty-second . . .

I pointed out to Bix the most notorious stolen-car fence in America, Warshevsky's, a used-car lot a mile and a half long, with an
estimated two million dollars' worth of secondhand cars bought,
traded, or simply stolen off the streets and out of garages. They
ranged from day-old Cadillacs to battered pieces of junk—for War-
shevky's biggest business was scrap metal, and no car was too far
gone for his roving squads to hype, bring in, and in twenty minutes
render unidentifiable. I got a real yock out of Bix, who had never
heard of Warshevsky's, when I quoted to him the popular Chicago
parody of a current song hit, *I've Got a Song for Sale (That My
Sweetie Turned Down):* "I've got a car for sale—that Warshevsky
turned down."

"We'll get off at Thirty-first Street," I said authoritatively.

We descended the long sweep of iron steps, down into the noise
and bustle of South State Street. We were right in the heart of it.
As always during the daylight hours, there wasn't a white face to
be seen for miles in any direction, except our own—at night it was
a different story. We started walking.

As I had promised Bix, it was like being in the Negro section of
some town like Memphis or Nashville. Block after block of frame
houses, most in need of paint and repairs, barbershops and beauty
parlors with names like Papa Charlie's and Miss Willie Mae's,
crudely handlettered signs, most of them decorated with periods
after each word. . . . We turned down side streets, Twenty-ninth,
Twenty-eighth. Tall black country fellows in "overhalls" lolled on
the curbs or on front-porch steps, or in ancient creaking rocking
chairs on the sidewalk. Women, their heads wrapped in bright-
colored kerchiefs, sat rocking and fanning themselves with pal-
metto leaves. Men whittled as they lazed in the sun chatting with
neighbors. One man lay stretched full length on the sidewalk, fast

asleep, a farm-style straw hat over his eyes; a rangy dog of no particular race slept beside him, on its side, dead to the world, its paws vibrating in a dream of pursuit. Two wrinkled old ladies, their gray-black chins sprouting white stubble, smoked corncob pipes and gossiped on a sagging front porch. "Chaw" tobacco was big with the menfolks; the dozen different brands with their picturesque archaic trademarks in violent primitive colors were in every store window; the sidewalks and gutters glistened with the little metal tabs from the tobacco plugs, and every place of business had its obligatory spittoon. From the open windows of a yellow wooden house, as we strolled by, we could hear a scratchy phonograph record; we both recognized that voice.

"Bessie," said Bix, pausing to listen.

It was Bessie Smith all right, singing *Aggravatin' Papa*—one of the few records she had made that wasn't a blues. I said as much to Bix, who was properly impressed. "You know that record?" he asked.

"Sure," I said promptly. "The other side is *Beale Street Mama*, Columbia A3877. That's Clarence Williams behind her on piano."

"For cryin' out loud," Bix said.

"I ought to know that record," I said. "It's one of the songs I do." I judged it was the right time to startle him with another of my precocious accomplishments, and told him about Jack Goss and the Jazz Juniors. I brought out the name rather haltingly; suddenly it sounded ridiculous to me for some reason. I feared Bix might laugh, at the name, at how we worked, which I detailed. But Bix only looked at me seriously and said, "Hey, that's the nuts. Where'd you say you guys work?"

"All around the North Side," I replied, my hat size increasing several inches. "We picked up thirty dollars one night in just one joint."

"That's the nuts," repeated Bix. "Hey, you ought to sit in with us sometime." (Another inch.)

But I said modestly, "Oh, I'm not that good!"

Bix made a disparaging gesture that seemed to include the whole universe of struggling, suffering, imperfect musicmakers—himself first. "Oh, shit, man, who the hell is?" he said, twisting his little mouth.

Somebody inside the house had put the record on again. We leaned against the picket fence, listening. I had another nugget for

Bix. "That was the first song I did with King Oliver's band," I said, very casual, picking up a stick to fool with.

"King Oliver's band?" said Bix. "When did you sing with King Oliver's band?" His eyes were popping.

"I don't mean I *worked* with them, I mean just sitting in. Vic used to go out to the Lincoln Gardens all the time, when Louie first joined the band. King would always ask Vic to sit in on drums."

"Jesus," said Bix. "Jesus, I'd like to hear Vic play with a band like *that.*"

"Yeh. Then the King would ask *me* to sing a couple—you know, blues and stuff—out on the floor."

"Hah! Wow! Hey!" Bix's eyes were bright as he "saw" the scene. "Hey, that's all right."

A woman came out on the porch and saw us standing there listening to the Bessie Smith. She had just turned the record over; *Beale Street Mama* was coming at us through the window in Bessie's emotional growl; she sounded like King Oliver with a cup mute.

The woman watched us for a minute and smiled back, showing big gold teeth. "Y'all like that music?" she said in a rich, back-o'-town Georgia accent.

"Sure do," I said, laughing. "We're musicians."

"Sho nuff!" said the lady, her eyes widening.

"I've got that record at home," I said. "I've got all her records. I also have the record Lucille Hegamin made of it last year on Cameo."

"Well, Ah *declayah!*" she declared. "Haow come you know all that good nigger music?"

I was in my element now—astonishing people with my arcane knowledge. I laid a few more little items on her for good measure, to an accompaniment of "Ah declayahs," &c.*

"Will you *listen* to this white boy!" she exclaimed at last, hands on hips. "Say now, y'all like to come on in and set a spell?"

Bix looked uncomfortable at this hospitality, but I accepted with alacrity, and we followed her in.

The moment we got into her parlor I realized there'd been some method in her madness. Three lightly clad whores, two of

*From this point on, I will spare the reader any real attempt to render phonetically the diction of this lady and other typical South Side residents.

them young, were sitting around, curled up in big plush chairs and on a big plush couch, digging the records. One was doing her nails. "Sit up and look real pretty for these whitefolks," said our hostess. "Dixie, get these gents a little taste." One of the young whores rose, smiling at me, went to a sideboard, and brought out a bottle and a couple of glasses. "Give all the gals a little taste. This heah's a couple of *musicians.*" The way she said it said a mouthful. The middleaged one was looking me over, and now spoke for the first time.

"How old is you, sonny?"

"Going on fourteen." I hated being asked my age.

"Sho nuff. Why ain't you in school?" she pursued, not unkindly, just sort of motherly and concerned.

"It's a long story," I said.

"I'll bet," said the old whore.

"Cora Louise, why don't you mind your own business?" said our hostess. "These whitefolks knows whether they wants to be in school or out heah on Twenty-ninth Street enjoyin' theyself on a pretty spring day."

"What you got in that bag?" the young one called Dixie asked Bix.

"A horn," said Bix diffidently, and for no reason gave a little short laugh.

"What kind of a horn?" Dixie cried. "Le's see!"

Bix pulled the cornet partway out of the bag.

"You play that horn?"

"Dixie baby, how come you act so dumb?" her mistress chided. "Didn't I just finish tellin' you these boys was musicians?"

"Can he play that horn!" I blurted out. "He's just about the best in the world, that's all!"

Bix flushed scarlet. "For cryin' out loud, Frenchy!"

"Well, he is." I couldn't bear the thought that anyone who dug hot music should not know who and what my hero was. "Ever hear of a band called the Wolverines?" It just came out.

"Child, I got somethin' heah to show y'all." Our hostess went to the table under the phonograph, shuffled through the jacketless stack, and came up with three records, which she laid in my lap. "Now just you read me what it says on that record," she said dramatically.

Three Wolverine records: *Copenhagen, Riverboat Shuffle, Jazz*

Me Blues. I was so excited I jumped up, waving the records about. Dixie was sitting on Bix's lap, saying in a high falsetto voice, "That's *you* playin' all that horn on them records?" The other young one, named Billie, was whispering to me. Somehow Bix prevented the madam from putting his own records on; another blues record was playing, Martha Copeland singing *Daddy, You've Done Put That Thing on Me* (Okeh 8091), and Dixie was pleading with Bix to let her hear him "blow that little old trumpet just one time. . . ." The contents of that bottle must have been pretty potent. My head was spinning. Billie was leaning her almost bare titties all over me and whispering in my ear, my nostrils full of her heavy violet perfume. *"You ever had a real good time with a pretty lady, sonny?"* And the old one, Cora Louise, heaving her bulk up onto her slippered feet with the pink feather pompons, looking offended & righteous, saying, *"My God, girl, ain't you shamed of yourself robbin' the cradle like this?"* and waddling out shaking her bleached & hennaed curls in disgust. Drunk or sober, I was in no danger of yielding to Billie's blandishments—my mother had infected me with a lasting mortal fear of venereal loose women. I saw Bix over in the corner taking his mouthpiece out of his coat pocket and Dixie pouring him another drink. The madam was laughing with those gold teeth and putting the other side on, *Penetrating Blues,* and Bix was playing some real soft fills behind Martha Copeland's voice—*Well, Bix,* I thought, *you said you wanted to get more into those real nigger blues; I guess I brought you to the right spot this time*—and the girls and the madam had become completely still just listening to Bix and staring as if they couldn't believe it, and then tears came to the madam's eyes and she said softly, "My Lord Jesus, will you listen to this white boy play these blues" or something to that effect and Dixie, who was a little drunk, said softly to Bix, who was just sitting there, "Baby, you can park your shoes under this girl's bed anytime," staring at Bix, who chose that moment to open the little leaker valve and shake the accumulated spit out of his horn.

Then the spell was broken as the front doorbell spring tinkled and the madam came back in with a couple of beefylooking men she whispered to me were dicks from the Precinct and for us to come back later & have a real nice time and somehow Bix and I were outside stumbling down the front porch steps in the blinding sun just going down in the west way out over the far end of

Twenty-ninth Street and Bix was carefully fitting his horn into the paper bag and after a while I looked sideways up at Bix and I burst out laughing at how he looked and all Bix said was, *Shit, this is some town*, shaking his head and blinking into the sun.

I stopped and said, "Wait a minute, we're walking the wrong way."

Bix said, "Oh? Where we going? You got some other friends you want to visit?" glancing at me in that sardonic way.

I shook my head and laughed, "No. Let's go down to the corner of Thirty-first and Calumet. There's always something going on around there," and Bix tucked his bag under his arm and said, "Lead on, kid, you're doing all right so far."

We walked up to Thirty-first, a main drag, then east across Prairie Avenue, Indiana Avenue with its shabby secondhand stores and storefront churches right out of some dusty Georgia crossroads village, then one more avenue (Giles?), and now we were approaching the corner of Calumet. That was quite an intersection, a drugstore on one corner and a cigar store on the other with a beautiful lifesize wooden Indian in front of it. (In those days every cigar store had its Indian and every barbershop had a striped red, white, & blue pole twisting eternally in front of it, two native American art forms—God knows we've always had few enough—now vanished with the village smithy.) The cigar store always had a half-dozen stout kitchen chairs ranged along its window on the Thirty-first Street side, Chicago's answer to the French sidewalk café, and the usual half-dozen down-home-looking black men lolling back in them taking in the passing show. But that wasn't all.

Every afternoon a couple of hours after school let out, a bunch of black kids, ranging in age from maybe twelve down to as young as five or six, would gather there from different directions, carrying homemade instruments: two or three kazoos; maybe one would have a water glass to blow it into, and maybe one would have a comb-&-tissue-paper kazoo substitute, also a water glass; a "string bass" consisting of an inverted buttertub with a broomhandle hinged to it, a length of waxed twine stretched taut by the broomhandle, the pitch of the note it gave out when plucked varied by the tension on the broomstick; two or three cigar box "guitars" strung with wire; a straw suitcase serving as a drum, beaten by a pair of whiskbrooms that had lost a lot of their whiskers, plus a whole assortment of other "drums"—pots, pans, wooden crates—and trash can covers for cymbals. Every one of these "spasm bands" had from three to six drummers, not counting a sort of "second line" fringe who stood in a half circle behind the band proper, clapping their hands in perfect time to the music ... and it was this fringe line that was actually the star attraction, as one after another trotted out, front & center, to dance.

These young dancers, who might be fourteen or might be four, were usually clad in nondescript hand-me-downs, barefoot or wearing shoes that were falling apart, tied with string, and several sizes too large. But they danced as if those broken clumsy sabots were the wings on Mercury's ankles. They boogied, they shuffled, they tapped and did buck-&-wings, and their time was perfect, their style serious, casually intense, negligent, and superb. They were the poorest of the poor, thin and ragged, but when they danced, or just retired to the circle of handclappers to keep time for their buddies, they had the style and authority of seasoned professionals. The music that drove their feet, their hips, and swinging, flailing arms, swung too, as effortlessly as they did; those eight or ten urchins with their cigar boxes, buttertub, kazoos and can covers laid down a beat, and a jazz sound, that was as compelling as any I ever heard.

Have I sufficiently conveyed the fact that (after myself, of course) Bix was the world's best audience? He stood with me, as close as he could get to the kids without getting in their way, following with his bulging eyes every step; every nuance of movement and music was reflected on his open-mouthed face; some of the others (all black except us) became as interested in watching Bix as they were in the dancers. After every "number" the oldest kid there, a boy roughly my age, passed an ancient felt hat around and collected whatever coins had been thrown on the pavement in front of them. I put a few coins in; I saw Bix contribute a paper dollar.

The crowd grew until it spilled off the curb into the street, at which point a huge black cop appeared and, after allowing the kids to finish their current selection (watching the performance himself with a tolerant grin), he routinely shooed everyone away. "O.K., folks, show's over ... let's break it up ... show's over." We drifted away with the others. Bix was looking at me with more excitement than I'd often seen him display. "Boy!" he kept saying, "those kids can really go! Boy!"

Once I had him hooked on "my" South Side, Bix went often. With the warm weather came the outdoor stands. Summer came hot and early that year; so did the outdoor street life. All night long, certain stretches along State Street, or perhaps it was Calumet, were garish with stands selling chitterlings, fried chicken and fish, barbecued pork ribs, and watermelon. The watermelon was in ten- and fifteen-pound wedges, sitting on blocks of melting ice, ten cents apiece. They gave it to you on big tin platters, along with a damp towel, and you needed that towel; you had to dive into the melon face first, spitting the seeds back onto the platter or into the gutter, which was black and slippery with them. The stands were lit by gas flares or hurricane lamps hung high and throwing grotesque shadows, each lamp the crematory of ten thousand delicately winged summer bugs. There were trees along the streets then, and bats flitting in and out under corner arc lights. Each stand was a little social center, swarming with folks lounging and strolling at ease, laughing and chattering in rich deep back-country accents, massive mothers holding tiny naked black babies, some of them nursing, quiet and big-eyed among the crowd & clamor; kids chasing in & out among the grownups' legs, pestering them for "a nickel for a ice cream comb." Bix and I were the only white faces to be seen. I'd give something to know what they said about us to each other, what the hell they thought we were doing there, digging the scene and eating ourselves into a coma.

The best thing of all I'd been saving. On a bright Sunday, one of the rare times Bix hadn't had a Saturday night gig and had stayed over, I managed to do something extraordinary—got him up and out in the morning. By quarter after ten we were on the Englewood Express, heading south. "Where the hell are you taking me now?" Bix kept asking, looking depressed, hung over, and only half awake. I had made him as neat as I could, at least his hair was well brushed, but I now noticed how wrinkled his suit was, and that he smelled as usual of alcohol, which worried me more than anything. I knew a drugstore that was open; we'd have to get him something for his breath.

We got off at Thirty-ninth Street and walked over to Wabash. Everybody on the street was all dressed up in black suits and snowy starched collars, families walking together very stately, the women in big highly colored hats—the French word is still best, *endimanchés*. It must have been quite a while since Bix had been in any such scene, but he recognized it immediately. "Jesus Christ, they're all goin' to *church*. What the hell time is it anyway?"

"Going on eleven," I said casually.

"*Eleven?* Eleven in the *morning?*" Bix moaned.

"Let's go in here a minute," I said, pulling him into the drug-store.

"I wonder if he's got any booze," Bix said, looking around. During Prohibition many druggists did.

"Shh!" I hissed sharply. "Why do you think I came in here?"

I got a package of particularly powerful mints, Life Savers flavored with cloves, cut into the roll with my thumbnail and urged one on Bix. "Better have one," I said. "C'mon, we'll be late."

Bix automatically took one and put it in his mouth. "Late for what?" he said. "Where the hell are you taking me?"

We had joined a couple of families converging on the ram-shackle hall at the next corner; the plain white-painted wooden cross on the roof, and plain colored windows, were all that in-dicated it was a church. Some of the people walking recognized me and called out, "Hello, brother!"

"Where are we going?" Bix groaned again. "All these people are going to church!"

"So are we," I said. "Shh!"

Bix stared at me, his jaw dropped, but he kept walking automati-cally. "I didn't know *you* ever went to church," he said sotto voce.

"Wait'll you hear the music," I said.

"Oh, yeah?" He revived a little.

We walked up the three wooden steps with the crowd. Just inside the door stood several elders and deacons or whatever they were, shaking hands. "Good morning, brother! Good morning, sister! Praise the Lord!" They pressed our hands, and Elder McGhee's face lighted up in a big smile. He put his arm around my shoulder and said, "So glad to see you here this morning, brother!" Three or four large ladies all in white satin greeted us inside; one of them ushered us down the center aisle to a place of honor right in front of the pulpit, in the third row of benches— there were no pews, just rough wooden benches painted a dark green. We squeezed past the seated parishioners—more greetings and golden smiles—people pressing our hands as we passed, with loud cheerful "Hello, brother"s and "Mornin', brother"s. Bix looked a little uneasy as we squeezed into our seats, our neighbors making room for us, but I knew he'd get over it once the service started.

It was pretty hot in there already, and the benches weren't even filled yet. The place had originally been some kind of an Elks' or Odd Fellows' Hall, and was as bare as a barn inside, with tarpaper insulation and a big potbelly stove with a rusty black pipe going right up over the middle of the floor and out through the shingle roof. Probably the only thing they'd changed were the windows, which now had colored glass in them; there were big oleo pictures of Jesus in violent colors nailed up between the windows, which were all open now. We could hear the L going by a couple of blocks away, and auto horns and kids yelling.

Up in front of us was a brand-new lectern draped in red satin, with a white satin cross sewn into the middle of it, and half a dozen plain kitchen chairs in a semicircle behind this pulpit, all this on a platform raised about four feet off the floor level. On the back wall behind the pulpit was a giant portrait, in pastel chalks, of the minister, with a hand-lettered legend under it: GOD BLESS OUR BELOVED PASTOR REV. GARVIN DRIGGS JR. and a gilt cross. Over it was another hand-lettered sign: FIRST.CHURCH.OF.BETH-EL.IN.-JESUS.OUR.LORD. Next to the platform was an old upright.

Bix was looking at everything and blinking. He didn't look sleepy any more. "Wow," he whispered to me, "church back home wasn't anything like this." I grinned. A lot of the people coming in were greeting me and waving.

"Glad to see you this mornin', brother, praise the Lord."

"You sure is welcome to see, brother! Praise the Lord!"

"You come here a lot?" Bix whispered.

"I've been here a few times," I said. "Mostly I go to those little churches in stores; there's a lot of 'em on Indiana Avenue."

"Yeah? How'd you happen to do that?"

"Just heard the music and singing, you know, and I was standing out on the sidewalk listening, and one of the women came out after me and said, 'Come on in,' and that was it. They're real friendly."

"Yeah," Bix whispered, "they sure are. Gee, this is really something." He was looking at the piano with professional interest.

The place was really full now. I was starting to sweat, but it wasn't a place where you took off your coat. The babies too were *endimanchés*.

There was a little stir, and everybody turned to look. It was the Reverend Garvin Driggs, Jr., coming down the aisle. Everybody was laughing and greeting him and he was shaking hands as he walked, right and left. He saw me and leaned way over to press my hand. "See you done brought you a friend today, brother," he said in his incredible basso. "Done snatch' a bran' from the burnin'!" and he laughed a deep rich bass laugh, and went on down and mounted the pulpit. He had been followed onto the platform by six elders or deacons including Elder McGhee. Driggs towered over them all like a giant. They draped his black robes over him; the congregation quieted down as he stepped up and gripped the lectern in his powerful long black fingers. He waited until there wasn't a sound to be heard but the traffic outside, and a year-old baby crying.

Suddenly he said in a soft, deep bass tone, "We all come here this mornin' to praise the Lord—ain't that right?"

There was a scattered response from the congregation. "You right!" "That's right!"

"We come here this mornin' to praise the Lord Christ Jesus— ain't that right?"

"Amen!" "Praise the Lord!" "Ain't it so!"

"Because you KNOW"—his voice rose a tone or two—"we all his children. *Ain't that right?*"

"That's right!" "Well, go on!" "Jesus!"

"Because I KNOW . . ." Pause. "I am *HIS CHILD.*" His head drooped suddenly on his chest.

There was murmured assent on all sides. "Well, my God!" "Yes! Yes!"

His magnificent head came up just as suddenly, and he shouted in a voice of thunder, "AM I his child?"

The response was equally thunderous. "Oh, my Lord!" "Oh, Jesus!" "Child of the Lord!"

"AM I his child?"

With every repetition of the question, the volume of response grew and grew until it filled the hall like a solid mass, vibrant and almost tangible.

"Let me hear you say Amen."

"Amen!" "Lord, Amen!"

"Let me hear you say AMEN!"

"Ayyyyyy-men!" "Amen!" "My God, Amen!" Some women were on their feet, waving at the preacher and chortling happily, dancing in place.

"I mean I wants to hear you SAY it!"

The answering shout was like a peal of thunder; the motes dancing in the shafts of sunlight from the open windows, the red and blue and yellow ones in the light from the lifted panes, seemed to leap in unison response.

The great head drooped again, fulfilled. "Well, all RIGHT," the deep basso intoned. "Well, all . . . RIGHT."

Murmured heartfelt grateful sighs of assent. The head jerked up anew.

"Do you feel good this mornin'?"

Response.

"Do you FEEL GOOD this mornin'?"

Tremendous response.

"So glad to be here today!" . . .

For another quarter of an hour Reverend Driggs continued to exult with them in that vein, then he began the sermon proper: "I take as my text this mornin' the words of the prophet Isaiah, the twenty-eighth chapter, the seventh verse and the eighth verse. *'But they also have erred'* "—he glanced at the open Bible on the lectern—" *'have erred through wine, and through strong drink are out of the way . . . they are swallowed up of wine, they are out of the way through strong drink; they err in vision, they stumble in judgement. For all tables are full of vomit and filthiness, so that there is no place clean.'* "

"Oh, my God." "Amen." "Well, go on and git it now."

"I am talkin' to all you people," he began in a low soft voice, "and you know I am talkin' to *you*. You know which of those among you has erred through strong drink. You know which among you has come home this very week drunk as a skunk, upsettin' your wife and your loved ones, who has to pour you into bed and take the clothing offen your body. You know which of you has tooken the rent money which was got in the sweat of your brow and of your wife's takin' in washin' and scrubbin' of the white folks' floors, has tooken that precious money and given it to the speakeasy. *Does you know?*"

Cries of approbation from the women, shouts of acknowledge-
ment from the men.

For the better part of an hour Reverend Driggs developed his
theme, while his congregation shouted and cried back at him;
halfway through it, his voice had gone from speaking to singing,
first a minor third up from the changed keynote and a full octave
drop, up and drop, and the congregation began to chant with him,
in unison or at the interval of a third; then the voices rose and fell
in frank song, a new "hymn" was created before our eyes and ears,
and as his voice fell into the rhythm the handclapping began, folks
were on their feet singing and shouting and clapping; a skinny
young girl, her black face almost invisible under her rose-pink hat,
was at the old upright piano, providing a backdrop of hard open
chords, open triads, sometimes with an added trill in the treble;
the whole hall jumped and trembled in tempo. A little wizened
black man with the gnarled hands of three-quarters of a century's
toil on the land was jigging soberly down the aisle, eyes closed,
hands raised aloft to Jesus; his fellow worshipers guided him till he
reached the little space in front of the platform, where he continued to jig back and forth, now on just one foot, one hand raised
aloft, the other behind his hip; some of the elders who had been
on their feet shouting and singing now joined him in dance. Many
of the congregation were dancing and shouting in place, the
women waving scarves and kerchiefs at the pulpit.

Bix and I were on our feet clapping and stamping with the rest,
and Bix had taken up the ground chant of *O my Lord* in a loud
clear tenor voice I had never heard before, above my hoarse
baritone. The large ladies in white satin with red armbands were
kept busy taking care of women who had fainted and fallen back
in their benches, or of those who had gone into a frenzy, flailing
their limbs about and jumping, in danger of hurting themselves or
others; their fellow parishioners would surround them protec-
tively, holding them gently until the ladies in white could take
care of them. And the piano was going like a triphammer, a live
voice with a life of its own. Bix was watching the four-year-olds
clapping and swinging in perfect rhythm with their mas. . . .

Bix had put five dollars in the collection basket. As we trudged
up the aisle, everyone around us pressing our hands and reaching
out to us—"God bless you, brother," "Thank you, brother, in Jesus'
name," "Bless you, brother"—I felt as usual dizzy and light-

headed. Only when I got out into the open air did I realize I was drenched to the skin with sweat; like everyone else in there, my collar & tie were wet rags. Bix's too. His eyes were vague, and he almost stumbled; the paper bag under his arm was damp, the outline of the horn showed.

We got about a block away; people had stopped waving and smiling; we found ourselves right in front of the L steps.

I had peeled off my coat & tie and opened my soaked collar & shirt halfway down my chest.

"How about that music?" I said triumphantly.

"Yeah," Bix said, shaking his head, still dazed. "They really give out, don't they? Wow." Then he added, "They ought to get that piano tuned."

For some reason, that struck me so funny I had to sit down on the curb, laughing until I almost cried; Bix watched me nonplused. "What the hell is so funny about that?" he asked, while I got my breath back. "The treble was about a halftone lower than the bass. Shit, it was driving me out of my mind."

"I know, I know. You're right. Only . . ." I was off again.

At last I stood up, feeling weak in the knees. "I don't know about you, but I'm starving. Let's go find us some ribs or something." I started walking toward Thirty-fifth.

"Christ I need a drink," said Bix, "after that sermon. You know any place around here?"

I thought a minute. "There's a place Vic always goes, on Thirty-fourth Street—I think it's between Calumet and South Park. A little hole in the wall, in a basement. Only I don't know if he's there on Sundays. We could try, I guess."

"Yeah, let's try," said Bix.

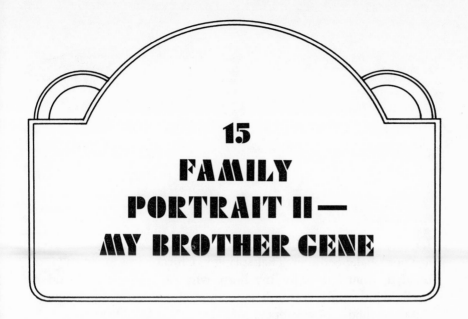

15
FAMILY PORTRAIT II — MY BROTHER GENE

Born for success he seemed,
With grace to win, with heart to hold,
With shining gifts that took all eyes.

Ralph Waldo Emerson, *In Memoriam E.B.E.*

Every idyll is by nature a temporary state of affairs; lotus leaves are not a balanced diet. That spring in Chicago was for me a kind of idyll; what it was for my hero, who can say? An interlude? perhaps intriguing, certainly enlightening, a glimpse of previously untasted modes of existence.

Examining those scenes today, I must be on my guard not to attribute to myself awarenesses I probably didn't have—such as that the idyll couldn't last. At thirteen, the day after tomorrow hardly exists, next week is hardly imaginable. But mightn't there have been, carefully tucked out of sight toward the back of my mind, a small worm or two of knowledge, eating into my brief desperate happiness—such as the knowledge that between Bix and me were seven years (i.e., more than half my lifetime), at an age when seven years represent the impassable gulf between boy and man? And another, sharper than the serpent's tooth, the knowledge that in some very short time my brother Gene would be returning from Europe? and there would be an end of my little brief authority in matters of classical music. I knew already that Bix was curious and impatient to meet him; and between Bix and Gene were hardly seven months.

One morning the fatal cable arrived:

SAILING TODAY SATURDAY NOON CHERBOURG SS MAURETANIA WILL WIRE FROM NY LOVE JEAN

"I see he must have telephoned that cable," I said. "Look how they spelled his name." But my heart sank. *Here we go,* I said to myself.

Naturally he arrived in Chicago dead broke; if we hadn't met him at the depot he wouldn't have had enough American money on him for a taxi home.

Once more our lives were turned upside down for a few days. *Gene was home,* with the usual trunkful of goodies for everyone, from London, from Paris, from Berlin, from Budapest, from Brussels—a gorgeous Spanish shawl for Mummy, given Gene by an amorous torero from Granada whom he met in a Marseilles saloon (Gene often liked rough trade*), a handcarved chess set for me, a set of pornographic photos for Vic—and about fifty pounds of new musical scores and libretti from a dozen Continental opera houses.

Once more the friends dropping in at all hours, hearing *Gene was home.* Our kitchen and livingroom looked like an anteroom of the Dill Pickle Club. Carlton Goodrich, "Queen of the Decorators," showed up with a bevy of aides from the Chicago Opera's corps de ballet, slim fellows with sinews of steel and pendulous wrists, who proceeded to redo the livingroom in batik drapes and the ceiling in midnight blue and silver stars; they even involved Bix in the project. Forgetting for the moment that Dick Voynow was obviously "that way," I'd been biting my nails about how Bix might react to Gene's being homosexual—but when Bix walked in on the batik scene, Carlton took command as always: "And WHO, may I ask, is THIS famous beauty? What's your name, young man, and what's your excuse?"

Bix just blinked at Carlton; I answered for him: "His name's Bix Beiderbecke, and he's a musician."

"Good God, what a name!—Very well, he'll do.—Here, gorgeous, take off that RIDICULOUS coat and grab a brush, there's an angel—join the mob. Mob, meet Bix Spiderback; Bix, mob." And within two minutes Bix, unobtrusive as ever, had been as fully integrated into the scene as if he'd known this crew all his life.

At the dinner table all attention centered on what Gene, shushing everyone, announced as "the latest dirt from the *cultural* capitals of the Old World." I wondered what went through the mind of my hero from Davenport, Iowa, as he listened, round-eyed, to my other hero (from the Cultural Capitals, etc.) toss the names and the glamour around. *("You'll never BELIEVE what*

*Working-class (& preferably muscular) males who, though intermittently homosexual, are not effeminate; sailors and truck drivers have always been traditional prey.

*Jean Cocteau was wearing. I met him at the home of the Comtesse
de Noailles—THE music patron of Paris these days—she now gives
ether-&-cocaine parties, help yourself, my dear, with a BOWL of
pills on the library table. . . .Berlin is ALIVE with White Russian
princes and dukes this season. One of them took over an entire
FLOOR at the Adlon to give this INSANE party—naked gypsies,
and a fountain flowing with champagne, all the time weeping
about how rich he USED to be, in Russia. . . . I met Max Pallenberg
there. He INSTANTLY offered me a comic bit in his new musical
at the Kaiser Wilhelm Theater, Orpheus in der Unterwelt—it's the
biggest hit in Europe. For three weeks I did this number every
night, and he never knew I was an American. My salary
was 100,000 marks a week, which is about $12 in American
money. . . .")*

"Gene Berton," said Carlton with decision, "I am aware that it
is two in the morning, and that these dear boys have ballet class
at ten, but wild *STALLIONS* will not drag me from this house until
you have favored us with a few *TINY* songs." He began dragging
Gene to the piano, amid a babble of agreement.

"Oh Christ!" Gene protested. "I haven't vocalized for a *WEEK!*
Nothing will come out of my larynx but a croak!"

"Splendid," said Carlton. "Roy here will dance the Frog Prince.
Gene—two songs! I promised! How do you imagine I persuaded
these poor lambs to come here and hang your *FEARFUL* batiks,
working for *HOURS* like Egyptian slaves?"

"Yes, yes, *ja, oui*, Gene, *Sie müssen!*" chorused the chorus.

Gene sat at the piano, and Bix listened openmouthed as he ran
through half a dozen of the latest song hits from the Berlin operet-
tas—Lehár, Kalman, Leo Fall. I was watching Bix—it was apparent that he was getting the message; his eyes shone in the lamp-
light; that unique organ of musical appreciation, Bix's face, pulsed
and rippled with every musical zephyr. Gene was no swinger, as
we know, but I never in all my life heard any pianist whose touch
for *this* kind of music equaled his. I don't know where it came
from, what to ascribe it to. Certainly not to technical polish; as
with most self-taught pianists, his fingering left a lot to be desired,
and like Bix he sometimes blurred a few notes in tricky passages;
but, mistakes and all, there was a lilt to his playing of operetta
music, a *lift* you could feel in your chest, that made the air you

inhaled taste of wine and glamour, of the gold-&-velvet of European music halls, the beer gardens of *alt Wien,* the perfume of Parisian courtesans—irresistible, even to an ear less sensitive than Bix's.

The two European boys couldn't get over it. *"Incroyable!" "Unmöglich!"* They begged for more, but Carlton raised his hand.

"You haven't heard him sing Debussy," he said, and now there was no faggot banter in his deep basso voice, only a kind of subdued reverence. "Gene—one song. From the *Chansons de Bilitis. You* know—*my* song."

"I know where they are," I volunteered, springing to the music chest.

There was a premonitory hush, a complete change of mood you could feel in the room like what happens onstage with certain light cues (all other lights dimmed out except a faint blue from the overhead pipe), as Gene silently turned over the precious pages. He cleared his throat, struck a chord and experimentally sang his top A flat—a rich, veiled tone that always sent a shiver through my bones. "Mm," he murmured, rather pleased. "All right. I'm glad Lehmann can't hear what I'm doing tonight—she'd excommunicate me." No one smiled; we just waited. I was conscious of Mummy and Bix at opposite ends of the couch, watching, mutely, two characters in an eighteenth-century allegory, Pride & Curiosity.

Gene touched softly the opening chords of *La Chevelure.* The room, the time, the world and century we inhabited melted away in a magic mist. I shut my eyes, lost instantly among the pan pipes and sensual flowerclad maidens of a Grecian urn, drunk with wine and love. The pain in one's heart was beyond bearing. Such thoughts, such thoughts—a thousand years removed from words or visions. Nowhere is the ineffable sorcery that is music's unique gift more intensely present than in these brief songs, whose strange, shifting, inevitable harmonies are the very core of the mystery. *What do they "say"? What is in the eyes of this "beautiful mute"?* And Gene's voice was like an element of those chords; something in its soft, strong, yet deeply reticent timbre seemed to merge with the very sound of the piano strings, then detach itself from them to breathe, on almost a speaking tone, the words as they fell in long cadences from his lips:

Il m'a dit
"Cette nuit, j'ai rêvé.
J'avais ta chevelure autour de mon cou;
J'avais tes cheveux, comme un collier noir
Autour de ma nuque et sur ma poitrine.
J'ai les caressais, et c'étaient les miens.
Et nous étions liés pour toujours ainsi,
Par la même chevelure, la bouche sur la bouche,
Ainsi que deux lauriers n'ont souvent qu'une racine.
Et, peu à peu, il m'a semblé que nos membres étaient confondues,
Que je devenais toi-même,
Ou que tu entrais en moi, comme mon songe."

Quand il eût achevé,
Il mit doucement ses mains sur mes épaules;
Et il me regarda, d'un regard si tendre
*Que je baissais les yeux avec un frisson.**

Once more a futile effort, with due apologies, to translate the untranslatable—French poetry; the virtues and vices of this rendering are my own:

He told me,
"Last night I dreamed.
I had your hair about my neck;
I had your tresses like a black collar
About my neck and upon my breast.
I caressed them, and they were my own.
And we lay bound thus forever, by the same tresses,
Mouth upon mouth, as two laurels often have but one root.
And, little by little, it seemed to me that our limbs mingled,
That I became yourself,
Or that you were entering into me, like my dream."

When he had done,
He gently laid his hands upon my shoulders;
And he gazed at me, with a gaze so tender
That I lowered my eyes, trembling.

When the song ended—but that song, like so many of Debussy's, doesn't really end; rather it pauses, and fades. . . .

All of us sat still, a stillness appropriate to the moment—except Bix, who jumped up and ran to the piano.

*Trois chansons de Bilitis, prose poems by Pierre Louÿs, music by Claude Debussy (Paris: Durand et Fils, 1907).

"Hey, those last three chords . . . Wow! What was that?" he exclaimed like a kid at a ball game. Gene looked up, amazed; everyone else stared incredulously. Bix all but pushed Gene aside, fumbling for the notes. And found them. "Yah . . . yah!" he exclaimed to himself, muttering. "Yah. Wow. Shit, that's some change there." He played them over again, softly, *con espressione;* nodded vigorously, straightened up, sighing. "Huh!" he said, to Gene's raised eyebrows. "That guy, Debyoossey, he really knew where he was going!"

Gene began to laugh; amiable laughter went round the room. Gene nodded in amused resignation. "That's one way of putting it!" . . .

Bix came even more often now. Gene, rehearsing for his coming recital, vocalized daily, steeping himself in his repertory—Debussy, Ravel, Poulenc, Satie, Fauré, and the Russians. He set great store by my criticism, and minutely trimmed and polished his interpretations by its light. "My best audience!" he said to Bix, who would sit watching, gazing eagerly from one of us to the other like an intelligent spaniel, his transparent face registering every nuance of Gene's performance and my commentary.

"Too slow!" I would cry, as Gene set to work on Erik Satie's *La Grenouille.* "Too heavy! That little *oom-pah* bounce in the accompaniment—it's satirizing a folk dance—" I broke off, singing the notes: *Bmp-ah mm-pah buddle-uddle-bah.* . . .

Gene did see. Mouth pursed in concentration, he did it over. "Good!" he exclaimed. "Ah! Yes! Oooh, that's better!" And started again.

"I don't like all that 'expression,' " I said. "Save that for the very end—

> *Et la nuit*
> *Les insectes*
> *Couche*
> *Dans sa bouche—*

I intoned in my hoarse accents. "Start out very 'flat,' like kids singing in a classroom—tongue-in-cheek of course . . ."

"Yes! Yes! Good!"

When he finished, I said, "Gene, remember what Satie said that day at the concert? 'My music never *says* what it is thinking—it sits, it leans back, ironically watching!' "

Gene nodded. He sang it all the way through this time, a finished, polished performance of such subtlety that the hair stood up along my arms. "Oh Christ, that's good. Do it that way, just that way!"

"Amazing what you can find in one 'little' song, eh?" he ruminated, turning to Bix, who hadn't opened his mouth once during our half hour's laborious polishing.

"That's some little song," Bix said. It was his strongest adjectival expression.

He would sit all afternoon taking in these sessions. He rarely spoke, except for his familiar exclamations of delight and astonishment. When Gene paused, he would go automatically to the piano himself, picking out what he had just heard. Sometimes he'd take out his horn and run over & over a figure, almost always part of something just played, a jazz development of it, which he'd play softly, over & over, smoothing it out, adding the indefinable lift that made it suddenly *swing,* in that unique tone that was my delight and despair.

Gene paid only the barest polite attention to these moments of Bix's. He too had been astonished by the swiftness and accuracy of Bix's ear, but I knew what he was thinking: What a pity he doesn't *do something* with all that marvelous musical gift! In Gene's eyes, jazz didn't amount to "doing anything" with it; and how far could anyone go, however intelligent, without *reading?* Actually he always felt "kind of sorry" for Bix, fumbling at the keyboard, a bit of Ravel here, a snatch of Debussy there, then (ugh!) *jazz.* . . . He didn't feel *he* could do anything about it—after all, jazz musicians were a different breed. He saw Bix as lost, groping—he didn't ever quite understand for *what.* Gene in short was as baffled, when he bothered to think about it at all, at Bix's commitment to jazz ("with all that *talent!*") as I was at Gene's total deafness to it, something the most continuous exposure never did anything to cure. A matter, obviously, of temperament, like my lifelong antipathy to Wagner.

I don't think Gene ever once took the trouble to go anywhere Bix was playing, to hear for himself what all the furor was about. He liked him well enough, but his professional side was without meaning for him.

Why *didn't* Bix do that simple thing, *really* learn to sightread, *really* develop his pianoplaying? I never once asked. Gene did, once—in a way. He was at first too tactful to come right out with such a fundamental question—like saying to a man who's been making his living as an artist, "Don't you think you should learn to draw?" All he said was "You don't read music at all, do you?" and his tone wasn't complimentary. Bix only gave a rueful laugh and shook his head. I felt defensive about it at the time—in those days there was a strong feeling among *white* jazzmen especially that there was something effete, sissified, about knowing how to read, something rough & ready and down to earth about not knowing; a rationalization that doubtless played its part in our kidding ourselves about Bix's musical illiteracy.

But that was only superficial maneuvering. There must have been, unsuspected by all of us, especially Bix himself, some deep-set block against his taking the comparatively small bit of time and trouble it would have cost him to become a reader, for, as was obvious from the first, Bix was no "mere" jazzman, was deeply affected by classical music, and only too evidently suffered from a sense of frustration over his ignorance of it, his never making it truly his own. All of us, each for his own reasons—tact, indifference, defensiveness, preoccupation—simply failed to face the fact, root out the trouble and cure it. I feel in my heart, today, that the chance was there, for anyone who would have had the wit and understanding to seize it, to help Bix get over that boulder in his path—and we all missed it, we all failed him as he failed himself, to the lasting remorse of his legion of mourners.

Meanwhile, what had become of my several apprehensions about Gene? I had dreaded Bix's scorn for Gene's tin ear for jazz; then, discovering his passion for the kind of classical music that was Gene's specialty, I had dreaded his alienation from me by Gene's superior authority and fascination; in both instances I had singularly misjudged reality. Bix seemed scarcely to notice Gene's indifference to jazz; I had reckoned without Bix's lack of ego, of pride in it, and in his own playing—he was far too interested in Gene's musicmaking to feel any injury at Gene's lack of interest in his.

As for my jealous fears, I had forgotten my own deep involvement with Gene's genius; I could hardly feel jealous of what was so much a part of myself.

Finally, there had been my uneasiness about Gene's sexuality, what Bix "would think." Ordinarily my attitude was that anyone who didn't like it could lump it (I was ever ready & bristling with all the familiar names of famous homosexuals—Oscar Wilde, Leonardo da Vinci, Michelangelo, Tchaikovsky . . .); now, inconsistently, I quailed before the supposed scandalization of this hero of mine from the wilds of Iowa. That anxiety too proved groundless. Whether Bix failed to notice, or didn't give a damn (he was the epitome of live & let live), I never knew, but if he had any negative feelings about it they were undetectable.

In any case Gene made no bones about inviting us both, one rainy evening, to tag along to a drag* some boyfriend of Ralph Shackley's was throwing, at his apartment out near the University. There was a regular colony out there, way out south, around Sixtieth Street, in the Jackson Park area.

It was quite a scene. Ralph himself had helped decorate it—all low dim lamps, candles in bottles heavily fraught with dripped wax like stalagmites on the floor of a cave, Turkish screens and hanging lamps, the air warm and close with perfumes and incense, a huge low studio couch taking up half the livingroom, covered with tie-dyed monk's cloth and varicolored cushions, the floor also strewn with large Oriental-looking cushions and low hassocks, and all quite dark—it took some time to adjust your eyes before you could see anything. Lying around on cushions were a dozen or so people of various sexes, mostly boyish girls and girlish boys, smoking, sipping wine, wooing, necking, or just chatting. Most of them were of the younger Chicago intellectual crowd that haunted the Dill Pickle Club, the Art Institute and Art Museum, the Chicago Opera, Orchestra Hall, and taught at or attended various art, music, and dance studios around the Loop and the Near North Side ("Chicago's Greenwich Village"), but there seemed to be a sprinkling too of what Ralph called Plain Janes—boys who might be stockroom help or shipping clerks at Marshall Field's, and whose only common bond with the other guests was their homosexuality —a rather firm bond, in those illiberal days—compelled by the square world they inhabited by day to play the role of "closet queens," able to breathe freely only in this night world.

A phonograph was playing softly, "sweet" jazz, and some were dancing, boys with boys, girls with girls—though that wasn't obvi-

*Party (or dance) where some or all guests may be "in drag" (in transvestite garb).

ous at first, as perhaps half were in drag—boys stunningly gowned and made up, girls in shortclipped hair and trousers, smoking "tough" at the corner of the mouth.

Carlton was there, and Ralph Shackley, in drag with high-swept hennaed blond hair; the ballet boys who'd done the batiking a few weeks previous; a beefy black diesel dyke* with her wispy blonde femme†—Ralph introduced the black one as a policewoman from Chicago Heights—and an even bulkier dame, very "society," Elsa Maxwell style, long cigarette holder and—yes—lorgnette, with an unexpected basso voice; it was some time before I could decide which sex she belonged to, either biologically or by preference.

Gene was surrounded at once, and one of the ballet boys, the German one, cried, *"Ach!* ve must to make him zing! He zings like an anchel!"* to which Gene smilingly shook his head and said, "Not here, dear." He explained that he never sang in any place where people were smoking. Bix and I escaped to a corner of the couch. Bix was taking it all in. He made only one remark, after fifteen minutes or so. "Shit," he said, "Davenport was never like this"; after that he just watched and drank, while I whispered various explanations and comments on the other guests (Bix hadn't realized at first that some of the girls were boys in drag & vice versa). We were, it turned out, the only heterosexuals there.

After our eyes got adjusted to the dimness and our ears to the babel, we could follow snatches of conversations from various clusters, thick with sibilants and shrieks of laughter.

". . . *SWEARS* on a *TUFT* of bibles she practically caught her in the *ACT* with one who shall be *NAMELESS!"*

". . . Whoops, my dear, *THAT* one!"

". . . some *DIVINELY* endowed creature . . ."

". . . showed up three days late, *MUCH* the worse for wear!"

". . . there she was, my dear, *HEAVILY* veiled!"

". . . Jesus! me beads!"

". . . *DEFINITELY* living in *SIN* . . ."

A smartlooking newcomer, somewhat made up but not in drag, was greeted by Ralph Shackley and immediately fastened on for

*Exaggeratedly "butch" (masculine) female who goes in for tough male garb & behavior.
†Feminine-behaving lesbian partner.

some specific piece of gossip he evidently had fresh off the faggot grapevine.

"Is it true that Harlow James is finally taking the veil?"*

"Utterly true. Some *WAN* little débutante from Oak Park who has *NO* idea of Harlow's *PAST*. But her mother has nearly two million dollars *SALTED* away in *TRUST* for her pet, so Harlow has learned to care."

"Is that 'little débutante' by any chance Tweeny Simmons, from Akron, Ohio?" asked a tall transvestite who had just joined the group.

"Simmons, yes, that's the girl."

"Oh-hohoho!" laughed the newcomer mirthlessly. "Little Tweeny isn't exactly a virgin herself, my dear. Except possibly between the left armpit and the right pinky. Didn't you know she was expelled from every girls' school in the East for teaching her dormitory-mates the forbidden joys? The mother had to virtually *BUY* the Briarcliffe School to hush it up! And they say the mother had *HER* moments, when *SHE* was a girl. Runs in the family."

"Our Harlow a fish queen!† I shall take *SLOW* poison!"

More hoots of laughter. "Poor Harlow! *WAIT* till they open the books on *THAT* one!"

"Don't be ridic," said the tall transvestite. "Harlow knows *ALL* and so does Tweeny. They say he laid her to FILTH‡ when he first heard the news about his *PRIM* little socialite, but dear little Tweeny had the goods on old Harlow too—seems her mama had put private detectives on his trail when they were first engaged, and had *SHELVES* full of details to regale her with."

"Ssssounds like the perfect marriage to me," said a slight, girlish chap who had just come up.

"*MADE* in heaven," said someone else.

The wispy blonde femme had draped herself on the couch next to Bix and tried to start a conversation with him.

"I've never seen you around before," she said, looking him over curiously. "What do you do?"

"I'm a musician," Bix said, and that was all he had a chance to say, because at that moment the black policewoman waddled over, murder in her eye.

*Getting married (heterosexually).
†Somewhat bisexual man who has occasional affairs with women.
‡Accused, upbraided.

"Lay off, Iowa," she said tersely to Bix. "This is *my* frail—go dig up your own," and grabbing her little friend by the wrist, she yanked her off the couch as easily as though she'd been a cushion, and started dancing with her.

"How did she know I was from Ioway?" was all Bix had to say, with such a twang that I went off into a fit of laughter. . . .

In the course of the evening, several people made discreet passes at us, but when it was explained to them that we only liked girls, they smiled and drifted away. "How old are YOU, beautiful?" one lissome hair stylist asked me. Going on fourteen, I told him. "And not been *brought out* yet?" he smirked. Later I heard him boasting about me to somebody else in the kitchen. "She can be had, dearie. Just *LOOK* at those lips!" One flaming drag queen tried to get Bix to dance with him, but Bix shook his head. We were getting restive; it was a relief when Gene came over, yawning, and said, "Ready to go?" Dawn was breaking over the Lake when we got out on the sidewalk.

"Pretty nutty bunch up there," Bix said.

Gene just laughed. "Oh, they're all right," he said. "Here comes our taxi, thank God."

16
VALUES! VALUES!

So they had met, Bix and Gene; a meeting I had feared because I couldn't foresee how it might affect my tenuous hold on Bix. It didn't—except perhaps to attach him more strongly to the Berton household.

Undoubtedly the whole family fascinated him. Like every musician I ever met, he was awed by Vic's fantastic drumming. I suppose he accepted my peculiar assortment of precocities as adding up to "a pretty smart kid," as I once overheard him describe me, and would have found me a more tolerable companion if I'd been better able to conceal my adulation, which always made him uncomfortable; I'm sure he envied us our mama, a combination of quiet stability and mind-boggling "freedom"; but in the end it was Gene who had the greatest impact.

It was Gene who was most thoroughly identified with the world of music Bix seemed most to hunger for, music after Debussy and the Russians, the music we called "modern" in 1924. No doubt the country boy in Bix was intrigued by the glamour of Gene's "career" and connections, his cosmopolitan life and celebrated circle of acquaintance, but that was only frosting; it was the music that got him; that, and certain aspects of Gene's career, which in turn threw a certain light on Bix's—as we shall see.

Gene's character was an intriguing fabric of contradictions. For all his deep and passionate commitment to the arts, he was in certain ways the most unabashed, anxiety-ridden snob I ever knew. Vic's early success as a drummer had brought us into the music business; Gene's career had landed us on the very fringe of what would now be called the Jet Set (Fine Arts Division). If we were still outsiders, financially and otherwise, that was no fault of Gene's; to be part of that world was his second greatest concern

222

in life, only a hair's width below his career itself. The intensity of these twin passions had made Gene the dominant force in our family. Vickie, five years his senior, remained the breadwinner and putative male head of the household, with a good deal of say in it; but it was Gene who decided how and where we would live, speak, dress; our social arbiter, with a pervading sense of what Joneses we were to keep up with.

In general, it was unlike Bix to pry into anyone's personal history; he was of that uninquisitive turn of mind so typical of the nomadic breed—seafaring men, cowboys, hobos. Ask me no questions, Jack, and I'll do the same for you. But he showed an abiding, shameless interest in Gene's "story," and looking back, one sees he had his reasons, more intuitive than conscious.

Wasn't Gene in so many ways what Bix *ought to have been*—the *Wunderkind* who, far from disappointing his early admirers, had gone on to fulfill triumphantly his early promise? Blinded as I was at the time by my admiration for Bix's unique jazz gift, I was worlds away from seeing things in that cold light, consciously anyway, though even I had my glimpses of the truth: that Bix vis-à-vis Gene was, among other things, precisely the prodigy *manqué* gazing with hungry eye and ear at the prodigy *accompli*, or at least well on his way. Though hardly the fellow to think such things out, Bix surely perceived that Gene's story was something that could only have happened in a family like ours, which believed in Talent to the exclusion of all else. "Shy" Bix was as persistent as a child in pursuit of that story; and it was a story Mummy was only too eager to tell.

Mummy had been not quite sixteen when Vic was born, twenty-one when Gene came. Social justice, three-volume novels, lectures and libraries and museums were her passions in life. Her biggest idols were E. V. (for Eugene Victor) Debs, the great Christian Socialist, who ran for President and once drew nearly a million votes; and Victor Hugo and Eugène Sue;* thus were her first two sons named.

At four, Gene could sing all the popular songs of the day *(Come Josephine, in My Flying Machine, If the Man in the Moon Was a Coon, Forty-Five Minutes from Broadway, In My Merry Oldsmobile, The Peek-A-Boo Rag, Meet Me in St. Louis, Louis)*, and—like

---

*Author of *The Wandering Jew* (1845) and other romantic classics, somewhat in the style of Dumas *père*.

Bix—pick them out by ear on the piano. He had a few lessons with his Aunt Sarah, a concert pianist, but was otherwise self-taught. At five he won an Amateur Night contest at a local variety house with his "impressions" of Lillian Russell, Anna Held, and Eva Tanguay, "The *I Don't Care* Girl."

In 1909 or thereabouts, when Gene was six (this was a year before I was born), our papa acquired a nickelodeon, as movie theaters were then called (admission five cents), in Logansport, a tough Indiana mining town full of fighting, shooting drunks (I have no idea what my family were doing in Logansport; probably got stranded there somehow). Little Gene provided between-films entertainment, billed as "The Boy with the Double Voice," singing ballads and ragtime ditties in two-part harmony—the second part contributed by cousin Lilly, aged eleven, secreted behind the movie screen—until one night the screen fell down, exposing the fraud, and the two baby tricksters, to a hail of fruit, caps, and profane abuse that ended the engagement—for the moment. Two nights later, having been hilariously forgiven, little Gene was back in the pit playing piano for the movie and singing between reels and whenever the film broke; every theater had a much-used slide that read JUST A MINUTE PLEASE!—PROJECTIONIST SPLICING FILM!

In those days of nitrate-based film and arc-lamp projectors, a nickelodeon's life expectancy was negligible. Papa's duly burned to the ground after a few months' service; needless to say, he'd never heard tell of such things as insurance, and we, or rather they (I hadn't been born yet), left town in a hurry—something Mama said happened frequently in my family's early years.

Vic and Gene then put together a slapstick comedy act—songs, dances, & snappy patter—touring the "Kerosene Circuit" (many tank-town vaude houses still had oil-burning footlights). I remember a fading sepia "professional" photograph, now lost, of eleven-year-old Vickie as straight man, in the obligatory straw hat & bamboo cane, swatting six-year-old Gene, in clown getup, over the head with a newspaper.* ("Christ! What a headache I had every night from that Goddamned newspaper!" Gene exclaimed when he saw it.) Behind them was the usual "street drop," a painted

*Sample joke: "You take sugar in your tea?" "Yes, I do." "You take sugar in your coffee?" "Yes, I do." "Here's a lump for your cocoa!" (Wham over the head with newspaper.)

curtain representing the main drag of some forgotten whistle-stop town (Doyle's Hardware, Schultz's Bakery, Archer's Drugstore), the rude early prototype of our TV commercials.

Mama had to travel with the act to look after them and wash and iron the required eight silk shirts a day (they were on the "grind," or four-a-day, time); and so I was born "on the road," raised backstage, sleeping in prop rooms and bass fiddle cases, and in due course (at about age three) joined the act.

How we fared, and for how long, are things now lost in the mists of time; the happy ending came when one of Gus Edwards's scouts caught us one rainy night in Cairo, Illinois. Edwards had a famous kid revue, a hardy perennial that played the "big time"* for thirty years; Groucho Marx, Ray Bolger, Georgie Price, Georgie Jessel, Eddie Cantor, and fifty others first tasted grease paint as Gus Edwards kids. The scout reported he'd seen a three-brother act that was nothing to scream about, but "one of the kids, the middle one, is unbelievable"; the next night Edwards caught the act himself, and, I presume, made Mummy an offer she didn't refuse. Vic went back to his real bag, the drums, and the rest of us entrained for New York.

Gene was teamed with six-year-old Lila Lee (she grew up to be a silent-film star) as "Baby Gene & Cuddles," and they were a sensation; Edwards also gave him several solo turns (his "impressions"). I don't know how long Gene toured with Edwards (he must have been with him during the Reisenweber's engagement in 1917, the night the Original Dixieland Jass Band opened in New York), but eventually Gene went out for himself on the big time as a single, with Edwards's blessing and active aid, including his own top material writers to help Gene put the act together. Don't let anyone tell you big-time show people are all shit-heels, upstaging each other and hogging the bows; there are also the Gus

*The Keith-Orpheum Circuit, operated by B. F. Keith, later by Keith & Albee, comprising the firstclass theaters in all major U.S. cities, with headquarters in New York's Palace Theater, the vaudevillian's Valhalla. Jokes of the period reflect its status during vaudeville's heyday, e.g.:

"Mr. Keith, I know you never liked my act, but this time you can't turn me down. I've written in a new sketch, in which I shoot myself at the end. Give me a week at the Palace, and you can advertise that for the last show I'll use a real bullet."

"Joe, you're willing to commit suicide to play the Palace? No dice, I can't let you do it."

"But, Mr. Keith, I want to—I'll die happy."

"Sure, Joe, but what would you do for an encore?"

Edwardses, who love talent and will do literally anything to give
it a break; not for nothing was he called "The Star-Maker." With
his help, Gene as a single was soon making $3,000 a week instead
of the $300 he made with Edwards, and played the Palace three
times his first year, playing piano, singing, and doing his female
impersonation bits and comedy monologues, later adding a light-
ning-cartoon routine and winding up with the final aria from *I
Pagliacci*, for what *Variety* calls a beg-off finish, with ten curtain
calls.

The reviewers ran out of adjectives; every notice was a rave;
Gene was nearing headliner* status and traveling with his own
blue velvet drop—the ultimate prestige symbol—in his meteoric
rush toward stardom. It would have been the classic tale of talent
triumphant, a perfumed ointment without a fly, except for the
central character. The sad fact was that Gene had discovered that
he hated vaudeville.

In the beginning it had been all play. All children not crippled
by shyness are born show-offs ("Daddy, Daddy, look what I can
do!"), and little Gene had rather more to show off than most. His
first professional efforts—the word is misleading, for he played,
sang, acted, mimicked, and cartooned as effortlessly as the average
child wets his pants—had been a lark. Clowning on the stages of
one-horse towns and hearing the yokels laugh had been a heady
wine. Even the Gus Edwards tour had had its thrills, the novelty
and glamour of the big time, and six-year-old Cuddles, with whom
he had fallen in violent love (as who didn't?) on sight. Above all,
show business had rescued him from those twin worms in the
apple of childhood, going to school and going to bed—no small
matter.

But going out as a single, facing that audience day after day,
night after night, an audience that had paid hard money to be
astonished, was another pair of shoes. For the first time Baby Gene
learned the meaning of the performer's cruelest nightmare—
stage fright, the icy grip of paralysis, like a stroke; he began to have
insomnia, and nightmares, the familiar terrors of the trade: face-
less audiences sitting on their hands, traveler curtains that
wouldn't close, mistimed laughs, "going up" in his lines, his mind
a blank.

*Billing was nearly as crucial a status symbol as salary. Those placed next to closing,
or near it, were also given top billing in announcements, hence *headliners*.

Mainly he objected to the "garbage" he had to sing. He fought to include a Mozart aria in his act, his agent telling him he was "out of his mind," which in a sense he was. The day came when he refused to go on, with Mummy standing in the wings next to me crying, the orchestra "vamping till ready" Gene's theme (the Gus Edwards song hit *Dimples),* and Gene raging, "Yechhh! I'll vomit if I hear that Goddamned song once more!"

Another crisis I remember became a family legend—Gene, made up and ready, standing in the wings refusing to go on until Mummy agreed in writing to buy him a Meccano set he'd seen in the railway depot. The house manager had to go out onstage and stall the audience while paper & ink were brought and the Meccano Treaty indited and signed—I was the witness. Only then did Gene go on (and killed them as usual).

Plainly this couldn't continue. Mummy held that no child should be made miserable, even by his own talent—and Gene's life took a new turn. He gave up vaudeville, retiring, so to speak, undefeated.

None of us could have seen it clearly then, but Gene was suffering from spiritual anoxia—in plain English, suffocation. Artistically he had outgrown his origins. What he needed now was a richer soil to take root in. He found it.

I don't know how or where Gene first met Marie and Esther Blanke, two spinster sisters who taught music and German at Lewis Institute, a Chicago day college that no longer exists: both of them monuments to culture, walking, breathing libraries of the arts.

I have no idea how old they were; age & sex weren't matters you associated with the Blanke sisters. To say they were plain hardly scratches the surface. Their plainness went much deeper than the mere absence of good looks; it was a thing sublime and monolithic, as imposing in its own right as any mere beauty. In their presence all thought of the personal, the sensual, simply evaporated like mist from a mirror. Jenghiz Khan's Huns, coming upon the Blanke sisters during a rape-&-pillage foray, would have respectfully dismounted, sat down, and taken a piano lesson.

They both played—the piano, the flute, the harp, and I don't know what all—with a passion, a penetration, that reached into the composer's soul and found there all that was noble in Man. Though they didn't personally dabble in the other arts, they revered them, and knew them, I think, as thoroughly as anyone could in only one lifetime. To see Marie's gentle amplitude seated at the piano, sister Essie's equally majestic bulk at the harp, you would never guess, in the moment before they touched the strings, what delicate poetry those sturdy German fingers could evoke, just as you weren't likely to think of them as female, except in the sense that the Statue of Liberty is female.

Their house, somewhere on Chicago's Near North Side, was exactly like them: large, clean, quiet, and artistic. Every room had its quiet treasures, yet it was at the same time as homey and cheerful as a peasant kitchen in a fairy tale. Their summers were spent, religiously, in Europe; always they brought some small tasteful treasures home for deserving friends; for if art was their religion, kindness was their mission. To do good, to someone, every day, was as necessary to them as eating, and they ate well.

The people one met at the Blankes'! The artiest faggots, the grimmest dykes, the dirtiest poets, shabbiest painters, shyest stammering composers, drunkenest actors, and most skeletal dancers, all found a welcome, a drink, a wholesome sandwich, a homemade cookie, in that Teutonically spotless salon. Their piano—"my first Bechstein," as Gene called it—was tuned twice a month, rain or shine. Paderewski had played on that piano, and de Pachmann; do not think they gave houseroom only to the struggling; even celebrities were welcome if they were true artists. Conversation at the Blankes' Sunday afternoons must have rivaled the famous "evenings" of Madame de Staël. Painters argued with composers the most recent and revolutionary ideas of the West; composers tried out their musical notions on the critical ear of the assembly; writers like Dreiser and Sherwood Anderson read new manuscripts aloud, and got candid opinion from their listeners.

Gene had always sensed that such a world existed. Now he knew; and the impact was devastating.

Marie Blanke must have felt some hidden force in this eleven-year-old variety artist with the apple cheeks and arrogant, oddly magnetic graygreen eyes. She made him come to her alone; sat down at the beautiful Bechstein, opened a volume of Schumann lieder, made Gene sit beside her, and said in her precise way, adjusting rimless pince-nez on her snub nose, "Eugene, I want you to sing something for me."

The song was *Mondnacht*.

It has no preamble or proper "introduction," but begins in the very middle of a thought; a thought so deep, so serene, so resigned to the beauty and heartbreak that is life, that to hear those first sixteen tones of Schumann's melody for the first time, and understand what they import, is to reconcile yourself in advance, as it were, to all the sadness that may be visited upon the unarmed heart, upon whatever part of us may be called "romantic." It is something you had always known—but Schumann has gently laid hold of it, brought it up into the daylight like a pearl diver, and set it there for us to hear, in the key of E natural.

Sixteen notes, comprising the "first subject" as the analysts would say. If you have never heard them you are to be envied; you have an experience in store.

Gene heard them, and caught his breath. Did he sense in this moment a turning point for him, of transition from what he had been and known, into a whole new world? He shut his eyes, listening, rapt, as the rest of the song unfolded.

Miss Marie had thought to teach it to the boy in the usual way —to see what this little creature from the strange world of show biz might make of it. He surprised her by saying he wasn't used to being accompanied this way (except by a pit orchestra), and preferred to play it himself. Somewhat taken aback, she made room for him on the bench. She didn't know that Gene, with his queer assortment of gifts and ignorances, could read at sight any normal piece of music as though it were a page of English. He did, intent, humming the vocal line to himself, and amazed Miss Marie by suddenly sobbing aloud; then said he would "really" sing it.

She was caught completely off balance by the depth and maturity of his reading of the song, his command of voice, his "presence."

"How old are you, Eugene?" she asked.

"Twelve in October," he answered, a little defiantly.

Miss Marie gazed at him a moment in silence, collecting her thoughts. Then she said quietly something like, "My dear boy, I don't know whether I have the right to say this to you, but—you are very young, and—well! I must say it. You are wasting your life. You are a great, great, great artist. It is a . . . a responsibility. And you are . . . wasting your life." She rose, rather red-eyed, and, blowing her nose quietly, left the room.

The Blanke sisters were not the sort to let such a matter rest.

"Eugene" became their new project.

They were artistic, but not softheaded. A singing career was no overnight affair. Years of hard work lay ahead; good teachers were expensive; Eugene would need a decent piano; he would undoubtedly have to go abroad for a time . . . and so on. There was only one solution to this kind of problem, the oldest in Western society since the Renaissance: patrons must be found. By what machinations they managed it, I don't know, but the next thing we knew, two resplendent patronesses had become Eugene's sponsors, and a new life began for him.

Lessons, lessons, lessons. Voice, French, Italian, German, fencing, ballet; Gene ate it all up like candy. Music, mimicry, languages were his forte. His teachers and coaches were prostrate with admiration; never had they seen such a prodigy. They foresaw a future on the opera and recital stage that would make music history. And as this was by common consent the most glorious manifestation of Talent yet seen in our family, thenceforth the lives of all the Bertons revolved around "Gene's career."

Around this time, Mummy divorced Papa. It wasn't as sudden as it sounds; she had yearned for many years to stop playing babysitter to a middle-aged child. But for quite a while I missed Papa, missed our midnight star walks, our map walks, and other impromptus, and the inexhaustible adoration he poured forth upon his sacred children whenever we were in range.

But I was a pretty busy seven-year-old, and if I never exactly forgot my love for Papa, there were soon other loves crowding it for heart room. At eight and a half, it was the ravishing chemistry instructress at Lewis Institute—I thought her so, anyway—inextricably interwoven with chemistry itself, which she taught me as quickly as Mr. Dauncey had taught me astronomy at six; at ten, Tom Seese—and in between, various jazz musicians, classical composers, James Joyce (Gene introduced me to him one night in Paris, as "his youngest reader"), Benny Leonard (my pompadour was directly inspired by his), Louis Armstrong . . . Quite a collection.

The Blankes' influence had given Gene strong views on having a "purpose in life." He himself, Gene now felt, had been, until recently, the horrible example of talent running wild; upon his return from Europe he turned a brooding eye on his gifted kid brother.

We didn't hold our tongues when it came to home truths.

"Christ! All those things, those things! Astronomy! Chemistry! Radio! Boxing! Chess! Jazz drumming! Singing your goddamn blues! Wasting precious hours in a lot of nightclubs with a ukelele! What the hell *are* you anyway?"

Bix's presence never prevented Gene from assailing my involvement with jazz, blues, etc., his unvarying theme being "You of all people!"

"I mean I can understand why a bunch of slaves on a plantation would express themselves in this sort of African style or whatever the hell it is—after all, what else have they got? I mean they're not exactly ready to go in for Ravel and Stravinsky, are they? But why *YOU?* You who can catch the most subtle nuances of a Poulenc song! . . ."

Only once did he bring Bix into these jeremiads, strangely enough—it wasn't like Gene to spare anyone his insights.

". . . You and Bix, farting around with this nigger plantation music—I don't understand your *values.* I mean what are *you* doing trying to imitate those poor bastards who grew up in tarpaper shanties and under freight cars? Let *them* sing the blues, or whatever they call them—God knows they've got something to sing them about! But you, and Bix, with your refined sensitive ear for *real* music—what the hell are *you* doing trying to be poor and black? What chain gang did *you* ever work on? Why don't you stay on your side of the tracks where you *belong?*"

Bix took refuge in his "vacant" look. But I leaped hotly to the defense.

"What the hell do you know about jazz?" I cried. "You couldn't tell Bix from Louis Armstrong! How much attention would *you* pay to someone's opinion who couldn't tell Ravel from Bach?"

"Oh shit! That's some comparison!"

We could get nowhere. But now Gene came out with: "I don't know why the hell all these jazz people are so afraid to learn how to *read.* I mean are they afraid they might find out Rimsky-Korsakov's music is a little better than King whatever-his-name's is? Look at Bix here. Jesus Christ, if anyone in the *world* ought to be *reading* it's Bix! With an ear like his . . . and he's obviously crazy about Ravel and Debussy and Prokofiev and . . . I mean why should he have to *sit* there while *I* play that music? Why should *he* have to wait for somebody else to play music he obviously loves? Now *there's* an example of fucked-up *values*. Just because the jazz world doesn't *believe* in reading, or maybe doesn't have to—I wouldn't know—here he is; here he is; and just like you, he isn't living by his real values. Values! Values! Believe me, brother, that's what it's all about. To know your own values, and live by them, *and nothing else.* If you deviate from that, you're right in the shit!"

The funny part of it is, Gene on that far-off day in 1924 struck very close to the bone, but perhaps had the truth upside down; that is, the reasons that Bix never learned to read were the same reasons he became a jazz musician—not that becoming one stopped him from reading (after all, it didn't stop a lot of others).

What was interesting, though, was Bix's reaction: a loss of countenance—an *Augenblick*—a rapid blink and wavering, as if a deep secret doubt had been touched on the raw; it lasted only milliseconds, but it was there, I didn't imagine it. What was that secret? No great mystery, as I now think. Jazz had rescued Bix, broken the deadly enchantment that had bound him to the square world he couldn't live in. God knows he gave jazz in return full measure, and then some. I suppose we may assume Bix loved jazz; but there are many kinds of love: joyous, zestful, desperate, anxious; there is a kind of love that is a gloomy, confused dependency, a continuum of almost-satisfactions and frustrations, never fulfilled and therefore insatiable, a love that asks more of the object than it can give. I seldom felt, even in Bix's best moments, that his love of jazz had much merriness in its composition. I did feel even then —and more surely now—that what Bix wanted from music, jazz never truly gave him; and that his fumbling overtures to classical music were an indication that he hoped to find it there.

But if that was indeed the case, why the vacillations and equivocations? Why *didn't* Bix, now a grown man earning his own living and living as he chose, forthrightly find himself some competent school or teachers, learn to read properly and play the piano properly—in short, become a full-fledged classical musician and have done with it—as composer, performer, or both? He might then have followed, in analogue, the advice of those little humorous signs seen in certain quick-&-dirties: EAT HERE AND KEEP YOUR WIFE FOR A PET—get his main spiritual nourishment from Debussy, Ravel, et al., and keep jazz for a hobby. Today, in the seventies, there are thousands of bilingual musicians—classical students or musicians who play jazz only on weekends. Something like that might have been the ideal solution for a man with Bix's temperament . . . *had he been able to manage it.*

I think now that this was the very core of Bix's problem, the one that at last killed him; that we are dealing here with a personality so damaged by early mishandling and unwitting abuse that no spontaneous recovery was possible. A child of Little Bickie's abnormal sensitivity, able to do such extraordinary things his way, unable to do the most ordinary things anyone else's way, just couldn't be forced into the mass mold of the public school system without serious pyschic injury. It would have been like putting a Cellini statuette into a baler.

Bix had managed to escape: first by inattention, falling asleep, detaching himself from all such situations as classrooms and lessons with Professor Grade; by (subconsciously) developing a calculated inability to learn such simple things as reading notes, correct fingering and position; finally by fleeing the school system altogether, by an equally (subconsciously) calculated violation of the rules & regulations, which Bix knew as well as any other student.

So Bix did avoid getting crushed in the baler—but, like a prisoner who has gone through barbed wire, not without permanent scar tissue. Perhaps it was something as simple as this: that all such things as reading, fingering, and "correct" practicing were so firmly associated in his unconscious with the world of formal instruction he had fled, that he could never "go back" to one without experiencing an overwhelming horror of the other. He had walked away from all that when he chose the road of jazz—he could never retrace his steps. It was too late.

Too late, that is, without the intervention of some psychological Intensive Care Unit—realistically, some extremely skilled (and hip) psychiatrist, someone on the order of a Wilhelm Reich, or my old friend Harold Greenwald, able to take the measure of Bix's whole problem, put things in perspective for him, smash up his elaborate defensive system of alcohol/jazz/nomadism-/solitariness/introversion. Whether any such person even existed then, I have no idea; anyway, none appeared on Bix's horizon— nor was Bix himself sending out any discernible SOS signals, unless indeed we can so interpret those almost subliminal *augenblick-liche* falterings.

Today, how quickly would I have so interpreted them! How glaringly they showed themselves at precisely those moments when *life goals, life values* were the issue! How equally clear was my impression of some deep guilt or shame, of a distinctly infantile emotional hue—as when a child has been caught in a fib.

But those moments passed; no one did anything; all of us just let things drift. It would have taken more prescience and temerity than any of us then possessed to cry *Halt!* to the career of a young jazzman who had already distinguished himself and was evidently headed onward & upward. It was Gene, with his (accidental) loathing for jazz, who came closest to challenging the rectitude of Bix's life course. (Values! Values!) But there was no direct sequel.

Did Gene's insight have any lasting influence? I suppose so, to a degree. Among other things, a deeper involvement with Debussy et al., of whom Bix never tired—a small clue was Bix's use, soon afterward, of the whole-tone scale* in "Davenport Blues."† Did Bix first hear that scale at 945 Argyle? It isn't a momentous question; he'd eventually have heard it somewhere. More important was the heightened Debussyesque coloring that quickly showed itself in Bix's musical thinking, especially in his harmonic ideas.

Bix made no secret of his admiration for Gene and "his" music. Not that he ever said anything, beyond his usual repertory of exclamations, but he looked volumes, and after Gene's homecoming came nearly every day, to sit silent and listen.

But in May everything changed. All of us got very busy. The Wolverines' jobs were coming almost continuously now—if they had three nights off in a row it was unusual—and then three events occurred in our family, in swift succession, that meant major changes in my life: a marriage, a summer idyll, and a permanent uprooting and departure from Chicago.

*Without semitones, e.g., C, D, E, F#, G#, A#, C, D. There is some question as to who first used such a scale, but Debussy was its best known exponent.
†Originally recorded by "Bix & His Rhythm Jugglers" on Gennett, January 26, 1925—the first of Bix's own tunes to be recorded.

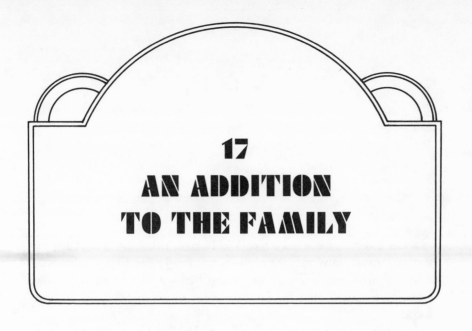

17
AN ADDITION
TO THE FAMILY

What ever made a man like Vic Berton think he was ready to marry—marry anyone, let alone a fragile flower like Gladys Stevens—is just another puzzle in the history of one of the most impulsive and foolhardy families ever allowed to walk around loose.

Her papa had been Hans Steiff until 1917, when under pressure of wartime anti-German feeling so many Germanic names were Americanized. They lived way out on Kedzie Boulevard, 3200 West, mile on mile of small frame houses and little stores; Papa's carpentry shop was right next door. The only imposing structure in the neighborhood was the new movie palace, the Senate Theater. Gladys, who worked as a secretary in some Loop insurance office, was a devoted moviegoer; she and a girl friend went faithfully every Wednesday and Saturday night, when the bill changed, oftener if the picture was especially romantic.

She was a pale blonde, with silky hair the color of iced champagne, wide gray eyes fringed by long dark lashes, classic straight North German nose and bony fashion-model face, wide pale mouth, lips the color of faded rose petals, tall slim body like an overgrown schoolgirl; shy, timid smile like Mummy's—she had no idea she was beautiful, which made her twice as beautiful. She made all her own clothes—her thrifty German mama thought it sinful to pay "store prices." Her only amusements were passionate love novels and movies.

She was one of those workingclass girls born, for no apparent reason, refined and delicate; she had never seen or met a boy or man who didn't scare or disgust her, until she fell in love with Vic, who, as fate would have it, was playing with Art Kahn at the Senate. It was her first, and only, aberration; in her twenty years

236

of life she had never done anything she wasn't "supposed to," along with every other girl in her school, Sunday school, and secretarial school. The first time she saw Vic playing tympani in the *1812 Overture* (Tchaikovsky's salute to the defense of Moscow —lots of tympani), she knew she wanted to marry him. Her "method" was simple. She just went every night and sat in the front row. Vic didn't need any blueprint. The third night, he took her home—his home—and was dumfounded to discover she was a virgin. Among his hundreds of affairs had been many virgins, but none who came home and to bed on their first meeting—nor, incredibly, none, virgin or not, more passionate.

We all liked her. I fell madly in love with her on sight; I am not over her yet. Her sweetness was beyond the poor power of words to describe; the simple nobility of her soul won even Mummy, who could usually find something "odd" about every girl her sonny boys brought home. Gene for some reason detested the name Gladys, which he said "sounded like a waitress in a boardinghouse in South Bend, Indiana," and renamed her Steve; there was something so funny about the most feminine creature that ever trod the earth answering to "Steve" that it stuck. For the sake of my erotic fantasies, I preferred Gladys.

Was Vic threatening to grow up? First had come the thoroughly un-Berton-like hankering to become an entrepreneur; now this twenty-five-year-old tomcat, the most notorious cocksman west of the Alleghenies, whose relationship to womankind had been that of a hawk to a henhouse, and who moreover was permanently bound to his family financially and emotionally, was actually marrying the girl.

It caused no revolutions in our household, hardly a ripple in fact. A quick civil "ceremony" at City Hall, and Steve moved the rest of her things from her home to ours—where she'd been living anyway for the past three weeks. That was all. She was to discover in the course of the next few years what a long way it was from Kedzie Boulevard to Argyle Street.

The real revolution took place in June, marking the end of our "Chicago period." Gene's New York recital was set for September; a major New York concert manager had acquired him; wires were being pulled at the Metropolitan Opera. Obviously we'd have to move to New York.

Vic was already negotiating the Wolverines' New York debut,

at the Cinderella Ballroom; meanwhile he'd landed them a summer job at Miller Beach, Indiana. Mummy had two brothers, Uncle Louie and Uncle Dave, who were said to own half of Gary (Mummy called them "my two crooked multimillionaire brothers"); I assume they had something to do with getting the job—if they did, it was one of the few times our wealthy relations ever did anything for us "gypsies."

It was decided that Vic would give notice to Art Kahn, at the Senate, and move out to Miller Beach for the summer to be (and sometimes play) with the Wolverines. I thought that was kind of strange, as they already had a drummer, Vic Moore; I didn't think he was going to enjoy very much playing behind Vic Berton every night. Steve too would give notice at her job and move out to Miller Beach.

The question arose, what to do with me? New York or Miller Beach? I loved New York. When I'd first gone there, three years before, on our way back from France, I'd found it the most romantic American city I'd ever seen. The miles of brownstones, smelling of history as Chicago never could, the distinctive flavor of lower Lexington Avenue, Gramercy Park with its European look, Washington Square, the two rivers and their waterfronts, had enchanted me, unforgettably.

I'd also begun a rather promising career on the New York stage, a year or so later, when I got a small part in a Ziegfeld musical, *Annie Dear,* starring Billie Burke, and also worked in a film being made at Cosmopolitan Studios, across the river in Fort Lee (the title is lost to my memory—something like *Mystery Island;* the stars were Hope Hampton and James Kirkwood).

All things being equal, I'd have opted unhesitatingly for New York. But they weren't equal. The two people I worshiped most in this world at the moment, Bix and Steve, were both going to Miller Beach.

Amazingly, I don't remember bidding Mummy and Gene goodbye, arriving at Miller Beach, and a lot of other things that must have happened. I think I stayed alone in the beach cottage the first week or two—Vic and the Wolverines were off somewhere; Wareing & Garlick say: "Berton led the band on a short tour of vaudeville theatres at Indianapolis, Louisville, Terre Haute and other cities. Moore took a short vacation, and at the beginning of August the Wolverines opened at the Gary Municipal Pavilion with two drummers."[24] They don't give their source of information; the fact is, I don't remember where the Wolverines were. I'm inclined to guess they must have gone farther away than that, so far that Vic felt he shouldn't spend the extra train fare to schlepp his kid brother along, railroad fares being a substantial part of road expenses in those days. But whatever the reason, for me it was a miraculous gift from the gods, the boon of one whole weekend completely alone in the cottage with Steve.

My passion for her was like a chronic dull ache in my chest. I'd decided this weekend was a kind of knightly ordeal by silence, to test my love. *She will never know, the secret will go with me to the grave:* so went my vow of chastity. I even did my best to exclude her from my nocturnal erotic fantasies. I must have dissembled well, for Steve showed no sign of treating me as other than her (handsome) kid brother. Well, I *was* handsome. I went through a period, from age twelve to about fifteen, of sudden good looks that was like the fabled frog turning into a fairy prince—and then, unfortunately, back into a frog again. But for those three years, I had them turning to look at me in the streets. Gladys, who stood half a head taller than I, was perfectly matter-of-fact in her admiration: "Gee," she said to me, lying on the beach that Saturday, "some girl's going to be awful lucky, one of these days, getting a boy like you," and gave my arm a squeeze, then went on with her crocheting. For at least a day I avoided washing that spot on my arm; I fancied I could still smell the scent of her fingers there. It was as near as I got to romance that weekend.

I suffered. Her nearness was physical torture. Thirteen, thirteen —what a miserable age for a hot-blooded lover! Any accidental touch, her hand on my shoulder—and she was an extremely affectionate girl—caused me a painful erection, which is no joke in a bathing suit.

The only tribute she paid to my precocity was to make me her confidant. Her excessive affection was explained when she revealed that she'd had a younger brother die of TB several years ago—he would have been just my age now. That brought tears of sympathy to my eyes, which made Steve throw her arms around me and kiss me emotionally, which in turn ... I suffered, I suffered. Mostly she talked about Vic. She worried, frankly and openly, about his drinking and about other women. She knew his reputation. He'd promised instant reform, but two nights later had come

in flushed with alcohol and smelling of perfume. Did I think she
could make him quit? She apologized for talking about things like
that, but I seemed "so grown up in some ways."

Before I knew it I had blurted out, "If a man had a wife like you,
how could he even look at anyone else?"

Gladys blushed. I could have bitten my tongue. Pledge of silence! Vow of chastity! Knightly ordeal! So much for good resolutions.

"Why, Ralphie! What a . . . what a sweet thing to say! Do you
really mean that?"

Did I! I looked away, almost angrily, but Gladys grabbed me (she
was some kind of swimming champ, and strong as hell) and kissed
me right on the mouth; reversing the traditional roles of the sexes,
I nearly fainted in her arms. Full of her own spontaneous emotion,
she never noticed a thing. It was a good thing we were lying
on our stomachs. I had to employ my usual detumescing devices before I could get up—mentally doing the multiplication
table, imagining a black-bordered telegram: YOUR MOTHER IS
DEAD. . . .

Somehow I stuck it out that weekend. Vic and the Wolverines
arrived the next day.

The obligatory "donkey shot," part of almost every American's childhood in the first quarter of this century. About eight years old.

Bix makes it to Davenport High: "Popular, full of fun and practical jokes, good at sports and music," but unable to see any real point in learning anything else.

Professor Koepke's big disappointment. Bix at Lake Forest Academy, with other members of the school band. Cy Welge holds his snare drum, Sam Stewart his sax. Dr. Koepke is at top center. About 1921.

Kicked out of Lake Forest, Bix's real life begins at last. His first full-time professional job was with The Wolverines in 1923. Seated left to right: Vic Moore, drums; George Johnson, tenor, doubling on baritone and clarinet; Jimmy Hartwell, clarinet and C-melody sax; Bix; Al Gandee, trombone; Wilfred (Min) Leibrook, tuba; Bobby Gillette, banjo. Standing, hand on Jimmy's shoulder, Dick Voynow, pianist, leader and den mother. (Wayne Rohlf)

Bix's (and The Wolverines') first record date, Gennett Studios, Richmond, Indiana, February 18, 1924. Standing at back: Jimmy, George; seated: Min, Bobby, Vic Moore, Dick, Bix; standing next to Bix: Al. Note recording horn just above Dick's head. Musicians played into the horn at various distances determined by trial-and-error. Note also absence of bass drum whose violent low-frequency vibrations would have knocked the cutting stylus clear off the wax master. (Wayne Rohlf)

A penny for Bix's thoughts, doubtless not particularly complimentary to himself. Probably taken at Miller Beach, summer of 1924. Standing left to right: Jimmy, Vic, Dick; seated: George, Bobby, Bix, my brother Vic. (Min Leibrook isn't in this picture, perhaps because he was busy taking it.)

We make it to New York: The Wolverine Orchestra at the Cinderella Ballroom, late 1924. Left to right: Dick, Bobby, George, Min, Vic Moore (drums and landscape), Jimmy, Bix. (Note, in this and other Wolverine shots, Moore's awkward pre-Berton method of suspending cymbals.) (Frank Driggs Collection)

Bix in 1927 at the peak of his powers. The band was Adrian Rollini's. Left to right: Howdy Quicksell, Eddie Lang, Bill Rank, Chauncey Morehouse, Bix, Rollini, Frankie Trumbauer, Bob Davis, Don Murray, Joe Venuti, Frankie Signorelli.

Riding the elephant: Bix as a soldier in the Whiteman army (probably late 1927 or early 1928). Whiteman stands (naturally) front and center; Bix, overweight and mustachioed, is third from right in the back row, obviously rather broken up by the scene. (Frank Driggs Collection)

Fragment of the Whiteman payroll in 1928, with signatures. Note Bix's wages and Bing Crosby's. (Thomas S. Pletcher)

America's impressive monument to one of her greatest artists (if you can find it): Bix's headstone at Oakdale Cemetery, Davenport.

18
MILLER BEACH

"The Barn," we called it—Gary Municipal Pavilion, to give it its official name. It was a lot bleaker than any barn I ever saw.

Picture a huge structure—brick or concrete, I'm not sure now which—a good city block long, maybe a third that wide, and (I find this hard to believe, but that's how I remember it) open to the weather on all four sides; at one end, a bandstand big enough for a thirty-piece orchestra, with an upright piano that looked as though it had been salvaged from a municipal dump—no front board, many "white" keys no longer white, having lost their ivory, and a generally warped and weatherbeaten air. The tone was in keeping—what my brothers called "summer resort piano," like a mechanical upright in a merry-go-round. The lake was about one hundred yards away; when the wind was onshore, you could feel the spray from the more sportive gusts; other evenings, when atmospheric conditions were right, a visible fog would creep up over the dunes, in out of the night, veiling the lights and band-stand, and making the dancers' clothing hang on them like damp dishcloths. What it did to the various instruments, especially those with strings or "heads," such as the drums and banjo, may be imagined.

At around noon that first Saturday, the band assembled in the pavilion to rehearse for their Grand Opening that night. I was there at the first meeting between that piano and Dick Voynow. There was nothing to be done. I had been present the week before when the tuner came out; as he had pointed out to me, the best piano ever made wouldn't hold its tuning under twenty-four-hour-a-day exposure to the weather. Eight of the keys had been stone dead; he'd fixed those, but out here you could expect things like that to happen again; obviously the Gary Parks Department

242

wasn't going to put a new piano out here either—in a few weeks it would probably look just like this one.

I duly reported all this to Dick, who shook his head morosely and sat down to give the rest of the band their A. They all started tuning up. Bix listened a second and said, "That's not A." He blew a note tentatively through his horn, tightened the mouthpiece a bit and blew again. "There's A."

"Thanks," said Dick. "What am I supposed to do? Carry a piano tuner around?"

"Vic used to be a piano tuner for a while," I volunteered. "Maybe he still has his starhead.* Want me to wake him up and ask him?"

They looked at me and at each other.

"No; the hell with it," Dick said. "We'll see. Meanwhile you may as well tune up to this mousetrap," and he kicked it, exasperated.

"Yeah, come on," George Johnson said, busy with his reed. "Tune up and let's play a little music."

"You mean tune down," Bix said, fiddling with his mouthpiece, while Dick continued sounding his A (or as near as that piano could approximate it) and the others tuned their instruments.

"This isn't the worst we ever had," Bobby Gillette said, tuning his banjo. "Remember the piano at ———?" He named some resort or roadhouse I don't recall. "The one the waiter dropped a tray of drinks into?"

"Take 'em the way they come," Vic Moore said cheerfully, putting his traps together. He tried a few thumps on his bass drum.

"Ouch," said Bix.

"This is nothing," said Moore-Moore. "Wait till after sundown; the whole set'll sound like a bunch of lead balloons."

"Grin and bear it," said Jimmy Hartwell. "It's all part of the job."

"Yeah," Bix said, "like mosquitoes." He blew a phrase, pointing his horn down toward the far end of the hall, or shed, or whatever you want to call it. As it always did the first few notes I heard him blow, a lump came up in my throat. Oh, that tone! But Bix said, "Wow. The sound just disappears here." I wondered, as I often did at those moments, whether anyone else felt the way I did—what they heard—whether anyone shared my emotion. I guess quite a few did, judging by their subsequent memoirs. Most of us just

---

*Wrench used by piano tuners to adjust the tension on the strings (so called from its hexagonal interior shape). Also called *tuning hammer*.

don't talk out loud about those things. Come to think of it, I didn't myself very much, at the time. (Whom would *I* talk to about it right then, for instance? Bix?)

They started playing, finally, around twelve-thirty. I pulled up a chair, unobtrusively, at the side of the stand, as near Bix as I could get without sitting right in front of him, listening ecstatically to what he did with a tune. I had learned already not to show my raptures unduly, especially in public; but at times I couldn't help myself, something he blew would lift me right off my chair, stomping in tempo and laughing like an idiot. Moore-Moore always got a kick out of my antics.

"Well, we've got one customer for tonight anyway." He grinned.

"Bring your friends," said Bobby Gillette.

Vic had come in toward the end of the rehearsal session, and sat down at the back end of the barn, where the toilets and checkroom were, and the soft drinks bar and food concession.

He came up now to the stand, nattily togged out in slacks and sport shirt, and smiling broadly. "That's quite a piano," he said. "I wonder if we can do anything about it."

"Grin and bear it," said Jimmy.

Eager to be important, I told Vic what the tuner had said, and asked if he still had his tuning equipment. He laughed and shook his head. "You sound pretty weak down at the other end," he said to them. "Maybe we can put some kind of a shell behind you before tonight." He turned to me. "How about it, guy? Want to rustle around and see if we can dig up something—piece of board or something?"

We spent the next hour or two, with the caretaker's help, getting together an improvised band shell—I'd found a pile of unused lumber lying under a tarpaulin out behind some sheds. Vic and I put on old pants and sneakers and helped the caretaker carry it up to the pavilion and nail it together into some semblance of a wall. We found a piece of muslin to tack over it, so it didn't look too conspicuous. "That ought to do it!" we told each other, nodding wisely. Vic went down to the far end again to listen while I banged out *Nothing Could Be Finer Than to Be in Carolina in the Morning* on the tinny piano; he came back, nodding approval. "At least you can hear it now," he said.

"Is that good or bad?" Bix asked.

Later I tried to find Bix to make him come swimming, but he'd gone back to sleep in one of the cottages the band was sharing. Steve had made a picnic lunch for us, which we took down to the water's edge; after lunch Vic and Steve and I played catch on the beach, swam, sunbathed, and slept. I couldn't believe I was in for two whole months of hearing Bix play every night. And swimming. And Vic. And Steve. Into such a paradise what evil could enter?

Opening night was weird. It was a perfect night, warm and still, just enough breeze off the Lake to keep things in the pavilion comfortable. But by seven o'clock there weren't more than thirty people in the whole place, lost in all that acreage, which looked like a railway station at two in the morning. The lighting was provided by thousands of bare sixty-watt bulbs strung all around the walls and festooned back and forth across the eaves under the slanted roof. It was like a cattle sale I once saw in a barn out in Oklahoma somewhere, and about as cozy.

The Wolverines began to play, and I forgot all about the lighting; so, apparently, did the other twenty-nine people present. They huddled around the bandstand, dancing in an automatic way, but mostly really listening, amazed, to the hot blast coming from those seven maniacs. Enthusiasm grew, and the dancing crowd grew too; as the stars came out, so did the residents of nearby areas. By ten o'clock nearly half the floor was filled with dancing couples, doing the fox trot, one-step, and two-step, the more enterprising doing the kind of dances more usually seen in the black-&-tan joints of the South Side—the toddle, the eagle rock, ballin' the jack, the mooche, the boogie-woogie (a term I heard applied to dancing at least two decades before the great boogie-woogie *music* upsurge of the forties)—steps that caused any older people present considerable anxiety for the moral safety of the younger dancers.

A good 10 percent of the "dancers" hardly danced at all. They were the real music fans, the alligators, who pressed close around the stand to watch and listen, clap and cheer and laugh with delight, following the music intently and encouraging the musicians to ever greater efforts of excitement and "hotness."

I reveled in their enthusiasm, since I could share it without being conspicuous. I noted though that my fellow enthusiasts seemed less critical in their appreciation than Vic and I. They

greeted Bobby Gillette's corny ragtime banjo breaks with the
same outbursts of applause and other signs of enjoyment as they
did Bix's most thrilling flights, and—this I particularly remarked,
though it should have been no surprise—Bix's more subtle and
musicianly ideas, whose effect depended not on a blast or pounding out of rhythm but on an unexpected turn of phrase, an ingenious inversion of a previous phrase, a neat and surprising omission
or understatement—such passages seemed to evoke little response.

I had two regular listening posts. Either I sat glued to my gilt
ballroom chair at the left side of the bandstand, which after a
couple of nights was left there for me—even the caretaker and
cleanup crew soon took to calling it "Frenchy's chair"—or, when
I could sit still no longer, I'd get up and join the other alligators
in front of the stand, rocking, stamping, clapping, and roaring with
the rest. Each position had its virtues. That in front of the stand
offered better acoustical balance, and a more piercing, soul-sear-
ing impact of Bix's peculiar tone; but Frenchy's chair gave me a
better observation point from which, without being watched myself, I could watch minutely Bix's every expression and gesture.

Bix seldom stood up to play. He generally sat either with both
feet squarely on the floor in front of him, one foot stomping out
the beat, or, alternatively, one leg crossed over the other, right
ankle on left knee, at a complete right angle. Unlike many jazz
musicians, Bix nearly always played with eyes open—wide open—
one of them anyway (at certain moments, usually when he was just
about to rip out an especially stunning thought, crescendo, the left
eye would flicker half shut, with a particularly sinister effect);
staring straight ahead, he always gave me the impression of a man
deeply involved in some urgent though cryptic panorama unfolding scene by scene, like a dream sequence in a film, before his
intense gaze—in which, every instant, some startling or unexpected plot twist might develop. The gaze was as at something
distant, another world, unseen save by this one solitary rapt on-
looker, its meanings and commands intended only for his gaze and
no other living creature's; swift as thought they flew, those distant,
terribly distinct and significant pictures, and even as they reached
the eager, anxious eye of the watcher, were instantly translated
into musical designs—now harsh, pitiless, now tenderly lyrical, at
the will not of the player but of those faraway constantly unfolding

tableaux—at one moment an elaborate, graceful arabesque, at the next some grand, simple cadence, resolving to the tonic chord, pure and inevitable as the proof of a geometric theorem, Q.E.D.

Six hours every night, six nights a week and Sunday afternoons, I sat or stood, watching Bix as raptly as he his inward vision—but hardly ever could I anticipate what was coming next out of his horn, penetrate even by the space of a beat to share that vision.

If I had secretly hoped that the respectable official auspices of the Gary Parks Department would curtail Bix's nightly drinking, I was soon disillusioned. He simply kept a quart bottle of "orange juice" (or "ginger ale," or something equally legal) behind his chair, swigging it freely between numbers; as the evening wore on, between choruses. Between sets, if necessary, he went out and replenished it from the abundant stores most of the musicians kept in their cottages. Between sets, also, they would meet outside the pavilion, usually out back behind the dunes leading down to the beach, to pass a joint around. I should add parenthetically that the "tea" available in those pristine days, at fifteen cents a joint, was of such quality and vigor that five or six souls could pass just one of those around, each getting perhaps four good pokes out of it before it reached the tweezers stage, and all five or six be flying like kites within five or six minutes—and *stay* stoned and flying like that for a couple of hours, sometimes longer, depending on circumstances. By the way, my recollection is that grass wasn't even illegal in Chi when I was a boy, only because the fuzz hadn't caught on yet to its existence among us—I don't know that anybody knew about or smoked it then except musicians and their friends. I believe it all came from Mexico, and it was dynamite; but friendly dynamite, giving you usually a laughing high, nothing frightening or paranoiac. My brother Vic was the biggest viper* of any musician I knew, but then he did everything that way— smoked more cigarettes (three to four packs a day), had more girls, worked harder, than just about anyone around him. He drank, I would guess, almost as much as Bix, the only difference being that Vic sometimes got drunk—silly, stupid drunk—whereas Bix never did, not in those days anyway. For that reason Vic, who was a professional of professionals, took good care never to do what Bix habitually did—drink on the job; he did his tanking up after hours,

*Habitual (in the sense of constant, not addicted) marijuana smoker.

and was saved from doing it constantly only by being so busy working.

This summer of 1924 was an exception, an unaccustomed stretch of comparative leisure between Vic's usual killing schedules, and consequently a period of heavier drinking than any I'm aware of before or since. His duties at the Miller Beach job were only token, consisting, so far as I recall, in taking his turn behind the drums a couple of sets every night—whenever he felt like it, I guess. That much he did, and the effect was magic. Vic taking over the drums from Moore-Moore was like suddenly turning all the lights up on a stage scene; the whole band sounded different, more intense, with a zing and drive it seldom had at any other time. I don't know how happy that made Vic Moore or even the rest of the band, who may well have sympathized with Moore. Moore-Moore was an easygoing, goodnatured guy like most of the others, taking life as it came, but on several occasions I heard him sigh as he came back to take his place on the stool once more, after a set or two of Vic Berton's fireworks: "O.K., party's over, old Stinky is back," or some such "jocular" remark.

I think Dick Voynow after a week or so began to worry about Moore-Moore's morale in the circumstances, and, by extension, the rest of the band's; after all, Dick was the nominal and official leader, the one who felt impelled to hold things together, to look after the rest, he who was always sober and responsible, even in the midst of frequent chaos. As I mentioned earlier, Dick was gay. (That in itself was extraordinary; it's a fact that in all my more than fifty years of intimate contact with jazz, I can literally remember only three other musicians who were; all, by the way, now that I think of it, were pianists—two of them very famous.) I thought nothing of it then, but it now strikes me that, considering how young and relatively unsophisticated were the other members of the band—quite ordinary American college kids, in fact—there was something very fine in the way they all simply accepted Dick's sexual preferences, live & let live, in the most relaxed way, casually kidding about it with him at times, mostly just ignoring it, like the weather. As I may have hinted, about the only way Dick's feminine ingredient was apt to show itself, apart from a certain softness of gesture (rather unexpected in a man of his Charles Atlas build), was in his motherly fussing over the others' health, punctuality, neatness of dress, and similar Eagle Scout virtues. He and my brother Vic must have worked out something on the morale question, because for the last half of our sojourn at Miller Beach Vic (Berton) didn't play at all until the last two sets, when Moore-Moore, released from duty, would promptly take off after some pretty admirer—he was nearly as "bad" as my brother that way, though in an engaging, boyish style, not the often sinister and intense way Vic Berton had, which rendered so many women of all ages helpless, in the fabled manner of birds fascinated by serpents.

Regarding my own sitting in with the band, for once I was in no hurry. I felt very ambivalent about displaying my drumming, such as it was, before my idol. On the one hand, I was eager just to experience the thrill of playing behind one of the most inspiring of all jazzmen; on the other, I felt so diffident in his presence that I hesitated to exhibit my accomplishments. On the one hand, I dreaded to "louse it up" with my uncertain technique and command of the drums; on the other, I reflected that I was probably no worse than Moore-Moore, about whom I'd never heard any of the band complain—but, as we know, the Wolverines were, in that respect, a singularly uncomplaining lot. I felt in any case that I had better "time" than Moore-Moore, and a few Vic Berton licks up my sleeve; if they didn't complain about him, why should I be scared to get on the stand with them? Sooner or later I knew I would.

My brother, who was always gently pushing me that way—for "experience"—saw to it that it was sooner. I guess it was the second rehearsal, probably a Tuesday afternoon; Vic had brought some new tunes with him from the city, publishers' stock arrangements he wanted to try. Moore-Moore for some reason wasn't around (probably off in a cabin with some thrill from the night before), and Vic sat in on drums while they ran the numbers down. Bix was really something on those rehearsals. Almost every new number sounded "terrible" to him at first (most of them were)— he'd greet each one with "Jesus, what a dog." Then he'd start to get "an idea or two" for it. Next thing, he'd be sitting at the piano with Dick, working out some "nice changes"; then, listening to his inner voices a moment, he'd suggest a different tempo—and then, all at once, he'd say, "Hey, let's run that down now," pick up his horn, and bite into the lead. I'd get the familiar chill up my back; Vic and I would exchange that comradely glance of comfort and despair, shaking our heads with an almost grudging grin—*Son of a bitch, that Bix*—and a new number would have been added to the book.

Today, having tentatively set the new number, Vic got up and said to me, "Take the drums, guy—I want to hear how it sounds from out front." He stuck the sticks under one of the bass drum tension rods and climbed down off the stand to stroll out into the hall. I got a little pale around the gills for a second, then told myself, *To hell with that—come on let's go*, and as casually as I could climbed in behind the drums. One of the guys said something kiddingly about "O.K., let's all 'get' Frenchy" and somebody else said, "Hey, Frenchy, you got your union card?" I must admit my chest felt a little tight when Bix turned around and gave me the eye, rather coldly I thought, but he didn't say anything; Dick smiled at me from under his single thundercloud eyebrow and winked encouragingly, Bix stomped off, and away we went.

I was careful as hell at first, trying not to "do too much"—Vic was always cautioning his pupils about that—just keeping a good steady swish with the brushes the way he'd taught me; not too much bass drum, just a good solid beat, a little tinkle on the top cymbal going into the breaks. All of a sudden I realized I wasn't tense any more. My gaze, which had been focused on my instruments in a kind of anxious blur, relaxed too. I lifted my eyes to look out at where Vic was sitting; he'd pulled a chair onto the middle of the dance floor. He grinned back at me and winked—I started to feel fine. I could feel my hands relaxing, my beat getting a little looser. George went into a sort of nice punching solo, and I added the backbeat foot cymbal behind him; Bix turned his head and half smiled back at me, and I knew it was O.K. What a great feeling! I knew I wasn't great, just getting by really, but that was plenty! What the hell, it wasn't a very demanding kind of band—just loose and comfortable. Jimmy had taken a clarinet solo; now it was Bix's turn. I stashed the brushes and switched smoothly to the sticks, putting an insistent shuffle beat behind him; he began to really climb into it, I felt a slow warm flush mount right up from my toes to my face, wow did that feel great, *That son of a bitch Bix*, I thought. *He's really laying it out, and here I am laying down the beat behind him!* We came up to his break solo and I sprung him into it just right, with one of Vickie's favorite licks, *ah-bip-i-di-paaaahhhh* on the top cymbal, holding the little Egyptian cymbal underneath, in my left hand—and, oh Jesus, Bix tightened my wig (as we used to say) by "answering" my little lick with a similar figure on his horn, using it to construct the next eight bars of his solo. . . . I don't think I'd have traded those ten minutes for any like period of bliss in the race's history. Whew! I went right down the line with the rest of the tune, broadening out on the final wrapup ensemble chorus with just enough razzle-dazzle on the cymbals, fell right into the false ending with the rest of the band, and took it on out with a *boom-crash,* bass drum to crash cymbal, just the way Vickie would do it.

Vickie was on his feet, laughing; Dick smiled at me under his brows, winking, and Bobby Gillette hollered, "Yeah, Frenchy, all right now!" Finally Bix turned around and cased me with his little half-sour-pickle smile, not even a smile really, more like a grimace; said, "Shit, now I've heard everything," scratched his ear and shook the spit out of his horn. I knew then for sure I'd done O.K. Nothing great—I wasn't within thirty miles of brother Vic (and never would be—I knew that too, always)—but just doing O.K. behind Bix and in front of Vickie and everyone—that was, as they say, worth the trip.

I didn't push my luck. I got out from behind there, and was happy just watching and listening. Late that night there was another opportunity, on the last set, and I sat in again, for three or four numbers.

Another time I started wailing some blues, in my inimitable foghorn, at first just to myself, but some of the alligators hollered, *Come on, kid! Sing those blues!* and started clapping in tempo. I cut loose, and I guess must have done O.K., judging by the whistles and encores, with Bobby Gillette laughing at me in his cheery way; Bix again thrilled me as only he could, playing some fine soft fills behind my vocal, real bluesy, and I remembered our little conversation in that Cicero club a few months back. I could see Vic was satisfied too, grinning up at me from a table at the side, where he was getting loaded again.

That was Vic's last night out there before Steve joined us for the rest of the summer, and he was making the most of it. He had this dark cute girl, their hands clasping under the table, the girl gazing into his eyes, so serious, as though this was for the rest of her life, whereas I knew very well it was only a one-night stand. They disappeared somewhere after the last set, as I put the covers on

Moore-Moore's drums and began moving them into the locked shed. Nothing'd ever been taken as far as we knew, but we couldn't take the chance.

"I wish they'd steal the piano," Bix said.

"No such luck," said Dick.

Bix would hardly ever touch that piano; he said it was like "banging a rock on a tin roof."

Every night that pavilion was crawling with single, available flappers; the musicians, all single except Vic—who might as well have been—were their natural prey, and vice versa. Knowing the personal peculiarities of each musician as I soon did, it was an interesting nightly show for an alert, prurient, precocious Peeping Tom like myself, just watching the byplay between (or among) the sexes.

The girls unfortunate enough to be attracted by Dick Voynow were always fascinating. As I've indicated, his homosexuality was anything but obvious, especially to the dumb little girls that hung around this Indiana beach resort; I imagine most of them had never seen a real live "queer" before. The time they wasted trying to flirt with Dick was inversely proportional to the aggressiveness of the individual girl. The bold, wicked type of flapper, skirt five inches above her knees, flask of gin in her coat, the kind who would walk right up to the stand after ogling him during a set and say, "Hi, tall, dark, & handsome, how'd you like to buy a girl a drink?" could get a short answer from Dick, depending on his mood, like, "Thanks, but I don't drink and I don't like girls." It could take another sort of girl all evening to get to that ultimate answer.

Jimmy Hartwell, who was goodlooking in a neat, dark, clean-cut way, was rather retiring, not a "chaser." Toward the end of the second week, I began to see him with a very quiet ladylike girl, who'd been "properly" introduced to him by one of Moore-Moore's girlfriends, and never saw him talking to anyone else after that.

Bobby Gillette and Moore-Moore both liked, and seemed to attract, the same type of wild, "fast," extreme flapper, and often double-dated at night after the job, gallivanting around the Indiana countryside in one of the band's noisy automobiles till dawn and winding up in some inexpensive roadhouse with "rooms upstairs." Min Leibrook, another quiet one like Jimmy, was something of a mystery so far as girls were concerned; always politely chatting and joking with them, but I never saw him getting practical with any of them after hours; I have a feeling now that his constant light badinage was a camouflage for a really extreme case of shyness, and that none of the rather ordinary types of girls that frequented the pavilion that summer ever figured out how to get inside it.

My brother Vic, who never knowingly wasted ten seconds on a girl who didn't "mean business," naturally tended to gravitate to the bolder, come-&-get-it, rolled-stockings-&-hip-flask girl, or the sophisticated, regal, statuesque rich widow or society woman, although he had actually no single "type" and just loved the female sex, period. Not many would consider him handsome, but there was something about him—his dark, "Arabian" eyes, his utter confidence that any private conversation between himself and a female could have but one conclusion—and the result never disappointed their expectations: it was indispensable to his image of himself that his partner of the moment, be she countess or waitress, emerge from his embraces swearing she'd never had it so good; "nothing was too much trouble." (Only much later did I come to realize what a driven man my apparently happy, successful, universally liked and sought-after brother Vic really was: driven to women, driven to alcohol, driven to chain-smoking, hard driving and hard driven, until he perished of lung cancer at fifty-two, still seemingly in the flush and prime of life and health, and still "on the God damned drums" until very nearly his last hour —they literally had to come and take him away from his last job [with the Los Angeles Philharmonic] in an ambulance, on a stretcher. No, I *don't* know the answer. I do know what he proudly replied when the doctors remonstrated with him: *But, Mr. Berton, how, how could you, how did you manage to finish out that concert at the Philharmonic? It was simple madness for you to stand at the tympani for two hours in your condition!* His reply deserves to be enshrined in the annals of the American Federation of Musicians, Los Angeles local: "Me, doc, after forty-six years—*send a substitute?*" It might have been his epitaph: Here Lies Vic Berton —He Never Sent a Sub.)

I took a keen interest, half jealous, half proprietary, in Bix's response (or lack of it) to the nightly presence of so much available girlhood. Except when Vic was sitting in on drums, Bix was easily the most conspicuous of the septet—not only because he was the cornet player and enjoyed a natural advantage in volume of sound, but because of what he played on it. Most of his auditors may not have appreciated its more subtle aspects, but they couldn't help feeling its compelling drive and swing right down to their toes. Between sets little throngs of admirers surrounded him, about equally divided in sex.

Knowing how uncomfortable Bix always was about even the most moderate of praise, it was no surprise to me to see him ducking and fending off these intemperate fans, male and female alike. One night, though, I noticed his gaze wandering frequently in the direction of a dark, slim girl who sat at one of the tables ranged along the sides of the dance floor. There were three other girls with her, but she often stayed at the table alone, sipping a bottle of Green River (a noxious "lime" soda of the period) through a straw, while the other girls were dancing with various boys who came over to the table. From Frenchy's chair, I remarked that whenever Bix wasn't looking her way, she was looking his way, and this game of Dodgem continued through at least one set, by which time I got bored watching. But a little later I saw the same girl dancing, passing in front of the bandstand. Bix was as usual gazing off into his private astronomy, blowing something pretty. The girl's partner was saying something, but she didn't seem to be listening; she was looking at Bix out of the corner of her eye. She was even nicer-looking close up, simply and quietly dressed, rather oldfashioned-looking among all the loud flappers with their dozens of strings of beads and skirts up on their bare thighs and what was practically stage makeup. This girl had long brown hair worn up around her head in braids, which made her rather conspicuous in that sea of bobbed and frizzy heads. Bix never looked at her all the time she was dancing—too busy playing—but she was looking at him, over her partner's shoulder, sometimes turning her head to get another look.

A while later she was back at her table alone, and the game started again. During the following set I saw a couple of her girlfriends and their partners alligatoring in front of the stand near Bix, while she still sat alone; between numbers they were leaning over, talking and giggling to Bix, who smiled a couple of times— I was dying to hear what they said, but there was too much noise and chatter. The next thing I knew, they were gone and Bix was playing again. I don't know what they said, but after a time the table was empty, the girl nowhere to be seen.

The next night she was back, alone. Again she and Bix played their game. It was getting so ridiculous I was almost tempted to butt in some way (I could hear my mother saying, *Oh for God's sake if you're that crazy about him dear why don't you go over and tell him so?*—she had no patience with that sort of thing)—but what way?

A little later I was standing with the alligators myself, yelling and clapping with everybody else at a particularly frenzied performance of *Muskrat Ramble* that had us all hoarse with enthusiasm; I was back on the outer fringe of that semicircle, and became aware all at once, between climaxes, that the brownhaired beauty was standing right near me, not yelling or carrying on, just looking, trying to edge a little closer.

When the set ended everyone drifted away to the tables, I with them; she disappeared somewhere too, I assumed to powder her nose. Then I saw her standing in front of the bandstand talking to Bix and he was showing her something on the cornet, not really looking at her but saying something and pulling out one of the slides. I guessed she'd made an excuse to ask him something about the horn. Just before the last set, I saw him buying her a Green River at the soft-drink stand. After the dance was over and the others had packed up, I saw Bix holding her coat for her and walking her out into the dark, taking her to the bus.

The next day I went by the cottage Bix shared with Jimmy and Min, to try to get him to come swimming with us. So far he'd always made some excuse or just looked sarcastic or something, but this time he was in the best humor I'd seen for a long time, and said, "Sure kid, why not."

He couldn't find a bathing suit to fit him, but Jimmy Hartwell had an extra one hanging on the line out back and at last he was ready, and we joined Vic and some girl down at the water. It was the first time I'd seen Bix swim. I could see he knew how, all right, but he complained that the water was too damn cold and didn't stay in long. Somebody had brought some sandwiches down, and Bix asked if anybody'd brought a jug. One of the guys went back to the cottage and came back with a milk bottle full of gin or the nearest facsimile; Bix took a big swallow and lay down in the sand, and pretty soon fell asleep. He could fall asleep faster than any adult I ever met.

Some of the other guys were horsing around and wanted to see if they could bury Bix in the sand without waking him, but I made them knock it off. They settled for planting a paper rose on his chest and a cardboard from a shirt laundry, on which Bobby Gillette or somebody had printed, with a piece of charcoal from a burntout bonfire, DO NOT OPEN UNTIL XMAS. Vic's girl thought it was the funniest thing she'd ever seen. She and Vic went back to the cottage, Vic whispering to me not to come up for a while, and I went swimming again with the others. Bix woke up in due course and found the flower and card. All he said was, "We ought to pin this sign on that piano." I tried to drag him into the water again but he said Hell no, it was too damn cold.

We walked back to his cottage. The sun was almost down on the dunes when we got there, and coming up onto the porch I finally said something about the girl last night.

"Holy cow!" Bix cried. "I was supposed to call her today before six! What time is it, somebody?" he called into the house. "Search me," Jimmy called back from inside. "My watch stopped again. Must be the damp out here."

Bix went into the house. I followed him in, and watched him rummage in the general disorder. "Where the hell did I put that phone number now?" he said several times.

"Did you look in your shirt pocket?" I suggested. "I always see you sticking things in there."

He started pulling shirts off a big chair that was full of clean and dirty clothing.

"You were wearing the light blue shirt with the stripes. Here it is," I said, pulling it from under a pile of other stuff.

He reached in the pocket. The piece of paper was there, with her name and phone number—Doris, Dora, some such name. Bix looked at me and laughed out loud. "This kid is the nuts," he said, and poked me in the stomach. " 'No job too large, no job too small,' " he quoted. " 'Ryan Brothers does 'em all.' " He turned back to me. "The telephone in your cottage working yet?"

I shook my head. "You'll have to use the one up in the pavilion."

After reminding him to take some nickels with him (he was starting out in his bathing suit, without any money), I went back to our cottage. Vic was writing some music on a manuscript pad; the girl was fixing dinner for us, wearing one of Steve's beach robes.

My radio receiver—a crystal set I'd built myself out of coils of wire wound on an oatmeal box to make a tuner, and homemade capacitors of glass and tinfoil—had finally arrived by bus. I went into my room to start setting it up. For the first time in a long time I felt really angry at Vic.

19
MIDSUMMER
NIGHT DREAMS

Being your slave, what should I do but tend
Upon the hours and times of your desire?
I have no precious time at all to spend,
Nor services to do, till you require.

Shakespeare, *Sonnet LVII*

Shaw said somewhere that if all the names of all the males (in England) were placed in one hat, and all the names of the females in another, and pairings made by a blindfolded chimpanzee rummaging in the two hats, the results could not possibly be worse than they are under the present system.

We can all think of examples that prove Shaw's point; the pairing of Victor Berton and Gladys Stevens would do as well as any.

How did such a mismatched couple ever choose each other? Blindly, the one as blind as the other. Actually it was Gladys who did the choosing, and on no more rational grounds than a romantic imagination, fed on trashy novels and the plot devices of Hollywood hacks—and of course the sinister dark eyes of a mysterious, glamorous being: a musician.

In one way, as it happened, these two were made for each other: this demure daughter of Lutheran piety bore within her maiden belly the fires of a Messalina, unsuspected and unkindled, awaiting only the magic touch of my wicked brother. Such creatures may be bred anywhere, even on prosaic Kedzie Boulevard. Once such a woman has, in the poetic phrase of an artist friend of mine, "put her little flower in your basket," it takes a mighty cool customer to pluck it out; wiser, cooler men than my hotblooded brother have found themselves unable to reject such a treasure.

Unfortunately there is more to marriage than bedroom and kitchen (ethereal-looking Gladys was also, thanks to her Old Country mama, an excellent plain cook). Outside them, poor Steve could no more keep up with Vickie's way of life than a tortoise can fly with eagles—to cite one of Aesop's ancient morals. Vickie continued to live it up, and discretion wasn't in his nature. In her trouble, Steve like a drowning animal sought a rock to cling to, and

260

there was none but her thirteen-year-old "kid brother"; not much of a rock, but better than none: I was precocious in "certain matters," furiously on her side, loyal & devoted; above all, I was *there*, with nothing better to do all summer than offer what consolations love could give. Not surprisingly, I soon became more than confidant.

It didn't happen overnight; I had first to suffer a bit more.

The first few evenings, she joined me enthusiastically in the Barn, sat at the musicians' table with me and Vic, enjoying every minute of this new high life. But a few nights finished her. Twenty years of "supper" at five-thirty and early to bed had ill fitted her for performers' hours. By nine-thirty she'd be glassy-eyed. "What time is it?" "Steve's bedtime" became a running gag around the bandstand.

One night a crowd of Vic's friends showed up—his famous "sweetie" Bee Palmer, inventor of the shimmy, vaudeville headliner, a real blues singer (in that day we used to call them "white niggers"), the Marilyn Monroe of her time, dazzling cream-white hair, incredible bosom, sexy sway and all, clad in a skin-tight silver gown that showed more than it covered; also the famous stuttering comic and hoofer, Joe Frisco, and the entire Carlisle Evans jazz band—"her" band, as Bee called them, which indeed they were said to be, in every sense of the word: Bee's reputation as a nymphomaniac was as big as her star billing ("fucked her way to fame and never quit" was the way Vic put it). It was a known fact that any time Bee's act played Chicago, neither she nor Vic "saw" any other sweetheart as long as she was in town.

I suffered for Steve as this flaming sex queen came breezing in with her entourage; she was graciousness itself as she kissed Vic on the mouth and cooed all over Steve in her Georgia drawl. "Why, Vic Berton, you double-crossin' cornfield rattlesnake, *Wheah* did you *evah* dig up such a *chahmin'* little wife?" and immediately made a play for Bix. "Hey now, ain't that that cute li'l trumpet player used to come out an' sit in with you at that roadhouse, Ca'lisle honey? My body an' soul if he ain't pretty-lookin'! Introduce me, Vic honey," poor Steve sitting there so lost and mournful. Bee wasn't exactly subtle.

To my great satisfaction Bix showed no interest in adding his scalp to Bee Palmer's collection, being too busy having shoptalk with the musicians. Bee as always dominated the scene, flirting and carrying on with Vic as though Steve weren't there. Steve got the message. She excused herself even earlier than usual, and refused to let Vic or even me walk her back to the cottage.

The Barn really jumped that night. Bee made Vic play drums, and angry as I felt, I couldn't help a thrill of admiration as I watched him drive that band like a string of freight cars. Bix outdid himself, playing *Original Dixieland One Step*, with the dancers going wild. Vic and Bix playing fours—wow! The way Vic made each of his four-bar breaks into a catapult that launched Bix into *his* four bars, like a steel spring—damn! The crowd cheering them on, waiting for the next one, breathless, the joy swelling from hundreds of throats like the roar from a fight crowd when some-body lands a solid punch. I stood next to Moore-Moore, yelling with the rest, two half-ass drummers watching the real thing. God! Even Bix had that smile on his face as he turned each time to watch Vic take his four, horn ready at his little red mouth to pick right up after him.

I'll say one thing for Bee Palmer: there was no bullshit when it came to jazz. She followed every note with intensity, and when they came back to the table after the set she grabbed Bix and Vic, near tears, and said in a choking voice, "Oh shit, man, are these two a couple of jazzin' fools? Ain't they a couple of jazzin' *fools?*" and everyone laughed again.

Joe Frisco said, "Hey, everybody, how ab-b-b-bout m-m-makin' Miss Bee s-s-s-sing some b-b-b-blues, right *now!*" The crowd took up the cry, which spread to the farthest corners of the Barn: *"Bee —Palmer! Bee—Palmer! . . ."*

Bee was in her element. She swayed up to the stand with a drink in her hand—they loved her for that—the crowd pressed in as close as they could and still leave her room to breathe. I forgot my animosity as she belted out the blues. (There were no mikes in those days—you had to *sing.*) She had 'em eating out of her hot little hand: *You may be fast, but your mama's gonna slow you down,* putting a funky growl into it like a real black blues shouter, Bix filling in behind her real nasty, using a derby hat as a mute. The crowd ate her alive. You have to picture this blazing blonde standing there half naked, her delicate beauty and amazing body as though offering themselves to all, wailing *Don't You Want to Touch My Mojo?, Eagle Rock Me Papa Till I Can't Stand Up,* and Bix and the band smearing and growling behind her like seven gutbucket blacks from a nigger whorehouse. . . . Bix wrapped it up by going into his intro to *Jazz Me Blues,* a Wolverines favorite, and Bee fell right in, screaming and pleading, *Yes baby jazz me, Oh honey come on and jazz me,* her gorgeous pelvis suiting the action to the words, and then into her world-famous shimmy, shaking her lovely shoulders and quivering breasts at that frantic tempo.

I really feared for one mad moment that the crowd would inundate her in a mass rape. It was really no more than a "shake dance" such as you'd see in any club floor show, but Bee had more to shake, and did it besides with a real dancer's grace and unsurpassed intensity. She *meant* every quiver; it was the nearest thing to a publicly exhibited orgasm ever seen—each man and woman in that crowd *knew* he or she was being symbolically fucked into a trance.

There were hoarse shouts of MORE MORE MORE like a collective cry of pain, but Bee Palmer always knew when to leave 'em hungry; with a burning glance all around, then lowering her eyes, she swayed the celebrated hips back to our table through the maddened mob, flanked by Vic and the others. I mentally thanked Fate that Gladys hadn't been there to witness Bee's triumph.

I undressed in the dark and flopped into bed. I was almost asleep when I heard Gladys's voice, clear and startling in the silence:

"Ralph? Where is Victor?"

I hesitated, just a heartbeat. "He . . . he went to see them off at the parking yard."

Silence. "Is he drunk?"

Again I tried to think what I ought to say.

"I guess so. Kind of."

She said no more. I don't know how long I lay waiting. The next thing I knew it was gray dawn. A crash of some kind had jolted me awake. I could hear Vic giggling and mumbling inanely, heavy creaking of the bed, then Gladys's voice loud and stark, *Get away from me, you stink of her!* and again Vic's silly laugh. . . .

It must have been well past noon when I came down to the beach. Gladys was swimming far out on the blue water. Some of the guys were lying on the sand. Voynow and Jimmy were batting a water ball back and forth. They said Bix was still sleeping.

I ran and hopped down across the blistering sand and plunged gratefully into the mild surf, swimming under water, out toward Gladys. When I surfaced she lifted her head and waved. She seemed to be O.K., her pale champagne hair floating behind her in the waves. We horsed around as usual; she'd just been teaching me the Australian crawl and gave me some more pointers now, telling me to keep my head down, don't splash so much, don't let my legs drop. . . .

We lay down on the blanket. "Where's Vic?" I asked.

"Went to Chicago," Gladys said. "Then he has to go to Indianapolis, to see some man Joe Frisco put him on to, about the band. He won't be back till Friday." Her voice told me nothing; she behaved as if nothing had happened.

I opened my new *American Mercury* and read to her for an hour (I had undertaken her "education"), making her laugh at H. L. Mencken's barbed comments on the "American booboisie."

"There's Bix," Gladys said, shading her eyes and pointing.

Bix had finally come out, and stood blinking in the sun in a swimsuit a couple of sizes too small. It seemed to be his fate to wear garments that didn't fit him.

I yelled. He trudged over to us, blankfaced and disconsolate.

"You look like an accident going somewhere to happen," I remarked (Vic's latest gag). Bix shrugged.

"Nothing a shot of firewater wouldn't cure," he said, yawning. "Got anything in the house?"

I said no, pinching Gladys's arm to give her a high sign. "Come on, I'm going in the water," I said. "Come on, Gladys." Bix looked doubtful, blinking at the sparkling water. "Come on, Bix, I want to show you my crawl."

"I'd like to crawl into a hole and pull it in after me," Bix said, as Gladys and I more or less dragged him down to the water.

He plunged in after us, and obviously felt better. He started horsing around, ducking us and splashing. "Wow, this feels great," he said. "It's hot as horse piss in that cottage," he murmured, first making sure Steve was out of earshot. We joined Dick and some of the others near the shore, tossing the water ball around.

Bix followed us up to our umbrella. Gladys made him take a sandwich, which he ate with obvious enjoyment. "When was the last time you ate?" Steve asked.

Bix scratched his head. "Search me, kid. Maybe suppertime last night."

"You better take care of yourself, Bix," I said. "You're not looking too well. You can't live on alcohol and orange juice, you know."

Bix looked at me sarcastically. "Jesus, Frenchy, you too? You sound like Voynow."

We all glanced involuntarily at Dick, who was standing a little away from everyone doing his exercises.

"He seems to be in pretty good shape," I said.

"Yeah," Bix conceded. "Yeah, kid, maybe you've got something there." He stretched out on the blanket next to me and picked up my *Mercury,* leafing through it curiously. "Isn't this fella Mencken supposed to be an atheist?" he asked. I gave my standard answer. "All intelligent people are atheists," I said.

"Wow," Bix said, smirking at me. "I guess that lets out saps like me, huh?"

Gladys was shocked. "Ralphie, don't you believe in *God?*" she cried.

"Do you believe in Santa Claus?" I countered.

"You . . . don't believe there's *anything* or *anyone* . . . up there?" she gasped, like a wounded bird, indicating the heavens.

I was extremely fond of such questions. (My style had been formed in great measure on Joyce's Buck Mulligan, an early hero —e.g., this little exchange in the first episode of *Ulysses:*

> The doorway was darkened by an entering form.
> —The milk, sir.
> —Come in, ma'am, Mulligan said. Kinch, get the jug.
> An old woman came forward and stood by Stephen's elbow.
> —That's a lovely morning, sir, she said. Glory be to God.
> —To whom? Mulligan said, glancing at her. Ah, to be sure.
> Stephen reached back and took the milkjug from the locker.
> —The islanders, Mulligan said to Haines casually, speak frequently of the collector of prepuces.)

"What do you mean by 'up'?" I asked. "Don't you know that where you're pointing now will be 'down' in another twelve hours?"

Gladys didn't follow. I explained.

"Hey, kid, that's pretty neat," said Bix.

"But if there's no"—it was hard for her even to say it—"no God, why is it everyone else believes there is? Can *everybody* be wrong?"

"Certainly," I said. "Everybody once thought the world was flat."

"Hey, that's right," Bix said, laughing. "How about that?"

"You believe in God," I said, "because your papa and mama did. You think whatever your parents thought."

"Doesn't *Mummy* believe in God?" Steve asked, aghast.

"Of course not," I said. "Papa and Mama are both socialists—atheists."

"Well, that makes us even, I guess," said Bix simply. "You think like *your* parents do—same as us."

Gladys tittered.

"That's really not the point," I said, getting a bit red. "The point is that the whole religion business is just a big fairy tale, like magic and all that crap."

Gladys gasped. "Oh, Ralphie! What an awful thing to say!"

"Ever think about this?" I said. "When you learn arithmetic, they give you *proofs* of everything they tell you. When you learn science, they give you the proofs. But when they teach you religion, all they tell you is 'Have faith, my child!' It's a sin to ask too many questions. Didn't you ever wonder why?"

Gladys looked up quickly. "Gee, that's so," she said. "Our Sunday school teacher always said that."

"Yeah," Bix said with unexpected feeling. "Leave the thinking to them."

I smelled a couple of converts, and brought out my most crushing arguments. . . . When Bix left, I had the satisfaction of feeling I had, as they say, put a flea in his ear.

All during "supper" I could see Gladys had something on her mind. Over dessert she said to me out of a clear sky, without raising her eyes from her plate, "Do you think married people should be unfaithful?"

I guess it was the first time I'd ever consciously pondered that insoluble problem.

"Well," I said. "It's like . . . Prohibition; you're not supposed to drink, but everybody does."

She was silent a long time. "Do you think a . . . a woman has as much right . . . that way . . . as a man?"

"Jesus!" I exploded, the outraged socialist. "I should hope so! God! What a question, Steve!"

She just squeezed my hand and said, "You're sweet."

We sat on the porch watching it get dark over the Lake. The shore runners appeared (where did they stay in the daytime? I wondered), darting in & out, just clear of the incoming wavelets, like little white puffs of smoke in the violet dusk. I couldn't look at her. She brought her knitting out and sat close to me in the swing. I wished something terrible would happen, the cottage would catch fire or an earthquake or something. It was really dark now.

"Aren't you going over to the Barn tonight?" Steve asked finally.

"I don't feel like it tonight," I said shortly.

"Oh, good," said Steve. "Neither do I."

When I heard the first mosquitoes I went into the house and started fooling with my crystal set. Usually all I could get was static, and one lousy Chicago station that played ricky-ticky "society" music—we must have been in a dead spot because of the dunes or something—but tonight I suddenly tuned in KDKA, Pittsburgh, loud and clear.

Gladys was at my door watching me. I pretended I didn't know she was there, and fussed with the crystal. She came in then, and leaned over close to me when I let her listen on the earphones. I could smell her hair, feel her warm breath. She listened awhile and kept asking me about how I'd built it and said something about how smart I must be. She was strange; I couldn't figure her out tonight. All I knew was being so near her was driving me nuts.

I was feeling pretty strange myself. I thought about going down for a swim all by myself—Gladys was already in bed; I could hear it creaking when she turned. I sat up in bed and pictured myself walking down to the shore, but the idea of all that black water out there made me shiver. I read a little while, then put out the light. I could just hear faintly the music from the Barn. I thought I could distinguish Bix's clear round tone, floating over everything. . . . I slept at last, an odd feverish sleep.

I know I had some maddening dream about Gladys . . . in my arms . . . under water . . . Gladys murmuring in my ear, *Oh, you're sweet, you're sweet.* . . . In my dream I knew I was dreaming and terribly anxious not to wake and lose it, lose the heat of her body that I could feel right through the water, *Imustntwake* I thought, but oh christ her hands slipped downward, I felt her soft firm fingers close around it . . . oh, not yet, I mustn't wake. . . .

Slowly I opened my eyes. Dark, dark, dreamdark . . . but there was a faint gleam of starlight right before me. The gleam was Steve's eyes; my own were looking into hers—and it was no dream; her fragrant face was an inch from mine, I could feel its heat, her breath whispering into my very mouth *O sweet Ralphie o my God help me Ralphie I can't stand it I can't be alone I can't* and her hot hot hands trembling fingers caressing my loins . . .

The sky was powdered with stars over all the vast blackness of the water; a fresh breeze stirred our hair, still wet with sweat. It was a little after midnight; we stood on the front porch naked, calm, drinking in the night, the cool, the stars. Far out on the black horizon a tiny row of yellow points of light glimmered, wavering, hung motionless—a ship bound up north for the Mackinack Islands. My arm around her warm slim waist (all at once I was her kid brother again, a head shorter, showing off), I pointed out the Milky Way, the first-magnitude stars, told her how some got their names, showed her how to find Polaris from the two pointers in the Big Dipper, by which sailors since the days of the Phoenicians had been finding their way, just like the ship we were looking at now. When I told her that the light from Rigel that we saw tonight had started on its journey nearly five and a half centuries ago, her eyes filled with tears. Awe and wonder and starlight shone in them as she pressed my head to her breast and murmured *O Ralphie I'm so ignorant, what do you see in me!*

What did I see in you! If I lived to be a hundred, I'd never meet a more marvelous apotheosis of pure femaleness than plain quiet beautiful incredible Gladys—this pagan love goddess from the antique groves of Aphrodite, mysteriously reborn and set down twenty-three centuries later in a little two-story frame house at 3317 Kedzie Boulevard, Chicago, Illinois, disguised as the daughter of a respectable carpenter. . . . What did I see in you! O Gladys, Gladys, your fragrant loins could have given lessons in love to Venus! How could I tell her, my mouth filled with her sharp perfume, my nymph, my Aphrodite, my teacher. . . .

(Later that morning I would read to her the opening sentence of Maupassant's most famous tale:

She was one of those pretty, charming young ladies, born, as if through an error of destiny, into a family of clerks . . . for women belong to no caste, no race; their grace, their beauty, and their charm serving them in place of birth and family. Their inborn finesse, their instinctive elegance . . . are their only aristocracy, making some daughters of the people the equal of great ladies.

Her gray eyes wide with wonder: *O Ralphie! Do you mean that?* Her look at that moment was payment for a lifetime of devotion.)

When I rose from my knees, aching, stiff, burning, the ship's lights had disappeared; shivering, we went back into the cottage, back into my strange and marvelous new life.

20

**JAZZING IT
UP AT SKIPPY'S**

Midafternoon.

We emerged, a little light-headed, into the blinding sunshine, stumbling down to the bright blue water. That onshore breeze was still blowing. Pounding surf, with a few whitecaps showing; Gladys cautioned me not to venture out too far. The Lake was notorious for its treacherous undertow.

I wondered where they thought we'd been. The whole band was down on the beach, Dick doing his barbell stuff for an admiring ring of teen-age boys out from Gary for the day; Bix too, sitting by himself with his back against an old ship's timber half-buried in the sand, bleached silvergray in the sun, his horn pointed down between his bare feet, running those triplets and arpeggios. The others were giggling and passing a joint around, laughing it up. Somebody had the Sunday funnies from the *Herald-Examiner,* reading them aloud as well as he could manage, weak with laughter. He'd come to a balloon and try to read it, and break up in such a laughing fit that he couldn't get it out for a couple of minutes, which would start everyone off again. I don't know if they'd even missed us, and didn't give a damn. The way I felt about our little secret, I was ready to hire a skywriter. The message would have been that I owned the world and everything in it worth owning. The central feeling—partly an illusion, no doubt—was that *I didn't feel like a kid any more.* Difficult to define, but palpable, pervasive as an elixir in my veins; a sureness, a feeling that *I knew something now*—about myself, about her, about all women and men really; I had tasted the outermost limits of pleasure, pleasure so intense it was an agony; it had been given me, and I had given it, again and again, until nothing else existed; again and again had transgressed the borders of sanity, crossed over into the only paradise realistically accessible, here on earth; again and again, until it had become a rightful possession. Had I been a Bible reader then, I would have understood the parable of Eden: I had eaten of the Tree of Knowledge, and nothing ever again could take it from me. And here was Eve, walking at my side through the sand, human, touchable—runner-up in the Interscholastic Fifty-Yard Free-Style Swim, West Side High Schools Division, Cook County (1921); my big sister, my Aphrodite, my bride.

I suppose it must have been a Monday, because it was the band's night off. We all stayed down on the beach, laughing and carrying on. There was a conspiracy to throw everybody, one by one, into the water, except "Muscles" Voynow, as Bix christened him that day, who was just too much man to tackle, even for that wild crew; everyone else got it, though, including Bix, who wasn't wearing bathing togs; he was tossed in in shirt, pants, and shoes, and came out swearing and flinging sand. Gladys and I were grabbed and thrown in together, which may have been a tacit recognition of something. Voynow as a rule disapproved of such horseplay as "dangerous," giving it his darkbrowed disapproval from a distance; but he was pretty busy himself, showing the fine points of weightlifting and gymnastics to one handsome teen-ager, which necessitated considerable contact with the Body Beautiful, Moore-Moore kidding him a bit and yelling, "Hey, champ, take it easy on the cradle," others placing mock bets on whether Dick would succeed in cutting the chosen one out of the acneous herd.

The next thing we knew, Bobby and Moore-Moore had disappeared somewhere without our noticing, because all of a sudden we heard a wild honking and sputtering, and one of the old jalopies owned (jointly, I imagine) by the band—I think it was a Reo six—an open touring car with the top down, came barreling down toward the beach between the dunes; one of them was driving, the other madly punching the klaxon, *ca-yoo-gah! ca-yoo-gah!*

"Come on, pile in, everybody!" they yelled. Moore-Moore had a police whistle that was one of his favorite toys, and he was blowing it now, yelling, "O.K., everybody into the bus!" like a camp counselor.

Did you ever see ten alleged adults packed into and hanging onto one Reo touring car? Steve was on Voynow's lap ("He can take the load!" they said as they dumped her there), everybody stacked like cordwood, Voynow's new friend and me standing on the running board, ready to roll—only she wouldn't roll. The rear wheels spun uselessly in the sand.

Moore-Moore shrilled his whistle again. "Everybody out! Stand by to lighten cargo!" We jumped off in all directions like fleas from a dog. Bobby tried again.

"Everybody push!"

We pushed and shoved, the tires shooting sand up into our faces, but the minute we stopped pushing, the car stopped; the wheels buried themselves anew in the sand.

Bix had the answer: "Let the air out of the tires, dummy." Four minions leaped to the task, there was a chorused hissing from four valve stems, a smell of stale rubber was wafted to us.

"Not too much—you'll ruin the tubes!"

"That's enough, try it now!"

The car struggled an instant, then took off like a stone from a slingshot as the rubber took hold, all of us running after it yelling, climbing in on the run. Somebody passed a flask around. Everybody (except Voynow) had a swig from it by the time we got down to the road. "Not too fast on these soft tires—you'll have a blowout!" warned Voynow as Bobby got her up to about thirty. The old Reo was swaying and careening anyway because of the soft tires; Bobby took the cue and began snaking it back and forth like some mad amusement park ride, everybody roaring in unison on each swing of the car, the two of us on the running boards hanging on for dear life. We passed cars coming the other way and yelled nonsense at them—"Whoopee!" "So's your old man!" "So's your Aunt Mabel!" "So's your anchovy!" "California, here we come!" "Got a match, mister?"

"This is a hell of a party!" George Johnson complained, swallowing the last of the hipflask. "Where are the women?"

"We've got one anyway!" "Yeah, we've got Steve!" "Everybody kiss Steve!" Packed in as they were, everyone scrambled to plant a kiss on Steve, wherever they could get to her, including head, arms, and knees. Two old men walking their dogs peered in astonishment as we careened past them yelling, "Buy a kiss from a pretty girl! Fifteen cents—two for a quarter!"

Bobby turned and headed back for the dunes. "Come on, let's see if this crate'll make it up the dunes!"

"Get 'er up to flying speed, Bobby!"

"Full throttle!"

"Get your foot on the floor and keep it there!"

At seventy miles an hour, the two of us clinging like burs to the running boards, we took off up a steep dune and just made it to the top, started down the other side—a startled pair of nutbrown rabbits leaped out of our way, one to each side of the car, as our laughter pealed after them.

"Out of the way, rabbit!"

"Gangway!"

Slowed by the sand, we swung drunkenly up and down the dunes, without the slightest idea where we were, dodging shrubs and scrub pine. Someone had lit up a joint. Bix handed it to me in my turn, remarking, "Hell, he's always with the band anyhow, he might as well get high!" I took a deep, professional drag, holding it down in approved fashion, trying not to cough. (Except for one experiment with cubebs* some years back, this was the first smoke of any kind in my whole life.) I handed the butt on to somebody else. Two or three more drags and I was flying. Steve had taken her turn too, and was already giggling like the rest of us at every nutty joke flitting back and forth.

By the time we were pulling up by the cottages, we were pretty stoned. As we clambered out, everyone complaining—"Christ, my leg's asleep!" "I'll never walk again!" "Hey, pull my arm, will ya?" —somebody said, "Hey, I've got an idea! Let's all go sit in somewheres tonight!"

"Yeah!"

"Right!"

"Shit yes!"

"Some roadhouse or something!"

"Let's find some black-&-tan joint!"

"Yeah, man, let's find us a real good nigger band!"

"Shit, I don't want to drive all the way into Chi!" said George Johnson, "I know a hell of a place right out here on the road to Crown Point. Hell of a band, too."

"Great!"

"Let's do it!"

"Can you eat there?"

*A now obsolete cold remedy formerly sold in every drugstore, consisting of cigarettes containing the crushed green berries of a tropical plant of the pepper family *(Piper Cubeba);* often used by kids in those days, since they were both legal and harmless.

"I'll tell the cockeyed world you can eat there!" said George. "The guy that runs it used to be a Pullman car chef!"

"What time?"

"About nine o'clock," George said. "That's when they really start jumpin' there. Wait till you see some of that dark meat," he said to Moore-Moore. "Some of them dusky beauties—mm-*mm!*"

"Oh, yeah?"

"Yeah!"

"Lead me to it!"

"Do they have liquor?" Bix asked.

"Are you kiddin'?" said George. "This guy's partner is the chief of police's chauffeur. He gets all the stuff he wants, right from the warehouse!"

"Meet you in the Barn at nine o'clock."

"Everybody—nine o'clock."

"You coming, Frenchy?"

"I'll say I am!"

Bliss, bliss. I'd never ask a bigger portion than was mine that summer afternoon and night. Gladys there to reach out and touch; Bix there for me to hear; love and music were fire in my veins, making me into a new being, taller, stronger—did it show in my face, my step, my voice? (Larry Hart, who died of heartbreak, said it as well as anyone:

> . . . grand
> To be alive, to be young, to be mad, to be yours . . .
> I'm wise,
> And I know what time it is now.)

At about nine that evening, Bix and the rest were straggling into the Barn with their instruments, some still milling around the pay phone. Several girls had already materialized out of the night, including Bix's Doris. (Vic had finally talked Bix out of the paper bag routine; he now carried his horn in a green cloth drawstring bag.) A quarter of an hour later we were on our way in two or three cars. A stick of *mota** was lighted and handed around. It was handed to me in my turn without comment; I guess the new me *was* showing after all. I took my drag and handed it on to Gladys. You have to remember being thirteen to know how that felt.

A few miles before Crown Point, George pulled off the state

*Marijuana.

blacktop onto a dirt road, the kind you used to see all over then, two wagon ruts with a grass crown between, one car wide—if you met another car one of you had to pull over. We didn't meet any; just the night and the Indiana farmland, stars reeling above us and the smells of night in the country, pine, skunk, honeysuckle, cowbarn, night mist.

The dirt road wound through flats of jackpine and at last up into the backyard of an old rambling white farmhouse; the others drove up behind us. Twenty or so other cars were parked next to a rail fence; we parked there too and got out. When we shut off our motors we could hear music and laughter from within. The back door opened as we trudged up to it; a black man opened it and stepped out on the porch with a shotgun. He must have weighed three hundred pounds.

"Who there?" he called amiably. "Friend or foe?"

"Hey, Skippy!" George yelled. "What you going to do with that thing, shoot you a chicken?"

"Who you, son?" cried Skippy. "Does I know you?"

"You do when you're sober, Skippy," George said, marching up the back steps. "George Johnson. Remember me?"

"Oh, yeah, yeah! Tenor sax man! You was here last time with Freddie—Freddie what's-his-name—little bitty cat plays all that piano! . . . Man, you ain't been here in a mule's age! Well, well, come on in, come on in! . . . These your friends, George?"

The old farm kitchen was huge; black iron wood-burning range, vast iron pots and cauldrons from which came delicious odors; the wall behind it—ancient faded wallpaper, now smoke-blackened— held a stovepipe that went up and out through a scalloped tin disk. Skippy leaned the shotgun in a corner and led us inside.

The boys in the band were digging the food. "Wow–ee!" cried Bobby, who lived to eat. "Sure smells good!"

"Yes, well, you know, I always gots something cookin' for the folks," Skippy said genially, waddling ahead of us.

The music hit us with a blast as we walked through the swinging doors of the diningroom into the big main parlor. There was no bandstand, but in one corner six or eight black musicians were blowing their ass off, a fast blues; a dozen couples were dancing, some white, some black, some black and white. Some thirty tables were ranged along the walls. In an adjoining room was the bar, where a very tall good-looking black man was pouring whiskey—

from a *whiskey* bottle, something you seldom saw in speakeasies.

Skippy's little pig eyes glistened as he saw all the instrument cases. "My, my, my, my!" he chortled, "look at all these fine young musicians! You fixin' to play some?"

"If nobody minds," George said.

"Mind!" chuckled our host. "Oh, Lord. Oh, Lord. Here, let me git you somethin' to wash the dust outen you mouf. What you folks like to drink?"

"What have you got?"

"Son," said Skippy, "if Skippy ain't got it, it don't come in no bottle. Just name your poison is all."

"You got bourbon?" somebody said.

"Has I got bourbon? Yes, I got bourbon. One hunnert and twenty-five proof, bluegrass Kaintucky bourbon, goes down so smooth you think you sippin' branchwater, and then—" He struck his open pink palm with his black ham of a fist. "Wham! You is *on* your *way.*" He looked at me. "You ain't drinkin' tonight, son, is you?" It was scarcely a question.

"Only if you've got beer, thank you," I said, very offhand.

"You means near beer?"* Skippy asked.

Bix spoke up. "It's O.K. He drinks beer at home. His ma makes it, real good. He can handle it." I could have kissed him.

"Fine, son, that's just fine. You going to like my beer better than you mama's. My beer ain't homemade, son—it come fum a *long* ways off! What erbout you, young lady?"

"I'll have beer too," Steve said.

Doris said she'd have the bourbon.

When Skippy waddled away to order our drinks, I looked around the table. "What happened to Dick?" I asked.

George shook his head. "He isn't coming," he said. "I think he has other plans."

Everyone laughed goodnaturedly, and I said, "Yes, I think I saw him . . . making them." More laughter.

Bobby grinned at me and said, "Frenchy, you're the bee's knees."

I was listening to the band now. Mm-*mm*. What a beat. No white band played like that, not even the Rhythm Kings. *What was it?* I knew what Vic always said when I asked that rhetorical question:

*Beer with all but .05 percent of its alcohol removed, offered for legal sale during Prohibition—without many takers.

"They're niggers, guy—that's all there is to it." And that's all there was to it, in those days; not until the mid-thirties would there be any considerable body of white musicians on a par with blacks.

This wasn't a dressup joint. Most of the patrons were black workers from the steel mills of Gary and East Chicago. Many were in pants and shirts, clean but not fancy. The black girls at the tables were all hookers. One of them saw Moore-Moore looking her way and soon joined us. "Hey there, good-lookin', move over and buy a lady a drink." There were two white cops, in uniform, drinking at the bar. They had hung their jackets over the backs of their bar stools; it was sweating hot in the place. With their holstered .38s and cartridge belts hanging off their hips, they gave the place a Wild West air that went perfectly with the gaslight fixtures and the fancy looking whores at the tables. They gave me a safe feeling, though, a lot safer than many other speaks I had been in with Vic, where all the guns were under somebody's vest.

The band was playing *San Sue Strut.* The piano player, a chubby man who looked to be in his early forties, had been grinning over at our table, watching us digging the music. When they finished the number he came up and said to George, "Hey, white boy, don't I know you? Ain't you the fella was out here last year playin' tenor?"

"That's me," George said. "I heard you swingin' up there. Sure sound good." He introduced us all round. "Ain't your name Bobo? Bobo, this is . . ."

We made room at our table; Bobo sat down. Skippy put the bottles on the table "for the serious drinkers," bourbon, rye, Scotch, gin, beer for Gladys and me. Skippy watched my face and grinned. "You mama never made that beer," he said happily. I was looking at the label: *Münchener Brau.* "That beer ain't even Milwaukee," he said. "That come all the way from *Germany,* son." He stood a moment longer, and said, "You mind my axin' you, son? How old would you be?" "Going on fourteen," I muttered.

"Fo' *teen!*" he exclaimed. I knew I looked more like eleven.

"He's really a midget," Bix said. "He'll be fifty-two next Tuesday."

There was general laughter, and Skippy waddled off to "tend to business."

"You play some instrument, young fella?" Bobo said.

"Drums," I said. "Just studying."

"Hey! Real fine!" he exclaimed.

"He's Vic Berton's kid brother," said George.

"Vic Berton! Oh, oh, *oh!*" said Bobo. "Oh my Lord. We going to have to git him over there, right *away*. I ain't never heard Vic Berton, but I done heard plenty *about* him fum them as has!"

I laughed wryly. "Well, you're not going to hear Vic Berton tonight either," I said.

"That's all right, son," he said. "We all got to learn sometime. We got to crawl befo' we kin walk."

"Don't worry," Bix said unexpectedly. "He won't louse you up. He's got nice time." *He said that—he actually said that,* I kept saying to myself. I think my head swam for a moment. *I should leave right now. Quit while you're ahead.* I saw Steve looking at me with such pride that I once more felt there was nothing I couldn't do if I tried. *I have to play with this band.* "We've got a drummer here," I said, indicating Vic Moore.

"The mo' the merrier," said Bobo cheerfully. He was looking curiously at Bix, digging his chewed-up lip. "You plays trumpet?" he asked.

Bix nodded. I couldn't refrain from saying meaningly, "That's Bix Beiderbecke."

"Bix? Is that you, Bix?" He laughed happily. "Well, shut my mouf! I knowed I seen you somewheres before. I can't rightly 'call where it was—somewheres South Side, I don't know—you was sittin' in. Plays a co'net, don't you?" Bix nodded again.

"Whoo-ee," Bobo said, closing his eyes for emphasis. "Yes you *does*. You sho did play. I knows where it was—little joint on Thirty-seventh and State—big brown-skin fella owns it—I just can't 'call the name, but you sittin' in there, and—whoo-*ee!*" He looked around the table. "This white boy, he make *everyone* quit."

Bix smiled uncomfortably, and found nothing to say. "Bix Beider . . . how's that agin? You know I got a couple records you made, yeah," Bobo said, and then it dawned on him. "Say—is this—hey, George, is these them Wolverines?"

"That's right," George said. "We're all here except the piano player."

"Well, shut my mouf! That's right, somebody did say you was playin' with the Wolverines! How about that? Oh, yes indeed, I got them records of yours, *Fidgety Feet* and *Jazz Me*—'scuse me, ma'am. . . . Well, let's git over there and play us a couple, what you say, boys?"

They got their instruments out and walked over to meet the black musicians, who were just wandering in from the bar. There was much handshaking and smiling and shoptalk and questions—"Weren't you working last year at Jimmy Riggs's place in Cincinnati?" etc. The girls and I were left alone at the table; I looked at Steve and knew there was nothing in this world I couldn't do. She gave my hand a squeeze under the table. *Nothing, nothing.* I was itching to get at the drums. Let Moore-Moore play a set first.

While they were getting set to play I looked around the place. It was a curious fact that the black-&-tan joints, which had the most scandalous reputation in the square white world—the very term was spoken in shocked tones—were actually a lot more "decent" than ninety-nine out of a hundred of the lilywhite cabarets, at least the ones that served booze. I'd actually seen gunplay in two of the white-owned joints, and heard of a lot more; and not only the owners but many patrons were obvious hoodlums. I never saw anything like that in any of the black-&-tans. You might see a couple of Prohibition raids, or police coming in and looking around, but both management and patrons seemed almost respectable by comparison. This one was no exception. The only really toughlooking customers were the two white cops getting quietly stewed at the bar.

Another noticeable difference was the jolliness of the colored joints. There were laughter and merriment at nearly every table and among many of the dancing couples, animated talk, loud but amiable arguments with much rhetorical wagering and appealing to bystanders for support, and of course when it came to the dancing there was no comparison. Next to the black-&-tans, the whites were a pretty glum bunch. As for the music—I hardly ever walked into a joint where a black band was playing without thinking of what Vic always said on that subject: "White jazz musicians are all right as long as they know their place."

So it was tonight. Except for Bix, the difference between the way the blacks and whites swung was glaring. The colored trumpet player blew a rough, sharp, thrusting horn something like Natty Dominique,* and generally it was that kind of band, the

---

*Early New Orleans trumpeter, recorded with Johnny Dodds and others; available (?) on Milestone 2002 and 2011 and RCA LPV-558.

kind you were likely to find in any of a hundred black cafés in and around Chi in those days—only a few steps up in sophistication and polish from a country jug band. The piano player was the best musician in the band, not a great swinger by any means—he was in that transition stage between the ragtime "professors" and modern stride piano—but with an insistent, solid beat in the left hand that gave a swinging horn a lot of support.

They politely invited Bix to "call it" for the first number. Bix said *Sister Kate.* I started singing the lyric to Steve, and Skippy walked by and paused to listen a moment; then he pulled me up by the arm and walked me over to a spot in front of the band.

"Ain't no use you cheatin' the rest of my customers," he said. "Come on, white boy, let's hear you sing it!"

I sang it. The dancers crowded around close, grinning and hollering encouragement. The band really socked it. I knew right then this was going to be my night. As I got into the second chorus, Bix and the colored trumpeter did something cute; they must have fixed it up between them. They took alternate fills behind my vocal, and the contrasting styles were something to hear; the customers on the floor found it irresistibly funny, greeting each one with an appreciative shout, like the congregation of a storefront church. . . . After that number, everyone was inviting me to their table.

I got pretty stiff on that *Münchener Brau.* I don't really remember some details of that evening. I played drums, I sang, someone found me a ukelele and I did one number (I don't remember which) from my Jazz Juniors repertory—all a happy blur next morning, or rather afternoon, when I awoke and tried to recall what I had said, done, and drunk.

Some great moments stood out, though, like sequences in a film. I had one tremendous insight, while they were playing some Dixieland standard like *That Da Da Strain* or *Shake It and Break It* or *Maple Leaf Rag.* The colored trumpet player and Bix had got into one of those amicable carving sessions. Bix was "answering" his fellow musician—curiously, he usually found himself in the position of the second man, the answerer, the counterpuncher as we'd say in the boxing ring; and indeed in a very deep sense Bix's entire output was a kind of commentary. This time, the style of his "answers" was subtly different from what they'd been in the session with Paul Mares, reflecting the sensitivity of his response to the company in which he now found himself. This black guy was playing real rough and lowdown. Bix was "replying" from another level, as he had before—but now I heard it all in a new aspect, saw it in a new light.

Something came to me, not exactly a thought, too brief and too vast to be called thinking, like a lightning flash illumining for one ten-billionth of a second a whole landscape. I sensed with utter clarity something it might take the rest of my life to "understand." I couldn't have said then what it was; I can hardly do it now—it had to do with the "meaning" of jazz, and how can that be put in words?—but I must try anyway.

What was Bix saying that no other musician had ever said? Simply that *this* jazz wasn't on the bottom looking up any more. It was out on the level now, reaching for the heights; not grinning sardonically or defiantly at itself as black and poor and dirty and barefoot: *Yeah, baby, I'm ugly, ain't I, I'm evil and lowdown and funky, ain't had a bath for a year, dig me!* Certainly that kind of jazz has its own strength (what honest art impulse doesn't?), but Bix's jazz was just *music*—a different kind, to be sure, from what the "decent" people had enshrined in their concert halls, but modestly, quietly, proudly *itself*, ready now to grow new wings, develop new visions, consciously seek new riches of harmony and structure. It didn't feel compelled to act tough any more, to poke fun at lyricism and sentiment. It could be just a clear look at reality, or fantasy, or what it chose. In that sense it had joined that other music, the music of Bach and Mozart and Debussy; it had joined the gods.

The latter half of that evening remained ever after not a blank, but a kind of surrealist landscape in which time became just one more dimension, laid out flat like the others, in which before and after were relative, not absolute, terms. I recall individual incidents and dialogue—Moore-Moore disappearing for about three sets with his black hooker, and my taking over at the drums, as in a dream, while the regular drummer, joined by one of the other black girls at the bar, did a fantastically funny dance in midfloor, a kind of caricature of the cakewalk, in combination with some real funky drag dance like a slow boogie: his dancing inspired me to more and more relevant solo breaks, until soon he and I were in effect "playing fours" like two musicians, greatly to the other dancers' delight. I recall dancing with Gladys—another dream sequence, with *her* leading *me,* her gray eyes swimming just above me—fat Skippy handing us bottles of *Münchener Brau,* asking, "Is she your big sister?" and my replying gravely, "Sir, not exactly," only just managing to choke back an impulse to shout with laughter at this ingenious reply, while points of answering laughter danced in Gladys's eyes but neither of us uttered a sound. I remember being drenched in sweat after a set at the drums, then finding myself out in the dirt road with Gladys holding me up— I guess I was staggering a little at that point—pleading, "Please please don't be so drunk, Ralphie," and realizing my silly laugh sounded just like Vickie's and that thought making me suddenly sad and almost sober, and my kissing her on the neck in the dark road, then looking over her shoulder, seeing something totally incomprehensible—a dark yellow lantern that turned out to be the moon rising, like no moon I ever recalled seeing, and saying to Gladys very loftily, "Madam, your moon has arrived," and thinking it was the funniest thing anyone had ever said. I remember Gladys clinging to me in a barn smelling of horse sweat and my kneeling to kiss her "down there" as she always delicately phrased it—my forehead pressing her belly and the world spinning and spinning, and then her trying to do it to me but I was too drunk. . . .

I don't remember going back into the house but Skippy must have let us in again through the kitchen; I was ravenously hungry; Skip gave us each a bowl of chili out of one of the huge pots and we ate standing in the kitchen like two starving maniacs, the best chili I ever recall eating in a long life intermittently devoted to eating chili, including my own. We ate other things, a whole sequence of eating in that bountiful kitchen: fried chicken, chitterlings, barbecued pig ribs, an enormous pickled pig's foot in jelly, big as a horse's hoof, washed down with more beer, hot yellow corn bread right out of that woodburning oven—Jesus, was that good with the fried chicken—a slice of sugarcured ham that must have been an inch thick on a slab of that same corn bread, then homemade apple butter washed down with homemade apple cider. That Skippy was some cook; he enjoyed our enjoyment like a true artist.

Then we were inside again dancing. We danced out of the big parlor into a hall: I glanced up the stairs and up on the landing in the dark I saw Vic Moore kissing the colored girl and she was holding him "down there" and he had his hand under her skirt, which wasn't hard to do, it only came down about six inches below her hips to begin with, and Gladys saw them too and quickly looked away as if she'd seen something dirty, and Gladys asked me what I was laughing at but I just shook my head, I couldn't explain.

I don't remember leaving Skippy's. I do remember everyone standing out in the kitchen with their instrument cases and taking out money; Skippy must have charged us a lot less than George thought he should—I have a picture of George trying to press an extra twenty on Skip, and Skip laughing and shoving it back in George's pocket and saying, "You a real gentlemen, George" several times and George saying, "You know what you are, you big so-and-so," and both of them laughing and shoving, only shoving Skippy was no laughing matter, it was like pushing a freight car. I remember being secretly humiliated because Gladys had the money for us and feeling like a little brother again; and it was true —I seldom carried any because I seldom had any use for it; I resolved to see to it from now on that I had some. . . .

Then we were in the car jogging and bumping over that dirt road with George or somebody singing at the top of his lungs the refrain of "Ja-da" and me remarking to myself the profundity of the lyric—

> Ja-da, ja-da,
> Ja-da-ja-da-jing-jing-jing.

and deciding that the human race was truly unfathomable—which in turn I decided was quite the most profound insight I had yet had the good fortune to entertain. "Ralph," I remember saying to myself in the depths of the car, somewhere on the road between Crown Point, Indiana, and Miller Beach, one night in June or July of 1924, "Ralph, face it: not *everything* has to *mean* something."

Out of the darkness near me Bix's voice said, "What'd you say, kid?" I believe I replied, "I have just discovered the secret of human life." Words to that effect.

Bix said something profound like, "Oh, yeah? How about that?"

And Gladys Berton, née Steiff, my Aphrodite from Kedzie Boulevard, said nothing at all; she was asleep, her head on my shoulder, as any sensible love goddess ought to be at 5 A.M. and not being made love to.

21
LESSONS

Yet you ask on what account I write so many love-lyrics
And whence this soft book comes into my mouth.
Neither Calliope nor Apollo sung these things into my ear,
My genius is no more than a girl.

Ezra Pound, from *Homage to Sextus Propertius (The Cynthia Epistles)*

I very soon received my next important lesson in that lifelong study entitled "Understanding Women," which was that I might never succeed in doing it; and my teacher was my love, my bride, my Gladys.

Vic returned from his trip—and with his return, it was as though our love had never been. It didn't go underground; it didn't become clandestine; it wasn't regretfully postponed or withdrawn. It simply vanished, like a mirage, like a name written on water.

She greeted Vickie, quite properly, with a shower of wifely affection; and from that moment on I was just her kid brother again. I had expected her to be "discreet" of course; but it was gradually revealed to me that so far as Gladys was concerned there was nothing to be discreet *about*. Not by the slightest look or sign did she betray any consciousness of the "madness" between us, even when we were completely alone. Amazing! I couldn't believe my own ears and eyes, but after my first unsuspecting attempts to behave as (discreet) lovers will, I withdrew, baffled and bewildered. I felt like pinching myself: had it all been a dream?

It might as well have been. I had to accept it. Gladys, so far as I could see, had nothing to accept.

I suffered like that for a week or more; then it happened that Vic had to go away again for a few days; Gladys kissed him goodbye as mournfully as a loving wife should . . . and, lo! that night all was as before, my goddess had returned, her sacred flame as consuming as ever; as before, I awoke from uneasy dreams to find her drawing my very soul out from between my lips, panting, desperate—in short, Gladys.

All my attempts to discuss our relationship rationally met a stone wall—her blank incomprehension that there was anything to dis-

cuss. I soon gave up; and had to admit she had once more taught
me something: among other things, that so far as women are
concerned, men talk too much. I learned from Gladys how to shut
up and make love—*whenever necessary and convenient;* hence,
that woman is above all *practical* in these matters; it is man that
tends to be foolishly romantic.

Nights when Vic was away, I was torn between Barn and bedroom—between my god and my goddess. I resolved the conflict
by dividing my time between them; when "Steve's bedtime"
came, I'd do just what Vic would do when he was around—walk
her back to the cottage, make wild love for half an hour or so, then
back to the Barn and Bix, then to bed again and my slumbering
nymph, who loved nothing better than to have her slumbers thus
interrupted, as frequently as possible.

One of these nights, returning to the Barn in a particularly
euphoric state, I saw Bix in unusually animated conversation with
a tall, goodlooking guy about his age or maybe a year or two older.
He turned out to be a classmate from Lake Forest Academy. They
were talking about tennis; he was recalling, with enthusiasm, Bix's
legendary massacre of "Rodney"; Bix, needless to say, was mini-
mizing his own role.

This was the first I'd heard of Bix playing tennis. I felt injured.
Off and on for a couple of years, I'd been playing tennis, or trying
to; with my bias against any kind of schooling, it hadn't occurred
to me to seek professional instruction, but, characteristically, I had
gone so far as to get tennis books out of the public library; Bill
Tilden had briefly been one of my sports idols. Here I had had a
real tennis player right under my nose for months without knowing it! What a waste! I really blew my stack.

"God damn it, Bix!" I cried. "Why didn't you *tell* me you played
tennis?"

"You never asked me," Bix said, reasonably.

I shook my head. "Boy, you're something. You're really something."

"We could play," Bix said. "Have you got a racket?"

"Sure," I said. "How about tomorrow?"

He scratched his head. "Yeah, O.K.," he said, "tomorrow. I'll
probably be lousy," he added.

"Don't believe him," said his friend.

It was no use trying to get Bix out of bed before noon, but shortly after that, Gladys and I, with our rackets, were on our way over to his cottage. I'd borrowed one of the cars that morning and made a special trip into Gary to buy balls and find out where we could play; there were some good clay courts behind the local high school; the nets were up and they were in excellent shape. I was determined to leave him no excuses.

In my later years in New York I chummed around for a while with a bass player, one Buddy Jones, who in his teens had gigged around Kansas City and been brought out under the tutelage of the great Charlie Parker himself. He told me two things that stuck in my mind, and always made me think of Bix. One was Bird's answer when a lady asked him what his religion was. "Madam," he said, "I'm a devout musician." The other was what Bird's neighbors said about him there: that if you ever passed Parker's house and didn't hear him practicing, you knew he was either asleep or not home.

I heard Bix's horn now as I came up over the dune toward his cottage. He was sitting on the front steps, just out of the sun, in dingy-looking BVDs and bare feet, his cornet pointed down between his knees, running some phrase over and over. Next to him on the top step was a tall glass of what I was pretty sure wasn't just orange juice.

He glanced up as I approached, went on a minute or two with his practicing, and paused to say, "Hey, Frenchy" and take a swallow from the glass. I could smell the alcohol from where I stood.

"First thing in the morning, Bix?" I made bold to say.

Bix twisted a faint smile. "Yeah, well, you know . . ." he said vaguely.

"How about coming swimming before we play tennis?" I said.

Bix looked at me, blinking. "Tennis?"

"Yes," I said, "tennis."

"Hey, that's a good idea," Bix said. "I got a racket in there somewhere. I haven't played for a dog's age, though."

"I know. That's what you said last night at the pavilion."

He stared. "I did?"

"Yes, you did. Don't you remember? When we were talking to your friend Bill."

A flicker of recollection showed on his face. "Oh, yeah. That's right. O.K. You got a place to play?" I nodded. "What about some balls?"

I nodded again. "I took care of all that this morning."

Bix laughed then. "Hey, Frenchy, you're all there," he said.

"Come on, Bix," I said, as he seemed about to pick up his practicing where he'd left off. "It's a great day for swimming and tennis and everything. Let's go swimming first. D'you eat anything yet?"

"Eat?" he said vaguely. "No, I guess not."

"That's fine. Steve fixed up a beach lunch. Come on, get your suit on."

He smiled. "O.K., Tarzan. Let's see if I can find one to fit me in this dump."

I followed him into the "dump." It certainly was. Every time I went into one of the musicians' cottages I had a golden opportunity to compare the housekeeping of my German-trained *Hausfräulein* and three or four bachelor jazzmen. In Bix's room, there wasn't a horizontal surface unoccupied, and to find anything you'd first have to move four other things; the trick was knowing which ones to move. Most articles were apparently owned in common; in the morning, or rather afternoon, it was a case of first-up-best-dressed. Vic and Gene and I were lucky, I decided, to have women like Mummy and Steve around.

While Bix was rummaging under a bureau, mumbling, "Shit, where did I see that blue bathing suit?" I happened to glance at his bed; there was a girl in it.

"Who's that?" I asked, sotto voce.

Bix followed my gaze and straightened up. "Oh, for Christ's sake," he said. "I forgot all about Doris." He scratched his head.

"What's the difference?" I said. "She can come along. Steve's coming with me," I added, not without a private glow of "maturity." "Does she play tennis?"

"Search me," Bix said. "I guess I better wake her up." She was already stirring; she opened her eyes, and was obviously one of those people who awaken in full possession of their faculties. "Hi, Frenchy," she said at once, smiling. "What time is it?" Very together, as we'd say now.

"Time to go swimming," I said. "You, Bix, Steve, and me. Picnic lunch, swimming, and then some tennis."

"Sounds great. I'm not much on tennis, but I'll watch." She

looked just as good in daylight, and waking up, as she had at night; not one of those girls that have to spend a lot of time putting their faces on; she woke up with one.

She and Steve got along fine, though I could see Steve felt a little shy and inferior; Doris was a pre-med student at Indiana University. *Well, honey,* I thought, *I bet I know one subject Steve could give you a few lessons in.*

When we all got into the water, I purposely made Steve give me some coaching, just to show her off. Doris watched with unconcealed admiration as Steve flashed through the water like a golden seal. She seemed to skim six feet ahead on every kick, like a horizontal entrechat, every movement graceful as a ballerina's.

"That's some crawl!" Doris murmured. I made her repeat it loud enough for Steve to hear.

"You ought to see her medals," I said, though I'd never seen them myself. I only regretted there was no diving board at Miller Beach.

It was my turn to *kvell* again when we opened Steve's picnic lunch. Michelangelo painting the ceiling of the Sistine Chapel couldn't have paid more attention to detail; it was just a bigger job. It was a quality so built into her by family training that she was unaware of it. She packed a lunch basket for a hundred-yard journey down to the water's edge as if for a party of Swiss mountain climbers. The meat cut in hearty slabs, lettuce and cucumbers clean and cold, dark bread sliced paper thin (there was no "sliced" bread then); each sandwich neatly wrapped, tomatoes carefully dried and separately bagged, little jar of Düsseldorf mustard with its wooden spreader rubber-banded to it, cold pickles and home-brew and cold washed fruit, all in waterproof oilcloth on a little block of ice—and to watch Steve set it all out on a clean square of cloth, with a stack of napkins in the center, was enough to make you want to get married. Steve really didn't understand our praise; was there another way to pack a lunch, sew a button, clean a house?

We went in Doris's car, a brand-new Dodge, Bix with a pair of old pants and sneakers that reminded me again of the Rodney story, and a couple of five-year-old Spalding rackets.

Doris sat on the bench watching. Neither Steve nor I could return Bix's service with any certainty—we were lucky to get a racket on it. Watching Bix's strokes, I sensed for the first time the difference between the strenuous labors of mediocrity and the effortless ease of talent. Steve and I on one side, against Bix on the other, had all we could do to cover our court, running panting from net to baseline, yelling, "O.K. I've got it," and "Take it! Take it!", missing half of his shots, or just managing to pop them back or out of the court. Bix hardly seemed to run, but somehow he was always there, the swing of the racket timed just right, its easy sweep just meeting the ball square, rifling it straight over the net, which it cleared by inches, to a spot just inside the baseline. When he saw we couldn't handle his placements, he stood back, hitting long balls to us alternately, one to me, one to Steve, with monotonous precision, low and flat, just enough top spin on them to make them leap solidly to your racket. I never knew I could hit that good a ball, stroke after stroke. I noticed he hit them a little softer to Steve. I'm not even sure he was conscious of it, it was more a kind of instinctive chivalry that required no thought; his attitude toward women, offhand as it was, would have made it impossible, I think, for him ever knowingly to do anything to make them uncomfortable. In the time I knew him, I don't remember his ever saying anything disparaging about women; never called them "broads" or "skirts" or "frails" or any of the other belittling epithets most men used at one time or another.

After a while Steve tired and went to sit with Doris on the bench, and I told Bix I'd like to play him a set, and he said, "O.K., Tarzan, serve 'em up," flipping all the balls over to me. I told him not to take it easy, I wanted to see whether I could ever get any points off him, and he nodded and said all right.

It was ridiculous. It was the first time in my two years of tennis, I quickly realized, that I'd ever been up against what you'd call a real tennis player. His serve looked so casual, but it came whistling into a corner of the service court like a bullet; the best I could do was try to block it back, but when I did Bix was right at the net to put it away; when *I* tried to come to the net behind a shot, he invariably passed me, right down the alley line, well out of reach of my racket. The score was six–love, and I don't think I had more than four or five points in the whole set—all of them on his errors, not one of them an earned point. But how could I expect him to play his best against me? I gave him nothing to play against.

Playing a second set would have been too silly; anyhow I was winded. I asked him to give me some pointers, watch my strokes. He wasn't an inspired teacher, but after a couple of minutes he did start pointing out some obvious mistakes. Give yourself room to swing, you're crowding the ball, you're swinging too late, you're not getting your racket back soon enough, racket back, hit it flatter, racket back, don't reach for the ball, step over to it, racket back, don't stop your follow-through, racket back, don't lean over to hit the low ones, crouch down, get your racket back sooner, get your racket back. . . . (Many years later I exchanged chess for tennis lessons with Elwood Cooke, a famous pro. Doing my poor best to return his negligent backhand drives, which I usually returned everywhere but in the court, I said to him one time, "Say, Elwood, am I getting my racket back soon enough on those forehands?" To which Cooke, who had no sense of humor that I could ever detect, replied with resignation, "No, you people never do." *You people!* Alas, there was no need to ask who "we people" were. The gods who invented tennis have also fashioned, for their inscrutable amusement, two kinds of people to play it: on the one hand, the Bixes and Cookes; on the other, "you people.")

Tired but happy, as the saying goes, we drove back the nine bumpy miles of the rutted, grass-grown road to Miller Beach. Bix drove, one hand on the wheel, the other arm over Doris's shoulder. As my gaze strayed from Gladys to Bix, it struck me for the first time how many traits they shared. Quietude, self-deprecation, but for all their mute modesty, the same tough invisible core of determination to follow their fate, even when it led right away from the path marked out from childhood by family tradition; tenacity, German thoroughness . . .

Half dozing in the sun's dying heat, lulled by the jouncing car, I mused: weren't they a better-suited couple than quiet Steve and boisterous Vickie, diffident Bix and determined Dr. Doris? To my hazy consciousness came that startlingly original thought common to bright adolescents: *How strange life is!* (Stranger than I realized: I had no way of knowing that my god and my goddess would share a common fate, would be dead and gone in their twenties, and I scarcely into mine.)

Very much the man of the house, I invited Doris and Bix (after due consultation with my woman) to sup with us.

"Supper" was up to Steve's standard: a great homemade mutton barley soup, fricasseed chicken, golden-brown homefried potatoes, vast green salad, crusted rice pudding studded with currants and raisins—how she managed all that on a rickety summer-shack kerosene stove is a mystery; and she *apologized* for serving store bread!

Watching Bix put it all away, I wondered, as Mummy had, whether this kind of cooking gave him any twinges of homesickness—for his home, or even *a* home. I didn't know how to elicit such confidences; but a little later that evening there was an obliquely related conversation, instigated by Doris, who must have been having parallel thoughts.

Doris and I played chess after dinner; a cozy domestic scene, Steve sewing on a pattern in one corner, Bix stretched on the windowseat with last year's best seller *Leave It to Psmith*. Like a kid with a comic strip, he found something to laugh at on every page; after a while he laid it down to ask, "Hey, Frenchy, who is this guy P. G. Wodehouse?"

"It's pronounced 'Woodhouse,' " I said automatically. "He's written lots of different things—Broadway shows and everything. He wrote one with Jerome Kern. My brother Gene met him in New York."

"Boy!" Bix said with feeling, "He's the ostrich's underpants," and resumed his reading and chuckling. Then he was quiet, and when next we looked up from our game he was asleep, the book open on his chest.

"How do you like being married to a musician?" Doris asked Steve, looking at her very straight.

Steve hesitated—a long moment. "I . . . I was raised very strict," she began. "My folks are from the Old Country, you know, and . . ." She paused, sewing and thinking. "Vickie was the first man I ever went out with. I . . . I don't know much about other musicians, but . . . Well, I don't really understand a lot of things about them." She seemed at a loss to go on.

Doris was also silent, gazing thoughtfully at sleeping Bix; then she said, "I have this feeling that—the ones I've met anyway—they never sort of . . . grew up. I don't think I could be married to one."

Steve raised her eyes and looked at her, her gaze clouded.

"I get the feeling," Doris went on, "that raising a musician husband—keeping him out of trouble, you know—could be a full-time job. And I'll already have a full-time job, once I get my M.D."

Steve dropped her eyes and went on sewing. It's hard to know what girls are thinking, half the time.

22
END OF SUMMER

In 1905, Judge Elbert Henry Gary, chairman of the board of U.S. Steel, which he helped organize, bought the land and built the town that would bear his name. Its homes were built for the workers in the mill; its shops and churches and government were there to serve the mill. Its workers were carefully recruited from the most illiterate immigrants and black Southern peasantry; they lived in carefully segregated zones, known locally as Dago Town, Nigger Town, Swedeville, etc. Crooked salesmen and petty con men had rich pickings in such communities, where illiterate housewives could be found paying installments on a sewing machine already paid for twice over. Judge Gary's workers had a trained incapacity to question authority in any guise.

In on the ground floor of this captive community, this human gold mine, were Mummy's brothers, my uncles Dave and Louie, who, I think, opened the first bank, real estate, and construction companies in Gary. They had half the city government in their pocket, appointed their friends to judgeships and school boards, and reaped the customary rewards of good citizenship. But not content with the legitimate profits of doing business in the fastest-growing industrial community in the Midwest, they were, according to my mama, constantly hatching schemes to do a little better, in collaboration with certain foremen at the mill.

As Mummy afterward explained it to me, a worker would be sold a home on a short-term mortgage—my dear uncles' own private Five-Year Plan—and just when he had only another six or eight payments to go, he'd find himself fired. There were no jobs nearer than Chicago for illiterate Polacks and Hunkies, and foreclosures were swift and final. Mummy said some of those homes had been sold five times.

One hot day toward the end of July, 1924, a six-foot-two black millhand who'd just lost his job and his home walked into Uncle Dave's private office carrying a short piece of lead pipe under his coat, and walked out a few minutes later, remarking to the girls outside that he'd just killed their boss.

Uncle Dave didn't die, but he was never the same afterward. Whether he mended his ways along with his skull was unclear; but when the millhand told his story to a church lady visiting the city jail, she promised to look into the matter. She had heard rumors of the machinations of "those two Jews" in Christian Gary, and liked nothing better than to catch them cheating honest goyim.

That opened a can of worms which was never closed again until half the city aldermen had been fired. Uncle Louie and Uncle Dave narrowly escaped going to prison, according to my mama.

Unfortunately for us, one minor by-product of this teapot tempest was that all recent municipal projects came under sharp scrutiny. One of them was the Miller Beach Pavilion, built (by my uncles) with city money and operated for the benefit of grafting aldermen and various suppliers of everything from hot dogs to toilet paper. A freeze was quietly clamped on any further disbursements to the Pavilion, and two of the church ladies paid an incognito visit to it the next Saturday night.

They reported with relish the shameless goings-on out there: the lascivious dancing of shortskirted flappers, the ubiquitous hip-flasks, the necking in cars and all over the dunes—all this "urged on to the highest pitch of excitement by the most immoral so-called music we have ever listened to." In incredulous tones they told how many Merry Widow* boxes they had counted, just on their way back to the road. We were lucky no squares knew anything about marijuana in those halcyon days, or we might all have wound up on the rockpile. As it was, the last few pay checks for the band were indefinitely held up. We didn't get them until sometime the next spring, in New York—a lovely surprise, but right now the delay was disastrous.

Nobody of course had, figuratively speaking, a nickel to his name; money wasn't regarded by young and healthy jazz musi-

*The cheapest, and universally used, brand of rubber contraceptives, then dispensed in every drugstore and men's room. They came rolled flat, three for fifty cents, in little round aluminum boxes stamped 3 MERRY WIDOWS—AGNES, MABEL, AND BECKY.

cians as something you "saved." Why bother? Next week there'd be more; if not, a pal would "lend" you enough to get by till the next gig, or the next pal. Dick and Jimmy were the only savers, and it did them little good; as soon as the others were broke, they got it all anyway. Now they were as flat as everyone else.

A good ten days or two weeks before Labor Day, the Pavilion was no more. All the help had left, after boarding it up against the weather—winter on Lake Michigan was no joke. As though the gods had been notified by their vicars in Gary, Indiana, we suddenly got a couple of days of cold rain, enough to persuade most of the summer cottagers across the inlet to pack it in a week early. Practically the only ones left were Vic, Steve, me, and the band. Then Vic got a three-day tour with the Chicago Symphony in Saint Louis. He accepted with alacrity. We needed every nickel we could lay hands on now, with the move to New York staring us in the face. Family finances were at a twenty-year low; Gene was in trouble with his patrons; Mummy had even been desperate enough to hint to Gene that he might consider going back into vaudeville "for a little while" till we could get back on our feet. (I could just hear Gene: *"Vaudeville!* Christ, I couldn't stand that shit when I was *eleven*—you think I'd love it any better *now?"*)

Such was the situation in New York as our Miller Beach summer drew toward its close: Gene and Mummy all but stranded in a new apartment, Vic forced to wire them the rent out of his own dwindling capital. The only sure commitment Vic had in hand at the moment was the Cinderella Ballroom contract for the Wolverines, due to begin soon. Vic of course never had to worry about employment anywhere, and was already a member of the New York local of the union, Local 802, which meant he could accept employment there the moment he arrived.   .

The trick now was to arrive.

23
HOW WE GOT
TO NEW YORK

. . . led by some wondrous power, I am fated to journey hand in hand with my strange heroes and to survey the surging immensity of life, to survey it through the laughter that all can see and through the tears unseen and unknown by anyone.

Nikolai Gogol, *Dead Souls*

Dick sat crosslegged in the sand, a pad and pencil on one bulging hairy thigh; the rest of us sat or sprawled in various attitudes of patience, interest, or worried concentration, except for Moore and Bobby, who were playing catch, and Gladys, who sat hunched over a basket of socks (not just Vic's but the whole band's) under the sun umbrella with a darning egg in one hand and a needle in the other. Vic squatted next to Dick, looking over his shoulder at Dick's calculations.

"From Gary to New York City," Dick was saying, "I figure in round numbers 900 miles—actually 840, but you may have detours and so on, and getting lost sometimes—say 900. Figure an average of 15 miles to a gallon is—15 into 90 is 6—60 gallons. But we have three cars, so $3 \times 60 = 180$ gallons. 180 gallons, or to be safe let's say 200 gallons, should surely get us there. 200 gallons at an average of 18 cents a gallon is . . . $36. Add ten or fifteen for safety—say $50 gas and oil, total."

Bix had picked up his horn again and quietly gone to sit against his log to practice.

"We have to eat, and sleep somewhere," Vic said.

"Right. Suppose we average 30 miles an hour, overall. That's 30 hours driving time. We spell each other driving, so we shouldn't have to stop anywhere."

There was a chorus of agreement.

"Well," Vic said, "I'm kind of fond of beds as a rule, but I'm game."

"We have to keep out enough for Steve's train fare," Dick said. "Steve, do you need a sleeper or can you make it by coach?"

"Oh, I wouldn't spend the money on a Pullman," Steve said. "I love trains. I've never been on a long train ride. I'm sure I won't sleep a wink anyway; I'd just as soon sit up and look out of the window!"

"It's a twenty-two-hour trip, you know," Vic said.

"Oh, that's all right. I can sleep when I get there."

Vic kissed her and said, "Attaboy."

"Coach fare is $31.85, and one of us can drive her in to Chi. She'll need some food too. Figure three meals in the diner—"

"Oh, that would be a waste of good money," Steve broke in. Mama will pack enough food to get me there."

Vic volunteered to drive her home and then put her on the train to New York. Dick went on, figuring next how much the rest of us would need to eat on, how many meals, how much for possible breakdowns on the road, trying to allow for every emergency. The total sum needed, it was finally agreed, was in the neighborhood of $400.

"What have we got right now between us?"

"*Among* us," I murmured automatically. That tickled Vic Moore, who turned and threw the ball at my head.

"Get this kid!" he appealed to the world at large. "We're trying to figure out how to get to New York alive, and he's worried about our English!"

We dispersed in all directions to rummage in pockets, wallets, and purses, reassembling a short time later to pool our findings. Dick carefully made a list of each one's contribution to the common fund, which was then added to the pile in the center of our blanket. All told, including a bottle of pennies I'd been accumulating for nearly a year, it came to $59.73, leaving $340 still to be raised.

"I've got about—let's see"—Vic consulted his checkbook and did a rapid calculation—"about sixty-five dollars in my checking account—say sixty dollars to be on the safe side." There were no credit cards in those days.

"We still need, say, $300," Dick said.

"Wait a minute," Bix said. "I'll be right back." He disappeared over the dune again, and came back with ten dollars and change. He had just remembered another pair of pants he hadn't worn for a few weeks.

"I've got some money in the post office," Steve said.

Everyone looked at her. "The *post* office?"

"Sure; didn't you ever hear of a postal savings account, dummies?" Dick said impatiently.

"How much?"

"Ninety-one dollars," Steve said. "I was saving it for . . ." She hesitated. "It's O.K., it doesn't matter," she said, blushing.

"Look," Vic said, "why don't you just use that money to get to New York, and let us worry about the rest?" There was general agreement.

The blanket collection was placed in a paper bag, while Dick made a final computation.

"We ought to have another $250 to play it safe," he announced. "There are eight of us; if we can each put the bite on somebody for about thirty dollars, that'll be it. Anyone got any rich relatives?"

Vic said, "I've got two uncles who own half of Gary, but Uncle Dave's got one foot in the grave and the other on a banana peel, and Uncle Louie isn't talking to me." He got up and stretched. "All right, the telephone up at the Pavilion's still working. Let's get on it." He rummaged in the paper bag for all the change he could find, and everyone headed for the Barn. . . .

Appropriately, it was a cold, drizzly day when I said a sad goodbye to our little cottage at Miller Beach, and to the old brass bed in which I had lost so many of childhood's illusions and abandoned myself to those of adulthood.

We set out that morning in our three valiant strugglebuggies, a mildly demented cavalcade, with scarcely enough among us for gas, oil, and hamburgers, and what had been hopefully reckoned an adequate supply of booze and weed stashed under the seats. Moore-Moore's drums and trap cases, Min's tuba, and a few other instruments considered redundant had been sent on ahead by rail (on Steve's ticket, a welcome economy of space and expense); all the others were taken along on our trip, "just in case."

As for Bix, it was hard to imagine him without his horn for more than a few hours. He wasn't a talkative companion. He slept a lot; as I've said, I don't think I ever met an adult—a word I've learned to use with caution—who fell asleep more suddenly, or in more singular times and circumstances; but whenever he wasn't asleep, he usually held his little green cloth bag on his lap. The moment we found ourselves on a smooth enough stretch of highway so the mouthpiece wouldn't knock his teeth out, whenever we stopped to fill our tanks or empty our bladders, Bix would have his horn out, running his exercises, or working out some idea he'd been kicking around in his head. Everybody got pretty fed up with the exercises after a while, and intimated that a little variety would be welcome. "For cryin' out loud, Bix, will you let up on the fuckin' triplets for an hour?"

We started making "requests"—*Flock o' Blues, Tin Roof Blues, Lots o' Mama, He May Be Your Man, Copenhagen, There Are Smiles (That Make Me Happy)*. Believe it or not, after a few minutes, when he got really warmed up and swinging, you hardly missed the accompaniment; his solid sense of time created the illusion of a rhythm section behind him, his beautifully timed "changes" the illusion of stride piano chording under the melody line; all that was really lacking for the full lift and drive of great jazz was the bass. The other musicians were getting the same message, hearing the same musical wizardry—you could tell by their looks of pleasure and unspoken admiration, their appreciative chuckles as he slid into a particularly graceful turn of phrase or soared into one of his rarer funky wails of bluesy anguish—solos often interrupted arbitrarily by George's warning, "Watch it, Bix —railroad crossing" or "Watch it—bumps ahead!"

Eventually, out came the other instruments, and so did the sun. At the next stop for gas we put the tops down on all three cars "so we can hear each other," and great was the astonishment of the good burghers in the towns and villages we passed through, as our jazz caravan rolled by. We took a particular joy in startling the peasantry (as my new god, H. L. Mencken, had taught me to call them) with funky and outrageous blasts of the blues and *fortissimo* Dixieland stuff like *Bugle Call Rag* and *Clarinet Marmalade*. I don't know whether it was the sunshine, the open road, the marvelous carefree hours, the agreeable consciousness of bringing jazz to the countryside, or all of them put together, but jazz never sounded better to me than it did ringing out under that Indian summer sky, during that glorious odyssey, west to east, with Bix and the Wolverines.

I believe it was Pascal—some Frenchman anyway—who once observed that "It is of the nature of human plans not to be realized." Dick's carefully worked out budget of time and costs was destined to go the way of a lot of other human plans.

The first item to go was the "thirty-m.p.h. average." That was fine as long as George Johnson and the other drivers kept bowling down the highway at sixty and sixty-five or better. But after they all started blowing jazz en route, no one wanted to play any kind of a horn at that speed, particularly Bix with that brass mouthpiece, and the cruising velocity inevitably slowed down to half of that, cutting the average accordingly. There were frequent halts as we pulled over to change drivers so everyone could get a chance to blow; and Bix took his turn at the wheel like everyone else. By nightfall of that first day we had got no farther than Defiance County, Ohio; we'd been on the road nearly nine hours and were utterly bushed.

Conference. All three cars pulled off the road into a little grove of sturdy old maples surrounding a picturesque pond that looked like a calendar painting of the Old Swimmin' Hole. It was a beautiful warm night and *nobody* felt like driving another yard. In vain Dick browbeat them with Jeremiah-like warnings of getting stranded halfway to nowhere. He couldn't drive all three cars himself, and no one else would budge.

The stores beneath the seats were visited; out came the cans of alcohol. Soon came the suggestion for a moonlight swim, here & now, far from the madding crowd and under the greenwood tree. Off came the clothes—all but Bix's—and "everybody into the pool!", to the sound of Moore-Moore's piercing whistle.

Nothing could have been more joyous than that scene, the naked Wolverines capering about in the moonlight, splashing and ducking each other; Bix too, after the others threatened to throw him in, clothes and all; no one really drunk, just spiffed enough to be feeling no pain (that pond was icy), drunk on moonlight and youth and general hell raising and camaraderie.

My brother tried at last to bring them to order. "Come on, let's push on!"

"Oh shit, who wants to drive any more tonight? Let's sleep here!"

"Yeah, we've got blankets!"

"Choose you for sleeping on the rear seat!"

"Enough of this stuff"—gurgle-gurgle from an alcohol can—"and you won't feel *nothin'!*"

"Yeah, put a little more antifreeze in your radiator!"

Nothing is perfect. We had reckoned without the mosquitoes. I had thought they were pretty bad at Miller Beach, whenever the breeze was blowing from the inland marshes; but that was a joke by comparison. These mosquitoes must have been twice the size of our little Miller Beach pets; they came upon us suddenly, in swarms, like a plague of locusts, darkening the face of the moonlit sky; they attacked in squadrons, twenty or thirty at a time; you had no chance with them—while you were slapping one, the other twenty-nine were sinking their saws, swords, hypodermic needles, and drinking straws into your hide; within thirty seconds your body was pebbled all over with itching bumps. We got our clothes on a lot quicker than we got them off; but it was a long time before everyone stopped scratching and cursing.

"What I'd like to know," Bix asked with some bitterness, "is what those mosquitoes live on when I'm not around."

The truth is—such is youth—even the Mosquito War, which we so ignominiously lost, was "great" too, part of it all, "an experience" that we reminded each other about, laughing and shaking our heads, incredulous, long afterward.

One thing those Ohio representatives of *Culex pipiens* did for us: they prodded us forward on our eastward journey that night —they got us as far as Cleveland, which must have pleased Dick Voynow.

True, the famous schedule was threatened en route to Cleveland. With a clamor of honking from the rearward car that brought us all to a roadside halt, one of the guys (probably Vic Moore), having studied a road map, discovered that our route would pass within twenty-five or thirty miles of Sandusky.

"Sandusky!" he pleaded. "That's where this great broad lives— she gave me her phone number that time we played the dance at ————." He named some college or other. "Sandusky! Jesus, we'll practically be going through it in a couple hours."

Dick tried reasoning with him. "For God's sake, do you know what *time* that'll be? It's after ten *now*. Anyway what are the rest of us supposed to do while you go chasing off after this girl? Assuming of course that you can find her."

"You don't understand," was the reply. "This gal is a real jazzer; and I never got to do it, because she had this God damned six-foot football player with her—she had to sneak her number to me when he was in the john. *It's a sure thing!*" His voice broke with emotion as he uttered the sacred words.

There was a chorus of sympathy from his fellow bandsmen.

"Come on, Dick—let the poor guy get laid!"

"Yeah, Dick, this is a serious matter!" said my brother, not really kidding.

"Yeah, Dick, how would *you* like it?"

It was the name as much as anything else that intrigued them. "Sandusky! Jesus, how can you turn down a broad from *Sandusky?*"

"What's her name?" Vic asked. "How come I overlooked her?"

"Wait a sec! I'm looking for it!"

"I bet you lost her number!"

"Are you kidding? Lose her number? You ought to *see* this jane —Christ, what a pair of tits! I almost lost my mind when she came over and . . . Here it is—Eileen McDuffy!"

"Shit, that's no good! Why not McClusky?"

"Right! McClusky from Sandusky!"

That settled it. From that moment on, her name was McClusky (from Sandusky). "On to Sandusky!" they cried.

Dick gave in, reluctantly. "Compromise," he said. "When we get close enough you try telephoning her—we haven't got any money to waste on long distance calls."

The map was consulted again.

"Fremont, I'll call her from Fremont—that'll be practically a local call."

"We don't go through Fremont," said Dick.

"That's what you think," said Moore-Moore (or whoever it was). "You didn't see the *tits* on this jane."

Dick sighed. "All right, Fremont. Come on, for God's sake, let's get going."

At Fremont we finally found one phone, in an all-night drug-store. (Yes, Willie, they used to stay open all night.) We waited eagerly outside, cheering his entrance.

"Go get'm, baby!"

"We want McClusky!"

He came out in two minutes, the picture of gloom.

"D'ja get her?"

"Huh. I got her *father.* Guess what? Guess where she is? Guess where she's been *all summer?*"

"A whorehouse in Saint Louis?" asked my brother Vic kindly.

"Working in Miller Beach?" asked Jimmy.

"Practically. *Chicago.* Can you feature that?"

"Chicago! For Christ sake, you could've been seeing her every night!"

"Jesus! Chicago!"

"All right, fuckit. Let's go."

"Yeah, you'll catch McClusky on the way back!"

"McClusky from Sandusky!"

For months after, "McClusky" or "Sandusky" was enough to cause giggles; her name became the symbol of almost-but-not-quite-getting-it, the girl you thought you had but it turned out different—a common enough occurrence, alas! in this complex world. . . .

No, we simply refused to go any farther than Cleveland this night. The supposedly foolproof idea of drivers spelling each other, nonstop, broke down at once; between the hilarity at the Old Swimmin' Hole, the mosquitoes, McClusky, and the freely poured antifreeze, we were lucky to make it to Cleveland, which we must have reached long after midnight. I was asleep by that time; my memory is a blur of several shabby hotel lobbies, a bare electric bulb hanging in the middle of a room with peeling wallpaper, and four of us—Vic and his hernia scars glaring whitely, Bix, and somebody else—in two enormous beds that rattled and creaked with every move we made—then oblivion.

Next morning I couldn't wake up; the first thing I recall was Vic literally carrying me over his shoulder down a long flight of carpeted stairs and dumping me into the car. I woke up at breakfast, some place out on the lake road, like an old farmhouse, a motherly woman bustling around getting us ham & eggs, nine coffees? toast? Looking out the window, at Lake Erie, she pointed and said, "Yep, that's Canada over there, if'n you could jest see forty mile. You're closer t' Leamington here than you are to *Dee*-troit."

Vic and Dick Voynow paid the woman and then sat at the cleared table counting up what was left of our money. We were getting dangerously low.

"Vic," said Dick earnestly, "we can't do any more of this! We've got to try to stick to our schedule from here on! No more sleeping over. We simply must spell each other at the wheel, and sleep the best we can in the between times when we're not. If we do that from now on, we should be in New York by tomorrow night the latest."

"I'm with you," Vic said with equal earnestness.

The first unscheduled occurrence was a sixteen-mile detour, somewhere east of the Pennsylvania border, near a city called Meadville or Meadowville. We were up in the mountains now; the air was quite chilly, we had to stop and unpack sweaters and gloves. We came off the detour and had no idea which way we were heading; the map was no help—nothing on it matched any road signs; we found ourselves in a wilderness where there was no one to ask. Road maps don't tell you about detours; they don't tell you that from here to here may look like an easy thirty miles on the map, but between them are two or three ridges sixteen hundred feet high, with your road crawling up, down, and around until the thirty gets to seem more like eighty. They fail to tell you how to recognize right and wrong turnings and forks—before you know it, you're good and lost. The few human beings we met on the road—walking or driving heavy wagons drawn by old farm horses—gave us directions we found we couldn't follow.

I don't know how many hours we crawled in and out of those roads, following signs to places we saw on the map—names we never heard before or since: Spartansburg, Saegertown, Centerville, Titusville, Hydestown, Guys Mills, Slippery Rock. The sun was behind some peaks as we finally got into a goodsized town called Oil City, bustling with oil wells and machinery, hardfaced men, and money; a hamburger in that town cost 75¢—five or six times what it cost anywhere on the road. We'd planned to have dinner there—we were all starving—but one look at the prices, in their plainest-looking eatery, made us change that plan in a hurry.

This time we knew enough not to try to head east; we settled for Pittsburgh. At least we knew we'd be able to eat there.

That was a memorable meal, in a little Italian family restaurant across from a railroad freight yard. When we walked in, the first thing we saw was an old upright against the wall. Without a word, without going to the john or washing his hands, Bix walked up to it and sat down and started playing.

It must have been past the railroad men's supper hours; there was nobody else in the place but the family, eating their own supper at a table in back. One of them was a girl about my age, or a year older—it was hard to tell; she was small and slightly made and dark all over: black hair, black eyes, face brown as a little hazelnut; but those eyes! She was the first to get up and go over to the piano and listen. Bix was fumbling through *A Pretty Girl Is Like a Melody*, putting his own odd notions into it, softly swinging, and *April Showers, Say It with Music, Do It Again, When My Baby Smiles at Me*—funny mood he was in, all these sweet tunes, but in his hands they had a queer edge to them; I knew what it was, too; I had sat enough hours on our couch at Argyle Street listening and watching him getting that edge together, and all summer long at Miller Beach doing something else with it on his horn—after one touch of the keyboard on that "summer resort piano" he had drawn back in disgust, and would never touch it again. Now he was making up for a lot of lost time.

The whole family was standing around the piano now, including Papa, who had finished taking our orders. When Bix stopped and looked up, the old man said in a rich Neapolitan accent, "Young-a man, you play-a nice, real-a nice." There was a heartfelt murmur from the rest of the family. Pretty soon the rest of the band had their instruments out. They played, ate themselves silly, drank good red wine out of coffee cups. The place at some point or other had begun to fill up with watchers and listeners, all men, some of them big and beefy, some short and squattylooking, all with rough hands burned reddish-brown in the sun, most of them wearing the pinstriped caps of railroaders, like the blue-&-white ticking of old pillows. After a while every one of them was holding one of those coffee cups. Brother Vic had rustled up an old leather suitcase somewhere, Vic Moore was carrying his sticks and brushes, and the two Vics were taking turns on the suitcase; Dick was on piano now, Bix was blowing hard, with his eyes shut. Some of the railroad men were dancing with each other, and I heard Dick talking to the old man, who was leaning over the piano, the old man saying, "Whats-a mat', you craze? I no take-a no money from-a you boys!"

She must have felt me looking at her, all the time we were in there. When I took my turn at the suitcase, I felt her looking at me; it didn't make me play any worse. Once I glanced up after getting off a sweet lick, and looked straight into her eyes. What eyes. Jet black, with a peculiar burning light deep in them, not a smile in a mile. She made you shiver when you looked at her.

Alas, that's all there was to our story—almost all. There was a last scene . . . very short. We were piling into our three old cars; it must have been ten-thirty or eleven by that time. We were full of the best wine and spaghetti and lasagna and veal parmigiana I could

remember. I stalled about getting in; I was waiting for her to come
to the door. She did, taking her time about it, with a slow, swaying
step I felt right in my groin. This time our gazes met and held. She
stood leaning against the doorframe in the weird light from the
streetlamp, her body silhouetted against the yellow interior. I
tried to think of some excuse to go over to her, and couldn't, and
then, probably because I'd had enough of her papa's wine, I simply
walked over and stood staring at her thin brown bony face; all I
could really see were those eyes, the faint bluish lights burning in
them, tiny reflections of the streetlamps, almost lost in the jet
blackness. You know Anouk Aimée's face? Hers was like that.

She said, "Where you going now?" very low.

I said, "New York."

Silence. "New York City?"

I nodded.

"You live in New York City?"

"Yes." Pause. "What's your name?" I asked.

"Angelina." Pause. "You leaving right now to go to New York
City?" I nodded, and she said, very very low, "You have to?"

Oh, Christ. I nodded, unable to speak. Christ. They were calling
me. I heard Vic's voice: "Come on, guy, pile in, let's go."

Without knowing I was going to do it I reached out and took her
hand. It was hot as a radiator. I swear I felt something flow up my
arm and into my body like an electric current . . . a terrible,
terrible moment, pure agony, and then a sharp pain as she sunk
her nails into my flesh so that I almost cried out; she clung to my
hand an instant more like that while I stupidly stared, trying to fix
her face in my memory forever.

Papa and Mama appeared in the doorway behind her, smiling
and waving and calling good-byes. She dropped my hand. I waved,
dazed, and got in the car and Vic reached over and snapped the
door shut. I made a careful mental note of the sign over the door
—HOME STYLE RESTURAUNT *(sic)*—and the number, 1172. (1172
what? I remembered the name of that street for . . . five years? ten
years? But that was forty-nine years ago.) Johnson or whoever was
driving put her in gear and stepped on the gas, and we moved
away, waving. When I looked back, Angelina was still standing
there, motionless, leaning so sinuously against the doorframe;
fourteen years old, maybe fifteen at the outside. For years I was
saying that address to myself, picturing those burning black eyes,

remembering the nailmarks in the flesh of my left hand, calculating how old she'd be now. I never did get back to Pittsburgh. As someone has well said, it's the things we don't do that we later regret.

That night was pure hell for me; I don't know about anyone else. Cold, bumpy; more crawling up and down mountains; somebody (Vic?) tucking a blanket around me. . . . Just before dawn I slowly awoke to the sound of soft music. It was warmer again, almost balmy; I struggled out of my blanket. The moon must have just set, or maybe the sky was starting to gray with the diffused light of predawn; only the first-magnitude stars were still clear. We were rolling through a sleeping village, just one row of ugly sooty two-story framehouses, as alike as slices of bread, lining both sides of the road, their backyards with washlines and junked cars right up against the steep sides of the mountain pass we had come down. There is nothing more depressing than these country slums. Somebody gave me an apple.

A few miles farther on . . . five-thirtyish, full dawn; in the sky ahead of us, at the end of a long valley of steep ragged hills, premonitory streaks showed where the sun would shortly be coming up. We were running slowly between the blackened wastes of a working coal mine; the hills scarred with cuts, metal scaffolding with tall towers, huge pulley wheels rotating back and forth, elevators and buckets on cables emerging from the bowels of the crags to dump their loads on clattering conveyors.

Suddenly we were in the midst of a marching throng, a silent cortège of black-visaged men in caps with lights in the visors. A shift of miners was just coming off, pouring out of the ground like ants, trudging along the black road between the black hills to their black homes, like the ones we'd passed an hour before, farther up the valley. Each carried a blackened pick and a blackened metal lunchbox, the kind with a round top and carrying handle, all alike. The whole procession looked like a long double file of toy soldiers that had just been sprayed all over with black paint—face, hands, clothes, and whatever hair showed beneath their miners' caps— all somewhat roundshouldered, trudging down the long hill. Only their eyes showed through their black masks, many of them light blue, the irises gleaming whitely; passing close to them, one also saw lightcolored seams and wrinkles in their black brows and necks, tiny cracks like the dry rivulets in a clay hillside.

When we first came among them, we all fell silent, frankly staring at them as at a strange species in a zoo, rolling slowly between their ranks; those who bothered to look up at us had a look of grim humor in their sooty masked eyes, as if to say, *Take a good look, fellas, this is what we really look like, how do you like it?* But suddenly, on an impulse, somebody said, "Come on, let's give 'em a little song, for Christ sake," and we broke into *Strut Miss Lizzie,* blasting and tootling from all three cars. Through the masks the blue-&-white eye holes, astonished, widened and blinked; then the black masks cracked into grins, and some waved lunch pails as we crawled, slowing, through the denser and denser throng. We were right down in the town now; the orange disk of the sun was halfway up behind a mountain, shedding a warming glow over the shabby houses and stores just starting to open up. We pulled up in front of a dining car (they were real ones then, old railway or trolley cars hauled to a roadside spot and put up on blocks, with wooden steps added); the boys finished *Strut Miss Lizzie* on a fine high flourish, then stowed their instruments and piled out. The diner was crowded with miners; they made way for us in friendly fashion, squeezing together at tables to make extra room, welcoming us in an assortment of East European accents. "Komm on, yung feller, here is chair for you." "Seedonn, seedonn, plen-ty room. Hey, Russki, move over." "Anton, geev you chair. You seet here." Hearty eating, good company.

On learning where we were, however—Slate Run or some such name—dismay smote Voynow. Innocently following that valley, we had by insensible degrees turned northward again, and were now only some forty miles from the New York border—the far western part of the state. In the night, we had missed our way once more, by one hundred miles or so—and our treasury was approaching zero. We literally didn't have enough money or gas to reach New York City.

At this point, it was quiet Min Leibrook to the rescue.

"Western New York, hm?" he said thoughtfully. "Dick, let me have that map a second." He studied it, and said, "Gee, we're not too far from where Babe Jones lives."

"Who the hell is Babe Jones?"

Lloyd Jones III was a rich college boy—I forget where Min knew him from—fanatically devoted to jazz, who lived in his ancestral home on Keuka Lake; his family had been in the wine business that clusters around the region between Olean and Bath, New York, since the Joneses had helped settle that part of the state before the Revolution.

"He's there all year round," Min said. "He runs the family business. He always said if I ever got to this part of the country, to be sure and come visit with him for a couple of weeks."

"Sounds like you picked the right time for that visit, all right," Vic said.

"I think he's got boats and things like that," said Min.

"Never mind the boats," Bix said. "Has he got any hamburgers?"

"What time is it?" said Min.

"Seven-fifteen."

"Jesus! That's too early to call *anybody*."

"I don't know about it," Min said. "He's like . . . very conservative. He probably gets to his office about eight."

"Oh, shit, call him quick!"

"I hope this isn't another wild goose chase," Dick said gloomily. "We need every cent we've got now for gas and food—*more* than we've got."

The phone was on the wall up front by the cash register. We could hear Min trying to locate him. . . . *That's right—Jones, somewhere in the vicinity of Keuka Lake.*

"Wait till he finds out Min has eight other people with him," said Dick. "I should never have let him waste money on this call."

Min returned, radiant.

"Well?"

"He's there. He has to go to his office now, but he'll come back right after lunch. He said come ahead and just make ourselves at home. He said we could stay as long as we feel like it."

"Did you tell him we were nine people?" Dick asked.

"Oh, sure. He said, 'Great! We'll give parties for the whole neighborhood!' "

"Hey, that's all right!" said Bix.

"He also said he'd loan us all the dough we need," Min added as an afterthought.

The house at Keuka Lake was like nothing we'd ever seen before. It was a castle, set back on broad lawns and overgrown wild terraces that ran right down to one of those incredibly beautiful mountain lakes scattered all over western New York, long and

narrow—you could almost swim across it. The house was four
stories high and very irregular, having been added onto in sections
since the first part was built 150 years ago. I have no idea how
many rooms it had—I didn't think of such matters then. I'd guess
now possibly thirty. It had a greenhouse full of rare tropical plants
—Babe told us his grandfather was "a nut on plants" and had
collected them all over the world. There was a picture of one of
the early Joneses in the hall, by some famous painter who also
painted Washington or Jefferson or somebody like that. A lot of the
furniture had been in the house since it was first built, around the
time of the Revolutionary War, and looked as if six generations of
Joneses had spent a good deal of time polishing it.

One of the oldest pieces was a square piano, the kind Beethoven
played on, every square inch of surface adorned with carving,
ebony (I guess) roses, lions' heads, and God knows what else—a
museum piece. When Bix sat down to it—it was the first thing he
did—it turned out to be in perfect tune, which Bix found incredible. "Hey, this Babe Jones must be something, all right," he said,
playing a verse of *Look for the Silver Lining.* A comfortable-
looking lady of middle age came in from the hall, wiping her hands
on her apron. "You must be the young musicians Mr. Lloyd was
expecting," she said cheerfully. "I'm Emma. Make yourselves at
home. I'm just fixing a nice lunch for you. Jim'll take your things
up to your rooms."

Babe Jones was a tall, angular beanpole of a fellow, mild and
noncommittal—a young Shepperd Strudwick—soft-spoken, seemingly absentminded, but he never forgot anything for a guest's
convenience and comfort. His unemphatic manner belied a passionate lifelong attachment to jazz and jazz musicians. I don't
know now whether he had met any of the other members of the
Wolverines before—Bix in any case was a new acquaintance. He
had all the extant Wolverines records and, I soon observed, knew
them by heart. I have never, before or since, known a more unobtrusive man. He did no more to call attention to himself than the
umbrella stand in his hallway. When we got better acquainted, he
would occasionally point out to me some favorite passage in a jazz
record, some extraordinarily beautiful view around the Jones estate, but so diffidently you were hardly aware he'd said anything.

You could never have guessed from anything he said at the time,
but I'm sure now that he simply couldn't believe his luck in having

us as his guests; and that as far as he was concerned, nothing would have made him happier than to have us announce that his house suited us very well, and we had all decided to spend the rest of our lives there as his nonpaying guests.

He lived alone there with his grandfather; I assume his father and mother were both dead. I seem to remember a picture of his father in a World War I army uniform in the hallway or the library —colonel or something on that order—probably killed in action in France.

I don't think I ever was in any house, my own included, where I felt more at home, though the old man was in most ways the exact opposite of his grandson: voluble, peppery, loudly opinionated, authoritative on a hundred unrelated subjects, animated, a noisy eater and drinker and walker—he even urinated loudly.

"A *man*," he proclaimed, "should make a *noise* when he makes water. That silent pissing is all right for the ladies—it's their nature. If God had wanted men to piss quietly He would have made us squat down like the God damn women—not that I believe for one solitary instant in all this bullshit about God. If there were by any slim chance such a thing as a God in this God damn universe, why wouldn't He have shown his God damn face to me just once in the ninety-one years I've been walking around on His God damn earth? If He's there, God damn it, what the hell is He hiding out for like a God damn Blackfoot Indian stalking a wagon train? I was on one of them wagon trains, too, when I was younger than you are now. One of their God damn arrows went right through my nightshirt and pinned me right to the God damn wagon tongue. Served me right too; I knew I wasn't s'posed to be out there gettin' a dipper o' water that time o' night, but I was a stubborn little bastard and didn't want to wake my pa. I figured one little dipper o' water couldn't git me killed, but it damn near did. And the fella was suppose to be standing guard was sleepin' tighter'n my pa. We both got our ass kicked next morning, from here to Texas and back."

"Did you see the Indian who shot at you?" I wanted to know.

"Hell, no," he said with the rising inflection of all rural Southern and many older Americans. "Didn't I just say you never could see a Blackfoot unless he wanted you to? You're not paying attention, young fella. Hell, no. The only time you saw a God damn Indian would be when he came up trying to sell you something."

He was equally positive on the subject of rubber heels.

"Clump! clump! clump!" he boomed, supplying the appropriate sound effect with his own heels, which were of leather—I wonder they weren't hobnailed. "A *man* should make a *noise* when he walks—you ought to be able to tell when he's home. Rubber heels! Pfaugh! What's a *man* doin' sneakin' into his own house on a pair of God damn rubber heels—hopin' to catch his wife doin' something she oughtn't? Here I come! Git out of my way, everybody, and if you're up to anything you better quit! Clump! clump! clump!" He marched back and forth, on loud bootheels, and sat down again with a thump.

Before we all sat down to dinner the first night, he showed us mushrooms he'd gathered that day in the forest around Keuka, and at Beaver Dams: a huge basketful, twenty different kinds— huge bright orange-yellow pads as big as pie plates, tiny mouse browns with little caps on them no bigger than thimbles, with long stalks swelling out like elephant legs, and every size in between, in delicately shaded pastel hues, violets, brown grays, mustard, grayish white like dead men's hands; some so soft you couldn't pick them up without bruising them, others tough as rubber and good only for making soup. He knew them all. "And a hundred more," he growled.

"How," he roared, handing the basket to Emma, "can anybody call those tasteless white things they sell in a store mushrooms? What forest did they ever grow up in? You want to know where those store mushrooms spent their lives? In a concrete cellar! Now how the hell can anybody put those poor undernourished cripples up against a natural fungus that was born under a wood violet, grew up all spring and summer in God's green woodland—not that I believe any of that bullshit—and got pissed on by skunks and foxes, and washed clean by evening mists and morning dew, and gathered in the prime of their mushroomhood by some keen-eyed old bastard like me? Call those white things mushrooms? You might just as well sauté a cotton handkerchief and eat it."

He was one of the most magnificent specimens I've ever seen, of any age. At ninety-one, he still had every hair on his head, snow white, and a Karl Marx beard, untrimmed, that fell to below his pectorals; tall like Babe, a good six foot three, and erect as a hemlock tree; he looked as though he could, as they used to say, fell an ox with a blow of his fist; every tooth still in his mouth, complexion like a baby, fine sunbrowned skin covered all over, every inch, with a network of microscopic wrinkles; the brownish frecklelike liver maculae on his long powerful hands, covered with golden fuzz, were almost the only other physical sign of aging; he walked, talked, and leaped from his chair to illustrate a point, like a boy of twenty.

There was hardly a place you could name that he hadn't been, or else had a sufficient reason for not going to. ("Poland? Why would anyone want to *go* there? Every Pole you ever heard of that was worth a God damn left Poland to go and live someplace else —I'll give you a thousand dollars if you can name one that stayed in the God damn place!") One night he started talking about India and the Orient.

"I've met men in India," he said, "who would see through you like glass. They could look at your hand, by God, and tell you more about yourself, what you did and what you were going to do, than you knew yourself."

"They could read your future? You believe that, Mr. Jones?" I said coolly.

"Yes, young man," he said. "I not only believe it, I know it. Hell, I'm a pretty fair hand at that stuff myself, though I'm out of practice now."

"I don't believe anyone can know the future," said I. "It's a scientific impossibility. Since any event can have an effect on any other event, you'd have to know all of them to predict one of them. Astronomers haven't even solved the three-bodies problem yet; how could anyone solve a problem involving an infinite number of bodies?"

"You're a smart young feller," Lloyd Jones I replied, "but you don't understand. You have to be able to see into a man's soul. When you can do that, you pretty well know what his life'll be, and sometimes his death too. That's what I'm talking about, and not any God damn nonsense about astronomy."

"Could you see into *our* souls? I mean us here, tonight?" I challenged him.

"Shouldn't be surprised if I could," he replied offhandedly.

"Mine, for instance?" I pursued.

"All right," he said. "But you probably won't care for it. Folks seldom do. That's why I stopped doing it, years ago. Only made trouble. But you want to be convinced. You're a skeptic. You

believe only what you can see, or prove 'scientifically.' All right,
set right there and give me your left hand."

He put on his glasses and scrutinized my palm for a few minutes;
then he looked up into my eyes, very intently, for several more.
No one breathed. Finally he dropped my hand and considered me
from head to foot, as if I were a horse he was buying.

"*You* sure got a head start with the women, didn't you?" he said.

I flushed. The others stirred, looking at us with interest.

"Is that bad?" I said.

"Nothing's bad or good," said the old man. "It's what you do
with it. But you're going to get yourself in plenty of hot water
because you'll never be able to keep your pecker in your pants.
And you'll always tell yourself you couldn't help it. Couldn't help
it! There's the sickness of mankind in three words: *couldn't help
it.* What are you now, young feller? Thirteen, fourteen? Well,
you've already done things you wouldn't want everybody to know
about." He saw my gaze waver, and said, "Touched a nerve there,
did I? Want me to go on with this little reading?" he said, looking
keenly at me.

I felt Vic looking at me, along with the others. What had they
seen all summer, what had they guessed?

"I . . . sure, go ahead," I said defiantly.

"No," he said finally, "no, that's enough," and leaned back—to
my intense relief. "I told you you wouldn't like it," he added.

I managed a sickly smile. *How could he know?*

Some of the others pressed him to "read their future" too.

"Now look," he said, "I'm no God damn fortuneteller, telling
you you're going to meet a dark lady and have six kids. But there's
things you can see if you got the right kind of eyes—that's all."

When he got to Vic, he shook his head in wonder.

"What's the matter?" Vic joked. "Same trouble as my kid
brother?"

"By Christ, is he your brother?" He threw up his hands. "Jesus,
what a family!" he cried. "How do you get it all in, all in the same
twenty-four hours?" He shook his head again. "Just what is it you
do? Musician?"

"I play drums," Vic said. "Drums, tympani."

The old man turned to the others. "Tell me something," he said.
"Isn't this fella here just about the best God damn drummer or
tympani-ist or whatever the hell it is in the God damn world?"

There was a murmured assent.

"Now I don't know one note of music from another," said old man Jones. "Never could understand what anybody saw in it. But these hands here . . ." He picked up Vic's hands again. "You must have started when you were a little child, I guess."

Vic nodded.

"And just never quit," he continued, peering into Vic's palm, holding it at arm's length like any far-sighted man. "Yes, by Christ, when do you sleep? And the women?" he said fiercely. "And yet you're not satisfied. Not one little bit! You're at the top of the tree, and you're just itching to quit! Say, isn't that true—what's your name, young fella?"

"Victor Berton." Vic smoothed his hair back nervously. "Yes, Mr. Jones. I am itching to quit. I've had enough. Just . . . had enough."

The old man stared at him like an eager boy. "You don't say. Quit at the top? Well, some fighters have done it—Jim Jeffries did it, and Philadelphia Jack O'Brien—but why a musician? Is it"—he stared again—"money? You think you can make more money some other way?" Vic didn't answer. "Never!" cried the old man. "Never in this world! *You* thinking of going into some business for yourself? . . . By Jesus, you are, I see it in your eye! Oh, mister, let me tell you—forget it. *You're* no businessman!" he said brutally. "*You* up against those fellas—it's a joke! They'll tear you to bits! You might as well try to make an Olympic weight lifter out of this string bean grandson of mine! Look at him—six foot two and don't weigh more than 160 pounds wringin' wet! It isn't in his nature, any more than buyin' and sellin' is in your nature. I wouldn't be surprised if you've been burned some already—is that the truth, son?"

Vic looked down and nodded.

"Face facts. *You are a drummer.* Don't fight it—you're not going anywhere else in this lifetime."

All insisted he "do" Bix. Somewhat to everyone's surprise, he shook his head, though Bix, smiling, "sat" for him willingly enough.

"No," he said shortly. "No need o' that. I know all about him already."

"Wow," Bix said wryly. "I must be pretty bad."

Old Jones slowly raised his eyes. In them was a look of such compassion, such deep sorrow, that I could only stare, baffled. His mood communicated itself. All the impulse to banter went out of us. I felt myself stiffen a bit; what had he "on" my hero?

After a long, searching look at Bix, he leaned back in his chair, staring at the fire. We waited, in a sort of suspended animation, hardly knowing whether he would speak.

At last he said, still gazing at the fire, "No, son. You don't have a 'bad' bone in your body. If a horsefly was bitin' you, you'd just as soon chase him away as kill him."

Bix blinked and looked uncomfortable. He uttered a slight forced laugh. "I don't know about *that,*" he said in his flat twang.

"I speak metaphorically, son. A figure of speech. Live and let live, isn't that it? All you ask of life? Just to be free to sit and play your piano, and . . . what else is it you play? Trumpet?"

Bix nodded.

"I wouldn't know how good or bad you play. It's all the same to me. But I sense what others think. You're a holy man to them. They revere you like a mystery. In a way, you don't have friends —you have disciples."

There was dead silence in the room. The only sounds were the hissing of a green log, the soft crackle of the flames, a cricket outside the open windows. Tears came to my eyes, I hardly knew why. Bix stared at him, bewildered, mouth slightly ajar, eyes wide.

"I've seen you drink our wine here, as a man crawling through the desert gulps down a dipper of water. You'd drink the contents of a fire extinguisher if it would put out your fire; but that's a fire you can't put out, son, never—not this side of the grave. Do you know what I'm saying to you?" He turned at last and gazed at Bix.

Bix's own gaze wavered but somehow held. There was silence.

"Christ, son," the old man grated, "you don't even get *drunk.* You just *damp down that fire for a while.*" Pause. "And what bothers me, son, is . . . you don't know exactly what it *is* you're trying to *do.* Something with that music, of course, but . . . *if you don't know what it is, how can you ever get to do it?*" He looked around at us all then, and put another log on the fire, a log I doubt anyone else there but Voynow could have lifted. . . .

Next morning I cornered Lloyd III and asked him about Grandpa's predictions.

"Oh," he said in his usual mild way, "I must say I've never known Granddad to be wrong. Not that I can remember."

I still didn't care for some of the things he'd said to my hero. Why, Bix had only been playing professionally for a year or two, and already people knew his name all over the country! And this was just the beginning. Where would Bix be in another six or seven years? I felt like telling that to that crazy old man, with his mystical visions and his talk about my future as a sex fiend. I didn't—he was too intimidating—but I vowed I'd come back when I was twenty-one, and Bix was on top of the world, and I was a famous . . . well, whatever I was going to be, and ask him how he liked his predictions now.

I don't remember how long we stayed at Keuka Lake. So many things happened there that were unforgettable: A visit to the family winery near Hammondsport—what looked like half a square mile of underground vaults, cobwebbed, cool, fragrant, row on row of ancient oak casks and dark green bottles. How did all this go on existing during Prohibition? I haven't the least idea. All I know is, we were there, tasting everything in sight, constantly warned by Jones I and Jones III to take it easy, just a sip, not a swig, but nevertheless we all got gloriously swozzled and came out into the dappled sunshine of the wooded surroundings blind, blinking into the daylight like owls. . . .

A mad ride around the lake in a racing car—one of Babe's college friends was a racing driver; he'd come up for the weekend in a car he'd souped up—I believe it was a Mercer roadster, which, believe it or not, in 1924 would do ninety-six miles per hour just as it came from the factory. I had rashly told him I loved speed, and had already had a ride in a training aircraft, and he bet me a dollar he could scare me more in his racer than I'd been by a stunt flyer. That road around Keuka Lake was dirt, or clay rather, and full of hairpin turns; it was the first time for me with a racing driver, who *skids* the turns instead of *wheeling* them—at least half a dozen times on those skid turns, our rear wheels were racing in open space over a sixty-foot drop to the water's edge; I can testify that there's no truth to the myth about hair turning gray in one night; if there were, mine would have been snow white when I stepped out of that car, after an hour with that crazy young man, whose handsome profile and wild blue eyes, gleaming in the light of the full moon, are printed in my head forever. . . .

A walk in the woods with old man Jones, who knew the name (and Linnaean classification) of every plant that grew there (have you ever wondered how many different plants grow in one five-mile stretch of North American forest? try counting sometime). I couldn't keep up with his heavy-booted stride, crossing fallen trees and leaping rocky brooklets like a deer, and was hopelessly winded in ten minutes. I hated and admired him more than ever. . . .

Best of all was the party Babe gave for everyone he knew who dug jazz, and quite a few he thought might. I never heard Bix play better; he kept switching back and forth from piano to horn, and drove everyone there nuts; he wouldn't let up. I played, Moore-Moore played, Vic played—Babe Jones, needless to say, managed a fine set of drums for the occasion, as well as a bass horn for Min Leibrook. And, to understate the case, there was wine. I don't know what the old man understood of what was going on musically, but he obviously enjoyed every moment of it, watching "the young people" (any one of whom, I'm convinced, he could have tossed through the window, three falls out of three), and putting away his share of the product of those transplanted French grapes.

There was a girl there, one of many I admired, who went out of her mind over Bix's playing. She was a musician herself, or a student anyway; I don't remember what instrument. She sat there very cool as the band lit into its first song, not—I would guess—a jazz fan, just tolerantly enjoying the goings-on. The song was a very ordinary standard, something like *Oh, Sister, Ain't That Hot?* You must understand that Bix had not been really sitting down and *playing,* for something like three or four weeks, that is, not since the Miller Beach gig's untimely end. He'd been practicing, of course, all the time as usual, working out his own peculiar ideas on his horn and on the keyboard, polishing his lip and his control; then those strange hours en route, then the nutty little session in the Home Style Resturaunt, and the blowing coming in with the cortège to Slate Run. All this out of the side of the mouth, so to speak, no drums, no bass, and all rather disorganized. Now he sat down at last to a feast of musicmaking, sharp-set, bent on making up for lost time, like a sailor on shoreleave.

He picked up his horn, crossed that leg over his knee, and blew a five-note phrase that sticks in my head yet. Oh Jesus, what those five notes said. Loneliness, and a witty sardonic view of loneliness, and a swinging bittersweet sting to it that would have sounded like a sneer at life itself if it had been any less lyrical and lovely. Tears burst from my eyes. *No, no, Bix, I heard you, I heard you, don't quit, baby, play it, play it for me, tell your lonely beautiful story.* Oh, of course nothing so articulate, so nice and orderly. I write this forty-nine years after the fact, not to mention fifty-one years of practice in getting things down on paper. This time it was Bix facing all of Life, whatever it was to be; gentle, silent Bix with his façade of tough sarcasm, very likely knowing the deep truth of everything the old man had said, facing Life and saying, *O.K., Life —go fuck yourself.* "It had a dying fall."

As I choked back a sob, something made me turn my eye and look at this girl. Her fists were clenched, she bit her lower lip, she'd gone pale at those five notes; she knew something now she never knew before, about what music can say.

Of course Bix hadn't stopped there. That was just the how-do-you-do-folks. He started in then to build that story of his, in his "simple" fashion, the phrase repeated—with a tiny difference, though, a syncopation removed and replaced with a precise, corny two-step march rhythm, a tongue-in-cheek comment on his own swinging opener. Then a two-note fragment of the same phrase, used as a stepping stone, or rather a magic rope ladder hanging from nowhere, with the climber pulling it up after him as he climbs—a third higher, then the next third higher, and once more, climbing just above the octave of the original—and then, just as you expected it to resolve on the next step up, you were left hanging in space, because Bix never went up there at all, but smeared *downward* in a cruel sneering funky blast that swung you right up out of your chair—and then on *that* note he did quit, uncrossed the leg, and leaned down to empty the spit out of his horn.

I looked at the girl, who was positively beating on herself, quietly, with her little fists, chewing her lower lip and staring at Bix. Our eyes met; hers were wet too. She turned away abruptly, sat down, "casually" lit a cigarette and went on watching and listening. In the pause before the next number she said to me with a perfectly normal smile, "Hello, are you with this bunch?"

I briefly explained my connection.

"Er . . . that trumpet player," she began.

"Cornet," I said automatically.

"Oh. Yes of course, cornet. Who is he?"

"That's *Bix Beiderbecke,*" I said, in a tone that caused her to say:

"Oh—should I know who that is? Is he . . . famous?"

"With musicians anyway," I said. "Very famous. The Wolverines. They've got a few records out on Gennett."

Between sets I saw them talking, and late that night I saw them walking down to the lake, two cigarettes in the dark. I must have heard her name, but I can't remember it.

Except for being thirteen, at a party where no girl was under nineteen or twenty, I had a marvelous time that night. I don't know how the others made out, but I feel sorry for anyone who felt the way I did about not having a girl of my own. To hell with what old man Jones said about me and women. I wondered if *he* ever had to drive away looking back at a girl like Angelina Home Style, feeling the marks of her nails in his flesh. Everyone's different. You do your way, I'll do mine.

24
AUTUMN
IN NEW YORK

All stops included, our journey—despite Dick Voynow's best-laid plans and meticulously marked maps—had taken a good three weeks and an unknown amount of money, a large part of which was contributed by Babe Jones, who would never agree to take any of it back.

The trip had been great, but it was good to be home again—home for the Bertons, in those days, being wherever Mummy was. Not once did it ever occur to any of her three boys, no matter what outside attachments we might form, and we formed plenty, even to dream of setting up housekeeping outside "our home." I can't even call it "unthinkable," which always implies consideration and rejection; this idea never entered our heads to begin with.

She'd taken this great apartment at 119 West Seventy-first Street, five huge comfortable rooms with the high ceilings and corner moldings still to be found, even today, on Manhattan's upper West Side—Mummy had taken it over, furniture, books, and all, from some lady writer who'd lived in it thirty-eight years, and was now retiring to her native British South Africa. As may be imagined, it was like a five-room museum, library, and curio den, several of its rooms crammed from floor to ceiling with auto-graphed first editions—only her piano, Gene said, was "a horror," and that was hurriedly given to the Salvation Army as soon as the lady was out of the house, to make way for the golden-voiced Mason & Hamlin.

While waiting for the Cinderella Ballroom job to begin, and until they could get their first pay, the Wolverines holed up any-where they could. Those who could get money wired to them, from home or pals, took hotel or furnished rooms; those who couldn't stayed with those who could. Bix stayed with us, and shared my bed. (As Alex Woollcott remarked in a celebrated Christmas story, the child's room is always the guest room.)

The famous Mason & Hamlin sat in the livingroom, and my brother Gene sat, much of the time, at the Mason & Hamlin; Bix had to grab it when he could. But now, instead of the Ravel and Debussy scores, the books of lieder and Russian songs, what was on the music rack was manuscript paper. Gene had quarreled irrevocably with his patrons and managers ("I just couldn't sing the shit they insisted on for public recitals! Never mind—fuck it, darling!") and, incredibly, given up his vocal career for good. He was now an operetta composer, working on his first show.

His involvement with that kind of music actually was nothing new; it had begun almost in infancy. As his musical development proceeded he had leaned increasingly toward such composers as Messager, Kalman, Offenbach, Leo Fall, Lehár, Sullivan, and lesser known men whose music he'd heard all over Europe (in *Mitteleuropa*, every little town had its own repertory company and local composers, some of them very fine), much of which he'd collected and brought back; so he wasn't exactly entering an unfamiliar field. The only American composer he admitted to this exalted company was Jerome Kern, whom both Gene and I placed on a level with some of the most revered classical writers. He now intended to add Gene Berton to that list.

The decision once taken, he hadn't let any grass grow. By the time Vic and I got to New York, he had found himself a lyric writer, written four songs, and was already discussing the plot of a libretto for which he himself had concocted the idea—"The Gorgeous Borgias," as it was tentatively titled. The lyricist was Edward Eliscu, who in later years did pretty well for himself in Hollywood—*Flying Down to Rio,* which he collaborated on with Vincent Youmans, was his best-known film credit, and *You Forgot Your Gloves* (music by Vernon Duke), his biggest song hit. Gene and Eddie had still to find a librettist and a producer. Until that happy day, naturally, it would once again be good old Vickie footing the bills.

Fortunately this was no problem. Vic's fame had preceded him to New York by some years. I don't think I knew this at the time, but Vic had—according to the discographies—as early as October,

1921, been brought to New York by Sam Lanin (a drummer himself) to make some records;* a number of other bandleaders, finding out Vic was in town, had hurried to take advantage of that fact to cut a few sides with him; the collectors will have to tell me who they were.†

There's no sure way now of telling just how many bands Vic did record with in those years between, say, 1920 and the time he returned to New York with us—or how many sides he cut; probably several hundred. From those record dates came, doubtless, a big part of the family income that helped support Gene's promising vocal career, as well as the rest of us, sending us to London and Paris, &c. Equally important, he met and played with various musicians (not to mention leaders) who never forgot what it meant to have Vic Berton sitting behind the drums. Now this reputation, which was bigger than any of us had realized, exploded in a shower of contract offers from which he had only to choose the most attractive; various leaders and contractors, in fact, had known in advance of his moving to New York, and had been impatiently awaiting it, with a good deal of maneuvering among them to be first in line for his services. And that, by the way, was the end of his "career" as an entrepreneur. In words made famous by a certain movie of our own day, they made him offers he couldn't refuse—and with the family needing desperately to be bailed out after the debacle of Gene's career, there was nothing else to do but "stay on the God damn drums." Thus promptly was old man Jones's prophecy fulfilled. Exit Vic Berton, businessman.

The family exchequer was soon replenished. Steve, being Steve, had quietly gone out and found herself an office job, a couple of days after getting settled in our New York home, and I immediately applied for membership in Local 802, and without waiting for formal acceptance, began looking for jobs, making the rounds of the sleazier "artists' representatives," otherwise known as agents, most of them scarcely above the class of Times Square pimps.

Because of my extreme youth, ordinary jobs were hard to come by; I spent some weary hours schlepping my instruments up and

---

*With "Bailey's Lucky Seven," a recording name, but also under numerous other band names—probably up to sixty sides in all.
†Names I recall offhand, rightly or wrongly, include Howard Lanin (Sam's brother), Boyd Senter, Cliff Edwards ("Ukelele Ike"), Frankie Signorelli, Freddie Rich, Ben Bernie, Vincent Lopez, and George Olsen.

down Forty-seventh Street, and up and down the stairways of the kind of buildings "my" class of agents had their offices in, many of which had no elevators.

The standard routine was about as follows. At around 11 A.M., any day except Sunday, you arrived at Forty-seventh Street and Broadway, across from the Palace Theater, and, in good weather, took up a position on the sidewalk anywhere in that block between Seventh and Sixth Avenues, as close to Seventh as the competition would let you, exactly like a hooker waiting for a john to proposition her; indeed the hookers weren't far away—they kept to Broadway itself, between Forty-second Street and about Fifty-fourth; we soon had nodding acquaintances with many of them, and would exchange gripes about the weather, &c.

At any time after that, a minute or three hours, a greasylooking little man might, after walking up and down a couple of times looking us all over, approach you and ask, "Whattaya, union or nonunion?" At this period I invariably answered, "I'm waiting for my card—I can go either way."

"Whattaya play, hot or sweet?"

"Either way. Dixieland, society, straight dance work."

"You read?"

"Read or fake, either way. By the way, I guess you heard of my brother, Vic Berton?"

"Oh yeah? You Vic Berton's kid brother? Folly me."

Then came the schlepping—the bass drum, in those days more than twice the size of today's midgets, in a canvas cover, and the trap case, containing the snare drum and accessories, and weighing about forty pounds. Some of the nicer agents would offer to share your burdens, but nice guys generally didn't become agents. More usually, when you showed signs of suffering on the way up those stairs behind him, he'd say cheerfully, "Didn't your mother ever tell you you shoulda been a piccolo player?"

Arrived in his shabby office (they were always on the fourth floor), you joined four or five other hopefuls, with their instruments—saxophones, trumpets, trombones—usually with one tired-looking "house man" sitting patiently at a brokendown upright, looking out the dirty window and yawning.

"O.K., Junior, set up."

I got so I could set up in less than four minutes—dug the bass-drum spurs into his rag of a carpet, torn and riddled by a thousand predecessors, placed my cymbals, clamped the pedal on. . . . The agent would hand out the parts from a publishers' stock arrangement of the latest bit of art from Tin Pan Alley *(Red Lips, Kiss My Blues Away*, or *I Can't Get the One I Want [Those I Get, I Don't Want]*, or *I Left My Sugar Standing in the Rain)*; the piano player would chord an intro, and our audition was on.

If the agent liked what he heard, came the next routine: "O.K., this is a private dance, Satiddy night, up in the Bronx, 178th Street, nine to two. Not much money but plenty of cunt. Pays eighteen dollars a man, take it or leave it. . . . You with me, Junior?"

"O.K."

"Got a tux?"

"Yes."

"Here's the *ad*-dress. Nine o'clock sharp, Satiddy night, if you're late you get docked five bucks. Payoff is at 2 A.M."

I played Jewish weddings, I played dances in the wilds of Staten Island, I played three months in a speakeasy-whorehouse on Fifty-ninth Street just off Columbus Circle; one of the whores, just turned twenty, was a dead ringer for my Ada. ("Hands off, you bitches!" she declared to her co-workers the first evening I showed up for work. "This lily* belongs to me!") But I managed to resist, my ardor still dampened by Mummy's dreadful warnings of the ravages of "social diseases"—one of the few times I succeeded in proving old man Jones could be mistaken.

I don't know now how long Bix made his home in ours. Two things, though, do stand out in my memory. One was his piano playing, which had in the space of a few days or weeks moved to a new plane of intelligence (though not, I regret to add, of technical precision).

The somewhat emetic sentimental sobriquet "young man with a horn," along with the now familiar studio photograph of Bix looking out at us with his Mona Lisa smile and his cornet on his knee, may have contributed to what I now regard as something of a historical paradox; namely, that Bix is remembered almost exclusively as a cornetist. I believe I yield to no one living or dead in my passion for what he could do on that horn; but for me, his most astonishing flights of imagination, his most far-seeking musical journeys in quest of new meanings, were made on piano. By com-

*Virgin.

parison, his cornet inventions, though executed with dazzling technical virtuosity and a command of his instrument he never remotely approached on the piano, were rather modest in scope.

The fact that even on cornet Bix never managed to record at anything like the aesthetic horsepower with which he normally played in person during his best years is of course an irreparable loss to the art; but here we do after all have a fairly extensive body of material that at least reminds us of the original. So far as the piano is concerned, the loss is even more tragic—it is almost total; of all the startling flood of ideas and breath-stopping explorations his fumbling fingers found on the keyboard, hardly a bubble remains. Had it been possible to capture even a significant fraction of their essence in permanent form, the art of jazz might well have taken a healthier and more interesting direction than any we have seen so far.

Again I must make it clear that no such opinion, no such realization, were mine to contemplate and articulate then; they are the fruit of a lifetime of exposure to, and reflection upon, what one writer has called the "reluctant art."[26] But the *sense* of what Bix was trying to do, and often enough succeeding in doing, was very vivid to me in those first few weeks on West Seventy-first Street, however remote my feelings were from any attempt at formulation. Whenever Gene wasn't at the piano, one might say in general, Bix was. That usually happened sometime in midafternoon, which was when Bix customarily awoke, and Gene, having spent the whole morning composing, was often out of the house; in fact very often no one would be home but Bix and me.

Our daily routine was somewhat as follows.

Bix would arise, having slept as usual in his BVDs, and—having stood blinking for a moment and, as it were, remembering where he was—go straight to the piano, like a person anxious to write down a dream before it slips away, hardly pausing to acknowledge my ironic "Good morning." Whatever else I'd been doing—reading, writing, drawing, practicing with my sticks and rubber practice pad—I would quietly abandon and come in to listen. My favorite spot was a throw rug just beyond the piano, where I could lie and look as well as listen. Bix might continue an hour or more, forgetting to eat or even go to the bathroom; if Mummy was home, she'd call in after a while, "Bixie, you'd better come and eat something," a summons generally preceded by premonitory whiffs of griddle cakes, sausages, eggs, or the equivalent. "Did you wash your hands?" she would ask automatically as he entered, having perhaps stopped to put on a pair of pants, or perhaps not, depending on how dazed and hung over he might be. Usually the answer was No, and he would retire—rather briefly—to the bathroom, emerging looking much as when he'd entered, owl-eyed and tousled.

He seldom took any part in the animated conversation between my mother and me, unless he had something very specific to say; otherwise he ate in silence, not hastily, but obviously anxious to get back to the piano. But he never forgot to say, "Thanks for breakfast, Mom." At that point, if we had any liquor in the house, Bix would generally take a glass in with him and a saucer to set it on; unlike many absentminded people, he was quite careful about such things, conscious of where he put a lighted cigarette, &c. He'd go back to the keyboard, I back to my lair under it; and now the real work would start.

In their indecent anxiety to explain why jazz isn't music, the official custodians (self-appointed) of academic culture have regularly damned it as "formless." That of course is simple cultural deafness on their part; the strictest form in Western music, as it happens, is the twelve-bar blues, which has from the beginning provided the structural basis for a good half of all jazz; the other half, until a few years ago, consisting of a form almost as rigidly defined, the thirty-two-bar, four-part, A-A-B-A popular song or "standard." In their ignorance, they were criticizing jazz for a reason exactly opposite to what they might legitimately have complained of: that jazz forms, being so *very* strict, simple, brief, and repetitious, imposed a heavy burden on the inventiveness of the jazzman; where would classical music be today if the only form it had ever developed was theme and variations?

I speak as though no jazz composers had ever transcended these formal limitations, which was never really true, and is even less so today, when the revolution against any form at all—taking its cue from the "respectable" arts—has reached the opposite extreme, known by the ultimate absurdity, the ultimate contradiction in terms, so-called free form (as if "form" could ever be "free").

But long before the present wave of babbling idiocy had attacked the arts, jazz among them, there were jazz composers who went outside the few established patterns—and Bix was one of the most interesting; his experiments had an inner logic, and inherent artistic fascination, that made them unique in their time; regrettably, they are still unique today, which means no other jazz composer ever really "took him up on" his method or developed it further.

It was this "method" that I heard suddenly come to flower in those sessions at the piano in Seventy-first Street, and that held me spellbound (literally at his feet) day after day, often leaving me so limp with emotion, so dazed, so drunk on that inexhaustible fountain of musical genius, that I would have been unable to describe the time of day, let alone the music I had heard. Let me see how well I can do a half century later.

Basically we are already acquainted with Bix's approach to these piano compositions, involving, as The Schnozz might put it, "a little of this-a and a little of that-a"—one cup classical, one cup jazz. But to say only so much is to say very little. It is never the material in itself that makes art art, but the way the artist employs it, not the what but the how and why.

What Bix had begun to do now was to fashion definite melodic lines—first in the jazz vein, then classical, and so on—choosing, by that subtle artist's instinct that defies anticipation, melodies in each idiom that at times mirrored, at times violently contrasted with each other, so that, inevitably, each passage became a commentary on its predecessor. The reader has surely remarked by now how frequently this concept of *comment* has cropped up in my attempt to reduce to words Bix's fundamental approach to music. Certain classical composers—Scarlatti and Stravinsky, Poulenc and Satie—also come to mind, and with reason.

Why does the music of some men strike us as being fabricated from some primary stuff, others as being a kind of music *about music?* The simplest answer would be found in music that is patent satire or "atmosphere," such as Stravinsky's use of a hurdy-gurdy strain in *Petrouchka,* or his *Ragtime for Eleven Instruments,* Beethoven's introduction of the peasant-clodhopping dance in the third movement of the Pastoral Symphony; all obviously and deliberately fabricated from previously existing materials. A slightly less obvious example may be seen in Scarlatti's keyboard *esercizi,* many of which are frankly "inspired"—if no more—by Spanish or Portuguese street music, but transformed in the crucible of a great classically trained mind and poured molten into the

shape of the baroque two-part "sonata." (For a spectacular example of the exact opposite, i.e., "primary" music, formed out of
nothing but Chaos and Old Night, I give you the opening movement of Beethoven's Ninth, any passage.)

Stravinsky, though, remains our best exemplar of the "comment" genre, on every level; virtually his entire output was *music
about music:* summing up, with mordant wit or profound paraphrase, the essence of all that went before him; in Shaw's potent
image, he swept the whole field like a giant reaper, leaving nothing but stubble for those who came after him. And that is indeed
what has come from those who have come after him—nothing.

Bix's piano improvisations—which presently began to "graduate" more and more to the status of remembered and repeated
compositions—were similarly music about music, in this case
about "jazz versus classical," so fashioned that each part was somehow "about" the other. Specifically this meant, at times, beginning
with a classical theme, something quite modest, pretty, and lyrical,
like a shy milkmaid in a Watteau *pastorale;* then without warning
swinging this theme, still prettily, not too funky—as though the
modest maid had unexpectedly winked at us—just that, the merest hint of a lascivious id peeping out, like the lacy edge of a
petticoat. Back to the lyrical again, this time with stronger, deeper
melodic appeal—the maid protesteth her undying, sweetly melan-
cholic attachment to virtuous Love—and then, *wham!* the same
figure hits us right in the gut with a swinging cathouse beat; our
modest miss has in an appalling instant, as by the wave of a witch's
wand, been metamorphosed into a painted (but beautiful) strumpet, false eyelashes, hip-length black net stockings and all, swinging her hips and beaded purse and murmuring, "Well, hel-*lo!*"
Can there be still another renascence, from this tough, swinging
B-girl back into our demure milkmaid? There can; and, surprisingly, something more. Our original theme recurs, this time on a
higher plane of subtlety—our maid has become a woman, serious
and tender, seeking new avenues of pride and desire, lyrical and
austere by turns. We seem to have left behind us such crass images
as began our journey—for even as the jazz pulse reasserts itself, it
has lost its "dirty," lowdown air and become light, lively, still
swinging but with a witty, dissonant edge to its intervals that is
itself a comment on the previous assaults of funk. And what has
become of our glaring contrasts? We find ourselves suddenly in a

place where a synthesis is taking place, the controversy has become a civilized discussion, and the ending is—shall we say inconclusive?

I hasten to apologize for the vulgar and rather rudimentary imagery of the foregoing "program," this coarse backpack with which I have ventured to burden the delicate ballerina that is music; but I wanted to make my point in the simplest, most emphatic way. Needless to say, such prosaic imagery invariably leaves out precisely the essence of a piece of music, that essence that can never be told in words, the *musical* part of music, if I may be forgiven the pleonasm, a phrase eating its own tail—but there is really no good way to deal with the problem in words; we bruise the meaning by trying to express it, like a steam shovel trying to pick up a violet. And Bix's music, when he was at his best, was *all* music; his harmonies flashed strange instantaneous fires like the transitory hues of a turning jewel, perhaps never to be repeated. Tears in my eyes, I could only gnaw my lip and think: *No one will ever hear this, no one will ever hear this. . . .*

Surveying Bix's whole musical life, I have no doubts at all that here, in his piano explorations, beginning back in the Wilbur Hatch days in the summer of 1919, when he irritated "his companions" with his revolutionary chords, continuing through what I heard at Argyle Street and now on Seventy-first Street, and right to the end of his life, we have the supreme key and clue to that elusive question *Who and what was Bix?* Many other writers have noticed this in their own way. My own principal feeling, which I hope I've sufficiently conveyed here, is deep sorrow and regret that so little of this revealing and provocative adventure was ever captured for posterity, or further developed by others.

The other thing that made Bix's stay among us memorable—trivial enough in retrospect, though at the time it caused me considerable distress—was occasioned by what I was pleased to call my mother's "hygienic neurosis." She was raised in a family she herself used to laugh at as being "crazy clean." The easiest way to describe their underlying philosophy, I guess, would be the implied rule: Never touch anything. As filth and "germs" are everywhere, on every conceivable surface, the less you touch the cleaner you'll be. In my aunts' homes, this view of life extended to the orderly arrangement of every household object. Visiting there, one had a perpetual sense of uneasiness lest one might inadvertently displace a chair, a cushion, a newspaper folded just so and awaiting the master's homecoming and privileged first touch.

Of course our own home was nothing like that; but it was *sanitary*, to a degree a well-run hospital might envy. Beds were intended not so much for sleeping as for airing; the moment the occupying body had vacated it, each bed was turned out, stripped, the linen consigned to the hamper, and everything movable exposed to the germicidal sun and oxygen. No one ever walked barefoot from bed to bath; no sheet or bath mat ever came in contact with the sole of a foot that had touched a floor or a carpet —slippers were obligatory even on the shortest journey. Towels were changed daily, fixtures always in spotless, showroom condition. Daily life began with a bath, and washcloths and rather stiff bath brushes were routinely employed; hands were expected to be (and were) washed after handling *anything* and, regardless, immediately before approaching that most sacred of all materials, food. The very floors and carpets were, in the popular phrase, "clean enough to eat off," being vacuumed and/or scrubbed every other day; it was almost impossible to find a speck of dust anywhere but on the very highest bookshelves; and, even though she mocked at my aunts for similar compulsions, I saw with my own eyes that my mother never overcame a lifelong habit, when visiting anywhere, of surreptitiously running a whitegloved finger over any suspicious-looking surface for a quick inspection, "to know what kind of a house she keeps." It goes without saying that she not only never in her life ordered a hamburger in any public eatery (my brother Vic's joke: Customer—"One hamburger, please." Waitress [calling order to cook]—"Clean up the kitchen!"), but also never purchased it, as such, from any butcher; if she wanted ground beef, she first selected the steak she fancied, made sure his grinder was clean, and only then had him grind it. Guests who wanted a piece of fruit were handed it on a plate, with knife and snowy napkin, then watched afterward in hopes it would occur to them to wash their hands before returning to the touching of other objects. And so on.

Her life situation, accordingly, presented something of a paradox. As the only civilian in the family, she had spent that life, from her twenty-first year on, watching over a brood of eccentric performers, from the wings of dusty stages or in indifferently cared-for auditoriums and other unhappy places, hitting all the knocks and bumps of the theatrical life, in town or "on the road." Of course a good many of Mummy's sanitary views rubbed off on her offspring, that was inevitable, but for the most part in attenuated and relaxed form; and we often did careless things just to tease her.

As may easily be imagined, she had seen in her time a remarkable assortment of house guests; temperamentally a woman who made a religion of "tolerance," she very nearly drew the line at Bix.

It wasn't that Mummy wasn't fond of him; she was; she'd taken to him from the first, regarding him after a short time almost as a kind of adopted son. It wasn't the drinking; she was, however sorrowfully, inured to that—God knows Vickie drank enough on occasion; and as for Bix, he never misbehaved; in fact, though plainly an alcoholic, he was definitely not a drunk: that hard core of sobriety no quantity of alcohol, seemingly, could dissolve; his capacity was phenomenal. The thing that bothered my mother, right from the start, was that Bix just hated to wash or change his clothes.

There are human beings who seem almost to have been born homeless. We see them celebrated in every Western; their numbers are legion—cowboys, seamen, hobos, skid row types—restless, rootless, unable to form genuine attachments anywhere. Any place they live always has a kind of temporary look; they are incurable transients.

All this didn't occur to me when I was thirteen, but it is painfully clear now that Bix was one of these unhappy creatures. I could never picture him with wife and children. And for reasons intimately connected with that rootlessness, he always, or at least when I knew him, exhibited a certain resistance to the social obligation to keep himself clean—it was as if he never felt he had anyone to keep himself clean *for.* More than once, when he staggered in at six in the morning, he managed to look like a bedraggled alley cat only a professional humanitarian would befriend. He slept in his socks and BVDs, avoided changing them as long as possible, and, like many alcoholics, was profoundly suspicious of water in any form and for any purpose.

It is extraordinary, but true, that I succeeded in remaining unaware of this shortcoming in my hero until my poor mother felt compelled to point it out—all the more because, as it happened,

I was myself at the time going through an exaggerated phase of the very hygienic mania we used to tease my mother about, bathing twice a day (more in warm weather), spending hours manicuring and pedicuring, &c. All of which caused Mummy to remark that evidently love was not only blind but also wore a clothespin on its nose. Worse yet, she concluded—after a family conference —that as I was the one who was sleeping with Bix, I was the logical one to inform him—as tactfully as possible—that a daily bath and change of linen were house rules.

Nothing in the world, of course, could have made me do such a thing—not even when she replied that in that case she would have to do it herself.

I found the imagined scene too painful to contemplate, but the reality, when it arrived, was prosaic enough. One afternoon at breakfast, Mummy simply said to Bix, "Bix dear, you're terribly dirty, and your socks smell. You must bathe and put on clean things at once."

The skies did not fall. Bix behaved exactly like a sullen schoolboy, and my mother ended the matter by leading him firmly to the bathroom and refusing to let him out until he shone like the fixtures. Bix wasn't even embarrassed; only resentful, then resigned. So much for imaginary terrors.

Another delicate scene was threatened when, one morning, I woke to discover *two* guests sharing my bed—Bix, and a female companion snoring alcoholically and fragrantly into my face, an octave higher than my hero. Again my mother thundered that the Line must be Drawn, but nothing came of it; at *that* afternoon's breakfast (nothing could supersede the demands of hospitality), the girl proved to be a harmless stray from some Westchester junior college, who had discovered at 2 A.M. that she didn't have her latchkey, and, having got quietly stewed with the quiet young fellow from Iowa she'd met at Roseland, had gracefully accepted the not unattractive alternative. She had no idea who Bix "was." When Bix repaired to the piano, which he did as quickly as he decently could, I soon heard her and Mummy, from the dining room, deep in conversation about socialism on campus. . . .

Shortly after that, the Wolverines opened at the Cinderella Ballroom, Bix got his first salary, and I believe moved to some Times Square fleabag with a couple of other musicians, bringing the West Seventy-first Street "period" to an end.

25
OUR
SEPARATE WAYS

What words, no matter how well chosen, can convey to anyone who wasn't there the flavor of that time in America? We try a kind of shorthand: "the Jazz Age," "the age of F. Scott Fitzgerald," "the boom years," "the Prohibition years"; adjectives like "hectic," "fast," "crazy" . . . but its flavor, its essence, were such a complex blend of so many things, acting together on our senses—perhaps the greatest multimedia happening of all time—that now only a rather empty abstraction of it can be communicated.

It wasn't only the new freedoms—it was the newness itself. Did we literally change homes, mates, professions, hair styles, politics, income status, more than ever before or since? I don't know. But there was a feeling in the air that *anything could happen,* and probably would if you gave it a chance, a feeling that amounted to a new definition of the possible. We *believed*—oh, we believed! Talk about your Ages of Faith! . . .

Was it money you believed in? We believed *anybody* could get rich, not in a lifetime but *by next year*—and by God, a lot of people did; waiters, busboys, elevator starters were buying & selling shares in Wall Street, taking their lunch hour in their brokers' board rooms, watching the quotations. . . .

Socialism? The U.S.S.R. was the workers' paradise, and *next year* capitalist imperialism would come tumbling down, to be replaced by peace, brotherhood, and free milk; and sunburned, stocky girls with high cheekbones, driving tractors and smiling, just like on the posters, would be raising their chubby clenched fists over the collective farms of Nebraska. . . .

No walls could stand against the new freedoms. Ladies don't smoke? Ladies don't take "certain" jobs? Ladies don't show their "limbs"? Ladies don't need sex? Ladies don't get divorces? Maybe not—but women do, and the ladies were all turning into women.

The headlines of that age tell what happened. I wonder if they tell why, to anyone who wasn't there.

DADDY BROWNING TO MARRY HIS "PEACHES"
AGE NO BARRIER, SAYS WARD

29 DAYS, STILL ATOP FLAGPOLE
SITTER "FEELING FINE"

LINDBERGH MAKES IT ALL THE WAY!
"SPIRIT OF ST. LOUIS" SAFE
AT LE BOURGET—33 HRS. 39 MIN.

LEOPOLD, LOEB CONFESS
"KILLED BOBBY FOR THRILL"

DANCE MARATHON STILL ON
14 COUPLES STILL "DANCING" AFTER 192 HOURS

A man who voluntarily chooses to sit on top of a two-hundred-foot flagpole has to be "crazy"—but why did so many things like that happen just in those years and no others? Precisely because we had to show that *everything can be done.* ("Don't tell *me* I can't dance for three weeks!" . . . P.S. They did.) Up in Harlem at the Savoy Ballroom, the night of May 22, 1927, Whitey's dancers* invented a new "flying" step based on the Charleston, and named it the Lindy Hop; in a month it had crossed more international frontiers than Lindbergh's airplane. And after about 1925, the maddest, jazziest place of all, where it all came together most typically and intensely, the very eye of the storm, was the Big Town, the "Big Apple" as the jazzmen called it: New York City.

The fragile relationship between Bix and me, between rising jazz star and obscure worshiper, between twenty-one and going on fourteen, couldn't long survive the impact of life in the Apple. The accident of Bix's bunking with us had artificially prolonged it by some days or weeks; when he departed, along with the bouquet

---

*Whitey (Herbert White) was "a sort of fringe hood . . . with ideals. He had been a prizefighter, a sergeant . . . in World War I, and bouncer at the Alhambra Ballroom in Harlem. . . . He was great as a choreographer. . . . In 1923 [he] organized the Jolly Fellows, one of many secret gangs in Harlem. . . . [It] became the club for dancers . . . all stars of the Savoy, while Whitey became head bouncer." —Al Minns (one of the greatest of Whitey's stars), quoted in Marshall and Jean Stearns, *Jazz Dance.*

of genius and unwashed linen, it became tenuous, sporadic. Actually there'd never been between us what today's elevated journalese would call a dialogue. I'd sat quivering while he performed, having learned not to irk him unduly by my ill-concealed enthusiasm; Bix in turn had gazed with some wonder of his own upon my, and my family's, curious way of life, had even accepted, in his offhand way, occasional guidings and proddings from me. Also there was no question but that he'd derived new musical riches from "Gene's" music. That was the sum of it. In the end he remained as in the beginning, quietly aloof, shut in his inner world, wrestling with—or surrendering to—his private demons.

In any case he didn't stay long in New York. A month or two later—the exact dates don't matter—he left the Wolverines forever; the next I heard he was in Charlie Straight's band, then in St. Louis with Jean Goldkette. I lost track of him. Sometimes he would blow into town and come by, suddenly, or just phone. I was always thrilled to hear his voice, but conversation wasn't his strong suit. Then he'd be gone again.

A couple of times he came in with tests of records he'd recently cut—*Flock o' Blues, Toddlin' Blues, Davenport Blues*—his own composition (was it a hint of homesickness?). I noted that *Davenport* used the Debussy whole-tone scale; a nod to Gene? I was always afraid to show any eagerness about them; I couldn't say if he valued my opinion or not. He was playing and recording with a fairly limited roster of musicians, all of them familiar to me through Vic—Tommy and Jimmy Dorsey, Miff Mole, Don Murray, Fud Livingston. I don't remember all the names they recorded under—Sioux City Six, Bix's Rhythm Jugglers, the Broadway Bellhops. He made several with my brother Vic,* but it was rarely Vic could afford such luxuries; he was too busy making money.

Curiously, Bix had quit the Wolverines, and the Cinderella Ballroom, at the very peak of a popularity explosion. It wasn't only musicians who were making the glittering Broadway dance hall a nightly rallying place. Most of the big dance palaces were tending toward a "sweet" music policy; the Cinderella quickly became an oasis for the jazzier-minded dancers—so much so that the management, to protect life & limb, felt constrained to put up signs

*The only ones I could recall and track down were *Three Blind Mice, Clorinda,* and *I'm More Than Satisfied,* recorded in late fall of 1927, and released on both the Perfect and Pathé labels (later reissued on HRS).

around the floor: POSITIVELY NO CHARLESTONING. THIS MEANS YOU.

What was eating Bix now? My guess is that he must have heard sounds in New York (or his own head) that made him more aware than ever, not only of his own dissatisfactions, but of the musical limitations of the company he kept, and that he was as usual seeking greener pastures.

What years those were for jazz! So many firsts . . .

First electrical recordings—gone was that giant horn the poor musicians had to play into, at varying distances having nothing to do with the balance they needed to hear each other and play properly together. There was a new sound, a new fidelity.

As 1925 careened and rocketed into 1926, came the first great *modern* hot jazz records; and what records they were, turning every jazz musician and listener on to a new conception—moving jazz at one leap from its Stone Age, the last hangovers of the ragtime era, into the modern world: the first Louis Armstrong Hot Fives, Okeh 8000 series—every title still gives collectors aesthetic gooseflesh—*Cornet Chop Suey, Gut Bucket Blues, Yes, I'm in the Barrel, Georgia Grind, Georgia BoBo, Drop That Sack, Oriental Strut, Struttin' with Some Barbecue, Muskrat Ramble, Come Back Sweet Papa,* and the first scat* vocal, *Heebie Jeebies.* Wow! Hello! Gone! We all wore out our first copies—just the parts with Louie's horn, then we'd lift the needle; we couldn't stand to listen to his Stone Age companions any more—Louie soaring like a modern airplane, hot, joyous, free, over the heads of those pathetic stone-wheeled oxcarts. . . . I guess we'd always known, way back in the 1922 King Oliver days, that someday this chubby black grinning kid from the slums and whorehouses of New Orleans would turn everybody around. Unlike Bix, Louie was no longer groping. He had his hand right on that 100,000,000-volt switch, lightning for the world. Jazz had found its Beethoven.

Lucky for me that I was at an age when heroes arrived regularly on my horizon. *Jurgen†* was suppressed by the censors, making it the sacred duty of every intellectual avant-gardiste to buy, read, and display it on public conveyances; Cabell became for a space

*Using the voice as an instrument, with nonsense syllables instead of lyrics—the jazz version of fa-la-la.
†Satiric-erotic romance by James Branch Cabell (1919), set in medieval (mythical) "Poictesme."

of months my model of prose style; my burgeoning correspondence with various literary figures—H. L. Mencken, Ben Hecht, Max Bodenheim, and Cabell himself—was now cast in the pseudo-archaic language of Poictesme, a burden I suppose they bore with the seasoned fortitude of public men.

Vic in those years was busy cutting some four hundred sides with God knows how many different bands; under how many names, only the hardiest collectors have been willing to untangle; much of the time playing nightly with Sam Lanin at Roseland Ballroom, opposite Fletcher Henderson (who for a while had Louie and Coleman Hawkins in his big band), plus his record dates and radio broadcasts, and, when he could steal the time, an occasional afternoon concert with the New York Philharmonic.

So busy I got his overflow, subbing for him, "the other Berton," not invariably to the leaders' delight. A society ball with Meyer Davis's orchestra at the Saint George Hotel in Brooklyn. A swank all-night party at a private house out on Oyster Bay, winding up at 6 A.M. on a cabin cruiser with the host's wife, *How jolly . . . d'you know you're my first musician? By the way what's your name child? Oh MY, where did you ever learn about things like this, what'd you say your name was darling?* Pushing thirty-five, I imagined, and in the dawn light didn't look a day over thirty-four: a first for me in terms of age. A jazz record date* with Willard Robison's orchestra—*Melancholy Baby/Nobody's Sweetheart* and *Nobody Loves Me/I Ain't Got Nobody.* The songs weren't the only sad note, apparently; when Willard was asked later how Vic's kid brother did on drums, he was said to have said, "The best thing about the kid was his last name."

I can no longer remember when we first knew that Steve's morning cough wasn't just a bad bronchitis.

A thousand things I was too young to see must have contributed to her destruction, which began with a gradual withdrawal from life, from the unequal struggle to hold her "marriage" together against the legions of New York show-biz cuties, in a world for which she was as unfit as she was for the prize ring, and with a man who was unfit for any "relationship" other than one with King Solomon's harem. From the little frame house on Kedzie Boule-

*Collectors please note. I've never been able to find these records, my own copies of which (tests) I lost years ago. I believe some discographers thought it was Vic on drums.

vard to Argyle Street had been a short but eventful ride, into a new, strange environment for which nothing in her upbringing had prepared her.

Not long after coming to New York Steve began to stop going out with Vic "socially," if that's the word for what a busy, tireless, hard-drinking dance musician and incurable tomcat does in New York after hours, especially what one did in New York in the mid-twenties.

Her easiest excuse was that she couldn't stay up that late. The truth was, Steve couldn't do anything Vic and his friends, male and female, did, and it wasn't long before she stopped trying. She went out less and less, just sat in the house and sewed. . . . Even had I had eyes to see what was happening, I couldn't have helped Steve. Her one little aberration with me notwithstanding, Steve was a girl with but one love to give in her life, and she'd given it. That was the essential part of her story, and the rest of it isn't terribly relevant.

The doctors called it galloping consumption, as good a name as any for what any self-respecting nineteenth-century lady novelist would have had the courage to call a broken heart.

I went to visit her for a weekend at the sanitarium in Saranac Lake, where they said they might be able to "arrest" it. I stayed five months, taking a room in a private house. Sex was on her list of forbidden acts (the curing TB crowd up there had a private name for it—"five miles"; the doctors had explained that each act of intercourse was the equivalent in exertion to a five-mile walk), but Steve was only going through the motions of trying to cure— all she wanted now was to live as much as she could in whatever time was left to her. Naturally the nurses didn't dream of forbidding her to spend her afternoons with her fifteen-year-old brother-in-law; in fact they remarked how much better she was sleeping since my arrival.

I literally didn't care, that mad summer when for once I had my insatiable nymph all to myself, whether I caught her "active" TB or not; I thought the world well lost for love, at a pitch of passion I was never to see surpassed. As for the doctors' archaic strictures, her "thirty-mile" per day average was evidently not what killed her, for by December they found her sufficiently "arrested" to go home to Kedzie Boulevard; some time later she quietly divorced Vic. But in 1934, passing through Chicago en route to Hollywood,

I phoned her home, and was informed by her mama that Steve had died six months before. She had paid a heavy price for that seat in the Senate Theater down near the orchestra pit.

The year 1927 was a busy one for the Bertons. It looked as though I had "become" something after all: despite sporadic writing and ghost-writing jobs, I had been leaning increasingly toward art; that summer for the first time my family took a house in Woodstock, New York, where I fell in with a number of artists who encouraged me to paint seriously, especially Peter Blume, with whom I shared a studio; the next year the Woodstock Association hung three of my paintings, which was accounted quite an honor for a sixteen-year-old boy.

Gene had found himself a producer for his first musical show— Horace Liveright*—and was heavily involved in getting a proper script for it.

For years the half dozen top commercial dance orchestras had been bidding for Vic's services like collectors at an auction. Early in 1927 Paul Whiteman, biggest (in every sense) of them all, finally outbid everyone, paying Vic some unbelievable salary like four hundred dollars a week—a lot of mazuma in 1927—with Vic retaining the right to continue his recording and radio dates with Red Nichols and other bands. As it turned out, Vic's being hired by Whiteman was one of the worst things that ever happened to either of them. Having won his prize, Whiteman soon discovered its drawbacks. Behind his genial-fat-man mask, Whiteman in those days was a ferocious egotist, not used to sharing the spotlight; and now the patrons of the Club Whiteman seemed to be paying more attention to the new flashy drummer than to his porpoise-shaped leader.

Whiteman tried in various ways to cut Vic out of the limelight: ordering him not to take those spectacular solos, reducing his array of accessories, altering, or dropping from his book, arrangements that featured "too much" drums, etc. Nonetheless, Whiteman was twitted about "his new leader, Vic Berton"; tension between them grew.

*Eccentric pioneer publisher and producer (1886–1933). Founded Boni & Liveright (1918), also Modern Library (low-price classics); produced *Dracula, An American Tragedy, The Firebrand, Hamlet in Modern Dress;* famed as host & *bon vivant.*

Between sets one night, in the men's room, Whiteman and Vic found themselves standing side by side at the urinals—Whiteman, six foot one and 300-odd pounds of hard fat; Vic, five foot six, 140, a bit paunchy like many ex-boxers but all muscle and wiry tendon.

According to Vic, Whiteman finished first and buttoned up, and as he walked past Vic, did something he was well known for in those days of his celebrated overweight: "accidentally" jostled him —it was like being jostled by a beer truck—so that Vic literally fell against the urinal, drenching his tuxedo pants and his shoes. Vic said the following exchange took place:

"God damn it, Paul! Look what you made me do!"

"You don't say. What are you going to do about it, little man?"

"Listen, you big tub of shit," Vic said between clenched teeth, knowing his own murderous temper, "do us both a favor and get out of here before I kill you, O.K.? And this is my two-week notice, right now!" and he turned away, buttoning his fly.

"Listen, Jew boy—you can't quit, you're fired, and get out of my way before I step on you. You're in *my club,* Jew boy!" and Whiteman shoved Vic as hard as he could; or tried to.

There were no witnesses to what happened next, but the next thing Vic remembered was Whiteman lying on the tiled floor bleeding profusely from nose & mouth, two of his teeth lying next to him, shrieking that his jaw was broken; Vic said he never heard such bellowing from a human throat—"he sounded like a full-grown hog stuck under a gate."

At that point half a dozen waiters, &c., burst in, also a saxophone player, Paul Cartwright, one of Vic's best friends, who'd been in the Navy with him as a judo instructor. A couple of the waiters grabbed Vic, and Whiteman, who'd lumbered to his feet, started kicking Vic in the balls, whereupon Paul Cartwright grabbed Paul Whiteman and threw him against the sinks with such force that one of them was wrenched loose from its moorings and smashed on the floor; water gushed from the pipes, Whiteman collapsed again, screaming that his hip was broken, waiters were grabbing at Cartwright two at a time and getting dumped on their heads by him, while Vic had also struggled free and joined the melee. Several of the kitchen help rushed in; Vic and Cartwright were caught and pinioned. One of the waiters, bleeding from the ear, drew a blackjack and went for Cartwright.

At that point Whiteman, directing operations from a safe corner, screamed at the waiter (according to both Vic and Paul), *"Hit him in the mouth! In the mouth! He's a saxophone player!"*

The waiter did. (For nearly a year afterward, Paul Cartwright used to visit us with his teeth in various phases of repair, having restorative work done. He told us Whiteman had offered to pay for the work if Cartwright would keep his mouth shut about the incident, but he preferred to pay the bills himself and tell the world about Mr. Whiteman.) Fortunately the police entered about then, or it might have gone badly for the two lightweight warriors. Vic said it wasn't until then that he realized his fly was still open.

I understand the Club Whiteman was dark for some time following that fracas, while the medics were patching the "Tub of Shit," as Vic always called Whiteman from then on. Vic, miraculously, came out of the battle unscathed except for bruised knuckles and a sore groin, and a few nights later was back playing with Roger Wolfe Kahn at the Hotel Pennsylvania, at a $10 raise.

One afternoon in the late fall of 1927, I was in my room, practicing my tympani, when the front-door buzzer sounded. It was Bix, looking pale and hollow-eyed, and with a bunch of test records under his arm. He looked as if he hadn't slept. The penciled notation on the blank white labels said BIX & HIS GANG on three of them, and the titles. The fourth just said BIX BEIDERBECKE— PIANO SOLO. Glowing with anticipation, I put one of them on the Orthophonic—*Jazz Me Blues/At the Jazz Band Ball*—and squatted to listen. Bix poured himself a drink and flopped on the couch, bleary-eyed. I was amazed by the power and authority of Bix's horn, utterly unlike anything he'd previously put on wax; so vivid was the impression that I pulled out the old Gennett version of *Jazz Me*, waxed three and a half years before, and put it on for comparison. It was like putting a fifteen-year-old kid alongside a grown-up man. I suppose I said something to that effect.

Bix made a face.

"What's the matter?" I said. "You don't think the new *Jazz Me* beats the old one by a mile?"

Bix shrugged, and indicated that that wasn't saying much in any case. "The drums sound a lot better anyway," he conceded. "And at least they don't put him in the next room."*

---

*In the old acoustic recording, the drums were always an acute problem; bass drum usually was omitted altogether, and the drummer placed at an extreme distance from the recording horn.

"I'm not talking about drums," I said impatiently. "I'm talking about *you*—you sound like you really got hold of something there."

Bix muttered something like "Yeah; my own foot." I put the other records on one by one, doing my best not to look enthusiastic: *Royal Garden Blues, Sorry, I'm Coming, Virginia, Since My Best Gal Turned Me Down,* all of them by several miles the best cornet Bix had ever recorded. I had all I could do to keep from crying out at the way Bix swung—and the son of a bitch sat there, completely dead, with that disparaging expression I knew only too well, actually *wincing.* I felt like slapping him. He didn't deserve to listen to anything as good as Bix Beiderbecke on cornet.

He "woke up" only when somebody else's solo was on—Adrian Rollini's ponderously "humorous" bass sax, Frankie Signorelli's feeble and precariously tempoed piano solos, Don Murray's adequate but undistinguished clarinet. I mean they were all O.K., and Chauncey Morehouse's drums really sounded good—but what were they all put together compared to Bix? Bix seemed to like *them,* chuckling and saying, "This is Paul Mertz now on piano" and "Listen to what Don came up with right here," and so on, in his usual way—until his own solos, at which point he'd once again bite his lip and say, *Oh, shit,* if he said anything at all. You could kill a guy like that. *What was he hearing?* I asked myself.

I put on the last of the band sides, *Goose Pimples.** Just before I put the needle down, Bix said, "Wait till you hear what I did on this one."

I glanced at him surprised; his face told me nothing. It was such an unusual thing for him to say that I listened with bated breath.

There was no doubt in my mind, right from the first notes of the intro, that this one was going to be not only the best of the lot, but the most swinging horn he'd ever recorded. As always, there wasn't enough Bix on the side; I of course begrudged every groove that wasn't devoted to his horn; but what he did play was so hot that this time I couldn't help simply jumping up and shouting. Bix just sat and stared at me.

When I got up to take it off, Bix said, looking at me coldly, "You *liked* that?"

*All the sides mentioned here, plus six others with certain changes of personnel, recorded 1928, are available in reissue on *The Bix Beiderbecke Story,* vol. 1 (Columbia CL 844).

"Liked it? For Christ sake, Bix! It's the best thing you ever put on wax!" I cried, throwing caution overboard without a lifeboat. "You don't like it?"

"Like it?" Bix said, returning my gaze with distaste. "I wanted to break the God damn thing. Jesus, kid, you must be deaf. Didn't you hear all the idiotic mistakes on that?"

"You mean where you started to come in on Frankie's solo, and then dropped out again? Sure, I heard that—so what? Who *gives* a damn? You played so great on it, what do I care about a couple of . . ." I shook my head, speechless.

Bix stared again. "How about where I spoiled the whole take by blowing sharp on purpose?" I had never seen him so angry. He actually jumped up himself and put the record back on, putting the needle down in the middle of the record. "And listen to this piece of corn, where I stuck in that phoney Charleston lick, as a gag; I was so upset about spoiling Frankie's chorus, I thought the take was n.g. anyhow, so—"

"I heard that, I heard that!" I yelled back at him. We were actually quarreling—the first and only time. "Who the hell *cares?*"

"You'd like to play piano that bad," Bix said nastily.

"So what?" I shouted. I broke off to listen to the record again, which had reached the spot where Bix blew sharp on a couple of high notes, high and fortissimo—an unusual register for him to be blowing in anyway. I couldn't help laughing as Bix winced and said, "Yeah, sport, how about *that?* Can you imagine their *releasing* a take like this? Damned if they ain't, though! They're all deaf! Outside of that, everything's perfect down at Okeh recording studios!"

"What happened, Bix?" I asked. "Why'd you blow sharp like that? Just trying to spoil the take on account of what happened before?"

Bix shook his head. "No," he said. "I went ahead and blew my solo anyway, O.K.? You know, I thought, What the hell, and I could see the guys in the booth are still waxing. So just as we're getting blowing good there, the engineer starts going like this. . . ." Bix made a rapid rotary motion with his hand, the signal for *Hurry it up and finish, we're short of time.* "I got so damn sore—that's when I blew those sharp notes. But they're as deaf as you are, kid —they *liked* that take." He shuddered and finished his drink. "*I* wanted to destroy the God damn master, but don't you think they decided to let it go through?"

I didn't feel like discussing it further, and put the last record on. "What's this?" I said. "You finally made a piano record? A solo?" I got excited again.

"Yeah," Bix said, expressionless. "I finally made a piano record. It's a real wet firecracker, but they'll probably release it, too, so now *everybody*'ll be able to hear how good I play," he finished with a sardonic smirk.

I didn't reply; the record had begun, and I squatted down again with my ear to the soundbox.

The record was *In a Mist,** Bix's only recorded piano solo. At last! There he was, Bix on piano, as I'd been listening to him since he first came to the house three years before. Oh, it was feeble, stiff, self-conscious, compared to what I'd heard him do hundreds of times in our living room—pale stuff for Bix, but still unlike anyone else; instantly, unmistakably Bix, nobody else in this world! Once more, the alternating strains of modest semiclassical melody and modern French harmonies, against the dirty jazz stomping— Bix's familiar Jekyll-&-Hyde personality, complete with uncertain tempo and a few blurred fingerings.

I played it over again, without comment. It was charming, mistakes and all. It wasn't high-power Beiderbecke by a long shot, but it was Beiderbecke.

When I finally took it off, Bix was silent a moment. Was he waiting for a reaction from me? Did he give a damn what I thought? At last he said, looking at me, "You like that too?"

I said slowly, "It's not as good as I've heard you play myself, but it's . . . some of it's great. When does it come out?"

"Oh, I'll get you a copy," Bix said. He seemed suddenly subdued. He went back to the sideboard and poured another drink. Then, in a voice in which for once there was no sarcasm, he said, almost to himself, as it were, "I figured I might as well make at least one piano side, you know? So I got hold of Bill Challis—he wrote it all down—I couldn't have done it at all without Bill . . ."

I nodded.

"I don't know when this other shit comes out," he said negli-

*Now on vol. 3 of *The Bix Beiderbecke Story* (Columbia CL 846).

gently. "Sometimes they release the whole batch at once. I never could figure out what a recording company thinks about."

"You going to leave these here for Vic to hear?" I asked.

"Oh. . . . Yeah, O.K.," Bix said. "Might as well." *Might as well!*

He sat down to the piano for a while, but his heart wasn't in it today, and he soon abandoned it. I had a chance to look at him carefully for the first time, and realized he looked odd in some way. He looked—I fished mentally for a word—*prosperous*. Brand-new suit, brand-new shoes, smart-looking quiet tie, fresh clean shirt, and from my post on the rug I could see his ankles clad in neat new silk socks, not folding down around his ankles for once but evidently held taut by garters. Bix in *garters!*

He got up to pour a final shot of booze, and I said, "Bix, you look like a Brooks Brothers ad. You must be in the dough."

He grinned. "Didn't you hear?" he said. "I joined the Whiteman band."

I blinked. "That tub of shit?" I exclaimed. "When?"

"Couple of weeks ago. The money is great, and I'm going to have to really do some reading, I guess. They haven't been too tough on me so far."

"I thought you were still playing with Goldkette."

"Yeah, well, that folded," he said. "Tram* and I talked to Whiteman before, and . . ." He trailed off. "It's quite an outfit," he said.

"I can't stand that son of a bitch and neither can Vic," I said coldly. "I don't know how you can work for him. As a musician, he isn't fit to shine your shoes, in my opinion."

Bix looked uncomfortable. "He ain't very jazzy," he said unwillingly, "but you gotta respect the way he holds that big outfit together. And the arrangements are stiff, man. I hope I can cut 'em."

"Good luck," I said sourly. "Just be careful where you stand in the men's room."

Bix laughed shortly. "Vic told me all about that," he said. "I guess it could've been worse."

"Yes. Lucky Paul Cartwright happened to walk in when he did, or it might have been Vic in the hospital instead of that big tub of shit."

Bix nodded, not too happy. "Whiteman's telling everybody Vic

*Frankie Trumbauer.

started it. He says Vic had a knife, or a blackjack or something."

I laughed. "That's pretty hot. Can you see Vic with a knife?"

Bix had to laugh too. "No, not exactly." He got up to go. "Oh, well, what the hell," he said—his favorite expression. "What the hell, I guess I'll be O.K. there if I just mind my own business and play when he points at me."

"Yeah, I guess," I said. I still couldn't picture Bix playing in Elephant Land, which was the way I always thought of the Whiteman organization. "You won't be making any records like these, though," I couldn't help saying.

"Oh," said Bix, "I don't know. I don't know what you're raving about. If I had my way, I'd destroy those masters and try again."

"Yes," I said, rather tartly, I fear. *"You would."*

"Well—so long, kid."

"So long."

It was the only approach Bix and I had ever made to a real confrontation.

I didn't know then that it was also the very last time I would ever see him alive.

He certainly seemed to me, that day, to be at the very top of his form musically and otherwise. Those tests he'd played me *were* the best Bix I'd heard on wax. He had never looked so well heeled or well dressed—positively a fashion plate. And however much I personally might deplore the association of such a talent as Bix's with such a crassly commercial behemoth as the Whiteman orchestra, which to me smacked of naked prostitution, it was plain that Bix wouldn't have agreed; he obviously regarded his being hired by the behemoth as a *musical* step upward, a door opened upon a new dimension in his own development; that impression has been borne out, I know now, by the investigations of the biographers. It would not be, I think, too much to say that Bix regarded his new job as a step toward the realization of his private dream—whatever we may think that was, and with whatever admixture of private confusion.

Confusion would ultimately triumph; the bright dream would end in final nightmare, like a star-shell burning out and dropping, extinguished, to its dark end—but only after a struggle that lit up the sky, filling it with a melody brilliant, unique, and brief, whose echoes have refused to die.

26
ZENITH,
DECLINE & FALL

Victory comes late,
And is held low to freezing lips
Too rapt with frost
To take it.

How sweet it would have tasted,
Just a drop!
Was God so economical?

Emily Dickinson

Pee Wee Russell:

He was a very gentle man. He had a very, very good sense of humor. For him there was nothing better than a good laugh. He was a perfectionist for himself in music.[25]

Louis Armstrong:
. . . And all of a sudden, Bix stood up and took a solo . . . and I'm tellin' you, those pretty notes went all through me. . . .

. . . Well, you take a man with a pure tone like Bix's and no matter how loud the other fellows may be blowing, that pure cornet or trumpet tone will cut through it all. . . .

After the show, I went directly backstage to see Bix . . . and when they went on the stage for their next show, I cut out and went straight to a music store and bought "From Monday On" *. . . and put it with the rest of my collectors' items of his . . . from* "Singing the Blues" *on down to* "In a Mist" *. . . they all collectors' items. . . .*

When Bix would finish up at the Chicago Theatre at night, he would haul it out to the Sunset . . . and stay right there . . . until the customers would go home.

Then we would lock the doors. Now you talking about jam sessions . . . huh . . . those were the things . . . with everyone feeling each other's note or chord, et cetera . . . and blend with each other instead of trying to cut each other . . . nay, nay, we did not even think of such a mess . . . we tried to see how good we could make music sound which was an inspiration within itself. . . . Bix would get on the piano and play some of the sweetest things . . . real touching . . . he was getting ready to record his immortal "In a Mist" *. . . the tune is still fresh today, as it was then . . . you couldn't* *find a musician nowheres in the whole world that doesn't still love Bix's "In a Mist."*[26]

Jimmy McPartland:

I got a call at eight one morning from Bix. He'd left his tuxedo at the cleaners at the last town, and he asked if he could borrow mine. Then and always he could have anything I had.

All during the date at the theater, (we) gathered between shows . . . and jammed. Bing Crosby would play the cymbals or the drums if there were no drummer. Bix always preferred to play the piano at a session, and this time he asked me to play his new Bach cornet. . . .

I fell in love with it, and Bix asked, "Would you like to have a horn like this?" He took me over to the Dixie Music House after the next show, put down one hundred dollars and said, "That's all the money I have with me. But I guess you can scrape up the other fifty. You can give it back to me sometime."

I never did see that tux again. Do you think I cared? I still have that horn, by the way. Bix warmed it up . . . for a few shows, then I used it. . . . Now my four-year-old grandson, Dougie, has it.

People have often asked me what Bix was like. . . . He was very reticent. His main interest in life was music, period. It seemed as if he just existed outside of that.

I think one of the reasons he drank so much was that he was a perfectionist and wanted to do more with music than any man possibly could. The frustration that resulted was a big factor, I think.[27]

Mezz Mezzrow:

Late in '27 sometime, Bix suddenly fell into town. . . . He came backstage with Bing Crosby (Bing was singing in Whiteman's trio, The Rhythm Boys . . .). The first thing he said . . . was, "Come on, let's go get a drink." Down through the Loop he led us, along State Street, until just off of Lake Street we met up with a . . . store that looked like it had been condemned before the Chicago fire. A peephole slid open, an eye appeared in the hole and gunned Bix; then the door swung open like a switch-blade. I guess the mug of that bottle baby was known to every peephole attendant in the Western Hemisphere.[28]

Pee Wee Russell:

I first met Bix I'd say in the latter part of 1926 . . . in the Arcadia Ballroom in St. Louis. Frankie Trumbauer had the band and had brought Bix down from Detroit. . . . I came home one afternoon and there was Bix with Sonny in the living room. . . . It gave me a big thrill to have Bix in my home. Among musicians, even at that time, Bix had a reputation. Very few of us understood what he was doing. . . . He drove a band. He more or less made you play whether you wanted to or not. If you had any talent at all he made you play better. It had to do . . . with the way he played lead . . . with his whole feeling for ensemble. . . . Records never quite reproduced his sound. Some come fairly close but the majority don't.

. . . He had a hard time with some of those records. I don't mean that the men he recorded with weren't musicians . . . but they didn't belong. . . . So it was all due to them that a majority of the records didn't quite catch what Bix could do. But Bix's disposition wasn't one to complain. He wasn't able to say, I don't like this guy, let's give him the gate and get so and so. . . .

Without a doubt, music was all Bix lived for. I remember we used to have a Sunday afternoon thing at the Arcadia . . . the band would complain about the extra work, but Bix would really look forward to it. He said he liked to see the kids dance . . . do things like the Charleston . . . because the kids had such a fine sense of rhythm. And, in their way, the kids knew what Bix was doing . . . something different, because he made them want to dance. . . .

Bix had a miraculous ear. . . . There'd be certain things he'd hear in . . . modern classical music, like whole tones, and he'd say, why not do it in a jazz band? . . . Music doesn't have to be . . . put in brackets. Then later it got to be like a fad and everybody did it. . . .

We would often order a score of a new classical work, study it, and then request it from the St. Louis Symphony. And we'd get ourselves a box . . . when they did a program we all liked. . . . We'd haunt them to play scores we wanted to hear. Stuff like The Firebird. *. . . We wanted to hear these scores played well.*[29]

Max Kaminsky:

I was seventeen and in my third year of high school when Bix

Beiderbecke came to Boston with Jean Goldkette's band that spring of 1926. . . . Mal Hallett's orchestra . . . went on first . . . then Barney Rapp's band . . . finally the Goldkette band came on. . . . They opened with "Pretty Girl Stomp," *went on to* "Ostrich Walk," "A Sunny Disposish," "Clap Yo' Hands," *and ended with* "Tiger Rag," *and they were such a stunning sensation that when . . . it was time for Mal Hallett's band to play again, neither his musicians nor Barney Rapp's men would pick up their instruments.*

"How can you follow that?" Mal . . . asked plaintively. . . . Nobody had heard anything like this music before.

. . . I just sat there, vibrating like a harp to the echoes of Bix's astoundingly beautiful tone. It sounded like a choirful of angels. When I did work up the courage to go over and speak to Beiderbecke . . . I was still so overcome I could hardly get a word out. . . . He kept his eyes fixed on his shiny black shoes and solemnly nodded his round blond head at each halting word. . . . Suddenly I remembered having heard that he liked baseball. . . . I blurted out an invitation . . . to a game the next day. At the mention of baseball, Bix's diffidence vanished. . . .

"Sounds fine to me," he said in a soft-pitched Midwest accent. . . . I asked him if he would write out a hot chorus of "Blue Room" *. . . he obligingly fished a piece of manuscript paper out of a pile of sheet music on the littered table next to the bed and wrote out a 32-bar chorus in about three minutes. Even in the heat of improvisation Bix was wholly aware of his sequences and afterward could reconstruct exactly what he had played. When I questioned him about a weird G# . . . he explained to me about . . . passing tones to give color or tonal accent to a phrase, and he went on to discuss anticipation . . . all a part of making the music swing . . . just getting to be understood then.*

I was terribly worried . . . about how to keep a conversation going with Beiderbecke, but eventually I discovered he had no need of small talk; he seemed to be busy all the time with his own thoughts. Aside from music and baseball, he had only one other form of communication, if you could call it that; he'd kind of turn aside and sing a little snatch from a Bessie Smith or an Ethel Waters blues record. "The whole song is right there in that phrase —hear it?" he'd say suddenly. A gentle, silent man with a dreamy, preoccupied manner, he was one of the most fascinating persons to be with that I have ever known, for no reason that can be explained except that his playing cast such a spell over you that you were irresistibly drawn to him, in awe and gratitude and love. He felt that, of course, and he responded to it in his own inarticulate way. All he ever really seemed to care about were music and whiskey. . . . When I met Bix again in Chicago at a speakeasy called the Three Deuces, he disappeared. . . . I discovered him later seated at a battered old upright in. . . . the darkened downstairs dining room. . . . I sat down at one of the tables and listened while he spun out notes from a silver spool. His piano style had the same crystal purity of tone, the same perfect taste, and the same melodic grace that flowed from his horn, but it was more impressionistic. . . .

Louis and Bix are the two great originators of jazz. . . . There was the ethereal beauty of Bix's tone, with its heart-melting blend of pure joyousness and wistful haunting sadness. There was his sense of form, his hotness, his shining fresh ideas, his lyricism, his swing, his perfect intonation, and his impeccable, matchless taste. His intervals were so orderly, so indescribably right, like a line of poetry. Listen to those intervals and try to explain how Bix could think to play like that. Whom did he have to hear? Bessie Smith? Louis? They knew what they knew, but who could teach Bix what he knew? Bix knew.[30]

Benny Green:

By 1927 Bix had reached the point of perfect balance between his inborn jazz gift and his artistic awareness of European music. . . . Before 1926 he was far cruder. After 1928 he suffered partial and inexorably advancing paralysis because of the relentless advance of those same sensibilities. The point of balance was reached in the handful of recordings he made with Trumbauer in 1927–28.

. . . The really significant thing about Bix's solos in "Singing the Blues," "I'm Coming, Virginia," *and* "Way Down Yonder in New Orleans" *is that the playing is the product of a completely confident and lucid mind. . . . For the first time the unbiased listener can . . . come to grips with the reality of Beiderbecke's greatness. . . .*

Like Hamlet, "Singing the Blues" *is full of quotations. It is the most plagiarized and frankly imitated solo in all jazz history. For trumpeters of the same school, like Bobby Hackett and Jimmy*

McPartland, it has become a set piece, a tiny fragment of improvisation that has come to achieve the unexpected dignity of a formal composition.

. . . The listening musician, whatever his generation or style, recognizes Bix as a modern, modernism being not a style but an attitude. . . . Bix's solo . . . with its formal logic, its subtlety, its sureness of movement from cadence to cadence, and its characteristic implication of a deep sigh in place of the extrovert passion of his coloured contemporaries, is musical literacy of the rarest kind.

The Bix solos of this period are museum pieces . . . the first peak reached by the white musician in his pursuit of what had been exclusively a coloured muse. In the person of Beiderbecke the contact of the white races with jazz blossoms for the first time into minor works of art. . . . In Bix, the racial exuberance of Louis Armstrong has been distilled through an alien temperament. There is melancholy in Bix's playing, but . . . not the extrovert melancholy of the blues. It is something unmistakably bittersweet . . .[31]

Richard Hadlock:

. . . "Singin' the Blues" *left an impression on virtually every saxophone and trumpet player and, with the exception of Louis Armstrong's* "West End Blues," *has probably been more widely copied than any jazz performance recorded in the twenties. With this record, a legitimate jazz ballad style was announced . . . whereby . . . songs could be played sweetly without sacrificing virility. . . . Bix Beiderbecke . . . changed the pattern almost single-handedly. . . .*

As usual in his best work, Bix's solo . . . is architectonically sound and as ordered as a written composition. It was, in fact, included in later orchestrations as originally played, and at least two cornetists, Rex Stewart and Bobby Hackett, recorded the Beiderbecke solo in later years. . . .

Thus surrounded by top musicians, good arrangers, and close friends, Bix was enjoying what must have been the most rewarding months of his life. True, he was a spoiled child, the pet of the band, but he was getting better and better at reading his parts . . . and was earning his keep as a widely known and most extraordinary jazzman.

*. . . Irregular hours, random diet, and too much alcohol were
beginning to tear him down. Conventional relationships with the
opposite sex were, as far as one can tell, not important enough to
occupy Bix's thoughts for very long at a time. . . . Even among jazz
musicians, a notoriously individualistic lot, Bix was regarded as
a rather odd duck.*

*Goldkette's band . . . collapsed in September, 1927 . . . but Paul
Whiteman stepped in to rescue Trumbauer, Challis, Steve Brown,
and Bix by offering them permanent positions in his lumbering
organization of thirty-odd performers.*

*Whiteman paid high wages. . . . In the case of Bix Beiderbecke,
he was buying a useful commodity, a man who could improvise
on any given piece of music and lend an authentically "hot"
sound . . . whenever the effect was called for. The price to Whiteman was $200 a week, plus putting up with occasional unex-
plained lapses and tolerating a third chair man who couldn't read
very well. For Bix, it was lots of money, an opportunity to improve
his reading, and intimate contact with light concert music, which
had always interested him. It seemed a fair exchange. There would
still be recording sessions under his and Trumbauer's names on
which to let off steam.*[32]

Marshall Stearns:

*If the Original Dixieland Jazz Band made jazz a household
word in 1917, Paul Whiteman made it semi-respectable in 1924.
That is . . . as respectable as high-powered publicity from coast to
coast could make it. . . . Rudy Vallee described the "new" music
as "symphonized syncopation," a reasonably accurate label for
the light classics played by Whiteman with a businessman's
bounce . . . diluted beyond recognition. . . . However, it sold well.*

*. . . He put together the largest band yet and played carefully
rehearsed arrangements which featured as many semi-classical
devices as possible. By 1922, he controlled twenty-eight bands
playing on the East Coast, received $7,500 a week at the Hippo-
drome, and grossed over a million dollars annually.*

*. . . Whiteman advanced the cause of jazz immeasurably. After
the [Aeolian Hall] concert, jazzbands—good and bad—had an
easier time finding jobs. . . . Whiteman's own tendency was toward
adopting European concert devices and blending them with jazz.
The result was striking, easily intelligible, and profitable. . . . It*

was simple for his own publicity men to crown him "King of Jazz."[33]

Jimmy McPartland:

Bix didn't talk much, and there was certainly no conversation when a record was on. After it was over, we'd talk about how the chords resolved . . . how different and interesting the harmony was.

. . . I remember, about 1929 . . . he took me to a Stravinsky concert at Carnegie Hall . . . by the New York Philharmonic. We used to talk about writing a jazz symphony. The plan was to give the soloists a terrific background with a good beat and then let them take off. Nothing ever came of the idea. . . . I wish he'd put down on paper . . . what I know was in his head. . . .

One thing about his jazz records . . . I think it's remarkable he sounded as good as he did, carrying all that dead weight he had for accompaniment.

Bix contributed a lot to jazz. . . . He made it more musical. . . . I think almost any jazz musician . . . has one way or another been influenced by Bix.

. . . People used to ask Bix to play a chorus just as he had recorded it. He couldn't do it. . . . "I don't feel the same way twice. That's one of the things I like about jazz, kid, I don't know what's going to happen next. Do you?"[34]

Dan Morgenstern:

"In a Mist" is a masterpiece, featuring Hubbard's glowing horn in a woodwindy setting beautifully crafted by [Don] Sebesky. Bix Beiderbecke's 1927 composition (for piano, not trumpet) retains its haunting essence, and Bix's love for wholetone scales gives it a "contemporary" flavor. It is the most challenging material for Hubbard on this set (I doubt that the other pieces . . . will survive for 45 years) and he rises to it; his lovely rubato statements at beginning and end are reason enough to hear this album.[35]

Gunther Schuller:

The Wolverines recordings made for Gennett in 1924 are eloquent testimony. Though his beautiful golden tone was to become even richer in subsequent years (and recorded to better advantage), it already stands out as a unique attribute, not equaled even by Armstrong. Bix's tone had a lovely unhurried quality, perfectly centered, with natural breath support and a relaxed vibrato. Here, in fact, Bix showed his independence from Armstrong. Comparing the two, we note the extra daring in Louis' solos, the almost uncontrollable drive, the rhythmic tension—in short, playing in which all technical matters are subservient to the expansion of an instrumental conception, the exploration of new musical ideas. By comparison Bix was a conservative. His ideas and techniques combined into a perfect equation . . . the demands of the former never exceeded the potential of the latter. His sense of time, for example . . . within its limitations he was almost flawless. He showed a sure attack and a natural feeling for swing. Thus each tone . . . was a thing of beauty: an attack perfectly timed and initiated by a pure, mellow cornet timbre.

Bix had a quality extremely rare in early jazz: lyricism . . . .[36]

Bix's fascination with large orchestrations and arranging techniques did not come upon him suddenly in 1927. Even in the Wolverines days, the recordings . . . disclose advanced riff-ensembles . . . that anticipate [Don] Redman's arrangements for [Fletcher] Henderson of "Copenhagen" *and* "Sugar Foot Stomp," *and even some of [Jelly Roll] Morton's Red Hot Peppers records . . . the 4/4 beat and swing of the arranged ensemble . . . in* "Tiger Rag" *is amazing in its own right, regardless of historic precedence.*

Beiderbecke had an artistic consistency and integrity that never left him, even as he became more and more surrounded by commercial bands and arrangements. His many recordings with various Trumbauer aggregations and Whiteman attest to this: he was never less than remarkable, especially as seen against his surroundings. Very often he was superb, as in his great solo on "Clarinet Marmalade," . . . "At the Jazz Band Ball," *or his extraordinary attack and bright, joyous tone on* "Sorry." *Occasionally there are even, inexplicably, moments of real discovery, as in the middle of his solo chorus on* "Sorry," *when Bix plays an "asymmetrical" between-the-beats phrase as naturally as if he had done it every day for years. . . . But his crowning achievements were the superbly timed, relaxed, mellifluous solos on* "Singin' the Blues" *and* "I'm Coming Virginia." *Here is the essential Bix, unspectacular, poignant, with a touch of reserve and sadness shining through. . . .*

Beiderbecke's career was too short and too checkered to permit

*a complete review of his work. The period between March 1925
and early 1927 is not represented on records at all* and, of course,
nothing remains of the hundreds of jam sessions he is said to have
played as an antidote to life with the Whiteman band. His premature death precipitated a legend. . . . But even on the basis of his
recordings alone, Bix deserves to be more than a legend fashioned
out of the extra-musical syndromes of the Jazz Age. He deserves to
be called one of the truly great jazz musicians of all time.*[37]

No matter where I was, no matter where Bix was, I continued
to hear news of him, and to acquire his records as fast as they came
out, if not before. I need hardly add that that was exactly how I
and all his other admirers felt about them: they were "his" records, regardless of whom he was playing with or whose name was
on them as nominal leader.

The records Bix made with Paul Whiteman must remain for all
time as one of the most peculiar series of bastardized, hybrid
concoctions ever perpetrated in the whole history of the very
peculiar, hybrid art of jazz. To understand them, fully to penetrate
them in all their unbelievable panoply of bad taste, barefaced
pretentiousness, stupefying, monstrous, limitless vulgarity, and
portentous triviality, is to understand some profound and ugly
truths about the curious uses to which art and beauty may find
themselves put in our curious, fucked-up society—and some
equally profound and beautiful truths about the blind persistence
and tenacity of the human animal in general, and Bix's creative
instinct in particular.

That a man who was never himself a jazzman, and couldn't have
swung a single bar of music to save himself from the electric chair,
should have become known to the general public as the "King of
Jazz," tells us a great deal about both Mr. Whiteman and that
public. The fact that, as Marshall Stearns correctly reports, the
title was invented and conferred upon Whiteman by his own press
agents, is incidental; what is significant is that the public enthusiastically accepted it, like bubble gum and Billy Graham; obviously
it struck them as exactly the right note.

I would go further, and assert that there was even a kind of

---

*This seems to be an error. According to Wareing & Garlick's discography
(*Bugles for Beiderbecke*, pp. 308–9), Bix cut at least twenty-four sides with Goldkette, all on Victor, in 1926.

inevitability in such a choice, as symbolically appropriate as the choice, by the mob, of Barabbas instead of Jesus as the man to rescue from execution on the cross. Given the unerring instinct of the public in matters of art, it would have been surprising—the student of our life & times would feel distinctly taken aback—if in the so-called Jazz Age the populace had been found calling an actual jazz genius like Louis or Bix "King of Jazz" rather than some self-promoting purveyor of musical chewing gum, without, so to speak, a jazz pore in his entire body, like Whiteman—somewhat as though the national thirst were suddenly to choose fresh fruit juice instead of Coke. Once we understand that, there is no real irony in the fact Stearns rightly noted, that it was Whiteman—"of all people!"—who most visibly "advanced the cause of jazz." Who else indeed? What other sort of man could as effectively capture the ear of such a public—a public that, interestingly, has year by year increased its per capita consumption of sugar (it is now roughly 125 pounds for each man, woman, and child); could have calculated so nicely how much real jazz it would tolerate in its normal diet of musical syrup? Mr. Whiteman, I presume, had no trouble at all; he had only to consult his own infallible taste buds.

Up until the time he joined the Whiteman aggregation, I'd only heard Bix playing straight jazz, with small jazz combos. Inadequate as they were to give him the kind of backing or reciprocity that might finally have made him happy, still they did allow him the freedom to speak his piece in an atmosphere of carefree improvisation—in a word, the *jazz* atmosphere. Now came a growing stack of recordings with Bix in a setting we'd never conceived —playing leads and solos in big "arrangement" bands. (Once you get beyond six or seven musicians, you have to have arrangements or the musicians get in each other's way musically.)

Arranged jazz is today so common, even in the smallest groups, that only die-hard Dixieland and New Orleans purists will know what I mean when I say that jazz people like Vic and me, in 1927, couldn't take the sound of arranged jazz at all. Even listening to Fletcher Henderson's and Duke Ellington's bands was a trial for us except in the solo spots, where their men were improvising; we lifted the needle from the arranged-ensemble portions of the record. That being so, it may easily be imagined how we felt about hearing Bix's cornet come soaring out of a Goldkette or Whiteman orchestration. The Goldkette records at least had a general jazz orientation, and a really inspired arranger in Bill Challis, who moved mountains to make the ensembles swing, which they actually did on occasion. But it was the Whiteman records that really threw us.

I can't remember now which Bix-Whiteman records I first heard —not that it matters much; they pretty much followed the same pattern. Probably the first one we got hold of was *Changes*—I forget what the other side was. We listened, we shuddered, as the nineteen-piece elephant got to its feet and tried to dance; winced at the molasses-harmonizing of the sizable vocal group, which included Bing and the other "Rhythm Boys," who made sure not to spare us a high-camp vo-de-oh-doh passage—and then we came alive as Bix slashed in with a solo, like a beautiful, familiar face emerging momentarily from the greasy garbage-covered waters at an East River wharfside, only to sink out of sight again as the real Whiteman sound once more took command.

Vic played it over again—doing his best to avoid all but the tiny Bix solo passage. Afterward, we sat in silence for a moment; I could literally taste my rage, but could say only, "Jesus. Bix, in *that band.*"

"Like a stained-glass window in a shithouse," Vic said, then added philosophically, "Oh well, he's only doing what I've been doing all my life—making money."

It was true. What couldn't money buy? But we were both unaware that poor confused Bix had actually viewed his joining the Whiteman army as a long upward step in his musical development.

One other thing bothered me, though, listening to Bix's solo in *Changes.* "What the hell is he doing there," I wondered, "using a *mute?* I never heard him do that before."

"That ain't all." Vic laughed. "They tell me he's growing himself a mustache and a potbelly."

"I don't believe it," I said. "I have to see that for myself. Where are they playing? Is the band in town?"

"No, they're on the road somewhere. Tell you what: next time they come into New York we'll go catch them. What do you say?"

We never did, though. I think now I might not have been too anxious for another confrontation with my fallen hero, as I viewed him now—the great white shining knight sold out to the Philistines and using his horn to sell souvenirs and belly dancers to a crowd in front of a Coney Island peepshow. (At sixteen I found such sins hard to forgive, never dreaming I would spend most of my own "career" selling my white body for as much as it would bring in the literary marketplace.) It's true I was now busy enough, trying to combine the professions of musician, painter, and prize-fighter (in addition to trying to lead the love life of a sultan), but —everyone somehow manages to scratch where it really itches— if I'd still felt about Bix as I had three years before in Chicago, I'd have damned well seen to it that I caught up with him in person, no matter how or where. Now the bright shield had been tarnished; apparently I had other things to preoccupy me than keeping tabs on the itinerary of the Whiteman band. What, indeed, would I have had to say to Bix if we had met backstage after the embarrassment of watching him sit taking orders from "that big tub of shit"?

I was in Cuba; I was in Woodstock; I took my own little jazz band (nonunion) into a borscht-circuit summer hotel, where our compensation was fifteen dollars a week (thirty dollars to the leader), room & lavish Jewish board, eager young housewives from the Bronx looking for a vacation romp in the hay, and my first brush with crabs and blue ointment; I fought several pro fights at five dollars a round, thoughtlessly K.O.'ing my opponents (all of whom were actually superior boxers) in the second or third round; I began exhibiting with the Woodstock Association as their only surrealist (Eugene Speicher, the strictly academic square who reigned there, had, I was told afterward, urged the hanging committee to give me house room on the grounds that "we really ought to have one wild man in this God damn gallery"); I fell in and out of love four times in ten months. I don't know where Bix was, but those records kept coming out, and I kept hearing about him and his drinking, his hilarious exploits, his losing battles with his own absentmindedness: taking the wrong train, or the right train on the wrong day; going out to find a speak in a strange town and forgetting what hotel he was staying in; falling asleep in the middle of a golf game after losing all his balls; showing up at a railroad depot in pajamas (he'd packed all his clothes and sent his trunk on ahead)—and a lot more I've forgotten now, some of which have shown up in various biographies and album notes.

It's strange now to realize there was no written jazz criticism in those days—jazz wasn't an art; you dug it or you didn't—and I was shocked, only a couple of years ago, to read in Charlie Smith's liner notes to RCA's LP reissue *The Bix Beiderbecke Legend* (LPM-2323) this appalling little fact; I quote:

He was to become a great name in jazz, but only after his death. Would prescience of this belated fame have eased his frustration, this composer of choruses, this artist who, in his own country, in his own lifetime, was praised perhaps twice in print, and then obscurely? "How can anyone know what it was like?" Pee Wee asked.

Now, forty-five years later, naturally I treasure those lousy Whiteman records just as all the other Bixophiles do. Like everyone else I listen with irritation, boredom, or amused tolerance to the vintage Jazz Age corn and "symphonic" drivel that you have to put up with before and after Bix's golden solos; like other jazz critics I now hear with new ears the amazing feats of arrangers like Bill Challis and Tommy Satterfield (the less said about Ferde Grofé the better), who managed against all odds to juggle the several incongruous elements—Bix's uncompromising jazz inventiveness on the one hand and shaky reading on the other, the enormous orchestra's many technical talents and relatively immovable bulk in terms of jazz swinging—and come out with some passages, quite apart from Bix's improvised solos, that actually sound like jazz, with Bix driving the entire brass ensemble, which they wrote around Bix's earlier improvisations and then taught Bix to repeat, *either reading his own written-down inventions or learning them by heart if that was too hard!* The results sometimes are sheer wizardry; there is no other word; and they testify among other things to the strength of character of guys like Challis, of the limitless love and admiration they must have carried around in their hearts for Bix and his amazing genius, how profoundly they understood that genius and its limitations, their determination to make something truly musical out of the mess when possible, in spite of everything.

A strange, tense, precarious situation for both Bix and his allies, votaries, and midwives within the band; but how long so delicate a balance could be maintained was a question. As the event proved, not very long.

I don't truthfully know whether Bix's downhill slide began before or after the great Wall Street Crash of '29, and I also don't know that it matters much. Whichever came first, the Crash cer-

tainly didn't help musicians any, especially jazz musicians. It signaled the end of the Jazz Age, the end of the carefree, reckless,
let's-do-it-now-tomorrow-I-may-be-somewhere-else mood of a
large segment of the American public, which had emblazoned the
device JAZZ on its shields and gonfalons.

Maybe the big slide really started for Bix toward the end of
1928, when Whiteman switched from Victor records to Columbia,
with a much more commercial policy, and at about the same time
took on a big radio network show, the Old Gold Hour, in competition, according to Ed Nichols,[38] with the B. A. Rolfe Orchestra on
the number one commercial radio music show of the era, the
Lucky Strike Hour. The arrangements got tighter and tighter,
more and more syrupy, "symphonic," and full of commercial bullshit. Bix's fellow trumpet section men and worshipers had always
helped him out with his faltering reading of parts, teaching them
to him by ear when he couldn't hack it himself, but they couldn't
teach him whole arrangements, and Whiteman was becoming
increasingly disenchanted with Bix's nonconformist style. More
and more of his time away from the bandstand was spent in
speakeasies lifting his elbow, or, out of town, in his hotel room
drinking. Ironically, if we're to believe Pee Wee Russell, one of the
most scrupulously honest of jazz's informal historians, it was Bix's
very popularity that helped rub his nerves raw, in what might
otherwise have been hours of quiet recuperation:

As for what caused Bix to destroy himself, well, in that era, naturally
where he started, around Indiana, there was that thing with the hip bottle
and the gin—the 20s and all that stuff. Later, when he'd acquired a name,
he could get a bottle of whiskey any time of day or night. Now Bix enjoyed
a drink but he was human too. Everybody likes privacy. Privacy enough
to sleep and eat. But it was impossible for him to get any. There were
always people in his room. They would knock on the door even at six A.M.
and it was impossible for him, because of the kind of person he was, to
insult anybody, to say get out of here.

I remember how, at one hotel, he used to leave word that he wasn't in.
So some fellows would check into the hotel, take a room on the floor below
Bix's room; then they'd come up and rap and pound on the door and you'd
have to answer. He even had a piano in the room, and, when he had a
spare moment, he'd try to get a composition started, but with all those
people always hanging around he didn't have a chance. In a sense, Bix was
killed by his friends. But I think the term is being used loosely. Because

they weren't his friends. They were the kind of people who liked to be able to say, "Last night I was up at Bix's and oh, was he drunk. . . ." You know that type. . . . They wanted to be able to say they were there. . . . And Bix couldn't say no. He couldn't say no to anybody.

I remember one Victor date we did. Bix was working in the Whiteman band at the time. He had hired me for the date but rather than hurt anybody's feelings he also hired Jimmy Dorsey and Benny Goodman and Tommy Dorsey and everybody.

Every time somebody would walk into the door at Plunkett's, the bar we hung out at, Bix would say "Gee, what am I going to do?" So he'd go up to the guy and hire him for the date. He didn't want to hurt anybody's feelings. So he went way over his budget and we had to scrape cab fare to get back from the date.[39]

The best proof that Bix hadn't joined Whiteman's orchestra because he loved money and security are the eyewitness accounts of his friends—his real friends—at the time, regarding his behavior toward money and security. Nothing about him had changed, in that department, since the early days with the Wolverines. We need merely compare two statements of Jimmy McPartland, his lifelong disciple—one about Bix in 1924, the other when Bix was nearing the end of his rope with Whiteman—the same old Bix:

(1) . . . Bix . . . had just about everything I looked for in a musician. . . . Those Wolverine records . . . we just wore the records out. We copied off the little arrangements, and what was going on in the ensembles. . . . I was tremendously influenced by Bix. . . .

I was going to join the Flyers [a jazz combo at Station WGN, Chicago] when I received a wire one fateful day from Dick Voynow. . . . The rail fare was $32.50 . . . to New York . . . third-class coach, no Pullman or anything. And that was exactly the sum Voynow sent me [that's Voynow, all right! —R.B.] . . . Well, I left that same night—with just my bag and my little beaten-up cornet. . . .

And Bix—as I say, I had never met him. . . . Let's call him the master and leave it at that. . . .

The Wolverines were rehearsing that afternoon, and by the time I got there I was plenty nervous. Of course, I had memorized all . . . the band's records. . . . I knew all Bix's lead parts. . . . I played their routine, took my solo where Bix used to take his. . . .

Now Bix . . . didn't say anything until the rehearsal was over. Then he came over. "Kid," he said, "I'll tell you what. . . . You'll move in with me. I like you."

. . . For about five nights we both played in the band. First Bix would take the lead, then he'd play second . . . to break me in. He was an enormous help and encouragement, and I got to admire the man as much as the musician.

I must tell you about his generosity to me, a complete stranger to him until I took his place in the Wolverines. After a few days he asked me, "How can you blow a horn like that? It's a terrible thing."

. . . Out we went to see Voynow, who gave Beiderbecke some dough. Then . . . over to the Conn company, where Bix picked up four or five horns and tried them out. Finally he said, "This is the one, Jim, for you."

He just gave me the cornet—period. So that I would have a good instrument to play. . . .[40]

(2) My last . . . association with Bix was in New York. The Pollack band hadn't been working for almost two months. Eight of us, including the Goodman brothers [presumably Benny and his brother Harry, who played bass], were in one hotel room, and we were really scuffling for food. Then at a cocktail party on Park Avenue I ran into Bix who'd just come back into town with Whiteman. . . .

Bix took me into a corner and pulled out two hundred dollars. I told him ten was enough but he said, "Don't worry about it, kid, you'll be making money soon . . . you can pay it back." I did, in about eight months. . . .

In the last months of his life, I'd see Bix quite often at a little speakeasy on Fifty-Third Street called Plunkett's. . . . Bix was ill, looked bad, all swollen up. He drank, didn't eat, stayed up late, got very depressed. Whiteman had sent him home to Davenport for a while, but it didn't seem to help.

I remember one night he had a very bad cold, and he was broke besides. I told him to go home and stay there until he got over the cold and lent him some money. "Thanks, kid," he said. "I'll be all right. I've got a job at Princeton in a couple of days." That was the last I saw of Bix.[41]

By that time I wasn't in New York any more myself except occasionally. During the 1927–29 boom days my mother had bought a great beautiful house in Woodstock (in Bearsville, actually, up in the woods a mile from the crossroads) called the Red Roof. We'd made maybe twenty-five payments when the Wall Street Crash hit. The whole family, all except me, migrated to Hollywood, where Vic and Gene both started working in the movie studios to try to retrieve our shattered finances; I stayed at the Red Roof with whatever girls were around after the Depression hit, and eked out a living modeling for other artists, driving a truck, chopping wood on shares, cleaning out privies, and anything else that came along. I had an old Winchester .38/40 rifle, and in the winter of 1930 used to go out in the morning and shoot rabbits, which I traded to the local butcher shop for other meat.

Around December first, the Red Roof was sold at auction, to satisfy the unpaid mortgage and other debts, with everything it contained except the clothes I stood in. That included the pretty little Mason & Hamlin baby grand, our vast record collection, Mummy's treasured exotic drapes, rugs, and furniture, worth possibly thirty thousand dollars at 1929 prices, not counting the house and its forty acres of woods. The sum it brought under the auctioneer's hammer was seventy-one dollars—not bad for the winter of 1930–31. It was enough to get me out to California anyhow.

Everything I know about Bix's life during this entire period is strictly hearsay or what others have remembered or researched.

Among the many curious facts I knew nothing about was one dating all the way back to 1925, when, it seems, Bix took advantage of one of his many brief visits home to make yet another attempt to pursue his formal musical education.

According to Benny Green,

In February 1925, already a professional musician of three years standing, Bix enrols at the University of Iowa, registering for English, Religion and Ethics, Music Theory, Piano Lessons and Music History. At his first interview with his freshman advisor, Bix asks to drop Religion and take more music instead. . . . The request is refused and instead Bix is ordered to enrol immediately for Military Training, Physical Education and Freshman lectures. Four days later Bix and the University of Iowa part company. . . .[42]

Green has some other remarks worth quoting, in a generally sensitive and perceptive sketch of Bix's life, spoiled here and there by a spurious posture of cynicism toward Bix's other admirers, and an affectation of finding Bix's tragedy essentially "comic"—on what grounds is never quite clear—but the piece is more than redeemed by passages like this:

So far from being a moral coward who sold out to the highest bidder, Bix was the blind unreasoning artist who followed his advancing sensibilities as only a blind unreasoning artist can, completely oblivious of the consequences. To the critics unable to appreciate the kind of musical compositions which had so fascinated Bix, this issue of his advancing sensibilities is an inconvenient fact to be pushed hastily out of court on the grounds of lack of proof. Bix was not a conveniently prolific letter-writer or diarist who chronicled his development for the edification of posterity. He was not even a conscious artist at all. Nonetheless the truth is as self-evident and as irrefutable as if he had left a signed statement. It is implicit in his movements from band to band, in the development from the Wolverines through Whiteman to his death, and above all in the later compositions for the piano.

It is the supreme irony of Bix Beiderbecke's stay with Whiteman that he came to the orchestra seeking after a state of musical grace, unwittingly endowing Whiteman as he did so with the only real musical grace that clumsy group ever possessed. Bix in the Whiteman band looking for pearls of wisdom was like Tarzan at a Keep Fit Class. To any intelligent jazz fancier the one letter Bix actually did write . . . to his mother telling how frightened he was at the thought of joining a band as renowned as Whiteman's, may seem comical enough. . . . Here is this gifted musician about to bestow on a mediocre vaudeville act his own talent, a musician so far above the jazz standards of almost all his contemporaries that today we only tolerate the horrors of Whiteman's recordings at all in the hope that here and there a Bixian fragment will redeem the mess. And here is that musician telling his mother that the Whiteman band over-awes him.

The summation of the whole Bix-Whiteman paradox is contained in the . . . recording of "Sweet Sue." Every indelicacy that might conceivably be crammed into a four-minute performance is included in what the sleeve notes to the American Columbia Memorial album describe with some restraint as "a real period piece." Quacking brass, lumbering tubas, the tinkling of bells and the clashing of cymbals, portentous slow movements and dashing fast movements, comically bogus profundity, saccharine harmonies, teashop violins and what sounds like a deadly parody of every singer, male, female and neuter, who ever sat in the ranks of a dance-band. In the midst of this farrago, the listener may discover a single chorus by Bix Beiderbecke which momentarily dispels the nonsense as though by magic. There is no clucking interference from the rest of the band. The rhythm section merely accompanies Bix for thirty-two bars, and everyone else, from Whiteman to the lowest menial . . . leaves it to him.

The result is that Bix, playing casually enough, never at any time approaching the intensity of "I'm Coming, Virginia," or "Way Down Yonder in New Orleans," still reaches his own level of invention, and by the effortless ease of his creativity, reveals the pitiful gulf between his own mind and the minds which conceived the holocaust preceding and following the solo. . . .

(There follows a particularly acute musical analysis of Bix's solo, celebrating his unique tone and subtle intuition.)

... Examples like this do illustrate Bix's curious individuality ... his rare ability to evoke in the listener a range of emotions not so common in jazz as one might think. The very nature of the melancholia he conjures is distinctively Bixian, sensitive and reflective, quite devoid of the element of self-pity which obtrudes in so much later jazz aiming consciously at the same effects Bix produced instinctively. The "Sweet Sue" solo is superbly musical. It has been conceived by a born musician, and that such a man could ever have seen any virtue in the feverish goings-on in the preceding and subsequent choruses, is only further proof of the mess in which the intuitive artist can land himself when he lacks the normal reasoning powers.[43]

The "mess" got no better when Whiteman had to face the fact that Bix could no longer be depended upon even for the smaller and smaller contribution he was making to the Whiteman circus. Whether from virtue or from other motives, there is no doubt that Whiteman behaved well in *l'affaire Beiderbecke*. At his own expense, he sent Bix to a well known sanitorium for alcoholics, the Keely Institute at Dwight, Illinois, to dry out. When Bix returned, thirsty and depressed, Whiteman made him go home to his folks in Davenport, hoping that would help restore him to normalcy (whatever that was for Bix). Both times Whiteman paid him his full wages during his absence, and, so it is said, kept a symbolic third chair in the trumpet section vacant, against the prodigal's return, something damned few bandleaders, then or now, would have done.

Bix's several returns to Davenport and the bosom of the family were intended, of course, as physical and emotional convalescences. Physically they seem to have worked well enough, mostly because, knowing his family's intense shame and horror over his alcoholism, he made every effort to stay on the wagon; then as always, he sought with all his heart to please them. And we must add, I believe, the good influence of Esten Spurrier, who ran around and got him jobs, helped make square band leaders and club owners in the area aware of the visitor's fame, and did his level best to keep him away from liquor—as well as giving him the best of moral support a sensitive soul like Bix's could use: the informed and sincere appreciation of a lifelong friend and fellow artist.

Esten thus was able to work alongside his idol and model, in 1930 and '31, for nearly five months, off and on. The physical well-being Bix enjoyed, in what were to be these very last months of his life, is attested by the fact that, according to this faithful companion, he never played better—"Christ," says Esten, "I never heard that much horn in my life, from anybody!" He and Esten also discussed several promising musical projects. One of them was the writing of a "Bix's Method" for aspiring trumpet players. At that period, there were a number of "Methods" being published, to teach (so far as that art can be taught) jazz improvisation, and Esten tried to convince Bix that now was the time to cash in on his enduring fame among musicians; he, Esten, would provide the labor of transcription if Bix would provide the material. Bix's response was predictable: "Shit, who'd want to copy my fucked-up ideas?"

More to his taste was his mounting ambition to "get off the Goddamn horn" (shades of Vic Berton!) and turn his full attention to the piano and composition, which in his mind went together like berries and cream. When he went back to New York, Spurrier swears, the first thing Bix did was to get himself fixed up with an apartment and to buy a brand new piano. In what may have been one of his very last letters to anyone—possibly *the* last—Bix wrote to Spurrier to the effect that his life was entering a new phase. Not only was his head filled with fresh ideas and a new slant on composing, but he had done something else even more unexpected, something no one who knew him previously had ever thought would happen: he had at last "found the right girl" and was planning to marry her and settle down. That letter, regrettably, has disappeared (Spurrier has never forgiven himself for losing it); but Spurrier, whose faculties are as keen today at seventy as they must have been at eighteen when he was playing with Bix, is very clear about its general content and tone: Bix, he could see from that letter, was moving toward a new peak of energy and professional competence: almost, one might say, toward a new career.

If this picture should happen by any chance to be a true one, it raises some new and puzzling questions. For one thing, it deals a shattering blow to that portion of the Bix legend—its last act—which for some thirty-five years or so has portrayed Bix, in the period after he left Whiteman and failed to get rehired, as a crumbling wreck, stumbling from hangover to hangover down a steeply inclined plane, bleak with unemployment and punctuated by professional disasters, burdened by a confused mind and a lip that just wouldn't function any more. On the contrary, says Spurrier, Bix told him he'd been turning down most of the jobs offered him because he wanted to concentrate on his new work of composing and getting his compositions down on paper, mostly with the help of Bill Challis, which doesn't sound much like a picture of desperation and dissolution.

The question then is, which picture is the right one? I am personally in no position to decide, not having been around Bix at the time; but I must confess I find it hard to believe that a man like Esten Spurrier, who probably had Bix's confidence as few others did, could be very far off the mark in his judgements about Bix, whom he'd known and worked with since boyhood.

On the other hand, there is no doubt that Bix was once again drinking very heavily just before his final collapse into "pneumonia" or whatever the proximate cause of death actually was—and *something* must have precipitated such a swift and terrible lapse. Did that mysterious "right girl" let him down with a crash? Did mere habit and the company of other lushes prove too strong for his new-leaf resolutions? Was his sudden onset of illness the result of mere accident or carelessness?

In themselves, none of these explanations somehow strikes us as adequate; not in view of Spurrier's very persuasive testimony as to Bix's state of mind and body right up to the time, early in 1931, when Bix left Davenport for New York, and of Bix's known attitude toward girls, and the place he assigned them in his scale of values. Regardless of how much this new romance meant to him, I simply cannot picture Bix abandoning all interest in life and in his musical career, especially at such a moment in it, merely because of the fickleness of some female, even one about whom he was "that way," as we used to say.

The habit hypothesis is perhaps more plausible, though again it doesn't sort too well with the mood of the alleged letter to Spurrier. As for his being carried off so suddenly by a mere chance illness—well, anyone can (in theory) get sick "in the midst of life"; but is it believable that a twenty-eight-year-old man with Bix's athletic background, a recent history of reform and rehabilitation, and a legion of admiring friends hard by would so insanely neglect himself, and above all so isolate himself, as to crawl into a corner and expire like a sick alleycat? It strains credulity. No, there must, it seems to me, have been a powerful death wish there, to have brought about such a conclusion to such a life.

Again I have my own theory—scarcely provable, I fear, at this late date, unless new and relevant facts should be turned up by some dedicated researcher, but nonetheless interesting and suggestive—and, if by any chance I am right, it fits all the facts of Bix's what-the-hell and don't-give-a-shit personality, and personal history, as neatly as glove fits hand. If I am right, it is certainly an appropriate ending to this work of speculation and psychological sleuthing; it has everything: dramatic correctness, poetic economy and density, and above all irony, the irony that is so typical of life's and literature's little jokes on the human race.

My theory, appropriately, intimately concerns Bix's relations with his family, especially his parents.

During Bix's lifetime, not even the good people of Davenport had any real inkling of how cruelly, how completely, the Beiderbecke family shut young Bix out of their lives, once his feet had trodden the disgraceful road of jazz, nor has it been generally realized in all the years since his death. Square and conventional to a degree that can only be appreciated by someone who grew up in a small American town, and firmly attached to the respectable musical traditions of their German forebears, the Beiderbeckes were far more anxious about the good opinion of Davenport "society" than about the fate of their one black-sheep son, who might as well have been a two-headed creature from Venus, for all they knew or cared about what was going on inside him, from babyhood onward. No one but Bix really knew, because, in the "set" the Beiderbeckes traveled in, one simply doesn't mention such things; if they didn't literally do what certain orthodox Jewish families do, to this day, when a child dares to marry outside the faith—proclaim "our son is dead" and sit shivah (the ritual mourning) for him—it was only because they were far too respectable to wash such soiled linen in public; and Bix was of course hardly one to talk about it to anyone, or even to acknowledge to himself, perhaps, how absolute was his banishment, how little concerned his own father and mother were, his own brothers and sisters, about whether he lived or died, as long as he didn't further besmirch the name of Beiderbecke.

Had Bix been the tough renegade such a family deserved, this excommunication might have had small effect; his reaction would have been a healthy *Fuck you too, Jack!* But Bix was too "good" a boy for that, too guilty about the pain and humiliation he had supposedly caused them by his defection. To the end of his life he tried to make friends again with that tribe of smug philistines, tried to persuade them in his own wordless way that becoming one of the two most famous trumpet players in the world was no crime. Right from the start of his recording career to its very end, he made it a point to mail home the first copy of each of his records as it came out, including, of course, the Whiteman sides, through which he had the most hope of impressing his square German elders—at least they had heard of Whiteman as a Big Name. In vain. We can only try to conceive what his feelings must have been, on coming home during his final convalescence and new-leaf attempt (at the tail-end of 1930), full of love and guilt, ready to try again to become their son, on discovering that not one of them—*not even his mother*—had even so much as bothered to listen to one of them. Every record was still in its original en-velope, unopened—gathering dust on the top shelf of a closet. They were ashamed of them.

Knowing Bix's feeling about his family, his unswerving loyalty (he never uttered a word of criticism against them) in the face of their prim indifference, one can only assume that this last wound went deep indeed. For Bix, failure in their eyes simply meant—failure.

(Once Bix was safely dead, and the Oakdale Cemetery became a shrine visited by pilgrims from all over the world, the bereaved Beiderbeckes rather more than made up for their previous ne-glect of those recordings. His older brother Charlie, in particular, became an overnight authority on Bix's music. In this connection, my favorite anecdote, firmly documented by several unimpeacha-ble sources, is of a scene that apparently was repeated whenever a musical visitor from the Big Time appeared in Davenport. Charlie would trot out Bix's records one by one, but saving the best —in his opinion—for the last: a Whiteman record "with the best chorus my brother ever played." That chorus, as one astonished jazz devotee and Bix-worshiper after another discovered at the very first note, not only wasn't Bix, it wasn't even a *jazz* man—on

the contrary, it was by Henry Busse, one of the corniest "legitimate" horn men who ever put brass to lip. No one was brutal
enough to tell Charlie the facts of life. He went to his grave, so far
as I know, "loving" that chorus of "Bix's.")

It is safe to assume, too, that this business with the records was
only one example of the kind of kick in the stomach, the hurts
large and small, that Bix got from his loved ones, in what was to
be his last visit home. Is it not within the realm of reasonable
possibility that this final "400 blows," coming at such a crucial
turning point in his life, might have preyed on his mind to a point
where he eventually felt he needed "just that one drink" to ease
the pain? Would it be unreasonable to assume further that an
alcoholic's "one drink" might easily turn into a final, fatal binge?

Bill Challis, the arranger who played a crucial role in helping Bix
put his musical ideas across, first in the Goldkette band, then the
Whiteman band, finally in writing down and arranging all of Bix's
piano works, starting with *In a Mist* (one critic has called him
"Bix's Boswell"), is still active in the field. As this book was being
readied for the press he told me, in simple, nonmelodramatic
terms, the way it was that last year.

"Jack Robbins was really the guy who made it possible for us to
get all that stuff written down and published," Bill said. "He was
ready to publish anything Bix composed. Bix would play it for me
on the piano, improvising, going over it until he got it more or less
the way he wanted it, then I'd notate it. He was very particular.
If I didn't have it exactly right, to his ear, he'd make me work it
over until it was. He knew exactly what he wanted, all the time;
with him, there weren't any two ways to do something right. Of
course Bix needed the dough too, the little advances Jack Robbins
kept handing out to him. Jack wasn't a bad guy that way—I imagine a lot of musicians were into him for quite a bit of money, but
where Bix was concerned he never liked to give him too much at
once—he knew what would happen to it. He'd just dole it out to
him. You had to do that with Bix, or he'd probably give it away or
drink it up, and there he'd be, flat broke again.

"It took nearly six months to get *In a Mist* written down just
right, to please Bix. After Bix made the record, Jack Robbins
wanted another, longer strain in the middle of it—he'd had such
a big success with *Rhapsody in Blue*, you know, and he was looking for another one with Bix; so Bix just improvised a whole new

section—fantastic. He was the most creative musician I ever knew, I guess. I wish I had had him around with me the last fifteen years or so now; he would have become known as one of the greatest American composers if he'd lived—unbelievable talent and ideas. Anyway it wasn't that easy to get it down on paper; every time I'd have him play it over for me and try to write it down he'd change it a little, improving it all the time; and of course Bix wouldn't settle for anything he thought could be better. Six months of that. Most of the time we worked at my place—I had an apartment at the Park Crescent Hotel on Riverside Drive and Eighty-seventh Street. Bix would call me up, sometimes at weird hours, and come over and start to play, and I'd start writing. Sometimes I'd have to fix the fingering—you know, so ordinary piano players could play it; Bix often didn't finger things the way anybody else would.

"That last year, after he came back from Davenport the second time and Whiteman couldn't afford to rehire him—anyway we were out on the Coast then, I mean the band was, making the *King of Jazz* movie—Bix was just waiting around, looking for jobs, and there weren't any jobs. It was hard enough for regular routine studio men to get jobs in 1930, '31, let alone a musician like Bix; who understood what Bix was doing, in 1931? He had no one to play to, or with. He must have been about the most frustrated musician that ever lived. There were just the two extremes then —hot Dixieland, and the sweet commercial big-band stuff on radio—and Bix didn't really belong with either of them. So he just ... God knows what he did, that very last year. After he composed *In the Dark* and *Candlelight* and *Flashes* . . . that was about the time I moved out to Greenwich, Connecticut, and I didn't see much of Bix any more. Sometimes when I'd come into town I'd run into him. But times were really tough then. That Wall Street Crash—it didn't hit us immediately, took about a year or two, but when it did, it really hit us. Whiteman had to cut his band down from about thirty pieces to sixteen. We all got fired—me, Lenny Hayton, Tommy Satterfield. Everybody was scuffling, not just Bix. But I think he took it harder than anyone else. He was so depressed. I remember him always carrying that horn around—he didn't even have a bag for it then—just carried it around bare, like a kid going to a parade. And nowhere to play it.

"I got him a job once with the Casa Loma Orchestra out in Detroit, but he only stayed about four days. He couldn't take the kind of mechanical precision they insisted on—it just wasn't his kind of creative music. Then I got him into, or I tried to get him into, a radio studio orchestra here in New York. I even wrote a special arrangement—I forget the tune now—that featured Bix in just the right way to show him off good. That was fine, but then what? Those other musicians didn't really know what Bix was, what he was doing. It didn't work out. He lasted just that one time, and then he was out again, without a job.

"I don't really know what anyone could have done. The guy was born in the wrong time. Maybe if someone with a lot of money and musical appreciation had come along and subsidized him—you know, just said, 'Here—just sit down and compose, take your time —never mind about money'—that would be the only thing. But even then, I don't know. He needed an outlet too, for all that music he had in his head—where was the outlet in 1931? Now is when he should be around."

Just about the time I talked to Bill Challis, mid-June, 1973, I had a curious encounter on a mountain road. It was dusk, and I was driving back toward New York from the Catskills, near Woodstock, when I saw an elderly man hitchhiking. I stopped and picked him up. I asked him what was wrong with his feet—I had seen he was lame—and he said he'd hurt them years ago, when he was a hoofer in vaudeville. We got talking; I told him I'd been raised in show business too; and finally got around to the book I was just finishing, about "a famous trumpet player of the twenties."

He wanted to know who; I told him Bix Beiderbecke.

"Bix?" said the old man. "I roomed with him at the Forty-fourth Street Hotel—and for your information, young fellow, he played a cornet, not a trumpet."

He began to reminisce about Bix. "He wasn't much of a talker," the old man said—his name was Bill Duffy; he danced under the stage name of Jean La Marr—"but what a musician. But he was in terrible shape that last year when I knew him. Ten in the morning he'd already be over at Plunkett's—did you know Plunkett's?"

I told him I knew Plunkett's all right; my brother Vic must have pretty well paid their rent some months. Duffy knew all about Vic too, from the time he first played in Sam Lanin's band at Roseland, opposite Fletcher Henderson.

"Ten A.M., eleven A.M., Bix was already there, with a snootful.

Jesus, he could put it away. Very seldom would you see him what you'd call drunk, though. Always a gentleman. Nice as he could be. And give his last dollar away if he thought you needed it—you didn't have to ask. Not that he ever had much when I seen him then. He couldn't even come up with the room rent, but what the hell, I didn't care. He was just nice to be around, even though he wasn't no talker. And I was making it in those days, booking bands, and all that.

"Only one time I saw him really bad. And that was the last time. I was just coming into the hotel, you know, and here comes Bix out. I don't know what it was. He seemed like he'd had some disappointment—something more than the usual. And he was drunker than I had ever seen him. Glassy-eyed. He just looked at me like he didn't know who I was, and started to walk by me, you know, out into the street—it was a rotten hot night too—and then he sort of come back inside and shook my hand, not saying a word, but Lord! he did look bad. And then he turned around and walked out and fell straight out into the gutter—just fell like a log. I tell you, man, my heart jumped: I thought he was a goner. I ran out after him, but do you know what? He just picked himself up like nothing at all had happened, and smiling that little smile of his, he walked away up Forty-fourth Street. It was the last time I seen him alive. Never even came for his few little things. A couple days later I was out on the road again, and then a month or so after that I heard . . . well, you know, I guess."

For a long time, there was a story that Bix had a bad cold, and was supposed to play a dance down at Princeton University, and that Saturday night there was a terrible snowstorm, but the people promoting the dance said No Bix, no dance, so for the sake of the rest of the band, Bix got out of bed, sick as he was, and traveled to Princeton in a car in all that blizzard, and played the dance, and that was how he got his fatal pneumonia and was dead a few days later.

It sounded a lot like Bix, and for years that story circulated in magazines and in biographical books, until someone thought to look up the date of his death, and started wondering what college boys would be doing running a dance in the middle of the summer, and how it happened to snow in August—but I still read more restrained versions of that story, here and there.

Hoagy Carmichael, who may have really been the last of the old gang to see him alive, told about some girl friend Bix brought around to his, Hoagy's, pad a few weeks before the end, Bix looking bad and the girl having no idea who Bix was or even that he was a musician; and the girl had (Bix said) fixed him up with an apartment out in Sunnyside, Long Island, just across the river.

Not that all that matters very much. Any or all of the stories could have been true, knowing Bix, knowing what sort of a guy he was, a guy who would without any doubt get out of a sickbed to play a date and not let the rest of the guys down; a guy who didn't live any particular place for any particular time, and who might just as well be out in Sunnyside as in the Forty-fourth Street Hotel or the kid brother's room at the Bertons' or anywhere else handy, and who wouldn't bother much about taking care of himself no matter where he was flopping, because somehow he'd been born into the wrong world at the wrong time, and it was time to leave.

27
AUGUST 11TH, 1931

. . . and when he shall die,
Take him and cut him out in little stars,
And he will make the face of heaven so fine
That all the world will be in love with night,
And pay no worship to the garish sun.

Romeo and Juliet, Act III, Scene 2

Sybil emerged from the shower, nude, glistening in the diffuse sunlight from the half-drawn blinds over the bed, ravishing as a Botticelli, gazing contented, while she toweled herself, on my sprawled nakedness; put on her smock again, kissed her fingers to me, and tripped back downstairs. A moment later I heard her machine going.

I emerged reluctantly from my dream, eyes glazed, to the shuttered afternoon heat; crawled to my feet; stumbled to the shower myself. My limbs revived in the cool stream. . . . How good life was! I didn't bother drying myself; the sun would do that for me.

I'd just picked up my brushes again when the phone rang. My mother.

"Birdie," she said, her voice very low and quiet, "you wouldn't know where Vickie is?"

I looked at the clock; two-thirty. "Probably at the studio, working. Why, Mummy? Is anything wrong?"

"No, no," she said, "nothing. I just wondered what time he'd be coming home."

I reminded her that this was Tuesday, so he probably wouldn't be coming home at all until tomorrow afternoon sometime. From Paramount he'd probably go right to the job at the Coconut Grove, and then, at 2 A.M., to the County Jail for the night.

"Oh, that's right," she said slowly. "I forgot." She hung up.

A couple of months back, Louis Armstrong, fronting Les Hites's big band, had opened at Sebastian's New Cotton Club out in Culver City, across the road from the MGM lot. Naturally Vic and I were at a ringside table. Louie and Vic were always a mutual admiration society—each knew, and said to anyone who cared, that the other was the greatest on his instrument in the world, ever. What a band that was. Lionel Hampton was on drums; he got up when we came in, with the usual ceremonial announcement: "Uh *uh*, I ain't playin' no damn *drums* in front of Vic *Berton!*" and presented Vic with the drumsticks, while Louie and the band looked on, grinning. . . .

Between sets, around midnight, Vic and Satch went out in the parking lot to light up. Vic had a whole can of new Mexican golden leaf he was going to lay on Louie. They were sitting in Louie's car, smoking a joint and rolling some more, when The Man came up behind them and flashed a light into the car, and a badge, and that was it.

Every musician had warned Vic that L.A. was a "bad" town. The cops took Vic and Louie downtown, where they spent the night in a cell, laughing it up—they were still high. They stopped laughing the next morning, when the judge gave them six months and one thousand dollars fine each. But even as the felons, handcuffed, were being led away to their fate, the *deus ex machina* appeared: Abe Lyman, Vic's leader at the Coconut Grove, with his brother Tommy, who was a wheel in L.A. County politics (rumored to be the bootlegger & procurer of the Democratic party boss), met with His Honor in chambers and explained the facts of life to him. Pointing out that by locking up these two giants of music, he would be throwing approximately a hundred Americans out of work, Tommy added that he had already "convoised" with Big Ed, and that Big Ed would be troubled to read in some Republican paper tomorrow "where a Democratic judge had added a hundred U.S. citizens to the ranks of the unemployed"—who, in 1931, numbered fifteen million.

His Honor was a rational man. Court was reconvened, the two felons brought back upstairs, and, in view of "new evidence," given modified sentences that wouldn't interfere with their working hours: for the next six months, they'd have to sleep in the jail hospital five nights a week. In practice this meant driving downtown after work every night, parking in the space marked VISITORS, signing in, fooling around with the night nurses, going to bed in private rooms, not always alone, sleeping till noon, breakfasting with the day nurses, signing out, and going about their business. Justice was satisfied, and so, I presume, were quite a few of the nurses.

I sat down again to my easel, but felt for some reason vaguely uneasy. I laid my brushes down and went back to the telephone.

"Mummy? Is anything wrong?"

She hesitated, tried to say something, and her voice broke. Alarm spread over me like a blanket of ice. "For God's sake, Mummy, what is it? What's wrong?"

"Ralphie," she said at last, and I could scarcely hear her, "Bix . . ." There was a pause; she gave a little sob. My heart contracted.

I said it for her. "Bix is dead."

In the last fifteen minutes, three different musicians had called, asked to speak to Vic, then told her.

I asked when, where, how. New York, she supposed; no, wait, Jackson Heights? Wednesday or Thursday of last week, she thought.

Without being told, I could picture Bix all alone in some rotten furnished flat. . . . *Finally managed to drink himself to death* bitterly crossed my mind.

"Oh, Ralphie, how sad." Mummy was crying softly. "Poor Bixie, so young, so young . . . what was he anyway? Twenty-seven? Twenty-eight? His poor mother!"

I said it was stupid to bother Vic at the studio. What was the point in upsetting him in the middle of a rehearsal? If in fact he hadn't already heard it from other musicians. *You hear about Bix? Oh, man, no, no!* . . . I could picture Vickie's emotional face: fierce unbelief, then violent grief. . . . There was surely no rush.

Gene. Gene would be over at UA now, probably screening the film, sketching out his preliminary ideas for the score. Tell them both tonight after dinner.

"All right, Sonny," Mummy said. "All right, whatever you think."

I hung up, sat back on the bed, clenching my fists, trying to focus my mind on the reality. Then at the thought of telling Vic and Gene it hit me at last. I started to cry, had myself a real *crise*, face down in the pillow, cursing life, hammering the bed till my fists hurt, *God damn you, God damn you*—whom, I couldn't have said. I stood up, biting my lip and tasting blood in my mouth, not knowing I'd done it. I felt all my muscles strung taut; I wanted to kill, to tear something apart, rip apart a veil and make them give back Bix.

Well, it passes. I sank on the bed again, panting a little. Sybil's machine going again, stopping, starting. I was glad she'd been downstairs when Mummy called, with her machine going. I didn't think I could stand anyone asking me at that moment, *Who was Bix Beiderbecke?*

I threw on a pair of pants and went across the street to Mummy. Gene was already home. He was raging.

"Christ!" he said, tears in his eyes. "Why *Bix?* Why not some no-talent son of a bitch like Joe Schenck?" (Joseph M. Schenck, head of United Artists and then of Twentieth Century–Fox, was the latest producer on Gene's shit list—probably something to do with ruining a picture score. Gene called him "one of the deaf elite.")

I telephoned Sybil to say I wouldn't be home tonight, there'd been a death in the family; I could hear she was hurt by my distant manner.

The three of us sat up late, gloomily pondering our own roles, what we'd individually done or hadn't done. Hadn't we all seen, or rather watched, the early stages of Bix's self-destruction? I recalled what Gene had once said, very early on—that Bix would never live to be thirty the way he was going. Dead at twenty-eight. Gene shuddered; he'd be twenty-eight himself in October. Two years older than Keats and Pergolesi were when they died, Gene remarked bleakly, two years younger than Shelley, three years younger than Schubert.

And Gene, who had never understood one note of Bix's immortal music, made a keen observation: "He always seemed to me like a man who's gotten off at the wrong station, and is trying to find out what time the next train leaves."

No one felt like dinner that night. But later, when I was in the kitchen alone with Gene, sucking an orange, he said something that really floored me.

"In a way," Gene said, as though to himself, standing with folded arms gazing out at the lights of Hollywood—our "view"—"in a way, you know, I blame myself more than anyone. My own God damn selfishness."

I said, wondering, "Why you? You had almost nothing in common. Not even music, really."

"We had more than you think. I don't mean just because of our little fling. I mean that in a way I was *doing* with my life what he *should* have been doing—and do you know something? He knew it too. Bix knew it. We never mentioned it—but *we should have.* I might have influenced him. He had great admiration for my music, even though his meant nothing to me."

"Wait a minute," I said slowly. "What do you mean by a 'fling'?"

"What?" Gene said, his graygreen eyes momentarily blank. "Oh. *That.* Don't tell me you didn't know?"

"No," I said, a little resentfully. "How would I know?"

Gene shrugged. "I don't know. It's unimportant. Why? Do you object?" he said challengingly.

I didn't reply for a moment, but turned away, cutting up my orange.

"By God, you *do,*" Gene said. "You of all people! I thought you prided yourself on your *enlightenment,*" he added acidly.

"I didn't say I objected," I said, vexed. "I just never thought of Bix as . . . being . . ."

"Homosexual? Is that the word we're avoiding? Bix was about as 'homosexual' as you are, brother. I mean let's face it—it meant absolutely nothing to him one way or the other. I don't even know how much girls meant to him, if it comes to that—or let's say sex. *You* know his favorite phrase: 'What the hell.' That was about where he stood, on nearly everything but his music: *What the hell.* He was . . . what? For God's sake, Rafe, you must know yourself Bix would do just about anything you suggested to him—if it didn't take him away from his God damn horn too long—just because he couldn't think of a really good reason *not* to. Isn't that true?"

"That's true."

"Maybe he was curious. Maybe I intrigued him. Maybe he just didn't want to offend me. I don't know. It's the sort of thing that can happen to *any*one—believe me—given the circumstances. Just ask me, brother."

I had to smile, unwillingly, in spite of myself, shaking my head incredulously. "Bix—and you. Son of a bitch, Gene, you're something."

"Oh, forget it for God's sake. I'm sorry I ever mentioned it. I'm sure *he* forgot it. I can hear him now: 'Huh? Who? I did? Oh. Yeah. Maybe I did. How about that? Oh, well, kid, what the hell.'" I couldn't help a wry chuckle. I'd forgotten that Gene had started his professional career doing "impressions."

Dismissing the whole subject as unimportant, he went on, "You remember that time I asked Bix why he hadn't learned to read or play piano properly, since he loved it so much—loved Debussy, loved Scriabin and Stravinsky. . . ."

I remembered very well.

"Now for a *jazz* musician not to read is one thing—I don't know anything about that and don't give a shit anyway—but I gather it doesn't really matter, they even seem to brag about it. . . ."

I nodded. " 'What would we do if the lights went out?' " I quoted.

"Exactly. But Bix wasn't satisfied just being one of those. He *yearned*—Christ, how he yearned—after *real* music. . . ." I mentally bristled but didn't interrupt. "Well, brother, you can't 'fake' *that*. Any more than an illiterate peasant could act Shakespeare. He never had an answer to that question."

I wasn't sure I had one either.

Around noon the next day Vic drove into the driveway. I saw at once that he knew. His eyes were red, and when he saw me the tears welled anew.

"Well," he said, speaking with difficulty, "the stupid son of a bitch went and died on us, didn't he?" He squeezed my hand hard, put his powerful arm around my shoulder, and we walked into the house. He went to the bar, poured a stiff shot of bourbon, and gulped it down, poured another.

"You want one?"

"O.K.," I said.

"We should have tried," Vic said huskily. "Tried to get him . . . out here in the sunshine. Being broke out here's not as bad as New York."

"Was he that broke?"

"Shit, he was always broke. Well—you know, whenever he had it he gave it away."

"You sure he's dead?" I said suddenly. I'd just had a vision: Bix, sick but alive, myself rushing back to New York, bundling him into a cab, nursing him all the way here on the Chief; saw him in a warm bath, scrawny and sick, then out in our patio soaking up the sun with Mummy bringing him a bowl of milk with fresh figs from our little tree—watching him get tan and healthy out here as I had. . . .

Vic said, his voice flat, "He's dead, all right. His body's on the way to Davenport right now in a baggage car, if I'm not mistaken." *Jesus.*

Wearily I walked back across the street. Climbing the steps to our splitlevel shanty, I heard, as from a distant observation post, every trite philosophic cliché that ever visited the bereaved come limping through my dull brain: how meaningless life was, how fragile, how short. I could hear Sybil's machine stop as I came up the steps.

I'd never thought of her as sensitive, but this time around she couldn't have been more appropriate: she just folded me in her arms. I felt her heart start to thump against my chest.

Incredibly, I felt my loins stir in response. And a shameful feeling: *glad to be alive.* This was what it was all about, this hot belly against mine, female, yielding, its heat felt right through the thin cotton, pressing, insistent as life. . . .

It was different this time. This time I didn't sink into my customary after-coma. This time it was Sybil who lay as if dead, mouth a bit open, beaded with sweat like tiny pearls, honey hair all over the pillow, damp and disordered. I studied her with new eyes, seeing as for the first time the creamy perfection of her skin, the just visible peach fuzz on her forearm, glowing yellow in one short tiny stripe where a pencil of sunlight struck through the closed blind, her slender limbs composed like those of a Modigliani nude. . . . I think for the first time I knew what it was to feel *reverence for life.*

I laid my head on her pneumatic breasts, slippery with sweat, hearing her slowed heartbeat as through a stethoscope, *k-thunk, k-thunk,* the blind insistent muscle pumping life, just that little muscle between her and death. The doctors must have listened like this to Bix's heartbeat, listened with professional intentness as it wavered, gave a last feeble *thunk* and paused . . . forever. So fragile, so pitiful, that little fistlike pump, that I wept for it, for her little heart pumping away in her sleep, wept because Bix was dead, because all of us someday . . . Well, my head at least was where it should be at such a moment of emotion: on a woman's breast, giver of life. And I too slept.

We awoke, showered, put on fresh shorts, and got into her Model A roadster, the leather seats burning our bare legs, the leather cracking and baking in the afternoon sun; it had lost its top long ago, but in California, ten months of the year, you don't need a top. We headed up into the hills.

Up a rocky dead-end road in the blinding sun, wild, deserted, lonely enough for murder or love, we got out and roamed, scrambled down gullies, tearing our palms on cactus and yucca; scrambled up a dry stream bed and came out on a rocky summit, a breeze feathering our faces. Sybil's shriek arrested me just as I was about to put my foot on a rattlesnake coiled on a rock.

"Killitkillit!" she screamed, but I was in no humor today to kill any fellow creature, not even this ominous-looking citizen. I just stepped backward carefully, to a safe distance, watching it as it watched us—self-sufficient, unafraid, courteously warning us with its dry whirring tail: stay off my turf, man. It was a Texas diamondback, *Crotalus atrox*, a really lethal species. Every scale glinted distinct in the sun like a tiny louver, the hard triangular body neatly coiled as a hawser, fitting exactly the curve of its rocky pedestal; amazingly thick in the middle part, sandcolored, crossed from end to end with an elegant black, cream, and red jeweled pattern like a beaded bag.

Never was anything more stylish. Alongside this chic, chaste design, our bodies seemed a formless, rather sloppy job. The flattened head with bulbed cheeks, like a jeweled ace of spades, rose up for a better look, its unwinking eye still as a jet button. The slender forked tongue, black and wet, darted out ceaselessly, probing the hot yellow air for information. Evidently a decision was reached. Gracefully, effortlessly, leisurely, it uncoiled; its whole magnificent length began to flow, a silent stream of undulating jewels seven feet long, over and around the rock, flowing uphill, tail and head delicately lifted, poised, uninvolved in the rest of the smooth ballet. Sybil had stopped shrieking to watch with me as the long leather-and-bead fugue glided up the slope and disappeared between two jagged boulders. . . .

We counted our money and decided we had enough for a crab dinner out at Redondo Beach. Sybil drove; I lay back with eyes shut, wind in my face, setting sun ahead, reveling in just being alive. . . . Dostoievsky's painfully accurate observation came to me like a thorn in the foot. Our first thought on witnessing a fatal accident: *It wasn't me.* I must have dozed again.

When I came to we were rumbling over the timbers of the fishermen's dock at Redondo. Inside the wooden shanty were long pine-board tables spread only with white wrapping paper from huge rolls. The crabs were big as dinner plates, cooked in caldrons that, it was said, had never stopped for ten years, spiced with cayenne peppers, oregano and cumin; all you could eat for a buck, with red garlicky spaghetti and Dago red in tall green bottles, fifty cents a bottle; a big trough of escarole salad in the middle of each table, help yourself.

We ate and drank and joked with the Lucchese kids. Mama Lucchese, fat and steaming, sat nursing the latest family addendum and urging Sybil, on, "Eat! Eat! Whatsamatta you so skinny?"

The stars were out over the black Pacific sky when we reeled out to get into our little chariot, now cold and clammy to the touch. We put on sweaters. I drove homeward along the empty highway between the miles of oil derricks looming black against the stars. A flood of remembered incident welled from my soul: Bix and Chicago, days and nights listening, New York, Miller Beach, Indiana Avenue and Thirty-first, Keuka Lake, crazy Old Man Jones, crazy like a fox. Sybil with her new marvels of sensitivity was silent, only resting an unobtrusive caressing hand on my back.

And because she never once asked me who was Bix Beiderbecke, I began at last to tell her.

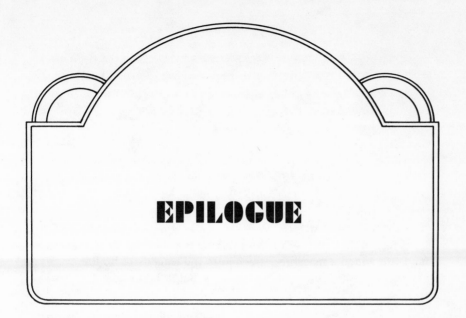

EPILOGUE

He was a man, take him for all in all,
I shall not look upon his like again.

Hamlet, Act I, Scene 2

Leon Bismarck Beiderbecke, the immortal Bix, died young . . . His youthful death added a macabre attraction to the tragedy of his life.

—Ralph J. Gleason, *Jam Session*

Bix was neither a tragic nor an heroic character.

—Rudi Blesh, *Shining Trumpets*

The saga of Bix Beiderbecke is not any more tragic . . . than the stories of dozens of jazzmen who lived through the Twenties. Romance aside, Bix died mostly from pneumonia.

—Richard Hadlock, *Jazz Masters of the Twenties*

The . . . tragedy of his life was . . . with the music itself.

—Benny Green, *The Reluctant Art*

I suppose it depends on how you define "tragedy." The classical view, as set forth in Aristotle's *Poetics*—"from which all Western appraisal of tragedy has flowed," according to one popular encyclopedia*—is that it is rooted in *character,* which must contain the fatal flaw that makes the hero's fall inevitable.

I hesitate, after 2300 years, to tangle with Aristotle (to say nothing of "all Western appraisal"), but I feel compelled to add the rather obvious postscript that character alone cannot assure defeat, or victory either for that matter, unless *circumstances*—that is, time & place—are there to cooperate. E.g., Ibsen could not have written *Ghosts* in the age of penicillin; ruined girls no longer appear on Father's doorstep in Act III, a tragic little bundle in their arms; there is no bundle; they are on The Pill. And in 1974, Joan of Arc would have ended, not at the stake, but on the David Susskind show.

My own favorite footnote to Aristotle is Marx's witty "Men do

*The Columbia Encyclopedia, 3d ed.; article "Tragedy."

make their own history, *but not just as they please."* Hardly as they please; rather, always in some unique context of circumstance, which may well determine whether they survive to make anything at all. Apropos, I certainly regard Bix Beiderbecke as an authentic figure of tragedy, but if he had been born in, say, 1953 instead of 1903, there would very likely have been no tragedy. Certain essential ingredients would have been missing. Reaching adolescence in our day, his alienation from his square family, in which he seems to have been the only beautiful soul, would have been nothing unusual. Today his elders would simply sigh "Generation gap" and go about their business; they would long since have learned to accept, because they could tag them with readymade labels (e.g., "dropout"), things that in 1918 were, at least within the middle class, rare and unnamed, therefore scandalous and unthinkable; today familiarity has dulled their edge. By age eighteen, as one of the Now Generation, Bix would probably have been living in San Francisco or the East Village, wearing dirty shoulder-length hair, leading a group called The Beautiful Soul and banking $2000 a week. With his native gifts, including his aversion to soap and conventional living, Bix would doubtless have been right at home in our contemporary LSD subculture. Except for his fanatic dedication to work and passionate perfectionism, it would not be altogether unjust to describe Bix as a premature hippy, born fifty years too soon.

In the loose and permissive seventies that may sound rather like a joke, but it surely was no joke to the anxious snobs that comprised the Beiderbecke tribe—nor, above all, to the bewildered little culprit himself. From the moment his elders became aware of the strangeness in Bix's character, his abnormal and singleminded dedication to music and only music—*his* music—they set out to kill it. In the end, the only way to do that was to kill Bix; and as we have seen, that risk doesn't seem particularly to have given them pause. Or so I read the record.

If no worse, they certainly succeeded in raising a boy so confused, so entirely lacking in any clear focus on his own identity, goals, or problems, that it was only a matter of time—not very much time, at that—before he became so baffled by the discrepancy between his aims and his accomplishments, so disgusted with himself and the world, that nothing mattered any more, not even his work: he simply gave up the futile struggle.

Whom can we blame? His idiot family is the most obvious (and convenient) target; but can we blame the blind for not admiring the Elgin marbles? Fully to appreciate their hierarchy of values, we need only stop and think for a moment about the most mind-boggling irony of all—I mean, of course, the origin of the very name "Bix." It was short for "Bismarck," which by 1903 had become a revered, obligatory family name, solemnly conferred upon one male scion after another (according to the school records, Bix was at first registered simply as "Bismarck Beiderbecke," the "Leon" being added later). Yes, reader, the culture hero chosen to symbolize the Spirit of the Beiderbeckes, the light that guided their footsteps through this vale, was none other than that latter-day Jenghiz Khan–Napoleon, Prince Otto von Bismarck, author and architect of modern German, or rather Prussian, military might; the man who first realized the unifying power of anti-Semitism, raising it for the first time in modern history to the level of an instrument of national policy; the man who gave us Real-politik, the Mailed Fist, the Big Lie, the deliberate instigation of wars with weaker nations, ruthless suppression of thought at home, bloodbaths for the political opposition, and thus, all in good time, the makings of Hitler Germany. That was the noble states-man for whom our Little Bickie was named; I imagine both parties to this immortal joke of the gods would have been somewhat disappointed in their namesakes.

My point, however, is merely—what could one have expected from such a family? How were they equipped to see into the soul of the gentle being they had mysteriously spawned, like a gazelle in a herd of buffalo? The rest of us, to our lasting shame and sorrow, in effect did no better. It is only now, after a lifetime of experience and the most thoughtful reexamination of the case by its light, that I myself have been able to see with any clarity just what kind of mind and soul we were dealing with. It was a soul totally and selflessly committed to a poetic vision, and to its own unique way of imposing order on the raw chaos of the seen and felt world; a mind and a vision uncluttered with irrelevancies and trivialities, unencumbered by ego, emulation, competition, or petty calculation of effect—in short, the mind of a saint and genius, hard as diamond and innocent as a child's, seeing all things in its own fresh perspective ("Make It New," wrote Ezra Pound in a later essay on the essence of poetry).

It was an arresting personality, one we have met before, in literature, especially since the dawn of the Romantic era, whose quintessence it in many ways embodies; but most remarkably, I think, in those two giant creations of pre- and post-Romantic writing, Hamlet and Stephen Dedalus.

Shakespeare's "mad" prince, Joyce's "unclean bard," differed from Bix, necessarily, in being classically introspective and articulate—in their cases, an indispensable literary device. All other major points they had in common: melancholy, introversion, a reckless sardonic wit directed as much at themselves as at the world, seeing both alike without fatuous admiration or illusion. I think it was no accident that both Joyce/Dedalus and Bix were hydrophobes—part, perhaps, of their rejection of the values of a world that soaps and scrubs its skin but lets its soul putrefy in peace. Though Bix, unlike Joyce and Shakespeare, had neither the ability nor the need to formulate in words his chill alienation from the philistine world that was so briefly his prisonhouse, his artist's eye saw through that world's vulgarities and banalities with pitiless clarity; and that vision, I have come to realize, found striking expression in his unique jazz style. The clarity is all there, in Bix's crystalline purity of tone and precision of attack—his *accent;* the wit is in his *dynamics,* the sure delicate balance of loud-&-soft within the single melodic sentence; the melancholy, the all-too-accurate foreboding of early death, are in the bittersweet beauty of his melodic invention, the startling harmonic implications, the casual, almost negligent tenderness of his phrasing, the subtle *diminuendo* that ended each individual tone, that was like a small dagger in the hearts of us who listened: "It had a dying fall." There was, you see, nothing really irrational in Bix's unyielding pessimism, his eternal discontent with his own efforts to describe the indescribable. Like Hamlet, he was "but mad north-northwest"; when the wind was southerly he knew a hawk from a handsaw.

As new generations of music lovers are everywhere rediscovering today, Bix was one of the rarest artists our raw American culture ever produced; inventor of a new musical sound, cool, lonely, inward-looking—as lonely as his own soul must have been in its solitary chamber; hardly aware of the hectic landscape in which he played such an anomalous role, born far out of his time, with scarcely a glimmering of his own part in it; an unpretentious,

dedicated figure of unconscious tragedy; a strange, careless, silent
saint of the Jazz Age; above all, a human being of exceptionally
fine grain and inward grace of spirit, worth remembering: Bix
Beiderbecke, born 1903, died 1931.

SOURCE NOTES

1. Richard Hadlock, *Jazz Masters of the Twenties* (New York: Macmillan, 1965), p. 76.
2. Ibid.
3. Quoted in Charles Wareing and George Garlick, *Bugles for Beiderbecke* (London: Sidgwick and Jackson, 1958), p. 6.
4. *Jazz Masters of the Twenties*, p. 77.
5. Marshall W. Stearns, *The Story of Jazz* (New York: Oxford University Press, 1956), p. 155.
6. Ibid.
7. Ibid.
8. *Bugles for Beiderbecke*, p. 10.
9. Ibid.
10. Ibid., pp. 11–12.
11. Ibid., p. 14.
12. Ibid., p. 15.
13. Quoted in Leonard Feather, *The Book of Jazz* (New York: Horizon, 1957), p. 27.
14. Quoted in Nat Shapiro and Nat Hentoff, eds., *Hear Me Talkin' to Ya* (New York: Rinehart, 1955), p. 63.
15. Ibid.
16. Ibid., p. 64 ff.
17. *Bugles for Beiderbecke*, p. 20.
18. *Hear Me Talkin' to Ya*, pp. 103–106.
19. Ibid., p. 115.
20. Ibid., pp. 122–123.
21. Mezz Mezzrow and Bernard Wolfe, *Really the Blues* (New York:

Random House, 1946), p. 59 and passim.

22. Eddie Condon and Thomas Sugrue, *We Called It Music* (New York: Holt, 1947), p. 82 ff.
23. Hoagy Carmichael, with Stephen Longstreet, *Somtimes I Wonder* (New York: Farrar, Straus, 1965), passim.
24. *Bugles for Beiderbecke*, pp. 42–43.
25. Quoted in *Hear Me Talkin' to Ya*, p. 161.
26. Ibid., pp. 158–159.
27. Ibid., pp. 160–161.
28. *Really the Blues*, p. 147.
29. Ibid., pp. 153–155.
30. Max Kaminsky, with Virginia Hughes, *My Life in Jazz* (New York: Harper & Row, 1963), pp. 12–23.
31. Benny Green, *The Reluctant Art: The Growth of Jazz* (New York: Horizon, 1963), pp. 33–35.
32. *Jazz Masters of the Twenties*, pp. 89–97.
33. *The Story of Jazz*, pp. 165–167.
34. *Hear Me Talkin' to Ya*, pp. 157–158.
35. Record review, *Down Beat* magazine, May 24, 1973.
36. Gunther Schuller, *Early Jazz*, vol. 1 (New York: Oxford University Press, 1968), p. 188.
37. Ibid., pp. 193–194.
39. Fred Ramsay and Charles Edward Smith, eds., *Jazzmen* (New York: Harcourt, Brace, 1939); chapter "Bix Beiderbecke."
39. *Hear Me Talkin' to Ya*, pp. 162–163.
40. Ibid., pp. 144–146.
41. Ibid., p. 162.
42. *The Reluctant Art*, p. 29.
43. Ibid., pp. 38–41.

BIBLIOGRAPHY, DISCOGRAPHY, END PAPERS

Never a real "collector," I am ill equipped by nature or circumstance to provide an exhaustive catalogue of the accumulated writings about Bix, and the many recordings which he made or is alleged to have made. Fortunately, there is or will shortly be in print a bio-discography that, if I may believe report, should rather more than make up for the deficiencies of mine. For some sixteen years, Phil Evans et al. have vacuumed the universe for Bixiana, and have come up with what promises to be virtually a day-by-day chronicle of Bix's life and works. Incomplete and as yet untitled as I wrote this, the book, by Evans and a British journalist, Dick Sudhalter, was to be published "soon" by Nostalgia Press, New Rochelle, N.Y. I haven't seen the manuscript, but feel I can safely recommend it to the serious reader.

THE WRITINGS

Dorothy Baker, *Young Man with a Horn* (Boston: Houghton, Mifflin, 1938; paperback, Penguin, 1945; also New American Library).

To her credit, the late Mrs. Baker warned us, in a frontispiece, that her book was inspired by "the music, but not the life," of the late Bix Beiderbecke. Apparently, no one but me ever bothered to read that disclaimer, for every printed reference to the book I ever saw either said or implied it was a *roman à clef* "about" Bix. A turgid little drugstore novel, with a hero like no jazzman living or dead (see my discussion of it, pp. 94–95). Recommended, for laughs, to any reader who knows music and musicians. Need I add that it was a best seller in its time and, I believe, is still doing good business?

Hoagy Carmichael, *The Stardust Road* (New York: Rinehart, 1946), *passim.*

The famous composer of *Stardust, Rockin' Chair*, and other hits virtually gives Bix and his incomparable music the credit for turning him onto music as a life profession. Many other writers have doubted Hoagy's facts because of his unabashedly melodramatic prose, but I've never been one of them.

Vittorio Castelli, Evert (Ted) Kaleveld, Liborio Pusateri, *The Bix Bands* (Milan: Raretone, 1972).

This ambitious recent effort by three overseas devotees—two Italians and one Hollander—of Bix's recorded music was plainly intended to be the best yet. As a non-collector, I was in no position to judge its merits, but I gather that its reception by bona fide discographic authorities has been a mixed one. One of them told me, as a sample of its defects, that on some of the "Bix" records it catalogues, Bix is nowhere to be heard; that some others, erroneously listed as alternate takes to previously issued sides, are in fact the same as the ones issued . . . and so on. I would guess that the forthcoming Evans and Sudhalter book will turn out to be much more reliable in this way as in others.

Eddie Condon (with narration by Thomas Sugrue), *We Called It Music: A Generation of Jazz* (New York: Holt, 1947), *passim;* see its index.

Another "rich slice of Americana," from another roughneck musician. Full of intimate glimpses of Bix by a man who knew him well and tells a story with plenty of tough Irish verve.

Otis Ferguson, "Young Man with a Horn," originally published in *The New Republic* (1936), reprinted in *Jam Session,* ed. Ralph J. Gleason (New York: Putnam, 1958).

One of the earliest appreciations of Bix to see print. A mere 1,300 or so words in length, it still holds interest today as a deeply felt tribute, by a man who knew genius when he heard it. Its somewhat strenuously rhapsodic tone is understandable; there were few writers, or readers either, around in those days to support the tastes of such as Ferguson. It also had the doubtful distinction of inspiring the best-selling novel of the same name.

Benny Green, *The Reluctant Art: The Growth of Jazz* (New York: Horizon, 1963). See "Bix Beiderbecke."

Another jazz musician (British) who can also write English, albeit occasionally flawed. Some reviewer must have once called Green "acid," or "trenchant"—heady liquor for a young critic, likely to fog his spectacles forever after. As a result, an essay that is in many ways acutely perceptive is repeatedly spoiled by Green's determination to be biting; for example, calling Bix's tragedy "comic," a word he employs without taste or judgement. To read his glib and authoritative pronouncements on what went on inside Bix's head, you would never guess they were being made by a chap who was three when Bix died, spent most of his life in his native England, and had only a reading acquaintance with either Bix or his environment. So much for the bad news. Now for the good.

Much of what Green has to say about Bix's music and its meaning is sensitive and to the point; he has a keen ear for some of Bix's extraordinary gifts, and says what he has to say about them very well. He also does a good job of showing that those who thought Bix was "selling out to commercialism" in joining Whiteman (I'm afraid I was one of them to begin with) were way off target. An uneven piece, but containing a number of useful insights.

Richard Hadlock, *Jazz Masters of the Twenties* (New York: Macmillan, 1965). See the chapter "Bix Beiderbecke."

A solid contribution by an experienced, knowledgeable jazz critic, with some good anecdotes and keen criticism of the records. Dick's insight into Bix's personality, however, leaves much to be desired; this may be as good a time as any to reexamine his "laziness" theory, this time on purely technical considerations. On page 77, he explains Bix's inability to absorb a conventional education, musical and otherwise, thus simply: "Bix got by on a vast natural talent for music and a quick, searching mind, *adding to these assets as little hard work as possible.*" (My emphasis.) I suspect Dick never studied a brass instrument. I did, and would strongly advise any boy looking for the "path of least resistance" not to seek it in that direction. Factually, it takes a conscientious student about five years, practicing a minimum of four hours a day, coached twice a week by a good teacher, to develop a reasonably serviceable lip—not to mention any real degree of grace or facility. Bix had no teacher at all, and within less than six years from the day he picked up his first horn was a recognized virtuoso, admired by innumerable fellow musicians, many of whom resolved to spend the rest of their careers as his disciples or frank imitators. That took more than talent and a quick, searching mind—at a guess, around 9,000 hours of tireless work. Whether you get them in in six years or ten is, to be sure, *your* problem—but I'd like to see the "lazy" boy who could do it, in six years or twenty. Bix's solution to the problem was simplicity itself: he just practiced most of the time he was awake. I never heard of any other road to success on a musical instrument, particularly in the brass family. I really don't know why Dick didn't figure all this out for himself. Apart from that one defect, this short, carefully desentimentalized sketch well merits the label "classic."

Wilder Hobson, *American Jazz Music* (New York: Norton, 1939), *passim;* see its index.

An almost forgotten book, this coolly accurate look at jazz still stands as one of the best, not only "for its time," and Hobson's quiet appreciations of Bix as some of the most evocative. A fine introduction to what jazz feeling is all about, by a man who felt it deeply himself and expressed that feeling to perfection.

Max Kaminsky with V. E. Hughes, *My Life in Jazz* (New York: Harper & Row, 1963); see entries in its index under Bix.

An absorbing, candid glimpse into the jazz musician's life and the music business, by one of its finest workers. Maxie's stories are as honest as his trumpet-playing, which was irrevocably influenced, or rather determined, by his meeting Bix while Maxie was still in short pants, but is nevertheless distinctively his own. What Max has to say about Bix's amazing, unforgettable sound *in person* has never been said better. Highly recommended.

Wingy Manone and Paul Vandervoort II, *Trumpet On the Wing* (Garden City: Doubleday, 1948), pp. 58ff.

The jacket copy rightly calls it "a rich slice of Americana . . . the uninhibited, racy story of an Italian kid who came up off the streets of New Orleans with a battered brass cornet and turned it into a horn of gold." It's all of that, and Wingy's roughneck view of our hero is "different," to say the least.

Mezz Mezzrow and Bernard Wolfe, *Really the Blues* (New York: Random House, 1946); see the various entries in its index.

The late Mezz Mezzrow (b. Milton Mesirow), was one of the more eccentric characters in a profession not exactly noted for stuffiness, a boy from a poor but respectable Jewish family who, once he caught the jazz virus, had but one goal in life: to become, in effect, a black jazz musician. Scorning all trappings of respectability, Mezz more than once got himself into jail; an open advocate of pot-smoking as a way of life, he once drew a six-month stretch on Riker's Island for selling it; up in Harlem during the thirties and forties, marijuana actually got a new nickname—"mezz." *Really the Blues* is worth reading for its lively opinions and bizarre anecdotes (and who cares whether Mezz made some of them up?); for its highly personal (and angry) views on what was wrong with Bix; and for its equally personal picture of the jazz half-world, from the bottom looking up. Mezz wasn't really much of a musician, and he surely wasn't a writer; but when you've heard some of the record dates he put together, and have read this book, you have to admit it doesn't much matter.

Fred Ramsay, Jr., and Charles Edward Smith, eds., *Jazzmen* (New York: Harcourt, Brace, 1939; since reissued in paperback). See the chapter "Bix Beiderbecke."

Charlie Smith, a valued friend of my teens, with whom I shared a shabby Woodstock studio long ago (it was our friendship that made him, eventually, a jazz critic), was one of the last great romantics, an early-nineteenth-century man to the core. Like Bix, he drank himself into a fairly early grave. *Jazzmen* was, for America, the first real pioneering work on the jazz giants, edited by two serious scholars of the subject. A period piece, dedicated and fervid.

Gunther Schuller, *Early Jazz* (New York: Oxford University Press, 1968, vol. 1). See the section "Bix Beiderbecke," pp. 187ff.

Close professional analysis of what was important about Bix's art, by a leading scholar of jazz who also happens to be that rare animal, a musician equally at home in jazz and classical music, and a competent, literate writer on the subject. The passages describing what happens inside a Bix solo are masterly.

Nat Shapiro and Nat Hentoff, eds., *Hear Me Talkin' to Ya* (New York:

Rinehart, 1955; also in paperback). See "In a Mist: The Legendary Bix."

Frank, unrehearsed words on Bix and his fantastic impact on the people around him, mostly his fellow musicians, by those fellow musicians and a few others; some I've quoted in this book, but there's more, and all worth reading. The rest of the book has the same format, covering most of the jazzmen worth talking to or about. (As evidence of how widely the editors ranged, they even went so far as to quote *me*.)

Nat Shapiro and Nat Hentoff, eds., *The Jazz Makers* (New York: Rinehart, 1957). See the chapter "Bix Beiderbecke" by George Hoefer, Jr.

Another very good short bio, again by a competent veteran jazz critic. Until his death some seven years ago, George wrote the "Hot Box" column in *Down Beat* magazine, "the musician's bible." Like Dick Hadlock's piece, this one devotes itself in part to showing that on the one hand, the legend-mongers had often overreached themselves, and, on the other, Bix's detractors—and they too have had a vogue—knew not whereof they wrote. More good anecdotes, and one more canny view of the music.

Charles Wareing and George Garlick, *Bugles for Beiderbecke* (London: Sidgwick and Jackson, 1958).

Written in a leaden and stilted pre-Victorian prose, but full of conscientiously gathered information which was probably the best available at the time, and some reasoned discussion of various points touching Bix's influences and disciples. I'm told its accuracy has been challenged in part. A revised, updated edition was supposedly in the works as we went to press. Don't miss the "poem" that begins the book, presumably by the same fine hand responsible for the rest of the writing.

John S. Wilson, *The Collector's Jazz: Traditional and Swing* (Philadelphia and New York: J. B. Lippincott, 1958). See "Bix Beiderbecke."

Brief but authoritative listing of Bix's recordings, or a representative sampling of them, with sharp commentary, by the *New York Times*'s seasoned jazz connoisseur. A reliable guide to a lot of good Bix on wax (or as good as there was), with no punches pulled concerning the relatively feeble musicianship of most of the men around him on those dates.

THE RECORDS

To contemporary ears, any jazz record made before, say, 1935, may well prove to be an acquired taste, and Bix's records aren't necessarily an exception. It is a highly individual matter; I've seen new listeners flip over them, and others whose first reaction is disappointment: Is this the sound that launched those millions of words? turned so many famous musicians on? changed their lives? created a whole new school of jazz thought? Yes and no. Many things must be borne in mind, among them, that the furor over Bix began among those of us who heard him in person as well as on wax, and that the Bix "sound" was, when we first heard it, a wholly new thing. It would be nearly half a century before that sound was imitated, absorbed, developed, and perfected by the then nonexistent army of musicians such as Lester Young, Stan Getz, Miles Davis, Art Farmer, Freddie Hubbard, and a hundred others whose sounds, however different from each other, all remind those of us "who were there" of the cat who started it all. All that *we* can hope for is that some of that original excitement has somehow been preserved on a few of the recordings, unsatisfactory as they are, and will come through to those who "weren't there."

The Dixieland format vs. the star system.
Bix's exaggerated modesty.

Not the least disappointing thing about Bix's records is how little there is of Bix on them, particularly of Bix as soloist. Except for *In a Mist*, his one full-length piano solo, Bix shares the meager three minutes of each recording with all the other men on the date, some of whom take up more of that precious time than Bix does. One waits, nursing one's patience and perhaps gritting one's teeth, through chorus after chorus, break after break, by his well-intentioned colleagues, to catch those few golden notes from Bix's horn—and very often it's well worth the trouble. There were two main reasons for this regrettable poverty of Bix solo horn on the records: first, the Dixieland format, an ensemble style in which Bix was trapped, as we know, during his brief career; secondly, Bix's almost unearthly modesty and self-effacement, which frequently resulted in the spotlight lighting up everyone in the studio more than himself. One cannot help comparing our good luck with Louis Armstrong, in that respect, with our bad luck with Bix. From about 1925 on, Louis, the first great jazz soloist, was presented on his records as the virtual star, while his mediocre companions receded more and more into the position of background support; by 1928, almost none of them ever took a full solo on any Armstrong side. Fortunately, many of the ensemble passages on which Bix merely plays "lead" cornet, i.e., carries the principal melody, are fair-to-good representations of his style.

Restrictions of early recording technology.

As the reader has seen, Bix was even more upset than most jazz musicians by the restrictive conditions imposed by the recording studio of the twenties. First of these was the three-minute time limit of the old 10-inch, 78-RPM record. Before the coming of the LP (33-RPM), the soloist who, like Bix, liked to "stretch out" in eight or more successive choruses, was severely hampered by this limitation, which might be likened to having to make love on an escalator, finishing by the time you reach the top. In addition, as has already been touched on, the pre-1926 acoustical recording method presented certain horrors and hazards now happily forgotten: the fearsome horn you had to play into (all take and no give; it may be significant that each performance into it is still called a *take*); the seemingly arbitrary placement of each musician by the recording engineer, not according to the musicians' preferences and convenience in hearing each other, but for "balance"; the nerve-racking knowledge, in those pre-tape days, that one clinker made by anyone spoiled an entire master, making it that much harder to relax and create; and, last but not least, the bleak certainty that even the most perfect performance would never come out sounding the way it went in—the fidelity just wasn't there. All these things must have bothered any jazz musician, to a degree; for reasons of personality, they bothered Bix more than any musician I ever met.

Despite all these and other difficulties, the fact remains that Bix somehow managed to "get some of it down" on wax, and that on the strength of the records alone, uncountable thousands of new Bix Beiderbecke enthusiasts are being created every year. Then there's the final fact that they are all we have.

What's Available

The *Schwann Record and Tape Guide*, or *Schwann* for short, purports to list, each month, all currently available recordings. But—to paraphrase one of my favorite lines from a Russian satirical novel of the twenties by V. Kataev—"Comrade, catalogues are written by sinners like you and me." As these words are written, the current month's *Schwann* shows only one Bix album as available, *Bix Beiderbecke with the Wolverines* (Jazz Treasury S-1003), which only proves the fallibility of this alleged "record dealer's (and buyer's) bible," for the fact is—according to those who *really* know—that nearly every note Bix ever blew in a studio is available on some album or another, mostly on the major labels; obviously someone at *Schwann* isn't doing his homework. I've listed those I know about here, with brief comments on those I know best.

Bix Beiderbecke with the Wolverines (Jazz Treasury S-1003). The first twelve recordings Bix made with the original Wolverines, on the Gennett label, all between February and October, 1924, and including those sides *(Fidgety Feet/Jazz Me Blues)* that my brother Vic first stunned me with. On *Jazz Me,* the high point is of course Bix's great solo. *Copenhagen* has rather a haunting quality, but the solo on *Riverboat Shuffle* tops them all, with Bix taking a couple of two-bar breaks during it that were the world's first clue to a whole new attitude toward jazz. *Royal Garden Blues* again has some beautiful solo Bix. *Big Boy* has a woefully undistinguished piano solo by Bix. In addition, this album has the two sides by "The Sioux City Six" cut afterward in New York *(I'm Glad/Flock o' Blues)* and "Rhythm Jugglers" *(Toddlin' Blues/Davenport Blues),* the last being the one on which Bix first used the whole-tone scale. An obligatory purchase for all readers desiring to understand Bix's musical beginnings.

The Bix Beiderbecke Story, vol. 1: Bix & His Gang (Columbia CL 844). These twelve sides, cut between October, 1927, and July, 1928, include some of the best Bix ever waxed. The "hottest" and hardest-swinging tracks, which most often suggest the level of creative freedom Bix usually reached only when playing in person, are *Jazz Me Blues, At the Jazz Band Ball, Royal Garden Blues,* made on the first date (October 5th, 1927), and *Goose Pimples, Since My Best Gal Turned Me Down, Sorry,* from the second (October 25th). The presence of a banjo in the rhythm section isn't a big help, though Howdy Quicksell played it about as jazzily as anyone could; but Bill Rank (trombone), Don Murray (clarinet), Adrian Rollini (bass sax), Frankie Signorelli (piano), and especially Chauncey Morehouse (drums), all contribute just about the best support Bix was ever lucky enough to gather around him on any commercial recording date. *Jazz Me* is fascinating, aside from the musical excellence of Bix's leads & solos, for the startling contrast it affords with the recording Bix had made of it three and a half years earlier on Gennett; in that period, Bix blossomed out musically and acquired the artistic authority of the recognized star; right from the opening notes, Bix is in command as never before. Among other highlights, note Bix's amazing wrapup of the second "verse," a run of six triplet-groups (from C# more than an octave down to Bb)—it's the one that comes just before Bill Rank's trombone half-chorus. Here we have the full-grown Bix, fleetfooted, with a structure of inevitable logic and surprise of a kind no one else then alive would even have conceived. *Jazz Band Ball* is a hard-swinging Dixieland standard, with Bix whipping the gang along from the first note, a good example of what the musicians who played alongside him meant when they said, "He made you swing, man!" But the "hardest" in my opinion is that same *Goose Pimples* that was the occasion of our only real quarrel. All the other sides here are loaded with representative Bix; one can only wish there had been more of him, less of his friends. *Since My Best Gal Turned Me Down* is an excellent reminder of how Bix could handle a pop-standard song. This entire album will repay close, repeated listening; it's the nearest you'll ever come to hearing the real Bix. George Avakian's album notes are accurate and informative.

The Bix Beiderbecke Story, vol. 2: Bix & Tram (Columbia CL 845). Another fine twelve, featuring Bix in a wide range of material, from February, 1927, to January, 1928, with varying support that often included the men heard on vol. 1, above. *Singin' the Blues* has always been, for most collectors, *the* Bix Beiderbecke solo on record, and no wonder; it's a masterpiece; one could write a sizeable monograph on it (some have), but I'll limit myself here to saying *listen. I'm Comin' Virginia* is one of the most profound and sobering statements to be found anywhere in the history of the art; appropriately, Bix's very last notes, a nine-note "codetta" launched by Eddie Lang's guitar "springboard," far from being any sort of afterthought, are a kind of startlingly beautiful, lyrical summation of his musical attitude throughout the entire record, especially his preceding cornet solo. Surprisingly, *Riverboat Shuffle*, which brought out the very best in Bix back in the 1924 Wolverines session, emerges here as an exercise in desperation and hysteria, one of the few recorded examples of Bix in which he actually sounded *hurried*, further marred by Bix's bad (and typical) judgment in giving most of the many two-bar breaks to his inferiors. But the wonder is never that bad things happened to Bix in recording, but that he managed to make so many good ones happen, despite all.

The Bix Beiderbecke Story, vol. 3: Whiteman Days (Columbia CL 846). This record would be an indispensable acquisition if only because it has *In a Mist*, Bix's only full length recorded piano solo, a composition that is still keeping jazz musicians all over the world busy. It has one track, *Margie*, from the previous *Bix & His Gang* dates (only issued long after Bix's death), according to George Avakian's liner notes; all the others, except of course *In a Mist* (cut on September 9th, 1927), were made in 1928 and '29, mostly with men playing with him in the Paul Whiteman orchestra. As always, Bix makes the performance, but some of his pals are hard to take. Twelve tracks, and Avakian's good notes.

Paul Whiteman & His Orchestra Featuring Bix Beiderbecke (Columbia CL 2830).

Paul Whiteman, vols. 1 & 2 (RCA-Victor LPV-555, LPV-570).

The Bix Beiderbecke Legend (RCA-Victor LPM-2323). Once you're really interested in Bix's records, all of them include something of interest, musically and historically. All these are in that category, and go to prove, if nothing else, how indomitable was Bix's independent, swinging musical spirit, which could continue to exist under the most unpromising conditions. Charlie Smith's informative album notes* contain a telling quote from Otis Ferguson: "But when Bix would get him a little opening and let that horn go, it really did seem as though the band was swinging, all seven acres." And Charlie adds, accurately, "A great deal is owed to jazz arrangements," meaning mostly Bill Challis and Tom Satterfield, who somehow wrestled the seven acres into a semblance of a framework for Bix, Jack Teagarden, and the other jazzmen who from time to time fought their way through the Whiteman Everglades.

Thesaurus of Classic Jazz (Columbia C4L 18). This is a mammoth four-album set, comprising fifty-two tracks in all, reissued, or in some cases issued for the first time, recorded between 1926 and 1930, mostly in 1927 and '28. The majority of them are by the Red Nichols band, with my brother Vic on drums and hot tympani; there are also three by groups that included Bix (*Humpty Dumpty, Three Blind Mice, Lila,*

*On LPV-570. My brother Vic, for his sins, is on a couple tracks on this album.

the last a real commercial stinker—the vocal is unbelievably dreadful). The ones with Red and Vic have stood the test of time well, if you accept Red's not very sensitive imitation of Bix. Many of the Nichols sides feature some of Vic's hot tympani, but it's regrettable that the age's recording know-how didn't allow a virtuoso like Vic to use his full instrumentation, without which he sounds, at least to me, like a man trying to play with one hand and both feet tied behind him. However, it's only fair to acknowledge that other jazz collectors don't seem to share my disparaging attitude toward Vic or Bix on wax. Certainly most of the people who have fallen in love with Bix's music have done so, perforce, exclusively through the records; and most of the enthusiasm that continues to be shown for brother Vic's work is also due to these waxworks, a poor substitute for the living model. In sum, this set of records is recommended as a valuable addition to our store of white jazz from the twenties.

In addition to the above American-made albums, I know of, but have never seen or listened to, there are a number of foreign-born LPs, listed below, some of them containing Bix recordings not available here, some with sides never before issued, as well as a good many sides included in the above American albums. Which means that the reader determined to acquire *all* the available Bix recordings will be in part duplicating already acquired tracks, not a real drawback to a serious collector. As I only know them at secondhand, the eager reader will have to hear them or examine them himself, and make his own choices; but, if he already likes Bix, he won't be going far wrong with any of them:

The Legend of Bix Beiderbecke (French RCA-Victor 731036 and -7). A two-record set, including about twenty-five sides from Bix's Goldkette and Whiteman periods, probably all with Frankie Trumbauer.

Great Jazz Trumpets (Joker 3122). One of the many "pirate" or "bootleg" labels, so called because they are manufactured without the formality of permissions or payment of royalties to publishers or other owners of recording rights to the music. Includes some Bix sides, sharked up from God knows where.

The following four albums on English Parlaphone are, I'm told, an invaluable treasury of Bix sides, some rare or entirely unavailable elsewhere.

Bix & Tram, 1929+ (Eng. Parlaphone PMC 7113).

Bix & Tram, 1927: The Bix Beiderbecke-Frankie Trumbauer Orchestra (Eng. Parlaphone PMC 7064).

Bix & Tram, 1928: The Bix Beiderbecke-Frankie Trumbauer Orchestra (Eng. Parlaphone PMC 7100).

Bix Beiderbecke & His Gang (Eng. Parlaphone PMC 1221).

The Victorious Bix: Bix Beiderbecke, 1926–'30 (Divergent 301).

Ibid (Divergent 302).

The Rare Bix: Frankie Trumbauer & His Orch. (Swaggie S-1218). This, on an Australian label, apparently includes some sides, e.g. *Humpty Dumpty,* available on other albums; but whether these are from the same dates (or masters) I don't know.

As we go to press, I learn that a new Bix album, to be called *The Unheard Bix,* consisting wholly of previously unissued recordings, is due to appear "soon" on the Broadway label, whatever that is.

So ends this partial discography; for more information, the reader is once more referred to *The Bix Bands,* and to the Evans-Sudhalter giant (see Bibliography, above).

END PAPERS

No book about Bix Beiderbecke and his extraordinary effect on people could be complete without a mention of the growing Bix cults, of which I can speak with certainty of only two.

The Annual Bix Beiderbecke Barbecue & Stomp has its headquarters in the home of one Bill Donahoe, a young advertising executive who was its begetter and guru, in Long Valley, New Jersey. Each summer the faithful forgather there, arriving in everything from beat-up Volkswagens to antique Rolls-Royces, most of them bearing bumper stickers that read BIX LIVES, to eat, drink, play, and listen to music live and recorded.

However, the definitive Bix society has at length been established in his old home town, Davenport, Iowa: the Bix Beiderbecke Memorial Society, formed a couple of years ago by local citizens and musicians in the Beiderbecke tradition, who flourish in and around Davenport, led by a chubby youngish cornetist named Don O'Dette, who has dedicated his life and career to playing like Bix and working to perpetuate his memory. Bix had been in his grave some five years when Don was born; but that hasn't prevented him from sounding enough like his model—according to many who have heard him—to fool some of the listeners some of the time. He has taken on what a lot of people would consider the rather thankless job of holding together and operating the Society he helped found; and, to date, is able to report nothing but success. Two years running, the Society has produced a four-day Bix Beiderbecke Jazz Festival, more than breaking even financially and attracting tens of thousands of visitors from every corner of the globe. The visitors have included several dozen surviving friends and fellow musicians of Bix's, who come to play, and reminisce publicly and privately about the quiet young guy they'd all known so briefly and had never been able to forget. The young guy would have been seventy if he'd lived, and some of these friends are now older than that. It must be a curious scene, as for the better part of a week the city of Davenport watches itself celebrate the memory of the bad boy, the hopeless dropout, the black sheep they'd done their best to disown half a century ago.

In Davenport there are other signs of belated atonement. The Free Public Library now has a Bix Beiderbecke Room, a sort of mini-museum. Bix's grave out at Oakdale cemetery (which for years was presided over by Bix's older brother Bernie, who was the caretaker there) has become an international shrine, its diminutive headstone visited by assorted devotees from Chicago, Copenhagen, and Yokohama, whose numbers seem to be growing.

The Bix Beiderbecke Memorial Society's membership is increasing. It now publishes a monthly newsletter, as well as brochures and other items craved by Bix fans, including T-shirts, signs, and bumper stickers. The address is BBMS, 906 W. 14th St., Davenport, Iowa 52804.

All over the world, among young people and those not so young, interest in Bix's music, his life, and the meaning of it, seems to be on the rise. The seeds he planted, at such cost to himself, many of the ideas he so earnestly and confusedly searched for, ignored and misunderstood during his short career, have found fertile soil. The world, the America that had nothing to offer one of its greatest creative artists in his lifetime is now, it seems, beginning at last to discover just what it was throwing away.

INDEX